William Lewis Fowler
#1639 South Grant Street
Denver, Colorado
November 11th, 1980

D1605755

The Samoan Tangle

THE
SAMOAN TANGLE

A Study in
Anglo-German-American Relations

1878-1900

PAUL M. KENNEDY

BOOKS
10 East 53d St., New York 10022
(a division of Harper & Row Publishers, Inc.)

First published 1974

ISBN 06-493635-X

© 1974 Paul M. Kennedy
All forms of micropublishing
© Irish University Microforms   Ireland

Published in the U.S.A. 1974 by
HARPER & ROW PUBLISHERS, INC.
BARNES & NOBLE IMPORT DIVISION

Printed and bound in Great Britain by
REDWOOD BURN LIMITED
Trowbridge & Esher

*To my mother and
to the memory of my father*

Contents

Note on Translations and Abbreviations viii

Foreword ix

Maps xiv

1　From the Earliest Times to the German Coup of 1884 . . 1

  i　*The Powers and Samoa to* 1877 1
  ii　*The Establishment of Treaty Rights in Samoa* . . . 12
  iii　*The German Bid for the Islands* 25
  iv　*The Reaction in London* 38

2　*'Furor Consularis'* and the Establishment of the Tridominium 1885-89　51

  i　*Salisbury, Bismarck and the Secret Anglo-German Treaty on Samoa* 51
  ii　*The Washington Conference and its Aftermath* . . 64
  iii　*The German-American Confrontation over Samoa* . . 76
  iv　*The Berlin Conference of* 1889 87

3　Tripartite Rule and International Relations 1889-98 . . 98

  i　*The Workings of the Berlin Act* 98
  ii　*Samoa and Anglo-German Relations* 1890-96 . . 108
  iii　*The Early Years of German* Weltpolitik . . . 122
  iv　*The American Expansion and the Changing Relations with Britain and Germany* 133

4　The Samoan War and International Politics 1898-99 . . 145

  i　*The Origins and Outbreak of the Samoan Civil War* . . 145
  ii　*Diplomatic Repercussions of the War* 155
  iii　*Relations with America and the Work of the Samoan Commission* 168
  iv　*Salisbury, Wilhelm and the Samoan Question* . . 178

5　The Partition of the Islands 1899 189

  i　*The German Pressure is Renewed* 189
  ii　*Samoa and the Coming of the Boer War* . . . 199
  iii　*Naval Memoranda and Political Considerations* . . 211
  iv　*Bülow's 'Free Hand' and the Settlement with Britain* . 225

6　The Aftermath 240

  i　*The Diplomatic Aftermath* 240
  ii　*The Samoan Crisis and Public Opinion* . . . 254
  iii　*Samoa and Tonga,* 1900-14 272

Conclusion: The Relations of Britain, Germany and the United States in the Light of the Samoan Question . . . 285

Bibliography 307

Index 317

Note on Translations and Abbreviations

Unless otherwise stated, all translations are my own. After a complete rendering on the first occasion, the following abbreviations have been used throughout:

A.A.	*Auswärtiges Amt*
Addit.Mss.	British Museum, Additional Manuscript
Adm.	Admiralty
A.M.L.B.	Akten der Missionen—Londoner Botschaft
BA	Bundesarchiv
BA/MA	Bundesarchiv-Militärarchiv
B.D.	*British Documents on the Origins of the War*, edited by G. P. Gooch and H. Temperley (11 vols., London, 1926-1938)
Cab.	Cabinet papers
C.O.	Colonial Office
D.H.P.G.	*Deutsche Handels- und Plantagen-Gesellschaft der Südsee-Inseln zu Hamburg*
F.O.	Foreign Office
F.R.	*Papers relating to the Foreign Relations of the U.S.*
G.P.	*Die Grosse Politik der Europäischen Kabinette*, edited by J. Lepsius *et al.* (40 vols., Berlin, 1922-1927)
L.M.S./S.S.L.	London Missionary Society, South Seas Letters
N.A.R.G.	National Archives, Record Group
N.D.	Navy Department
Reichstag	*Stenographische Berichte über die Verhandlungen des Reichstages*
R.M.A.	Reichsmarineamt
R.Kol.A.	Reichskolonialamt
S.D.	State Department
St.A.H.	Staatsarchiv, Hamburg

Foreword

'Historians in Britain', observed Professor Ward in a recent bibliographical essay, 'have shown little interest in writing the history of the distant, scattered islands that comprise the British territories' in the Pacific despite their ready access to 'some of the best sources for the task'. The reason for this neglect, apart from the obvious attractions of studying nearer and more populous lands, is not hard to find: it lies in 'the complexity and extent of the sources that have to be studied for a region of inconsiderable land area and small population'. This feature is especially true for the period of international rivalry in the Pacific,the last quarter of the nineteenth century, which, as Professor Ward notes, has resulted in the fact that

> in the history of what are now the British territories in the Pacific, strands of American history, French history, and German history are often mingled with the records of British and colonial action and the role of the indigenous inhabitants. As a result, the historian who works on the British territories in the Pacific may need sources from many countries.[1]

These words are most apt with regard to the study of Samoa, which in that period was the subject of the longest-lasting and most important controversy in the Pacific, involving three great powers, the dominions of Australasia and the natives themselves. Over 300 volumes on Samoa before 1914 are contained in the Potsdam archives alone, and the British total is over 100. In addition, there are the American official records, the enormous deposits in the various West German archives, the many materials in Fiji, New Zealand and Australia, missionary and trading company correspondence, well over forty private collections, and finally the Samoan records, both oral and written.

Faced with this mountain of material, the historian is very quickly forced to abandon early hopes of producing an account that is satisfactory in all its aspects and to address himself to the humbler question: 'What *sort* of history of Samoa should I write?' The answer in this case was partly influenced in a negative way by a desire not to duplicate the recent researches either of Professor Davidson, who has most ably dealt with the political development, reactions and attitudes of the Samoans themselves, or of the late Dr Gilson, who has produced a wonderfully detailed study in *The Politics*

1   J. M. Ward, 'The British Territories in the Pacific' in *The Historiography of the British Empire-Commonwealth*, ed. R. W. Winks (Durham, N.C. 1966), pp. 197-98.

ix

of a Multi-Cultural Community. On a more positive note, it seemed that a historian living on this side of the globe would be in a better position, certainly with regard to archival sources, to deal with the Samoan question from the point of view of the international relations of the three great powers involved in that group up to 1900. Finally, and the most important influence of all, was my abiding interest in *die grosse Politik*, in imperialism and international affairs before 1914, in the relationship between foreign policy and strategy, and between government actions and public opinion.

The essence of this work, therefore, lies in the sub-title: 'A Study in Anglo-German-American Relations, 1878-1900', for its main aim is to place the lengthy dispute over Samoa in a wider diplomatic and imperial context. Though this story rightfully begins with the establishment of treaty relationships between the Samoan government and the individual powers in 1878-1879, it does not really assume this wider significance until 1884, where Sylvia Masterman left off her account, acknowledging that the German bid for the group in that year had 'placed Samoan affairs on a new footing' and turned them into a matter of 'international importance'. After seeking to fit this bid into the general framework of Bismarck's colonial ventures, I then attempt to show how the Samoan tangle partly reflected, and partly contributed to, the very important changes in the relationships of Britain, Germany and the United States between the early 1880s and the turn of the century. These developments, particularly the worsening of Anglo-German relations, emerge so clearly in the final crisis over the group in 1898-1899 that I felt it necessary to examine those two years in greater detail, although it is true to say that this reflects the proportion of documentary evidence pertaining to the collapse of the tridominium and the final partition of the islands. As the concluding section of this study indicates, it seems fair to assert that the Samoan story is not only of importance from the point of view of the indigenous population itself and the growth of a multi-cultural community, and as providing one of the most interesting examples of great power rivalries in the Pacific, but also as a mirror of far larger trends in international relations and imperialism in the late nineteenth century.

The Samoan Tangle grew out of an Oxford doctoral dissertation which dealt more specifically with the partition of the group. As such, it owes much to individuals and to official bodies, for financial assistance, archival help and academic advice. I gratefully acknowledge the financial help given to me by the Northumberland Education Authority and by the Department of Education and Science. Twice I received the generous support of the Beit Fund, for my trip to the United States and for my visit to Potsdam. The Theodor Heuss Research Fellowship, granted me by the University of Oxford and administered most efficiently by the Alexander von Humboldt-Stiftung, made possible my twelve months' research in West German archives and libraries. Finally, St Antony's College, Oxford, not only assisted me in my United States trip and in the purchase of microfilms and books, but gave additional help for domestic purposes and, above all, provided a friendly and stimulating residence and base.

My debt to archives and archivists is particularly heavy, for this study is based almost exclusively upon original sources, in the securing of which I have bothered a large number of people. I am heavily indebted to the trustees, librarians and staff of the following institutions: the Public Record Office (especially Mr Franklin at the Ashridge Branch); the British Museum; Birmingham University Library (Mr D. W. Evans); Christchurch College Library, Oxford (Dr J. F. A. Mason); the Bodleian Library, Oxford; St Antony's College Library, Oxford (Miss A. Abley); the Seeley Historical Library, Cambridge; the National Library of Scotland, Edinburgh; the libraries of the universities of Newcastle-upon-Tyne, Southampton and London, and latterly that of East Anglia; the Institute of Historical Research; the *Times* archives, Printing House Square; the Naval Historical Branch of the Ministry of Defence (Mr J. D. Lawson); the Foreign Office Library; the library at Chatsworth (Mr T. S. Wragg); Gloucester County Record Office; the Royal Commonwealth Society Library; the Historical Manuscripts Commission; and Australia House (Miss P. Mander-Jones of the *Guide* to Australasian records, and Mr P. H. Saunders, Liaison Officer for the National Library of Australia.)

My debts in the United States are fewer, since the records there were less widely separated. I acknowledge with pleasure the assistance received from the ultra-competent staff of the National Archives, Washington; from the Manuscript Division of the Library of Congress; from the U.S. Navy, for permission to use the General Board records in the Navy Yard, Washington; from the Massachussetts Historical Society; and from Brown University Library.

In the Federal Republic of Germany, my thanks must go to the directors and staff of the *Auswärtiges Amt Archiv* in Bonn (especially Dr Gehling); of the *Bundesarchiv* in Koblenz (Dr Kahlenberg); of the *Bundesarchiv-Militärarchiv* in Freiburg (Dr Sandhofer); of the *Staatsarchiv* in Hamburg; of the

Capt. W. D. M. Staveley

university libraries of Bonn and Freiburg; and of the *Militär-geschichtliches Forschungsamt* in Freiburg. Oberstudienrat G. Ebel was most generous in allowing me to view and use the Hatzfeldt papers and his photostat copies of the London Embassy files.

To the director and staff of the *Deutsches Zentralarchiv* in Potsdam, German Democratic Republic, I am most grateful for assistance during my research into the *Kolonialamt* records.

I am pleased to acknowledge the gracious permission of Her Majesty the Queen in permitting me to reproduce extracts of the correspondence between Lord Salisbury and Queen Victoria, both from the Salisbury Collection at Christchurch and from the photographic copies in the Public Record Office of the Prime Ministers' Letters from the Royal Archives. Unpublished Crown copyright material in the Public Record Office and India Office Library transcribed in this book appears by permission of the Controller of Her Majesty's Stationery Office. I am also deeply grateful to the following individuals and bodies for allowing me to quote extracts of unpublished material to which they hold the copyright: the sixth Marquess of Salisbury (the Salisbury papers); Birmingham University Library and Colonel Terence Maxwell (Joseph Chamberlain papers); the Trustees of the Chatsworth Settlement (Devonshire papers); the Trustees of the British Museum (Balfour papers); the second Earl of Midleton (Midleton papers); the *Times* archives (Saunders papers, and the *Times* Foreign Letter Book); Captain W. D. M. Staveley (Sturdee papers). Every effort has been made to trace and to secure permission from owners of all manuscript material under copyright quoted in this book; if I have inadvertently trespassed upon such rights, I offer humble apologies.

Finally, I wish to acknowledge the kind help and advice of a number of academics, in particular that of my thesis supervisor, Mr G. F. Hudson. I am also deeply grateful to my former Newcastle lecturer and teacher, Mrs J. M. Taylor, whose perceptive criticisms were greatly appreciated, and to Professor James Joll, Professor A. J. Marder, Professor G. N. Sanderson, Miss Agatha Ramm, Mr A. J. Nicholls, Dr J. C. G. Röhl and Dr C. W. Newbury, all of whom provided, where necessary, references, advice, ideas and encouragement. Professor Dr H. Stoecker assisted my application to work in the Potsdam archives, and I am grateful to him for that. Dr H. Pogge von Strandmann and Mr S. J. Firth allowed me to use pieces from their own research which proved useful to my thesis. Understanding and tolerance of the ways of the author have been shown to me in large measure by Irish University Press, and especially by Mr Lalit Adolphus. My greatest debt is to my wife, not only for acting as my unpaid typist, but also for her general encouragement and for bearing with the affairs of 'that miserable archipelago' (Sir Thomas Sanderson) for the past years.

PAUL M. KENNEDY
Bad Godesberg, October 1972.

The Samoan Tangle

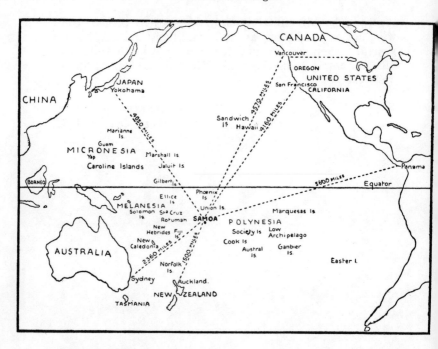

Map 1 The Samoan Islands, as usually shown in nineteenth-century maps of the Pacific. Reproduced from p. 107 of S. R. Masterman, *The Origins of International Rivalry in Samoa, 1845-84* (London, 1934).

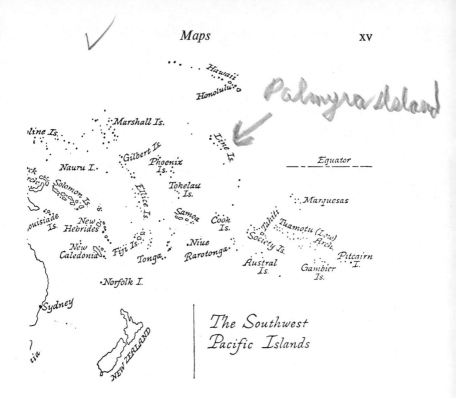

Map 2   The Samoan Islands, as they actually lie in relation to the other groups of the Pacific. Reproduced from p. 191 of C. H. Grattan, *The South-West Pacific to 1900* (Ann Arbor, 1963), by permission of the University of Michigan Press.

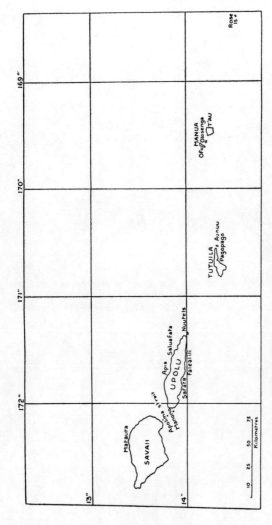

Map 3 The Samoan group. Reproduced from p. 18 of S. R. Masterman, *The Origins of International Rivalry in Samoa, 1845-54* (London, 1934).

1

From the Earliest Times to the German Coup of 1884

i *The Powers and Samoa to* 1877

Almost 1,600 miles north/north-east of Auckland lies a string of islands, fourteen in number stretching along an east-west axis. The group is built up on a long submarine ridge with deep channels between the individual islands, which are in fact the visible tops of a single mountain chain.[1] Volcanic in origin, they all rise steeply out of the sea and are rugged in character. The highest peak, in the centre of the largest island of Savai'i, has an altitude exceeding 6,000 feet and even some of the smaller islands are well over 1,000 feet high. This, together with the thick tropical jungle which covers all the islands, restricts habitation to the coastal regions, where native settlements abound; travel between villages is usually undertaken by means of small boats. A relatively constant high temperature and a heavy precipitation, particularly in the 'wet' season from December to March, account for the luxuriant verdure of the vegetation. Coral reefs surround the group, which, although known to the early explorers as the Navigators Islands, was more commonly referred to later as the Samoan Islands, or simply, Samoa.

The Samoan Islands lie almost 2,300 miles south/south-west of Hawaii and about the same distance north-east of Sydney. Yokohama and San Francisco are some 4,000 miles from the group, which is also 5,700 miles from Panama, a connection which assumed great importance during the nineteenth century as writers speculated upon the changes which the proposed Central American Canal would bring to the Pacific and its trade. But although the archipelago occupies a central position in the south-west Pacific, it lies too close to neighbouring groups, such as the Fiji, Tongan and Cook Islands, to possess any particular value in that respect. Being but one of a cluster of island groups, Samoa cannot be said to have the strategic

1 The physical characteristics of the Samoan Islands are summarized in the Admiralty's *Pacific Islands: Eastern Pacific*, Geographical Handbook series, vol. 2, B.R.519A (Naval Intelligence Division, London, 1943), pp. 582 91.

importance which was, and is, naturally attached to the
Hawaiian Islands.[2]

Of the islands in the Samoan group, only three can be said
to have any significance; Savai'i, Upolu and Tutuila: the
remainder are scarcely more than islets, five of them unin-
habited. Savai'i, the most westerly island, is also the largest,
being some 700 square miles in area. Owing to its lack of even
a moderate harbour, however, it is the least valuable of the
three and has always been more sparsely populated.[3] Strategically and commercially, its prospects were never rated as being
very high. Upolu, the next island of any size to the east, is
somewhat smaller in area (400 square miles) but much more
important, being the commercial and social centre of the
entire group. The native population was (and still is) mainly
concentrated in a series of villages along the north coast of
the island, where the native capital of Mulinu'u was also sited.
Close to this place lies the only town of any significance, Apia,
where the vast majority of the Europeans resided. Although
its anchorage was indifferent, the town was commercially
supreme in the group. Sixty miles east of Upolu lies the island
of Tutuila, only fifty square miles in area, but possessing the
fine natural harbour of Pago-Pago. Its strategic importance
was therefore far greater than its commercial worth.

The Samoans, a friendly and healthy race, were famous
throughout the islands for their internal politics, which had
earned them the title of 'the Irishmen of the Pacific'. The
native political and social structure was one of some complexity, being founded primarily upon family and regional
groupings rather than upon any form of central administration
or national organization.[4] Basically, Samoa was a tribal
society with chiefs as the local figures of authority and the
districts as the areas of government in which they ruled, rather
like the Scottish clan system in some respects. The heads of
various households in a village possessed the right to participate

2 Too many works have tended to dwell upon the suggested or apparently *exclusive*
position of the group, a tendency emphasized by accompanying maps with lines drawn
showing the distances between Samoa and the major ports of America, Asia and Australia
e.g., on the inside front cover of G. H. Ryden's *The Foreign Policy of the United States
in Relation to Samoa* (New Haven, 1933) and on p. 107 of Sylvia Masterman's *The Origins
of International Rivalry in Samoa* 1845-1884 (London, 1934). This was doubtless a
reflection of the exaggerated significance attached to the Samoan Islands by politicians
and public opinion in the late nineteenth century, but it needs to be stressed from the
start that the archipelago possessed no strategic or geographic advantage which the
surrounding groups did not also enjoy. See maps 1 and 2.

3 Savai'i, Upolu and the surrounding islands were reckoned to have a population of
some 28,000 natives in 1881, the majority living on Upolu; but all figures are very
approximate until the 1900 census. F. M. Keesing, *Modern Samoa* (London, 1934), p. 33.

4 This complex topic is best handled in J. W. Davidson, *Samoa mo Samoa: The Emergence
of the Independent State of Western Samoa* (Oxford, 1967), pp. 15-30. See also R. P. Gilson,
Samoa 1830 to 1900: The Politics of a Multi-Cultural Community (Melbourne, 1970).

in its councils or *fonos*, where the important decisions were taken. This process of deliberation by the chiefs, which was always an occasion for their orators, or subordinate 'talking chiefs', to demonstrate their conversational abilities, was continued at a higher scale by the district *fonos*, where each village was usually represented by its chief. In ancient times there were fourteen such districts, all based upon a collection of sub-district or village groupings. But if this pyramidal structure appeared in theory fairly regular, or even relatively democratic, practice and the developments in native power politics had tended to create a certain imbalance by the mid-nineteenth century, when four of the districts came to be regarded as of greater importance than any others.[5] Consequently the titles which these particular districts could confer upon their leader were greatly coveted by the rivalling Samoan chiefs, and if one person were able to obtain all four titles, he was regarded as the *Tafa'ifa*, the paramount head of the group.

In practice this struggle for the ceremonial headship tended to be centred around the two predominant families, the Tupua and the Malietoa, each based in Upolu. The early white settlers in the islands immediately made the mistake of confusing the *Tafa'ifa* with the more normal form of European monarchy. But there were in fact great differences between the two, as the American Consul-General Churchill tried to point out to the State Department in 1897:

> No king as such is king of Samoa in any sense comparable with better known monarchies of the present and ancient world. A king here is king over those who gave him the royal title which it is in their power to bestow together with those, who without the right to bestow this royal name are yet bound by the iron force of custom to obey the holder of that name. There are four such royal names in Samoa and the person who receives all four is king of all Samoa until one or more of these is withdrawn by those who, having it in their power to bestow, have equally the right to take away.[6]

Such withdrawals, which were in fact rebellions and treated accordingly by the *Tafa'ifa*, occurred fairly often in Samoan politics and this was the major cause for the chaos which so exasperated the white settlers and their governments. Apart from the Samoan leader's insecurity of tenure, the succession system was also a matter for dispute. From the lowest political roots (i.e., the family) upwards

5 Keesing, *Modern Samoa*, pp. 48-60; Masterman, *Origins*, pp. 19-23. The latter, however, asserts that there were in fact *five* districts of greater importance, but the commonly accepted number is only four.

6 Churchill to S.D. (State Department), no. 45 of 11/1/1897 in N.A.R.G. (National Archives, Record Group) 84, Apia Consulate despatches (C38-8a), vol. 1.

Louis de Bougainville [handwritten annotation]

La Perouse Strait an entrance to Japan inland Sea [handwritten annotation in left margin]

> succession to a title is elective within a family, and while heredity is a contributory qualification general ability, popularity and the capacity to make a good speech are the principal considerations borne in mind when a title has to be filled.[7]

This meant that, even in the later decades of the nineteenth century, when the Malietoa family tended to be the chief possessors of the *Tafa'ifa*, there existed no recognized manner of succession to the reigning head. Instead, the title was fought for between the various claimants within the family, with the districts, including those who had formerly supported the Tupua family, taking sides in the dispute. It was a swiftly-changing and chaotic state of politics, although the natives themselves do not appear to have complained much of it. Its real weakness lay in its potentiality for exploitation either by unscrupulous white traders, who were ever at hand to sell arms to both sides, or by established European firms, which sought commercial security and advantage by backing one of the rival candidates in a succession quarrel in the expectation of being able to influence, or even control, the *Tafa'ifa* they had placed in power.

The growth of white interest in the group was, however, slow and hesitant, at least in the early part of the nineteenth century.[8] The first explorers known to have sighted the Samoan Islands were Dutchmen, the members of Jacob Roggewein's expedition, which arrived in the archipelago on 14 June 1722, on its way from Tahiti to New Guinea, but as his journal was not published until over a century later, the Frenchman Louis de Bougainville, who came upon the islands in 1768, was for a long time credited with their discovery. It was Bougainville who, marvelling at the skill of the native boatsmen, gave the islands the name of *L'Archipel des Navigateurs*, a title which was in frequent use until the end of the nineteenth century. Neither expedition landed, however, and it was left to another French party, under Perouse, to claim this honour and then to be attacked by the natives, losing in the process twelve of its crew. The reputation which the Samoans acquired by this action was sufficient to keep most exploring parties away from the group for many years.

The first genuine and lasting European contact occurred with the arrival of the famous missionary John Williams in 1830.

---

7   *Pacific Islands*, vol. 2, p. 613.

8   This following section is a synopsis of an extensive and interesting period of Samoan history, which has been covered in much more detail by Masterman, *Origins*, pp. 29-193, and by Ryden, *U.S. Policy in Samoa*, pp. 1-207. Also extremely useful are W. P. Morrell, *Britain in the Pacific Islands* (Oxford, 1960), pp. 53-57, 205-38; J. W. Ellison, *The Opening and Penetration of Foreign Influence in Samoa to 1880* (Oregon State monograph, Studies in History, no. 1, Corvallis, 1938); and C. H. Grattan, *The South-West Pacific to 1900* (Michigan, 1963), pp. 179-242, 453-88.

This representative of the London Missionary Society, who had been working in the nearby Tongan group, was fortunate enough to be introduced to the Samoans by a relative of Malietoa Vai'inupo, the victor of a recent native war for the *Tafa'ifa*. Williams was thus allowed to leave behind eight Tahitian teachers and the mission flourished under the king's patronage, even if the first stage of conversion was nominal rather than real. Regular teachers, a printing press, numerous schools and a special educational centre were established in the next few years, and the majority of the inhabitants eventually joined the Church, although the Wesleyan and Catholic missionaries also gained some support later.[9] Williams and his successors, who built up Samoa to be the geographical and spiritual centre of their activities in the south-west Pacific, contributed significantly to the spread of the English language and culture in the group, a fact which the Germans were later to lament.[10]

Government interest in the Samoan Islands was small at this stage. They were visited and closely surveyed in 1839 by the United States Exploring Expedition under Captain Wilkes, who drew up a series of commercial regulations and appointed John C. Williams, the son of the missionary, as acting American vice-consul.[11] In 1845 he was joined by George Pritchard, who became British consul after his unceremonious expulsion from Tahiti by the French. In neither case did these creations indicate any inclination upon the part of the American or British governments to interfere in the internal affairs of the islands. The former saw their agent's task as being purely to assist the whaling vessels and distressed sailors and to apprehend deserters. British concern about native affairs was equally negative and Aberdeen promptly turned down an offer of cession by the Tutuilan chiefs in 1845, although suspicion of French designs caused him to add that 'Her Majesty's Government would not view with indifference the assumption by another Power of a Protectorate which they, with regard for the true interests of the natives, have already refused.'[12]

Despite the wishes of both the missionaries and the two

9   According to Masterman, *Origins*, pp. 29-35, neither the Wesleyan nor the Catholic missions obtained more than 8% of the population in their respective congregations. The Wesleyans were in fact first in the group but they agreed to withdraw to Tonga in 1835, returning again in 1857.

10   See, for example, the Promemoria of 21/12/1882 by Captain Schering, pointing out the need for German missionaries to do the same, in BA/MA (Bundesarchiv-Militärarchiv) 4348, XIX.1.1.2, *Auswanderungen und Colonisation*, vol. 3.

11   Ryden, *U.S. Policy in Samoa*, pp. 19-23. Williams' post was not recognized by the State Department until 1844, when they gave him the title of 'Commercial Agent of the United States for the Navigators Islands'.

12   Masterman, *Origins*, pp. 49-50, quoting Aberdeen to Pritchard.

governments to keep the islands out of the arena of international politics, important developments in Samoa, and in
the Pacific generally, in the decades following gradually
frustrated this policy. Although British and American warships
were very infrequent in their visits to the group, Samoa was
becoming of greater and greater importance in the field of
Pacific trade and communication, particularly for the large
numbers of American whalers. However, the greatest boost to
commercial activity in Samoa was the European demand for
coconut oil after the discovery that this could make better
soap and candles. The oil was first exported from the group in
1842 but this trade was hampered by the many disadvantages
involved in transporting it to Europe, and it was twenty-five
years later before it really developed, after the introduction of a
new method of preparation by a German company which had
arrived in Samoa in 1857.

This company was the famous Hamburg firm of J. C. Godeffroy and Son, which had already acquired extensive trading
experience in areas as far apart as Hawaii, Valparaiso, Victoria
and California.[13] Under the drive of their vigorous agent,
August Unshelm, Apia was quickly built up into the Godeffroy
centre for their Polynesian commercial operations and the
town served as an entrepôt for trade in oil, tortoise-shell, pearl
and copra which was brought there from smaller agencies
established in Fiji, Tonga, Tahiti, the Gilberts and the Mar-
quesas. As a consequence of these developments, a Hamburg
consulate was established in Apia in 1861. In retrospect these
activities were small compared with the Godeffroy expansion
after 1864, when a new and even more energetic agent replaced
Unshelm. This was Theodor Weber, a dynamic and ruthless
organizer, who can truly be said to have dominated Samoan
politics for the next two decades. His idea of drying the coconut
in the islands and then shipping the copra to Europe, where the
oil was extracted and the residue turned into cattle-feed, was
a great improvement upon the old system and this enterprise
boomed in the years following: the oil export of £14,000 in
1859 soon became the copra export of £121,360 in 1875.[14] It
was Weber, too, who in 1865 established the firm's first coconut
plantations in Samoa, in order to avoid dependence upon the
irregular native production of copra. From that time onwards,
the Germans dominated Samoan trade.

13 The two most detailed histories of this firm are R. Hertz, *Das Hamburger Seehandelshaus J. C. Godeffroy und Sohn* (Veröffentlichungen des Vereins für Hamburgische
Geschichte, vol. 4, Hamburg, 1922) and K. Schmack, *J. C. Godeffroy und Sohn, Kaufleute
zu Hamburg* (Hamburg, 1938).
14 Masterman, *Origins*, pp. 57-63; Hertz, *Godeffroy*, pp. 51-53; Schmack, *Godeffroy*,
pp. 113 233.

The significance of this commercial intrusion into the Samoan group cannot be too strongly emphasized. It was later to acquire great fame as Germany's first colonial enterprise, a fact fostered by the enthusiasts of expansion at home and used by the German government as the key argument in their claims to political control or predominance in the group. The crucial factor which led to the formation of a German interest in the internal politics of Samoa, was Weber's purchase of land upon a large scale for plantation purposes. Doubtless their concern was purely commercial at first; but as soon as the Godeffroy company was firmly tied to plantations, the question of their protection from the depredations which inevitably accompanied the native wars became a vital one. The greater the destruction, the more the Germans were to become convinced that the maintenance of law and order was impossible under a solely native government, and thus the more they were to turn to the idea of control by Germany.

Such a proposal would have been to Samoan minds the worst event which could possibly happen. The Germans were too strongly associated with the fortunes of the firm and its disregard for native rights. German rule, as everyone in Samoa was aware, meant Godeffroy rule. Moreover, much land had been acquired by the company under dubious circumstances, a fact strongly resented by the natives. The final and most telling point against the Germans was their use of imported labourers. The plantations necessitated a large labour force but the Samoans themselves were not disposed to work all day when the natural produce of the islands gave them all they required in the way of food, clothing and habitation; and thus Weber resorted to recruiting the natives of the Solomons, New Britain and the Gilberts, a cause of much trouble in Samoa.

As Pacific trade developed, other countries revealed a greater interest in the Samoan group than had been shown previously. The importance of communications in that ocean grew rapidly after the gold discoveries in California, Australia and New Zealand (1849, 1851 and 1853 respectively) and after the construction of the railway across the United States in 1869. New Zealand in particular began to focus her attention upon the islands, which were regarded by many as mere adjuncts to their own country. Such interest was increased by Governor Grey's schemes for the Pacific islands and by the activities of the New Zealand missionaries, sent out by Bishop Selwyn and others.[15] The spectacular growth of trade with the islands in the 1860s was also a significant factor. In 1869, Auckland's

---

15 The growth of New Zealand interest in this period has been well covered in A. Ross, *New Zealand Aspirations in the Pacific in the Nineteenth Century* (Oxford, 1964), pp. 1-69.

imports from the Pacific alone totalled £74,350, whereas in 1858 the total value of all New Zealand imports from that region had only amounted to £601.[16] Nevertheless, the key to the New Zealand interest in the islands was not based upon commercial or humanitarian grounds, however much these factors were ventilated in the press, but upon considerations of strategy. The desire for security in the Pacific, which in fact meant the annexation of all groups to prevent other powers from obtaining control in them, runs through New Zealand policy from the early nineteenth century to the present day.

This was hardly an attitude which recommended itself to the imperial authorities in London. Their policy in these years was quite definitely one of colonial retrenchment. Trading and missionary activities were encouraged by Her Majesty's Government: annexations were not.[17] Consequently, the agitation of the New Zealand Treasurer (and later prime minister) Julius Vogel in the early 1870s for British or colonial control of Samoa received a frosty reception from Gladstone's government: 'We have quite enough on our hands in all quarters of the world without adding to our responsibilities', minuted the Colonial Secretary, Lord Kimberley, in 1873.[18] This uncompromising attitude in turn led to the beginning of the Australasian colonies' disillusionment at what they judged to be the home government's apathy towards the dangers to British interests in the Pacific.

American interest in the Samoan Islands was also growing in 1860s and 1870s and, while less ambitious and vocal than the New Zealand claims, its stake in the group eventually turned out to be far more substantial. This was because the United States, although unwilling to annex, was not averse to obtaining trading and naval station rights which would assist her expansion into the Pacific. The fine harbour of Pago-Pago in Tutuila, whose value had been pointed out by Wilkes during his survey, was not attractive commercially because, unlike Apia, it possessed no trading establishments or hinterland; but with the growth of steamship services from America to Australia it would serve ideally as a coaling station. With this idea in mind, the steamship owner W. H. Webb began his campaign to secure Pago-Pago for the United States and, as an indirect result of this agitation, Commander Meade of the

16   Ibid., p. 57. This rate of increase tapered off later and in 1870 goods from the Pacific only formed 2.2% of the country's total imports, see pp. 57-60, 89-90.
17   This negative policy has been well shown with regard to Africa in R. Robinson and J. Gallagher with A. Denny, *Africa and the Victorians* (London, 1961), pp. 1-52.
18   C.O. (Colonial Office Records, London) 537/122, Kimberley minute of 23/10/1873 on paper 101 Secret, Fergusson to C.O., tel. of 22/10/1873; Ross, *Aspirations*, p. 114; Masterman, *Origins*, pp. 87-102.

Cmdr, Meade Mal. U. Col. A. B. Steinberger

U. S. S. *Narragansett* concluded a treaty on 14 February 1872, with the local Tutuilan chief, whereby America was granted the exclusive privilege of establishing a naval station there.[19] Although this delighted Webb and a certain coterie of Californian land speculators, there was little chance of ratification. The Senate refused to act when President Grant passed the treaty on to them but the administration in Washington was swayed at least to allow a special agent to visit the group in 1873 and to report upon conditions there.

The result of this mission was a fiasco. Colonel A. B. Steinberger, the agent chosen by Grant and a friend of Webb's, made a great impression amongst the islanders by his concern for their lands and welfare, and by advising them upon the proposed native constitution. Both he and they regarded his mission as but a preliminary to American annexation, whereas the United States government, with its eyes focussed upon the Senate, refused to act upon this suggestion. Steinberger, who was apparently eager to become the first white premier of the islands, saw more danger to his ideas in the extensive Godeffroy interests and travelled to Hamburg where he obtained their support in return for guaranteeing the company's lands and assuring them of a virtual monopoly of the native-produced copra.[20] Keeping the details of this arrangement secret from his own government, Steinberger persuaded them to allow him to return to Samoa for a second time. Then, with gifts from the American government but without either official or diplomatic status, he masqueraded as a fully-powered American envoy and soon became the power behind the new native government. Although many of his reforms were commendable, especially as they protected the rights of the natives and supported the Samoan's attempts to create a unified political body, existing interests in the islands resented them and soon had the backing of the American and British consuls against him. After almost a year in Samoa, Steinberger was peremptorily deported in March 1875 by the commander of H. M. S. *Barracouta*, at which the natives promptly turned upon their king, Malietoa Laupepa, who had allowed himself to be bullied into agreeing to his premier's forced departure. Although the two consuls and the naval commander consequently lost their jobs for their unauthorized actions, Steinberger's experiment in personal rule had come to an end.

19 Ryden, *U.S. Policy in Samoa*, pp. 42-48, covers the details of Meade's treaty.

20 Ibid., pp. 83-147; Morrell, *Britain in Pacific*, pp. 215-18. By this agreement, dated 16/9/1874, Steinberger was to obtain $2 for every ton of copra sold to the firm by the Samoan government and people, and 10% upon every purchase by the government from Godeffroy's.

Cuder Meade U.S. II.

Apart from an early indication of an American strategic
interest in Samoa, the real significance of these activities in the
early 1870s was that they formed the starting-point for a chain-
reaction of suspicion and intrigue on the part of the white
interests there who favoured annexation by their own government, or at least feared a similar move by a rival government.
In 1871, Weber, by then German consul, had unsuccessfully
proposed a German administration to his superiors and he
greatly feared that Meade's treaty of the following year would
lead instead to an American protectorate. Although the Godeffroy treaty with Steinberger revealed that the company's main
concern was still the securing of commercial advantages, their
ideal remained a German rather than an American administration. Moreover, the rule of the American adventurer had
aroused deep suspicion in New Zealand, where the agitation
for annexation was renewed although failing once more to
attract the British government.[21] In turn, these colonial aspirations became of ever greater concern to the German traders
in the Pacific, who were increasingly to look to their own
government for support. Thus three parties existed, anxious
for annexation of the group by their respective governments,
and it was solely the reserve and unwillingness of those latter
bodies to make a positive step forward which prevented the
assumption of political control in Samoa by one of the powers
a decade or more before the real period of imperial expansion.

Nevertheless, the inherent weaknesses of the native political
system and the patent inability of the Samoans to resist the
encroachments of the white commercial interests were pointing
clearly in the direction of some form of more regular (i.e., non-
Samoan) administration, if only for the sake of the natives
themselves. The debilitating effects of European financial and
moral influence upon African regimes in the nineteenth century
has been shown clearly.[22] In the Pacific the effects were the
same, although the causes were rather different. The key
development here was the securing of large tracts of property
in various island groups by white entrepreneurs, some of whom
were undoubtedly rogues, which reduced whatever resources
and power the native governments possessed for the proper
administration of their territories. These commercial interests,
whose viability depended upon peaceful conditions and
regular government, found it impossible to tolerate the natural
state of native anarchy and lack of organization which often
existed. The inevitable petty thefts and depredations of white
property by the natives usually produced an over-reaction, with

21 Ibid., pp. 214-16; Ross, *Aspirations*, pp. 111-12.
22 Robinson, Gallagher and Denny, *Africa and the Victorians*, pp. 41-52, 76 89.

the naval commanders or consuls demanding excessive compensation from the chief or king, whose authority and resources were thereby further weakened; while the flood of complaints which followed a civil war, when the warriors always 'borrowed' from the plantations as they had no time themselves to grow or collect food, would often be enough to cause a native leader to lose his position. Moreover, as trade in the Pacific expanded, so too did the white intrusion into the islands; and so, correspondingly, the native control was further reduced. The feebler this control became, the more resentful the natives felt and the more incidents this led to, the louder grew the demand of the white settlers and firms for metropolitan intervention. It was a vicious circle which continually worsened as time went on, until the home governments, often with a great deal of reluctance, finally took over.

Such was the series of events in Fiji and Hawaii. Yet the story of their absorption was, as Grattan points out, 'straightforward and pellucid as compared to that of Samoa'.[23] The presence of three rivalling foreign elements in the latter group made the situation there much more complicated than in Fiji and Hawaii, where British and American influence respectively predominated. Moreover, the state of Samoan native politics was even more complicated than normal in the Pacific and 'peculiarly vigorous and productive of the disorders of war'.[24] The death in 1841 of the London Mission's protector, Malieota Vai'inupo, was followed by the disintegration of his 'kingdom' and by years of unrest and intermittent strife which ended in 1857.[25] Repeated attempts by the consuls or by the visiting warship commanders to establish some general system of laws for Samoa broke down under the twin assaults of rebellious natives and undisciplined white traders. Nor were the efforts of the British consul Williams to support Malietoa Laupepa any more successful, and the latter was overthrown by a combination of the district chiefs in March 1869. In the war which followed, the rival groups readily granted their (and anybody else's) lands for ridiculous prices in order to obtain arms and ammunition. Between 1869 and 1872, for example, Weber bought land estimated to total 25,000 acres for his firm, while a San Francisco syndicate—the Central Polynesian Land and Commercial Company—claimed that it had bought over 300,000 acres at this time. Native autonomy suffered a further, and very considerable, reduction.[26]

23 Grattan, *S. W. Pacific*, p. 482.
24 Ibid., p. 483.
25 Morrell, *Britain in Pacific*, pp. 285-87.
26 Ibid., pp. 212-13; Davidson, *Samoa mo Samoa*, pp. 43-45.

The harmony among the Samoans which had been arrived at in 1873 and which was cemented by Steinberger's encouragement of a unified body politic, lasted only as long as he did. The *Ta'imua* and *Faipule*, those twin councils of chiefs organized by Steinberger, decided not to appoint a successor to the deposed Laupepa, possibly because of their own disunity. The latter, however, was too influential to be fully crushed and he therefore remained 'a potential focal point of anti-government feeling'.[27] Once again, a situation existed in which the white interests manoeuvred between the Samoan groupings in order to secure political and commercial advantage, while at the same time the various native bodies themselves were endeavouring to strengthen their hands by obtaining the support of one of the great powers. By the beginning of 1877, the Samoans seemed to be turning more and more to the idea of throwing their islands under the protection of either Britain or the United States—if only to avoid being ground between the many external and internal pressures. There is little evidence to suggest that the independently-minded Samoans ever appreciated the legal and political implications of formal rule by a great power; but their publicized offers of cession or a protectorate led to the most frenzied negotiations and stimulated the conflicting white interests and their more reluctant governments into a race to obtain recognition by treaty of their 'rights' in the group.

ii   *The Establishment of Treaty Rights in Samoa*

In July, 1877, Laupepa's party, which had founded its own seat of government in the *A'ana* district and was being encouraged in its opposition by certain German and British adventurers, attempted to overthrow the *Ta'imua* and *Faipule* but was very swiftly dispersed in battle. Yet the latter's success, as Gilson notes, could not compensate for their failure to carry out satisfactorily their 'main function as a government, the conduct of relations with the powers'.[28] Their hopes were pinned high upon the new American consul, Griffin, who on arrival in late 1876 had urged them to maintain Steinberger's ideals and then promptly left for Washington to interest his own government in a quasi-protectorate. This journey so alarmed Weber that he pressed for the recognition of German rights and property in the group, threatening to employ a

27   Gilson, *Samoa 1830 to 1900*, pp. 332-42.
28   Ibid., p. 345.

warship to recover a damages claim of $14,000 if these de-
mands were not acceded to. The *Ta'imua* and *Faipule*, in turn,
became so desperate that they hastily despatched a delegation
to Fiji to request Sir Arthur Gordon to grant a protectorate.
He insisted upon a full cession of sovereignty, however,
explaining that this would turn Samoa into a crown colony
like Fiji, and this the delegates refused to accept; relief from
pestering firms and threatening consuls, not complete political
subjugation, was what the Samoans desired.

Unable to gain British protection, the *Ta'imua* and *Faipule*
capitulated to the presence of a German warship in July 1877
and, besides promising to respect German property rights,
also declared 'We are bound not to give superiority to any
of the great Governments over Germany'. Weber had thus
pre-empted another power from taking over the group. These
German actions, and the fact that the recently-arrived British
consul, Liardet, had (unknown to anyone at the time) a 'disease
of the brain' and was acting in the most reckless manner against
the Samoan government, again produced the inevitable reaction in favour of the United States. Supported by the American
consul and by the Californian land speculators, the *Ta'imua*
and *Faipule* sent the chief Le Mamea to Washington to ask
the protection of the United States. There was little prospect,
however, that this request would be granted or that the various
intrigues in the islands would be dashed by such a move.[29]

The policy of the United States towards Samoa at this time
was, to say the least, confused. There were groupings in the
country—publicists, businessmen in the western states, naval
officers, and politicians like Seward—who favoured expansion
and who looked forward to the day when the Pacific would be
an American lake. However, they could make little headway
against the majority of Americans, who, led by Congress,
regarded with suspicion and hostility any hint of overseas
colonization; it was out of respect for this feeling that Secretary of State Evarts had rejected Griffins' earlier pleas for a
protectorate and insisted that the American policy had always
been 'absolute non-interference with the domestic politics and
government of the Samoan Islands'. Interference in this
instance was more abhorrent than most, for it might also
involve a degree of co-operation with Great Britain, a step
which would be sure to call forth furious criticisms from all
Irish-Americans and their anglophobe allies in Congress. A
single or joint protectorate by the United States was excluded
from the start, therefore; but the mission of Le Mamea, which

29 Ibid., pp. 344-50; Masterman, *Origins*, pp. 141-43. The quotation is from F. O.
(Foreign Office Records, London) 58/159, Gordon to F. O., Confidential, 22/11/1878.

attracted public opinion and culminated in a warm reception
in Washington by President Hayes, could not be rejected out
of hand, particularly when the Samoan envoy offered to cede
the rights of Pago-Pago harbour which the U. S. navy keenly
desired. The end result was the signing of an American-
Samoan treaty of friendship on 17 January 1878, by means of
which the Hayes cabinet hoped to placate the Samoans and
the American expansionists without alienating a strongly
isolationist Congress. In this latter respect it certainly succeeded, for the treaty was promptly ratified although an
application for funds to build a coal-yard at Pago-Pago was
refused by the House of Representatives.[30]

The treaty of friendship gave the United States consular
jurisdiction and most-favoured-nation privileges in Samoa.
The right to construct a naval station in Pago-Pago harbour
was also granted, although this was not the *exclusive* privilege
outlined in Meade's 1872 treaty. Perhaps the most important
clause of all, at least in retrospect, was Article V of this new
agreement, which promised the good offices of the United
States if differences should 'unhappily' arise between the
Samoan and another government. Not only did America
establish claims by treaty to a direct naval interest in the group,
but she also committed herself to an undefined form of special
relationship with the native administration. All subsequent
American intervention in Samoa under Bayard could be
justified by this article, which, though hardly noticed at the
time, was afterwards seen as the starting point for an 'entangling alliance' and as a great contrast to the usually uncom-
mitted policy of the United States.[31]

In the meantime, the jockeying for position in Samoa itself
continued. Having at last received the high commissionership
which gave him jurisdiction over British subjects in uncolon-
ized groups throughout the western Pacific, Sir Arthur Gordon
arrived in Apia from Fiji in March, 1878, to investigate affairs
following the sudden death of Consul Liardet and to collect
the fine imposed upon the *Ta'imua* and *Faipule* arising from
the *Barracouta* incident in 1875. It appeared clear to him, as he
told the Foreign Office, 'that without foreign intervention of
some kind, not only is domestic anarchy inevitable but a
violent collision with the white residents highly probable'.
However, since he continued to insist upon a full cession of

30   C. G. Bowers and H. D. Reid, 'William M. Evarts' in *The American Secretaries of State and their Diplomacy*, ed. S. F. Bemis vol. 7 (New York, 1963), p. 246; F. R. Dulles, *Prelude to World Power* (New York, 1965), pp. 98-102; Ryden, *U.S. Policy in Samoa*, pp. 188-200.
31   Ibid., pp. 297-98, 301-03, 388-89.

zweral Bartlett

sovereignty, the Samoans preferred to await the return of Le Mamea and to decline to sign any agreement with a power other than the United States or even to correspond with foreign representatives without first consulting the American consul. With signs of genuine regret, Gordon ordered the seizure of the Samoan government's steamer as security for the *Barracouta* fine and then returned to Fiji.[32]

This act, which completed the Samoans' temporary dis-illusionment with Great Britain, was answered by Griffin's proclamation of an American protectorate. While this did not prevent the acting British consul, Maudslay, from negotiating with the Samoan government until they gave way under threat of force and agreed to pay a reduced fine of $1,000, it certainly did cause consternation among the non-American residents and jubilation amongst the *Ta'imua* and *Faipule*. These feelings were only short-lived, for on 28 June Le Mamea arrived on the U. S. S. *Adams* with the news of the much amended treaty with the United States and of Griffin's transfer to Fiji for exceeding his instructions. While the numbed Samoans digested this information, Weber, whom Maudslay recognized as 'undoubtedly the real power in the place', was preparing his counter-move. The Godeffroy manager was determined to prevent American intrigues from prejudicing his company's flourishing trade and growing exploitation of Samoan land, and was merely awaiting the arrival of the next German warship to make more specific demands upon a now much weakened *Ta'imua* and *Faipule*. When the *Ariadne* passed through the group in July, therefore, the Germans seized the harbours of Saluafata and Falealili in the eastern half of Upolu and forced a helpless Samoan government to pay off old compensation claims.[33]

This, as far as Weber was concerned, was only a holding measure. As such it was very effective, for the pro-American *Ta'imua* and *Faipule* party had thereby suffered such blows to its prestige that many of its followers went over to the Malie-toan camp; in any case, the attitude of the new American consul, Dawson, was very reserved and the only American support the Samoan government could obtain was that of the speculators now led by a General Bartlett. Satisfying though these developments were to Weber, both he and the German government recognized that a complete and detailed treaty was necessary in order to regain their 'most favoured' position and to obtain security and protection for German land claims

32 F.O.58/159, Gordon to F.O., nos. 7 and 8 of 4/3/1878.
33 Ibid., nos. 9 and 20 of 26/3/1878 and 12/5/1878, enclosing Maudslay report and private letter respectively; F.O.58/160, Swanston to Gordon, 17/7/1878.

before a native civil war broke out again. Consequently, the warships *Ariadne* and *Albatross* returned to Samoa at the beginning of 1879 to effect such an arrangement. With this powerful backing, and the threat of permanently holding the two Samoan harbours, Weber coolly overrode the protestations of the Bartlett clique and a German-Samoan treaty of friendship was signed on 24 January 1879. Following the American example, most-favoured-nation rights, freedom from import and export duties and the right to build a naval station in the port of Saluafata were granted. In addition, all Samoan laws relating to German subjects were to be submitted first to the German authorities and could only come into force when the latter's approval had been obtained. The reference to later arrangements regarding the treatment of crimes and misdemeanours by Samoans against Germans had almost as much potential for future German interference in the group as the 'good offices' clause of the United States treaty had for American involvement. Finally, Germans were guaranteed 'peaceable possession of all lands in Samoa' acquired in a 'regular manner' from the natives—an extremely vague phrase—thus further interference in this matter by Samoans or anyone else was excluded. Concern for the property of the firm was ever Weber's prime motive.[34]

The same was true of the German government itself, though in a much more general and disinterested way. Protection of German trading interests in the Pacific was the main, perhaps the only, ground for Bismarck's support of Weber in these years. This was to be achieved solely through the influence of consular officials, police action by visiting warships and the securing of commercial rights by treaty to prevent foreign interests from gaining undue advantages in the islands. Annexations were excluded, not only because of Bismarck's own distaste for colonies, but also because of the strong opposition this would meet with in the Reichstag. Influential deputies like Bamberger accepted the German-Samoan treaty in June 1879 as a means to assist German trade but warned that it would have been opposed had it implied the beginnings of a colonial policy. An equally weighty consideration to such a supreme *Kabinettspolitiker* as the chancellor was the need to avoid irritating the other two powers with interests in the group. Although their commercial rivalry (especially the pork question) was just beginning to assume some political import-

34 On the German treaty, see F.O.58/164, Maudslay to F.O., nos. 17 and 18 Confidential of 29/4/1879; Masterman, *Origins*, pp. 150-52, 216-18; A. Weck 'Deutschlands Politik in der Samoa-Frage' (phil. diss., Leipzig, 1933), pp. 21-24; B. v. Werner, *Ein deutsches Kriegsschiff in der Südsee* (Leipzig, 1889), pp. 290-98, 463-66.

ance, German-American relations had been friendly if distant throughout the nineteenth century and Bismarck had no wish to see this altered. A good understanding with the British was more important still, due to Russia's hostility following the Congress of Berlin, and indeed in September 1879 Berlin made its famous alliance offer to London.[35] Bismarck, therefore, had no wish to alarm Britain's sensitive Australasian colonists by a forward policy in the South Seas. Weber was informed that the chancellor would not countenance the annexation of, or the creation of a German 'adviser' for, the Tongan Islands; and, whilst approving the German-Samoan treaty, Bismarck disliked any interventions by force in Samoa which might provoke foreign protests or even annexation with its detrimental effects for German trade. The most that could be hoped for was a form of *joint* protectorate administered by the three consuls.[36]

The British government's policy towards Samoa was even more reserved. Like Bismarck at the time, Disraeli and Salisbury were never men to risk prejudicing good Anglo-German relations and the delicate Eastern Question by causing a colonial quarrel which in this instance might also arouse the resentment of the touchy Americans. There also seemed to be nothing to be gained by annexing Samoa or even by getting involved in its seamy internal affairs, with which, as the Foreign Office reprovingly told Maudslay in consequence of his efforts to protect certain chiefs from the *Ta'imua* and *Faipule*, 'Her Majesty's Government have no wish to interfere further than is necessary for the protection of the rightful interests of British subjects in that island, or the general maintenance of peace and tranquillity.'[37] Nor was a joint protectorate administered by the consuls favoured, one Foreign Office clerk felt that 'It is a sort of happy family idea which would never work.' Although Gordon's fear, that a German or American administration of Samoa would soon detract from Fiji's commercial importance, had aroused Under-Secretary Lister's sympathy in 1878, by the following year Gladstone's public criticisms of the British government's colonial policy were beginning to make their mark. As acting High Commissioner Gorrie put it, 'the aspect of affairs in

---

35 R. J. Sontag, *Germany and England: Background of Conflict*, 1848-1894 (New York, 1969), pp. 158-63; W. L. Langer, *European Alliances and Alignments* 1871-1890 (New York, 1964), pp. 185-90.

36 R.Kol.A. (Reichskolonialamt, Deutsches Zentralarchiv, Potsdam) 2819, A.A. (Auswärtiges Amt) to Admiralty, 29/7/1879; BA/MA 625, PG65069, *Die Entsendung von Kriegsschiffen nach den Südsee-Inseln*, vol. 2, A.A. to Weber (copy), 3/3/1879; Weck, *Deutschlands Politik*, p. 29.

37 F.O.58/159, F.O. to Maudslay, no. 9 of 12/8/1879.

other parts of the world does not encourage any one to entertain a hope that a new question of acceptance of increased
territory would be favourably regarded'.[38] Thus the ill-timed
agitation of Sir George Grey for a more forward policy in the
Pacific was greeted with reserve by the Colonial Office and
even Gordon momentarily confessed that it would be 'scan-
dalous to intervene' in either Samoa or Tonga.[39]

Events in those groups themselves, however, were pushing
the British in an opposite direction. Gordon was urgently
pressing for a treaty of friendship with the Tongan Islands,
whose proximity to Fiji made foreign interference there most
undesirable.[40] In Samoa, the American and German treaties
had placed the British in an inferior position and Maudslay
was reduced to suggesting that the easiest way out might be a
German protectorate with equal legal and commercial rights
for Britons. However, the feeling in London (probably
because of Gordon's temporary presence there) was that
treaties should be negotiated with both Samoa and Tonga to
protect British subjects and interests. After some discussion,
it was decided simply to ignore the early fear that a recognition
of these native governments by a treaty would prejudice the
jurisdiction of the Western Pacific high commission, which
technically was not to function in the territories of 'a civilised
power'. Instead, extraterritorial jurisdiction was to be secured in
both groups, especially Samoa, whose native courts were 'a
grotesque burlesque on the administration of justice'.[41] The
British government also hoped to negotiate an agreement with
the Samoans and the other consuls, creating a municipal
administration for the township of Apia, which would be a
neutral zone in time of civil wars. Despite Gordon's suspicions
of an American coup in Samoa, it was decided that such
negotiations would await Gordon's return from leave to the
Pacific.[42]

By the time the high commissioner arrived in Samoa in
August 1879, local political conditions had greatly altered. The
power of the *Ta'imua* and *Faipule* had been steadily declining

---

38 F.O.58/167, C.O. to F.O., 15/7/1879, enclosure Gorrie's report of 28/4/1879. For
Gordon's earlier fears, see F.O.58/161, C.O. to F.O., 9/4/1878, enclosure Gordon to
C.O., 28/12/1877, with the contrasting minutes of Lister and Buckley thereon.

39 C.O.225/4, paper 8467, Gordon to Herbert, 27/5/1879, and minutes thereon.

40 F.O.58/163, F.O. to Gordon, no. 8 of 4/7/1879 (probably instigated by Gordon
himself, then in England), and F.O.58/163, Gordon to Tenterden, Confidential, 6/6/1879.
On the significance of Tonga, see below, pp. 211-215, 282, 284.

41 F.O.58/164, Maudslay to F.O., no. 18 Confidential, of 29/4/1879; F.O.58/159, Gordon
memo of 6/12/1878; F.O.58/161, C.O. to F.O., 20/12/1878, with enclosures.

42 F.O.58/163, F.O. to Gordon, no. 9 of 4/7/1879; F.O.58/164, Gordon to Salisbury,
12/4/1879.

since the signing of the Samoan-German treaty while that of the Malietoans, who had selected as their leader Tavalou, Laupepa's uncle, was growing rapidly. The Malietoans were tacitly encouraged by Weber, who was so eager for a regular administration that he was beginning to regard even an English annexation as preferable to the continual anarchy.[43] In May 1879 Tavalou had been invested with the *Tafa'ifa* at Mulinu'u, which the *Ta'imua* and *Faipule* abandoned without resistance. On the other hand, fear of native disturbances led the three consuls to unite in demanding from both parties recognition of Apia as a neutral zone—an erosion of Samoan sovereignty which was soon to be more formally developed. While this implied consular acknowledgement of two native governments, Weber was now throwing all his weight against the *Ta'imua* and *Faipule*. When Tavalou was taken by his enemies from a chartered Godeffroy schooner during a visit to Savai'i, the warship *Bismarck* threatened action unless he was returned, and as soon as this was carried out, the Germans levied a fine of $2,500 on the offending district and took away four local chiefs as hostages, blows which further drained the resources and prestige of Steinberger's 'old party.'[44]

The rise of the anglophile Malietoan party, and with it the increasing possibility of cession to Great Britain, had been welcomed by Under-Secretary Herbert in the Colonial Office, who at this stage was toying with the idea of a Polynesian confederation, possibly under New Zealand control; but such a scheme was crushed by his political chief, Hicks Beach, and would in any case have provoked a strong reaction in Berlin, where the high commissioner's visit was being watched with some anxiety.[45] To his credit, Gordon, upon arrival in Apia, swiftly recognized that the treaty rights of the other powers blocked any unilateral attempts to obtain control of Samoa. Advised by all three consuls that the Malietoan party should be regarded as the de facto native government, he began negotiations with Tavalou and very quickly received a secret request for a British protectorate, an offer which was immediately turned down, Gordon advising that some form of joint control was now the only possibility remaining. While Tava'ou then issued triplicate invitations to the powers to take over the group, Gordon completed his negotiations for an Anglo-Samoan treaty of friendship, which was signed on 28 August

43   R.Kol.A.2820, Weber to A.A., no. 2629 of 17/5/1879.
44   Ibid., Adm. to A.A., 2/9/1879 and 6/9/1879, enclosure *Bussard* reports; F.O.58/164, Maudslay to F.O., nos. 22 and 25 of 19/7/1879 and 7/8/1879.
45   C.O.225/2, paper 14020, Gorrie to Hicks Beach, 23/6/1879, and minutes thereon; R.Kol.A.2820, A.A. to Münster, 31/10/1879.

1879. Under it Britain obtained most-favoured-nation privileges, freedom from import and export charges, extra territorial jurisdiction, confirmation of lands acquired by British traders in a 'legal' manner, and the right to erect a coaling station in any Samoan harbour other than Apia, Saluafata and that part of Pago-Pago selected by the United States for its own station.[46]

Gordon's most notable achievement was to conclude, with the help of the German and American consuls, an international convention establishing an independent municipal administration for the town, harbour and neighbourhood of Apia. A Municipal Board, consisting of the three consuls and their three nominees, was to legislate for this area with a magistrate to enforce their decrees. Public order, sanitation, civil works, rates and harbour control were their major concerns. Such a body was doubtless very useful in helping to develop the commerce of the township and in controlling the activities of the many whites within it (although in many cases the latter could still appeal to their own consular courts) and it was even more important at a time of impending civil war to establish formally a neutral zone which would be recognized by the combatants. Nevertheless, the creation of this 'largely self-governing enclave' was a further blow to the autonomy and financial strength of any future Samoan government. Native sovereignty was in shreds, despite Article VIII of the municipality treaty, which claimed to preserve the territorial integrity of the islands.[47]

The same was true to an even larger degree of the treaties which the three powers had individually negotiated with the Samoans. As Maudslay pointed out in a very perceptive memorandum in the following year:

> On looking over the correspondence one cannot help noticing that no representative of a foreign power ever misses an opportunity of telling the natives that there is nothing his government desires to see more than the establishment of a strong and independent Government in Samoa, yet some of the stipulations of the treaties which the 3 Powers most interested have concluded with whatever semblance of a Government could be found to treat with, are such that, even if the Samoans had the highest capacity for government, the formation of a strong and independent Government is rendered impossible.[48]

46   F.O.58/164, Gordon to Salisbury, nos. 1 and 2 of 15/9/1879. On Gordon's interventions in Samoa in these years, see also D. Scarr, *Fragments of Empire: A History of the Western Pacific High Commission 1877-1914* (Canberra, 1967), pp. 53-64.

47   Gilson, *Samoa 1830 to 1900*, p. 361.

48   F.O.58/171, Maudslay memo of 20/10/1880, enclosed in Hill to Lister, 26/10/1880. Cf. Masterman, *Origins*, p. 150.

The treaties of the powers had freed their subjects from customs duties, which offered the only possibility for substantial governmental revenue in a land where direct taxes did not exist. Whites were tried in their own consular courts. Most of the lands were claimed by foreigners and, although for the most part acquired under dubious circumstances, their ownership could hardly be challenged in consequence of the German and British treaties. Naval station rights had been ceded away, and Apia was now outside the jurisdiction of the Samoans. In view of all this, it would be no exaggeration to conclude that, though admittedly a vague and very irregular form of supervision, the group was in reality under the tripartite control of the powers from 1879 onwards.

Yet even this shadowy, unofficial control proved too much for the home governments to accept. The State Department acutely disliked the Apia municipality treaty which their consul had signed and made no attempt to ratify it, informing Dawson that he could participate in the municipal government solely on his own responsibility.[49] Clearly, there was no chance of American agreement to a Samoan tridominium, and in fact United States warships became ever less frequent visitors to the group even though a cargo of coal had been dumped on the shores of Pago-Pago harbour. The British minister in Washington found Evarts unwilling to discuss Samoa, ostensibly because of the traditional aversion to overseas entanglements and colonial rule; but a more potent reason may have been the fact that any such form of joint support as requested by Tavalou would obviously have involved co-operation with Great Britain. An understanding with Berlin was not impossible, the German minister reported:

> but as soon as England comes into the question, the Yankees' old antipathy towards his British cousin shows itself, and the thought that the Stars and Stripes should appear as an ally next to the English flag in any sort of foreign action is a fearful one for every American statesman.[50]

In London a similar policy of reserve was to be found, and the advent of Gladstone's government merely strengthened the existing imperial policy of avoiding further commitments in the Pacific. Thus the high commissioner's suggestion of convening an international conference to consider the possibility of Britain administering the group was promptly squashed and he was informed that 'the joint protectorate now established is preferable to the Sovereignty of any other Power, and that it

---

49 Gilson, *Samoa* 1830 *to* 1900, p. 366.
50 R.Kol.A.2822, Schlözer to A.A., no. 4 Confidential of 8/1/1880; Masterman, *Origins*, pp. 153-54.

is not expedient to entertain the question of the annexation of Samoa to this country'.[51] Yet even this was too much when it was learnt that the three consuls had assumed ministerial positions in Samoa and were summoning warships to support Tavalou's government. The Foreign Office understandably felt that it was highly questionable whether the shelling of Samoans would lead 'to the development of trade, the moral and physical improvement of the natives, or the protection of British commercial interests', while the scheme for a governing council of the three consuls appalled Granville, who wrote to the German chargé that it

> would exercise so preponderating an influence over the affairs of Samoa as practically to throw the Government of the Islands upon the three Governments who would be represented upon the Executive Council. Such a result would be attended with many inconveniences . . . It is in view of such considerations that Her Majesty's Government must decline to commit themselves to any agreement which would entail a joint Government by the three Powers of the Islands of Samoa.[52]

Thus it appeared that only in Germany, where the Reichstag struggle over the Samoa Subsidy Bill was being fought at this very time, was there much interest in obtaining control of the group. The origins of this bill lay in the drastic deterioration in the value of the Godeffroy firm's European investments after the 1873 depression, and in the failure to attract new capital after the formation in 1878 of the *Deutsche Handels- und Plantagen-Gesellschaft der Südsee-Inseln zu Hamburg* (hereafter *D.H.P.G.*) to control their Samoan interests. Equally unable to obtain government support the new company pledged most of its shares to the London bank of Baring & Co., which gave rise to the fear that the extensive holdings of the *D.H.P.G.* would soon pass into English hands and German trade and prestige in the Pacific thereby suffer. Prompted by Godeffroy and by Hansemann, the head of the *Diskonto-Gesellschaft* and brother-in-law of Kusserow, the *Auswärtiges Amt* counsellor for overseas affairs, the German government announced its intention of guaranteeing a $4\frac{1}{2}\%$ dividend for twenty years of a new company, the *Deutsche Seehandels-Gesellschaft*, which was to take over the *D.H.P.G.* Yet despite this backing, the bill was rejected by the Reichstag. Distrust of Kusserow's influence, of potential colonization and, above all, of state intervention to rescue a bankrupt firm, combined to defeat Bismarck's proposal. The 'Manchester School' still dominated German

51   F.O.58/168, Granville to Gordon, no. 22 of 27/5/1880.
52   F.O.58/171, Hill memo of 31/7/1880, following Adm. to F.O., 28/7/1880; C.O.225/6, paper 14021, F.O. to C.O., 7/9/1880 Confidential, enclosing Granville to German chargé, 7/9/1880.

economic thinking, at least with regard to *foreign* trade. Nevertheless, a surprising number of newspapers and commercial journals regretted the Reichstag's attitude.[53]

Although this change in attitude by the government has been seen as the first indication of Bismarck's colonial policy, it was motivated more by ideas of trade protectionism (in 1879 Germany itself had gone protectionist) than by a wish to annex overseas territories. In fact, at this very time Berlin was attempting to erect a *joint* supervision of Samoa and ignoring Weber's renewed suggestion of a German protectorate. Bismarck was in no way convinced that colonization was a necessity for Germany and his aim here was the negative one of warning other powers, particularly Britain (Gordon was much suspected of extensive annexationist plans throughout the Pacific), not to seize the islands; 'we are not seeking anything *exclusively*, but wish to protect our interests there', he minuted.[54] After the Reichstag's decision, which he appears to have taken rather personally, he was even more opposed to the idea of a German protectorate over Samoa. Later suggestions of formal control put forward by Hansemann, Weber and the new full-time consul Zembsch were all flatly turned down; 'It all costs money and the Reichstag has refused to grant money', he wrote upon Weber's scheme of administration.[55]

Nevertheless, with an unequalled show of unanimity, virtually every colonial and naval official who visited Samoa in the years 1878-1880 reported that the only solution to the problem would be rule by one power. Perhaps the best-argued plea came from Maudslay, who outlined the enormous effects upon native politics of white entry into the Pacific, and repeatedly emphasized the fact that a Samoan 'king' had none of the powers of his European equivalent. With great prescience, the acting consul concluded:

Matters may be left to drift on for a few years yet and we shall hear more of native disturbances—for it is always worthwhile to encourage a native dispute when it creates a demand for muskets and lowers the price of land,—the taste for gin will increase, and when the natives have become hopelessly demoralised and have lost all claim to their lands, and a mixed government have (sic) succeeded in involving the country in debt,

53 Morrell, *Britain in Pacific*, pp. 224-25; Hertz, *Godeffroy*, pp. 59-65; Schmack, *Godeffroy*, pp. 239-44, 256-76; A. Zimmermann, *Geschichte der deutschen Kolonialpolitik* (Berlin, 1914), pp. 17-20.

54 R.Kol.A.2821, Weber to A.A., no. 2919 of 19/9/1879, and A.A. to Münster, 7/12/1879; ibid., H.Bismarck to A.A., 21/12/1879, enclosure A.A. to Bismarck, with minute thereon; ibid. A. A. to Zembsch, 27/12/1879.

55 R.Kol.A.2807, Holstein to Zembsch, 12/8/1880; R.Kol.A.2927, Hansemann memo of 9/9/1880 and minute thereon, Weber memo of 2/12/1880 and minutes thereon, Kusserow memo of 31/12/1880 and Stirum directive of 26/1/1881.

there will be an outcry from the *owners of the soil* against native depredations, and a demand for Chinamen and Indian coolies, and the large
estates and interests of Germans or Englishmen will be urged as a strong
reason for foreign interference and annexation.[56]

However, no amount of memoranda by local officials to their
respective superiors could alter the metropolitan attitude
towards this 'rich but most uncomfortable country which no
civilized Power will consent to annex and which bids fair to
be of more trouble to the 3 Powers concerned in it than it
would be to the one that annexed it'.[57] Kimberley's minute that
'the sooner we leave to those who have large interests the duty
of taking the chestnuts out of the fire (or keeping them out
rather) the better' captures much of this mood of reluctance
and even hostility.[58] As Masterman puts it:

> Annexation, protection, or participation in the native Government by any
> single Power was passed over—not because it was not the best solution,
> but because it involved most trouble at the time. The Great Powers
> determined to temporise.[59]

It was left to the consular and naval officials themselves,
therefore, to attempt to encourage and preserve through unofficial rather than official co-operation a certain degree of
order and government in the group. The treaty-making of the
Malietoan party during Gordon's visit had caused its prestige
to rise still further, since all three white powers, and especially
Germany, appeared to consider Tavalou as the de facto
monarch; 'his supremacy', Gordon wrote 'affords a prospect
of *rather less disorder* than would otherwise prevail.'[60] Thus
when war broke out in October 1879, Weber employed the
warship *Bismarck* ostensibly to arrange a cease-fire, in reality
to maintain the Malietoan party in power. On 15 December
both sides signed an agreement which recognized Tavalou as
king and Laupepa as regent, and allowed for the re-creation
of a more representative *Ta'imua* and *Faipule* to contain chiefs
from either party. A cautious recognition of, and promise of
support to this new government by the powers, was followed
in March 1880 by a more formal recognition and, a much
greater development, the establishment by the consuls of a
three-man executive council comprising an American minister
of justice, a German minister of finance and a British minister
of public works. As mentioned above, both this scheme, and

56   F.O.58/171, Hill to Lister, 26/10/1880, enclosing Maudslay memo of 20/10/1880.
57   C.O.225/6, Fuller minute on paper 14021, F.O. to C.O. Confidential of 7/9/1880.
58   Kimberley minute on ibid.
59   Masterman, *Origins*, p. 168.
60   F.O.58/168, Gordon to Granville, no. 30 of 13/9/1880.

ringtao China also

the employment of naval force in the following months in support of the Malietoan régime, was soon vetoed by the home governments. In any case, the former was breaking down due to the lack of enthusiasm on the part of Tavalou himself. Only in the administration of the municipality was there much sign of co-operation and progress.[61]

On 7 November 1880, Tavalou died, plunging the islands once more into a state of confusion and rivalry. When Laupepa was crowned king in his place by the Malietoan party in March 1881, the 'old Party'—virtually all of whom were members or adherents of the Tupua family—predictably decided to establish a government of their own. Only in July was the matter settled by an agreement signed on board the U. S. S. *Lackawanna*, where Laupepa was recognized as king and his rival Tupua Tamasese as vice-king, although these positions were to be rotated after an undefined number of years.[62] Whilst this understanding brought a much desired period of peace to the islands, there was nevertheless little firm hope to be gained from it that the inherent weaknesses of the native monarchy could be cured, or that order, justice and good government would be established. Yet the longer this unsettled political situation continued, the greater the possibility developed of Maudslay's gloomy predictions coming true. The *Lackawanna* peace provided no lasting solution, but rather the calm before the storm.

iii   *The German Bid for the Islands*

Of all the events which occurred in the decade after the Congress of Berlin, probably nothing has attracted more historical attention, or claimed more conflicting interpretations, than Germany's colonial expansion in the years 1884 and 1885. With one fell swoop, or so it appeared, places as far apart as the Cameroons, Togoland, South-West Africa, East Africa, New Guinea and the Bismarck Archipelago were annexed to the German Empire on the bidding of the chancellor who had for years previously assured everyone that he was '*kein Kolonialmensch*'. Yet, having seized overseas possessions five times the size of Germany, he then regarded them with coolness, if not positive distaste, for the rest of his life.

61   On the executive council, see F.O.58/168, Gordon to F.O., nos. 6 and 15 of 2/2/1880 and 28/4/1880; F.O.58/169, Graves to Granville, nos. 12, 25 and 38 of 24/3/1880, 5/6/1880 and 7/10/1880; R.Kol.A.2822, Zembsch to A.A., no. 1 of 5/11/1879; R.Kol.A.2824, Adm. to A.A., 8/6/1880 and 10/6/1880.
62   F.O.58/174, Graves to Granville, nos. 6, 19 and 27 of 22/1/1881, 12/5/1881 and 16/7/1881.

It is in trying to explain this peculiar stop-go-stop policy of Bismarck's that so many scholars have engaged themselves since the end of the first world war and the debate shows little sign of coming to a halt.

Many historians have rejected the simple economic interpretation of Miss Townsend and other early writers, and suggested instead that this sudden expansion can only be explained as a tactical move in Bismarck's complex European policy, i.e. that Germany was attempting to draw nearer to France by quarrelling with Britain. An equally formidable body of scholars maintain that the key can be found in the domestic political situation and that Bismarck sought to hit both the pro-English grouping of the crown prince, and the Radical Liberals in the 1884 election, by provoking popular colonial quarrels with London. An extension of this view is that the chancellor, ever suspicious of a Gladstonian cabinet and enraged at their slow and clumsy handling of his first colonial requests, was striving to discredit liberalism in both Britain and Germany by humiliating the British government.[63]

Although later opinion, recognizing the inherent complexity of this whole question and particularly the difficulty of adequately explaining any of Bismarck's major moves, has tended to turn from a single explanation towards a synthesis, it would be true to say that since the 1930s the expansion has been generally seen as a tactical move, aimed at securing a short-term object and having little to do with the colonies themselves. In recent years, however, more attention has been directed back to the possibility that, under strong persuasion from financial and overseas trading circles, Bismarck 'simply changed his mind and decided there must be German overseas possessions'.[64] In particular, the increase in annexations by other nations of tropical areas where German merchants had previously been free to trade and operate as they liked stimulated a fear, which the chancellor gradually came to share, that the markets of the non-European world might be closed to German commerce.

In the most recent interpretation of all, this concept of a *Torschlusspanik* has been linked with other factors, particularly the serious depression which hit Germany in the years 1873-1879 and 1882-1886 and the growing conviction at home that

---

63 By far the best synopsis of the various interpretations can be found on pp.709-22 of the essay by H. Pogge von Strandmann and A. Smith, 'The German Empire in Africa and British Perspective: A Historiographical Essay' in *Britain and Germany in Africa: Imperial Rivalry and Colonial Rule*, eds. P. Gifford and W. R. Louis (New Haven/London, 1967). See also C. J. Lowe, *The Reluctant Imperialists*, 2 vols., (London, 1967), 1, pp. 60-64.

64 H. A. Turner, 'Bismarck's Imperialist Venture: Anti-British in Origin?' in *Britain and Germany in Africa*, p. 50.

colonial expansion would help to solve both the commercial and the socio-political ills of the *Reich*. The latter argument, it is maintained, was the most important one of all for Bismarck, who never at any stage in his life showed much enthusiasm for colonies but was solely out 'to assure a continuous economic growth and social stability by promoting expansion, which in turn was meant to preserve the social hierarchy and the political power structure'. It was, in fact, 'a manipulated social imperialism', with its roots in the precarious political structure, where a conservative élite led by Bismarck was attempting to 'defend the traditional social and power structures of the Prusso-German state, and to shield them from the turbulent effects of industrialization as well as from the movements towards parliamentarization and democratization' by diverting public attention overseas. Although this complex eclectic interpretation is more difficult to document in all cases, it certainly deserves serious consideration.[65]

In view of these conflicting theories, the case of Samoa is well worth examining in the hope that it might shed some light upon the general controversy. Part of the difficulty in discovering Bismarck's true motives in his overall 'bid for colonies' has been the fact that these actions did indeed take place at a time when the chancellor had his eye upon the Reichstag elections and the influence of the crown prince's party at home on the one hand, and upon Germany's relations with France and Britain in overseas matters on the other. Not surprisingly, therefore, his correspondence in this period is a confused mixture of references to all of these developments, since he was attempting, in his usual dexterous manner, to kill a number of birds with one stone. A further difficulty is that the German move, when it eventually came, was so swift, particularly in such places as Togoland, the Cameroons and New Guinea, that there has been relatively little correspondence to guide the historian, who is thus left with the suspicion that reasons unconnected with the territories in question might have played the greater part in their annexation.

Not so with Samoa: the group was the only important territory in the Pacific which Bismarck failed to obtain in his colonial lunges against Britain of 1884-1885, but this did not deter him from seeking to achieve control of the islands in the years following. For a further four years, in fact, Germany attempted to realize this aim, through negotiations at the diplomatic level and action at the local level; and in the mass

---

65 H.-U. Wehler, *Bismarck und der Imperialismus* (Cologne/Berlin, 1969); idem, 'Bismarck's Imperialism 1862-1890' in *Past and Present*, no. 48 (August, 1970), pp. 130, 147, 153.

of correspondence over this affair, Bismarck was forced time and time again to explain his policy both to over-zealous consuls in Samoa and to the suspicious and often anxious governments of the other two powers involved in the group. In so doing, he also throws light upon his more general ideas about colonialism throughout the 1880s.

At first sight, the Germans would seem to have had little to worry about in their commercial position in the Pacific, for they dominated trade there from the 1860s onward; in fact, although exact figures are impossible to obtain, firms such as Hernsheim, Ruge and particularly the *D.H.P.G.* possibly controlled as much as 70% of the commerce of the South Seas.[66] What was alarming to these companies was not the challenges of their trading rivals but rather the extent to which their commercial interests and rights had been, or were threatening to be, restricted by the deliberate actions of foreign governments. In 1875 the Spanish government attempted to assert its theoretical control over the Caroline and Palau groups, and in the following year began raising customs difficulties for German traders in the Sulu Archipelago. In both cases, Berlin's earnest representations persuaded Madrid to give way, but this method of defending German overseas interests through diplomatic action did not prove very successful elsewhere. At virtually the same time, the United States obtained an exclusive trading position in Hawaii by virtue of her 1875 treaty, hurting German commerce in that group. In 1879 the British took over North Borneo and by 1881 it was administered by a chartered company, which gave rise to some regrets in German newspapers. Meanwhile, in the central Pacific the French annexed the Society Islands in 1881 and a little later assumed de facto control of the Leeward Islands; on both occasions, German trade was severely affected.[67]

It was in Fiji, however, that the greatest blow to German merchants and planters seemed to have been dealt in these years. The British, in annexing the group in 1874 when the native rivalries and white involvement had proved regular government by the Fijians impossible, felt obliged to subject all previous land purchases to a close judical scrutiny, in the course of which less than half the land claimed by the whites was allowed to stand. While Bismarck generally welcomed the coming of law and order in the group, local German land-owners and officials felt much less grateful. The commander

66 E. Suchan-Galow, *Die deutsche Wirtschaftstätigkeit in der Südsee vor der ersten Besitzergreifung* 1884, Veröffentlichung des Vereins für Hamburgische Geschichte, Bd.xiv, (Hamburg, 1940); Wehler, *Bismarck und der Imperialismus*, pp. 208-15.
67 Ibid., pp. 208-10; Morrell, *Britain in Pacific*, pp. 191-92.

of the S. M. S. *Gazelle* went so far as to press for the establishment of a fleet base in the south-west Pacific to protect German commerce and for the seizure of an important strategic point, which would only be given up again 'when the English government binds itself not to make further annexations without the permission of the German government'.[68] Although no overt action was taken upon this suggestion, the German-Tongan treaty of 1876, whereby the former obtained most-favoured-nation privileges and also coaling station rights in Vavau harbour, may well have been a response to the British annexation of Fiji. Moreover, moved by petitions from the Germans in Fiji, the chancellor agreed to intercede for compensation for the lands returned to the natives; but these requests were virtually ignored by London for ten years.[69]

Compared with these events, German interests in the Samoan group appeared to be reasonably well protected after the powers had established individual treaty rights there which prevented any unilateral annexation without due consultation with other interested governments. Moreover, the *D.H.P.G.* was liquidated and then revived with an infusion of capital from private financial circles in Hamburg and Berlin, and it continued to dominate Samoan trade despite the fears of British financial control, which did not fully subside until Baring's shares were bought back in 1884. In the meantime, however, the German firms encountered a number of increasing difficulties in the group itself, the most obvious of which was the continuing ineffectiveness of the Malietoan government's enforcement of law and order after the *Lackawanna* peace of 1881.

Because the Germans were the only foreign group with large areas of *cultivated* land in the islands, they were particularly sensitive to the repeated losses through wilful damage and thefts on their plantations in these years, and painfully aware of the mockery with which such acts were treated by the native 'police' and in the Samoan courts. Offenders from villages friendly to Malietoa were handled lightly by the government judges, who had no wish to see popular support for the régime further eroded; while those from Tupua-influenced areas were simply never caught or tried at all. Less important, though still very irritating to the *D.H.P.G.*, was the half-hearted and irregular manner in which the islanders approached the cultivation of Samoa's copra, three-quarters of

68 BA/MA 4349, RMI/V 578, *Die Errichtung überseeischen Flottenstationen*, vol. 3, *Gazelle* to Adm., no. 869 of 15/1/1876.
69 Morrell, *Britain in Pacific*, pp. 388-91; M. Townsend, *The Rise and Fall of Germany's Colonial Empire* (New York, 1930), pp. 69-70.

which came from native sources and upon which the firm's profitability so heavily depended. Malietoa's lack of interest, and failure to encourage his subjects either verbally or by instituting public works, contributed to Weber's gradual alienation from the party which Germany had played such a large part in establishing in power. These feelings, needless to say, were mutual and the Samoan government in its turn resented Weber's drive to regiment their way of life through threats of direct action by gunboats and his introduction of more plantation labourers from Melanesia and Micronesia. Finally, Malietoa was educated and influenced by the London Missionary Society (hereafter L.M.S.), and this to German minds meant that they could never fully trust the monarch, for they suspected (quite correctly) his pro-English leanings.[70]

That a confrontation between Germans and Samoans did not occur earlier was due, not only to the widespread knowledge that Bismarck desired harmony in the group and to the rather natural hopes on both sides for more lasting peace and progress after the *Lackawanna* settlement, but also to the person of Captain Zembsch, who had replaced Weber as German consul at the end of 1879. The newcomer showed an acute dislike of internal intrigues and arms sales by German commercial interests, an attitude which infuriated the *D.H.P.G.* and may have led to his eventual recall in 1883 but which won the praise of other officials and of the Samoans.[71] Yet even Zembsch himself found the situation in Samoa insufferable. The Malietoan party had ratified the German-Samoan treaty in 1879 with a great deal of reluctance and only after Gordon had advised the chiefs that it would be both insulting and rash not to do so. In the period following Tavalou's death the German consul had consequently inclined towards the idea of recognizing two separate native governments until dissuaded by instructions from the *Auswärtiges Amt*, which shared the British view that one strong monarch was the best guarantee for peace.[72] Doubtless aware that Malietoa Laupepa had complained of his attitude to the German emperor via Weber, Zembsch became so disillusioned that for a while he advocated English annexation as the only cure for the group's ailments; but as Berlin, and still less the German firms, showed little desire for this latter step, he was

70 R.Kol.A.2827, Zembsch to A.A., no. 28 of 21/4/1881; ibid., Oertzen to A.A., no. 41 of 12/7/1881.
71 R.Kol.A.2807, Zembsch to Holstein (private), 4/6/1880; Gilson, *Samoa 1830 to 1900*, p. 285.
72 F.O.58/174, Graves to Granville, nos. 6 and 7 of 22/1/1881; R.Kol.A.2826, A.A. to Zembsch, no. 22 of 9/5/1881.

forced to carry on under the dual though differing criticisms of the Samoan authorities and his commercial compatriots.[73]

Although these differences were seemingly settled by Malietoa's promise to act in a friendly manner towards German interests and by the disappearance of the possibility of a general civil war, the native government's known inability to preserve law and order continued to be a constant irritation. Even on the day after the *Lackawanna* peace, German sailors were landed in the municipality to keep the peace, and the warship S. M. S. *Möwe* was soon required in Tutuila to protect the property of a dead German there. In the spring of the following year, Zembsch was forced to offer the king repeated assistance in quelling minor disturbances in Savai'i and Upolu since American and even British warships were infrequent visitors to the group in this period. Outrages occurred against plantation workers, and several districts declined to send representatives to the newly-created *Ta'imua* and *Faipule*. It was clear that the kingship question remained unsolved and, at the first full meeting of that native assembly in December 1882, the Tupua party pressed for a regular seven-year rotation of the *Tafa'ifa* between the two families without, however, obtaining general assent to their idea.[74]

In the spring of 1883 Zembsch, whose efforts to preserve order had by then won the praise of Malietoa, was replaced as consul by a Dr Stuebel, a man of very different attitudes. Already in his first reports to Berlin, Stuebel revealed an obsession with the preservation of *Deutschtum* in Samoa, Tonga and elsewhere in the Pacific, and he continually stressed the need for more consular officers and greater naval protection against the threats from other nationalities, especially the English. Moreover, by that time Weber had returned to the group as manager of the *D.H.P.G.* and was arguing for firm action to preserve German rights and property in a situation where the native government possessed no administrative system, no finances, a deplorable judicial system, an inefficient police force and no gaol. In addition, native support was steadily growing for the Tupua party and although Tamasese showed no signs of wishing to provoke a conflict, it was clear that the Samoan government's writ only extended over half the group and that even here there was little law enforcement for fear that more villages might leave the

73   R.Kol.A.2827, Weber to Holstein, 23/5/1881, with enclosures; ibid., A.A. to Zembsch, 12/5/1881.

74   R.Kol.A.2828, Adm. to A.A., 31/10/1881 and 8/12/1881, enclosing *Möwe* reports; R.Kol.A.2829, Zembsch to A.A., nos. 25 and 62 of 22/4/1882 and 28/11/1882; F.O.58/177, Churchward to Granville, no. 18 of 31/12/1882.

Malietoan side. By the end of 1883 Stuebel reported that Samoa was *unofficially* divided into two political regions and that there were frequent discussions in the villages over the future of the kingship.[75]

While the internal situation continued to prove unsatisfactory to German interests, new threats from other directions were also raising their heads. In the first place, the D.H.P.G. was threatened with the drying-up of the Melanesian labour supplies upon which their plantations so desperately depended. In his 1882 trade report, the British consul noted 'the disinclination of natives to come to Samoa to work and the greater advantages and comfort offered them in other parts, such as Queensland and Fiji'. By the following year, he reported that the D.H.P.G. was so worried about this that it was refusing to send home labourers who had completed their contract, although it was hoped to obtain fresh supplies from New Britain and New Ireland.[76] However, at almost the same time those areas were flooded by labour ships from Queensland and Fiji and the supply drastically reduced just as the D.H.P.G. was beginning to rely upon it above all others. Despite countermeasures, the number of plantation workers in Samoa fell from 1,476 to 1,192 in the twelve months of 1882, and totalled only 1,057 by 1884; and the German consular representative, Oertzen, pleaded for action by Bismarck since 'in two or three years' time it can and probably will be too late.'[77]

Most alarming of all was the strident agitation for annexations in the Pacific which arose in the Australasian colonies in 1883. Queensland went so far as to proclaim the annexation of New Guinea and the adjacent islands by herself, an act which was promptly rejected by Gladstone's cabinet in London but which worried the Germans. Later that year the representatives of the Australian colonies, New Zealand and Fiji attending the Sydney Convention, pressed for annexations in New Guinea and the Pacific, declaring that foreign acquisition in those regions 'would be highly detrimental to the safety and well-being of the British possessions in Australasia and injurious to the interests of the empire'.[78] Meanwhile, a New Zealander named Lundon had landed in Samoa and urged the natives to

75   R.Kol.A.2830, Stuebel to Bismarck, nos. 42, 49 and 69 of 31/7/1883, 31/8/1883 and 11/12/1883.

76   *Accounts and Papers* (1883), LXXXIII, p. 88; ibid., (1884), LXXX, p. 645. This is confirmed in R.Kol.A.2830, Zembsch to Bismarck, no. 9 of 16/1/1883.

77   Staatsarchiv-Hamburg, D. H. P. G. Archiv, Bilanz-Berichte, 1882/84. (I am grateful to Mr. S. G. Firth for giving me these figures.) See also Oertzen to Bismarck of February 1883 on the labour situation in Samoa in the White Book, *Deutsche Interessen in der Südsee I*, copies of which can be most easily seen in *Das Staatsarchiv*, vols. 42, 43 (1884/85), pp. 342-47.

78   Morrell, *Britain in Pacific*, pp. 250-58.

Wellington = New Zealand Capital

appeal to Wellington for protection. Being an ex-member of the New Zealand House of Representatives and a contact of Sir George Grey, Lundon attracted both German and American attention, especially when his ideas were taken up in loud cry by the Auckland press. Disapproving statements on the British side failed to convince Weber and Stuebel that their interests and rights were not in some danger. At the same time, New Zealand firms began to take steps to challenge the *D.H.P.G.'s* commercial hold over the islands.[79] Counter-action seemed to be imperative.

Lundon's intrusion brought together the three separate factors which caused the Germans in Samoa most worry: annexation by a foreign power, the labour supply, and the unsatisfactory government of Malietoa. Given the British free trade policy, annexation by London or Wellington would not in theory have injured German commerce in the group; but it would have meant a much closer supervision of the *D.H.P.G.'s* plantations, where they were now desperately over-working their labourers due to the shortage of supply; and it would have caused a sharp rise in wages to bring them up to the levels in Fiji and Queensland. It would also have hit at the firm's vital small coastal trade by requiring all vessels to deal through a port of entry, a regulation which had caused the *D.H.P.G.* to abandon its operations on Rotuma Island after the British annexation of Fiji and the adjacent areas. Worst of all, it would probably mean a close scrutiny of all the land acquired by Weber in the civil wars of the 1860s and 1870s and possibly the return of much of this to the natives, as had also happened in Fiji. Weber was very alarmed, for example, to learn that the Sydney Convention representatives had resolved that in their opinion no purchase of land made before the establishment of British sovereignty in the Pacific should be acknowledged, except for small plots for trading or missionary buildings. This he saw as being aimed solely against the German plantations and he pleaded for government support to thwart such a move. After 1883 he had a firm ally in Stuebel, who was much more eager, chiefly for nationalistic reasons, to defend German (i.e., *D.H.P.G.*) interests than ever the sceptical Zembsch had been. In the consul's reports, in fact, one can detect an early example of that emphasis upon national glory and 'cultural' prestige which was to be the hallmark of colonial enthusiasts in the following decades. For Stuebel it was crucial to oppose any signs of an Australasian Monroe Doctrine in the Pacific and to build up instead the bases for an extensive German colonial empire, capable of withstanding the insidious encroachment of the English language, laws, culture and ideas.[80]

The German exasperation at Malietoa's patent inability to prevent depredations upon their plantations was redoubled by their fear that his pro-English proclivities and Lundon's urgings would lead him to appeal for British annexation; which he did in fact do in 1883, although this was not known until a year later. It became vital therefore either to control Malietoa or, in the last resort, arrange his deposition. Stuebel strove vigorously to influence the Samoans against Lundon and frequently complained to the British consul Churchward about the blatant New Zealand intrigues. Malietoa was repeatedly warned to improve the police and to erect a gaol and, when this was not carried out, he was forced to agree that natives convicted of offences against Germans should be sent to the municipal gaol—which was on *D.H.P.G.* land and in which hard labour was the rule. In late 1883 Weber obtained a further means of pressure upon the king when he managed to acquire the claims of an American settler to the ownership of Mulinu'u Point, the traditional native seat of government, possession of which was usually an important appurtenance of the *Tafa'ifa*. Although these claims had long been disputed by the Samoans, the chance of securing recognition of their own rights to that land was now nil and Weber could easily turn Malietoa off it if his requests were not met. The *D.H.P.G.* manager, Churchward thought, held the key to power in the islands. Despite this, Stuebel reported at the end of that year that the king had had the temerity to suggest a joint investigation into the validity of certain old land purchases by the *D.H.P.G.*; a request which was immediately refused.[81]

Alarmed by the continuous Australasian agitation for annexations and annoyed that Malietoa was proving so unresponsive to German wishes, Stuebel and Weber cast around for fresh means of pressure. Throughout 1884, however, the lack of naval backing forced them continually to postpone any action until the chance arrival of a German warship off Apia in early November of that year. On 10 November a most reluctant Malietoa was summoned to sign a German-Samoan treaty, a copy of which he was not allowed

80 On Weber's fears of losing the D.H.P.G. lands, see R.Kol.A.2929, Oertzen to Bismarck, no. 16 of 10/2/1884. On Stuebel's own fears and suggestions, see R.Kol.A.2830, Stuebel to Bismarck, nos. 42, 49, 61 and 67 of 31/7/1883, 31/8/1883, 1/10/1883 and 11/12/1883; and Stuebel to Bismarck, 18/2/1883, in *Das Staatsarchiv*, vols. 42, 43, pp. 323, 328.

81 Ibid.: R.Kol.A.2831, Stuebel to Bismarck, no. 72 of 18/12/1883; C.O.225/15, paper 4335, Thurston to C.O., no. 5 of 28/1/1884, enclosure Churchward's despatch of 6/12/1883.

to retain afterwards. By this agreement, a German-Samoan state council, consisting of the consul, two other Germans and two Samoans, was to be created for all affairs pertaining to German interests; a German secretary/adviser to the king was to be appointed; a German was to run the treasury and decide the taxes; Germans were to appoint and control the police force; and, perhaps most significant of all, wrongs against German subjects and property were to be immediately punished with hard labour sentences imposed by the secretary, who would administer the new prison and its inmates. With Weber as the major candidate for the post of secretary, it was obvious that the Samoans who damaged German interests would end up working on the plantations. With one drastic blow, the Germans sought to control Malietoa, prevent Australasian intrigues and solve the labour problem.[82]

It is difficult to avoid the conclusion that this coup, with its intended consequence of placing Samoa firmly under German control, was a contingency measure which Weber had for long contemplated in some form or other. Even when Gordon was in Apia, declining Tavalou's plea for a protectorate and arranging the British-Samoan treaty of 1879, the *D.H.P.G.* manager had urged his own government to take the lead in the group and to persuade the other two powers to agree to Germany administering it for a period of five to ten years, during which time the German 'adviser' would ensure that Germany would move towards a position of unchallengeable influence. One year later, after Weber had left his consular post, he repeated his plea for a German resident along the lines of the system in the Malay States. The Reichstag's rejection of the Samoa Subsidy Bill and Bismarck's disinclination for further colonial enterprises closed the door upon Weber's hopes for the time being, but upon return to the islands he became convinced that this was the only solution. With Stuebel's accession as consul, he soon found a ready ear for this scheme. As early as 1883, the new consul was commending to Berlin Weber's plan for the creation of a German adviser with virtually unrestrained powers, one of which would be the control of police and the supervision of enforced labour by Samoan prisoners on the plantations. In fact, Weber had already drafted a German-Samoan treaty in December of that year, arguing that it was merely a corollary of Article VII of the 1879 one, which referred to future arrangements between the two countries in relation to crimes and misdemeanours of

82 Details of the treaty are in F.O.58/199, Churchward to Granville, nos. 23 and 24 of 11/11/1884 and 17/11/1884; and in R.Kol.A.2832, Stuebel to Bismarck, no. 69 of 11/11/1884. See also, Scarr, *Fragments of Empire*, pp. 66-67.

Samoans against Germans, and of Article VIII, which referred to German approval of Samoan legislation. Malietoa had naturally baulked at agreeing to this new scheme when approached privately about it and for the eleven months following the two Germans had repeatedly postponed insisting upon it until they had a warship to back up their demands. By the time this did occur, Stuebel and Weber had learnt of the German annexations in West Africa and hoped that Bismarck could be persuaded to act similarly with regard to Samoa.[83]

Impressed by the flood of reports about the annexationist designs of the Australasian Colonies in the Pacific, Bismarck had gradually come to share Stuebel's worry about the threat to German interests and urged that steps should be taken to protect their commerce and plantations in Samoa while warning London yet again that great value was placed upon the independence of the group.[84] Although Stuebel may have used these general instructions to carry out the treaty with Malietoa, the chancellor had not advised or even implied annexation and he still adhered to his former views on the matter. Moreover, he knew nothing about the consul's plans to make such a special agreement with the king, a fact which may be attributed either to Kusserow's negligence, deliberately not sending the earlier despatches on to Bismarck, or to the latter's concern with more important topics, particularly at the end of 1884: the words 'What is that?' at Stuebel's mention of the treaty, was Bismarck's first comment in years upon a Samoan consular despatch, while a report from London at the same time earned only the remark: 'How is this matter? I have no time to read the enclosures.'[85] Possessing only an unclear telegram from Stuebel about Malietoa's petition to England and New Zealand's intrigues, Bismarck acted—as he had done in the previous six years—by asking London for assurances regarding the independence of Samoa; and when he had received these, and responded with a similar promise, he seemed content once again.[86]

Nevertheless, certain factors were at work which were inclining Bismarck in a different direction. He was in the midst

---

83 R.Kol.A.2821, Weber to A.A., no. 2919 of 19/9/1879; R.Kol.A.2927, Weber memo of 2/12/1880; R.Kol.A.2830, Stuebel to Bismarck, no. 67 of 11/12/1883; R.Kol.A.2832, same to same, nos. 60 and 69 of 7/10/1884 and 11/11/1884.

84 R.Kol.A.2830, A.A. to Münster, 3/1/1884; *Das Staatsarchiv*, vols. 42, 43, Busch to Oertzen, 29/9/1883.

85 R.Kol.A.2830, Stuebel tel. of 21/11/1884, and minute thereon; ibid., Münster to A.A., tel. no. 192 of 5/12/1884, and minute thereon.

86 Ibid., Kusserow memo of 1/12/1884, and Bismarck to Münster, 11/12/1884; F.O.58/199, Malet to Granville, tel. no. 34 of 1/12/1884, and F.O. reply, no. 29 Consular of 2/12/1884.

of his running battle with Gladstone's government over Germany's claims to territory in Africa and New Guinea. Not only had a combination of internal and external reasons persuaded him to change his mind about the value of colonies, but he was also aware that he had the upper hand in this diplomatic struggle because of Britain's weak position with regard to Egypt. Furthermore, a special commission was about to meet in London to delimit the spheres of interest of the two nations in the Pacific and New Guinea regions, and this could offer a suitable opportunity for a wide-ranging agreement and for obtaining Samoa if this was considered desirable. Stuebel's reports about the near-anarchy in the group and his own Reichstag promise to proclaim a protectorate over all unannexed territories where German commerce was predominant doubtless also influenced him into re-thinking his earlier negative attitude towards the acquisition of Samoa. However, since the other powers had rights there too, the status quo was to be maintained until the chancellor had discussed the various possibilities with them.

All this could be done at a later date for it was much more important in December 1884 to secure Germany's interests at the Berlin West Africa Conference and in the dispute over New Guinea than to raise the question of Samoa, where Stuebel appeared to have foiled New Zealand intrigues even though the methods employed in achieving this aim were not yet known. Despite the suspicions in Wellington and London, there had clearly been no intention on the part of the German government to introduce the Samoan question deliberately at a time when the Gladstone cabinet was reeling under the combined Franco-German diplomatic assault in Africa and was in no position to offer an effective reply. The timing of Stuebel's coup had been a pure coincidence and certainly cannot be seen as forming part of any premeditated move in Bismarck's European policy. The causes of the Samoan crisis were local rather than metropolitan in origin, although it is true that Bismarck, before taking any decision in the matter, was aware that Germany's international position was secure and a colonial policy was popular at home.

What kept it from sinking again into a decent obscurity was not the attitude of either the British or German governments, but fresh developments in the group itself. Not surprisingly, the Samoans had taken alarm at the arrival of a German warship off Apia in November and had endeavoured to forestall the designs of Stuebel and Weber. Joining together in a display of solidarity remarkable for them, the Malietoa and

Tamasese factions appealed to Queen Victoria on 5 November for protection. Six days later, and only one day after he had been compelled to sign the German-Samoan treaty, Malietoa renewed his pleas.[87] It did not take long before knowledge of these letters came to Weber's ears and his reaction was immediate and predictable: Malietoa had to be replaced or German interests would never be secure. It was with this thought uppermost in mind that the local German authorities were to strive for the next few years; and as a result, to bring the islands into the realm of international politics.

iv   *The Reaction in London*

In dealing with colonial topics in the 1880s which did not vitally concern them, such as Samoa, the British government always had to attempt to balance the expansionist demands of its self-governing colonies with the need to avoid disturbing its relations with another great power, particularly Germany, upon whose diplomatic support in Europe and the Near East it greatly depended. The two variables in this delicate situation were the extent of the colonies' agitation and excitement, and the degree to which events nearer home affected British dependence upon Germany. Were one factor strong and another weak, decisions would have been relatively easy to arrive at; but the local Samoan crisis of 1884-85 assumed much more embarrassing proportions in the eyes of the British government because it occurred precisely at a time when both variables had reached their highest point.

Although British dependence upon Germany had not been noticeably great in the 1870s, New Zealand's campaign for the annexation of Samoa had failed to gain the support of Her Majesty's Government because of a third factor, which was soon to disappear: the ingrained reluctance of both a Colonial Office and a Cabinet imbued with the traditions of nineteenth-century laissez faire liberalism to assume control over fresh territories unless, as in the case of Fiji, it became unavoidable. In the years following, though, this policy of doing nothing and of sitting upon the expansionist schemes of the Australasian governments was considerably modified as a result of the French and particularly the German annexations in the Pacific, which provoked a roar of protest in the antipodes. Possibly the inter-colonial convention at Sydney first made Whitehall aware of the strength of feeling in Australasia; it

---

87 Ross, *Aspirations*, pp. 183-84; W. B. Churchward, *My Consulate in Samoa* (London, 1887), gives an eye-witness account of these developments in late 1884.

uffican Pass ✓

even caused such stalwart defenders of colonial retrenchment as Gladstone and Harcourt to shift their position somewhat, and forced that arch-priest of inaction, Lord Derby, to offer support for the idea of a protectorate over New Guinea in 1884 provided that the colonies paid for its administration.[88]

Unfortunately for these Australasian aspirations, that other variable, British dependence upon German diplomatic support, also rose to a peak at this time. This assistance had not become crucial or continuously necessary until the British occupation of Egypt in 1882. Since France and Russia showed themselves bleakly hostile to this move, Gladstone's government realized that without German (and thereby Austrian and Italian) backing for their proposed financial and administrative reforms, they would never escape from their 'bondage in Egypt'.[89] However, after mid-1884 Bismarck demanded a heavy price in colonial concessions for his benevolence and, when this was not forthcoming as swiftly as he desired, joined up with France to give the British a vigorous buffeting in many areas of Africa. By August a bewildered and sorely-pressed Granville was already crying for a halt and retreating from his previous stand on various colonial matters; but the punishment continued for another eight months. With the Cabinet split from top to bottom over Egyptian policy and the Irish question, Gladstone and his colleagues were gasping for a break in the long row of difficulties which had beset them since the formation of their ministry; but instead, on 5 February 1885, they learnt of the fall of Khartoum and the death of Gordon. In the outcry and confusion that followed Gladstone was obviously telling the truth when he admitted to the Commons 'that the difficulties of the case have passed entirely beyond the limits of such political and military difficulties as I have known in the course of an experience of half a century'.[90]

His statement turned out to be too optimistic: there was worse to come. On 21 February Russian troops established themselves at the head of the Zulficar Pass, threatening not only Afghanistan but also the security of India. The Anglo-Russian war, which Europe had anticipated for over two decades, was in sight and it appeared to be a virtual certainty when London received news on 8 April of an Afghan defeat by the Russians at Penjdeh.[91] Germany's attitude, especially in

88 Morrell, *Britain in Pacific*, pp. 253-54; M. C. Jacobs, 'The Colonial Office and New Guinea' in *Historical Studies: Australia and New Zealand*, 5 (1952), pp. 112-18.
89 Superbly described in Robinson, Gallagher and Denny, *Africa and the Victorians*, pp. 76-159; Lowe, *Reluctant Imperialists*, 1, pp. 52-75; Langer, *Alliances*, pp. 281-318.
90 Robinson, Gallagher and Denny, *Africa and the Victorians*, pp. 143-44.
91 Langer, *Alliances*, pp. 309-15.

view of British plans to force the Straits, became more vital
than ever as the crisis loomed. Only in May did it pass and
serious negotiations for a compromise settlement get under
way; but by the following month the Gladstone ministry had
resigned, broken by internal strife and by sheer fatigue. It is
hardly surprising, therefore, that London should have regarded
Samoan events as a side-show, whose importance lay in that it
affected Anglo-German relations rather in that it necessitated
direct action. For every expression of concern about Australasian opinion, there were two about the need to placate
Germany.[92] Only amongst the staff of the Colonial Office was
much concern ever shown for the former during these months
of crisis.

On the other hand, it had been clear to London for a long
while that something would eventually have to be done to
solve the increasing chaos and maladministration in Samoa in
the years following the *Lackawanna* peace of 1881. Six months
after that treaty, the British consul warned Granville that
'there is small chance of the Samoans succeeding in establishing
any Government worthy of the name without the assistance
of some honest and capable foreigner';[93] yet all knew that the
creation of such a post would be bound to provoke suspicions,
if not objections, from other nationalities. While Gordon
wrote in 1882 of 'these unfortunate people, upon whom the
presence of Europeans has forced responsibilities which they
have no means of adequately discharging', he could think of
no way to improve the situation and was indeed simultaneously
fining them for depredations upon British property.[94] By the
following year, Consul Churchward's comments upon the
state of government in the group were as scathing as his German colleague's and for this reason the Apia municipality
treaty of 1879, which included a provision for the reversion of
the town to native control after four years 'if the internal state
of Samoa at that time will admit thereof' was quickly renewed.
It was a measure of the pessimism felt by the powers that a
fixed time limit was no longer placed upon the duration of
their control of the municipality, which was now to be maintained 'until such time as the internal state of Samoa will
happily admit of the District again passing under the control
of the Samoan Government'.[95] Thus one of the few opportunities

92 See, for example, A. Ramm ed., *The Political Correspondence of Mr. Gladstone and
Lord Granville*, 2 vols., (Oxford, 1962), 2, pp. 242, 292, 297, 309, 343.
93 F.O.58/177, Graves to Granville, no. 2 of 10/1/1882.
94 Ibid., Gordon to Granville, no. 24 of 8/11/1882.
95 F.O.58/182, same to same, 27/8/1883; ibid., Churchward to Granville, nos. 15 and
24 of 6/5/1883 and 30/9/1883.

to boost the latter's sagging prestige and influence had been made impossible by its own weaknesses.

Malietoa's secret petition for British annexation in 1883 placed Whitehall in a quandary. Unaware of Lundon's part in this appeal, certain members of the Colonial Office felt this to be a great compliment to the neighbouring Fijian administration and recalled Gordon's urgings in 1877 that a bona fide offer of cession should not be refused; while from Fiji itself the Assistant High Commissioner Thurston recommended either single British control or complete political abstention in Samoa. In view of the treaty rights of the other powers and of the Australasian agitations, neither of these solutions appealed to Herbert or his political chief Derby, who proposed instead a form of 'united protectorate', with equal treatment of all foreign nations, to the Foreign Office.[96] When the latter requested a justification of such a radical reversal of Britain's firm opposition to that particular scheme in 1880, the Colonial Office was swift to reply. As one of the clerks noted, Kimberley's earlier minutes against annexation

> could not now have been written, for the idea of allowing any of these islands to fall into the hands of other European Powers (which might have been the consequence of the action referred to in 1880) might almost drive the Australasian Colonies into revolt since the resolution of the Sydney Convention.

There seemed, as another minute put it, 'to be nothing better than a joint protectorate—confined if possible to England and Germany'; America's obvious disinterest and isolationist policies would preclude her participation.[97]

This bald assumption that Germany would be willing to co-operate in such a venture was soon to be badly shaken but at the time seemed well justified. In the few years following the defeat of the Samoa Subsidy Bill there was little fear in London that Germany might unilaterally annex the group; Bismarck's attitude towards colonization, faithfully reported by the British ambassador on a number of occasions, was too well known for that. As a Foreign Office memorandum reminded the Cabinet when the crisis in Samoa became known, 'During the years 1881, 1882 and 1883 the greatest cordiality existed between the German and British consuls and govern-

---

96 C.O.225/12, paper 1842, Des Voeux to Derby, 19/12/1883, with enclosures, and the various minutes thereon; C.O.225/15, paper 4335, Thurston to C.O., no. 5 of 28/1/1884, and enclosure no. 3.
97 F.O.58/199, C.O. to F.O., 23/2/1884 and 27/5/1884; C.O.225/17, paper 4779, F.O. to C.O., 20/3/1884, and minutes thereon.

ments, and very little was heard of Samoa';[98] and while Gordon had intervened to press Malietoa to ratify his treaty with Germany, Zembsch had encouraged King George of Tonga to ratify his with Britain. A suggestion for the joint protectorate of Samoa would probably be welcomed in Berlin, where it was known that the government 'is increasingly anxious that the interests of German subjects in the Western Pacific may be effectively protected'. But the prospect of actually doing something positive required 'much consideration' by Derby and by the time he had agreed to move (seven weeks later) Whitehall was no longer so sure that it would secure German co-operation for their scheme. Bismarck's bid for colonies had begun and in mid-June London was informed of his intention to establish a protectorate over Angra Pequena. As a consequence, Herbert felt that

> the new departure taken by Germany has again altogether changed the situation and until we know better how we are to stand with that country with regard to Colonial questions it seems inopportune to make a proposal for joint action; and it may be better to let the matter drop.[99]

Nor was it the German policy in south-west Africa alone which caused the British government to drag its feet over Samoa in the latter half of 1884. During the summer months they were forced to forego the ratification of their treaty with Portugal over the Congo river mouth; obliged to recognize the German annexations of Togoland and the Cameroons; forced to abandon the Egyptian conference upon discovering that Bismarck was wholeheartedly supporting France's proposals; and were beginning to fear that this hostile combination might manifest itself again when the question of the control of the Niger was discussed at the forthcoming West African conference in Berlin. In the Pacific, too, the German pressure was being felt; under the threat of the *baton égyptien*, Whitehall had at last been forced to agree to a joint examination of the thorny question of the Fiji land claims, and by September Bismarck was already making vague noises about the question of New Guinea, over which the Australians were extremely sensitive. When he suggested a special commission to examine and delimit spheres of interest for the two nations in the Pacific and New Guinea regions and to clear up the Fiji land dispute, London was eager to comply. Compared with all this,

---

98   Cab. (Cabinet Papers, P.R.O., London) 37/13/52, F.O. memoranda on the communications which have passed with the German government respecting the Islands of the Pacific, no. 3, 24/12/1884.
99   Turner, *Bismarck's Imperialist Venture*, p. 76; C.O.225/17, paper 4779, F.O. to C.O., 20/3/1884, and Herbert minutes thereon.

Samoa was unimportant and, as Derby pointed out, 'If we end up by assuming the protectorate of New Guinea, the Germans may very likely take Samoa: which will settle the matter, & do us no harm.'[100] Even if such a division proved undesirable or impossible, everything argued against discussing the Samoan problem, which was relatively minor since the first news of the German treaty did not reach London until 19 December 1884.[101]

It was therefore Bismarck himself who opened up the topic, in a conversation of 1 December with the British ambassador Malet, by asking for positive assurances that Britain would reject Malietoa's petition and respect the independence of Samoa and Tonga, an assurance which London was only too ready to give provided the chancellor gave a similar undertaking; they were, no doubt, responsive to Bismarck's hint that an unfavourable answer would affect 'our entire policy towards England'.[102] In fact, Derby personally believed that 'we might let them (Samoa and Tonga) go in consideration of no objection being made to our extending the New Guinea Protectorate over the whole east of that island. That would be a *'quid pro quo.'*[103] Granville even told Münster, the German ambassador, that Britain did not want the two groups, 'which we don't—In fact Samoa is half German already', while Herbert, speaking for the Colonial Office, said virtually the same thing to the Foreign Office a few days later. Only when he heard that Germany had hoisted her flag over New Guinea did Herbert feel that they should answer this blow by accepting Malietoa's offer—but only to be 'in a better position to retrieve the loss of that part of New Guinea taken by Germany contrary to our anticipations'; even this was too strong for Derby, who felt that 'We are pledged not to take Samoa and we don't want it.'[104]

This view was gradually modified by further knowledge of the German-Samoan treaty, by the howls of protest from New Zealand and by the general discontent felt in the Cabinet at Bismarck's tactics; but it still remained a question of balancing

---

100 Ibid., Derby minute of 27/6/1884; Robinson, Gallagher and Denny, *Africa and the Victorians* pp. 172-76; J. Lepsius et al., eds., *Die Grosse Politik der Europäischen Kabinette*, 40 vols., (Berlin, 1922-27), (hereafter G.P.), 4, nos. 736, 743, 745.

101 Morrell, *Britain in Pacific*, pp. 259-60, relying on parliamentary papers, puts the arrival of the news of the treaty at an even later date; in fact, Churchward's no. 23 arrived on 19/12/1884.

102 F.O.58/199, Malet to Granville, no. 43 of 1/12/1884, and F.O. to Malet, no. 29 Consular of 2/12/1884; R.Kol.A.2831, Kusserow memo of 1/12/1884.

103 P.R.O.30/29 (Granville Papers)/120, Derby to Granville, 11/12/1884.

104 Ibid., Granville to Derby, 11/12/1884; F.O.58/199, memo of 16/12/1884 by J.W.W.(?); C.O.225/17, paper 21898, Herbert and Derby minutes on F.O. to C.O., 19/12/1884; Morrell, *Britain in Pacific*, p. 258.

the two variables. On the one hand the British consul was instructed to be cautious and the New Zealand government was warned that Germany would have a strong case for annexing the group if Wellington persisted in its scheme to send a minister there; on the other, the Colonial Office wanted Malet to say that Her Majesty's Government expected that the German treaty would not be ratified, and pressed for the Admiralty to send a warship to Samoa immediately.[105] In private, though, they found themselves able to do little about the German-Samoan arrangement. Although Gladstone found himself, 'as to Samoa, unable to understand in what way the late proceeding is consistent with its independence', the Foreign Office librarian Hertslet pointed out that this treaty was not inconsistent with Article VII of the 1879 German-Samoan agreement; and that the only thing the British could do would be to obtain a similar one from Malietoa, an act which could only make a difficult situation more difficult.[106]

The German government based their answer to Malet's representations upon this defence and declared its intention to ratify the treaty in order to secure 'greater legal security and an improved penal system'.[107] Though Stuebel's action had come as a surprise to Bismarck, the latter agreed that firm steps were necessary to correct the chronic state of disorder in the islands from which only German interests suffered, and to forestall Australasian attempts at annexation. Nevertheless, Stuebel and Weber's next move caused him considerable embarrassment and went far beyond what the chancellor thought was necessary. Unable to subject Malietoa to his will and enraged upon learning of the renewed secret appeals for British protection, the manager of the *D.H.P.G.* threw all the weight of German influence in Samoa in favour of the vice-king Tamasese and, when the king protested against this, Stuebel had marines land in January 1885 and take over Mulinu'u Point, raising the German flag there. Disregarding the protests of the British and American consuls, the Germans then proceeded to occupy Apia and proclaim Tamasese king.[108] As the despatches of the powerless British consul did not reach London until ten weeks later, the first intimation Granville

---

105 F.O.58/199, draft to Churchward (sent 5/1/1885), following his no. 23 to Granville of 11/11/1884; F.O.58/200, C.O. to F.O., 8/1/1885; C.O.537/136, paper 6/85 Secret, F.O. to C.O., Confidential and Pressing, 9/1/1885, and minutes thereon.

106 P.R.O.30/29/129, Gladstone to Granville, 3/2/1885; F.O.58/200, memo by Hertslet of 12/1/1885.

107 Ibid., German Embassy to F.O., 28/1/1885; R.Kol.A.2832, A.A. to Stuebel, no. 4 of 3/2/1885.

108 F.O.58/200, Churchward despatches nos. 5, 7 and 8 of 29/1/1885, 4/2/1885 and 9/2/1885; Ryden, *U.S. Policy in Samoa*, pp. 284-87.

received of these events was when Herbert Bismarck explained them to Malet on 9 February, assuring the ambassador that these were solely a 'reprisal' for acts of violence by Samoans and that Stuebel was to be asked why he had thought it necessary to raise the German flag at Mulinu'u.[109]

Although he did not show it to London, Bismarck was in fact highly annoyed at these reports and at Stuebel's extremely vague references to New Zealand intrigues as justifying his gunboat diplomacy: 'Representatives who proceed militarily upon such gossip are only employable at home' was one of the chancellor's fierce minutes, and Kusserow himself was sharply reprimanded for attempting to support the consul's explanations. This fury is partly to be explained by Bismarck's intense dislike of having his hands forced and his very complicated and delicate diplomacy prejudiced by the misdeeds of unthinking consular officials—*furor consularis* as he was soon to label it. At the beginning of 1885 the chancellor had received urgent entreaties for state action from the *D.H.P.G.*, which cleverly reminded him of his Reichstag promise to proclaim a protectorate over all unannexed territories where German commerce was predominant. Such arguments, together with the reports of chaos in the group, caused him to come around to the idea that German control of Samoa was both desirable and necessary; but he still did not consider it to be urgent. This aim could best be achieved through the Pacific demarcation talks and he had moreover promised London that the status quo would be respected. A change in Samoa's status, Stuebel was quickly informed, could only come about through negotiations and not through military force in the islands.[110] While agreeing to the consul's request for the presence of a naval vessel, Bismarck specifically told the Admiralty that 'it is not intended to prepare for a German protectorate in Samoa by sending a warship'.[111] Possibly his differences with the French during the Berlin West Africa conference, and a growing disbelief in the likelihood of a New Zealand coup, were further considerations in his decision to obtain Samoa through diplomatic means. He had, in any case, no wish to establish a precedent by disregarding the treaty rights of the other powers.

109 F.O.58/200, Malet to Granville, no. 75 of 9/2/1885, and F.O. to Malet, no. 105 of 12/2/1885.

110 R.Kol.A.2831, D.H.P.G. to Bismarck, 9/1/1885, and draft despatch to Alvensleben, January 1885; R.Kol.A.2832, A.A. to Stuebel, no. 4 of 3/2/1885; R.Kol.A.2833, Stuebel to Bismarck, no. 8 of 3/2/1885, and minute thereon; R.Kol.A.2834, Kusserow memo of 20/3/1885, and minutes thereon.

111 BA/MA 625, PG65072, *Die Entsendung von Kriegsschiffen nach den Südsee-Inseln— Ganz Geheim*, A.A. to Adm., 10/2/1885.

On the British side, the desire for better relations was far more urgent and simply overrode all other considerations, especially after the disaster in the Sudan. The opportunity of settling colonial differences offered by the visit of Herbert Bismarck to London and the possibility of an arrangement over Egypt with France, however disadvantageous the terms of both agreements might be, were seized upon by the British government with great fervour.[112] Hard-pressed all over the globe, Gladstone insisted that they 'wind up at once these small colonial controversies' and on 6 March Derby accepted an 8° south latitude boundary line in New Guinea, ignoring the expected Australian protests with the excuse that 'the question of Egypt overrides all others'.[113] Under these circumstances, the Colonial Office felt that the best that could possibly be achieved was a neutralization of Samoa and Tonga; and Thurston, brought home from Fiji to negotiate the Anglo-German demarcation arrangement in the Pacific, was instructed to seek this end. At the same time, Derby told New Zealand that he was confident that it would 'recognise frankly the good claims of a great friendly power'.[114]

Herbert Bismarck and the German commissioner Krauel therefore found their work in London proceeding very smoothly and every member of the Cabinet falling over backwards to please Germany.[115] In both Africa and New Guinea the British gave way and by the end of March the Fiji land compensation dispute, after a decade of desultory negotiation, was also settled. Samoa was more difficult to solve. Bismarck, still concerned about the Australasian agitation, maintained his desire to protect Germany's predominant trade position in the Pacific. If Tonga could not be secured, Krauel was instructed, it would be better to neutralize that group, where the native government was fairly competent; but the situation in Samoa was so chaotic that a 'civilized' power must step in and restore order and, in view of the extensive nature of her interests there, that power could only be Germany. Although the chancellor was now beginning to feel that the November 1884 treaty was a mistake and inconsistent with the obligations

112 Robinson, Gallagher, Denny, *Africa and the Victorians*, pp. 150-51; K. Eberhard 'Herbert von Bismarcks Sondermissionen in England 1882-1889' (Phil. diss., Erlangen, 1949), pp. 113-51.
113 P.R.O.30/29/120, Derby to Granville, 6/3/1885; Ramm, *Political Correspondence*, 2, p. 343.
114 C.O.225/19, paper 4419, C.O. to F.O., 12/3/1885, with instructions for Thurston; Ross, *Aspirations*, p. 192.
115 A.A. (Auswärtiges Amt Archiv, Bonn)/*Akten der Missionen: Londoner Botschaft* (hereafter *A.M.L.B.*)/*Krauel: Neu Guinea & Südsee*, vol. 1. Krauel to A.A., no. 1 of 25/2/1885; G.P., 4, no. 760.

to respect Samoan independence, he had also definitely decided to try to obtain the group by negotiation.[116] While Thurston was not opposed to this idea and endeavoured to secure British control over Tonga as compensation, the Colonial Office itself was much less enthusiastic. New Zealand would not consider that to be a fair exchange and, in any case, the reports from Samoa at last arrived in London and provoked much indignation and suspicion that the German government had been assuming an innocent pose during the negotiations, while its agents were causing chaos in the group itself. Herbert warned Krauel that, despite the chaos and the German commercial predominance, all three nations must be equal in Samoa; two years previously he would have accepted the German argument. Strengthening the native government was the Colonial Office's only solution, 'having regard to New Zealand' and being 'the only way of our regaining the position which we have probably lost by the recent action of Germany'.[117] Even if the Germans were to have two members on a board of foreign advisers, and the British and Americans one apiece, a detail Thurston recommended in view of the German agitation upon recognition of their trade predominance, it would be far better than a totally German administration.

It was while both governments were analysing the separate reports of their commissioners that the Gladstone ministry came to an end, on 9 June 1885. It was replaced by a Conservative Cabinet under Lord Salisbury, who also assumed the post of foreign secretary. The change was very important, particularly in regard to Anglo-German relations, where a thaw followed almost immediately. This was partly due to Bismarck's relief at the fall of Gladstone and to a certain coolness in Franco-German relations; partly to the settlement of most of the major Anglo-German colonial disputes, and the passing of the possibility of an Anglo-Russian war over Afghanistan, where Bismarck would have been compelled to adopt a very strict neutrality; and partly to Salisbury's determination to strike at the root of Britain's diplomatic weakness by convincing Berlin that his government was eager to be friendly. The 'cement' to this understanding was provided by the news from Bulgaria in September, with the ominous implications

---

116 A.A./A.M.L.B./*Krauel: Neu Guinea & Südsee*, vol. 1, A.A. to Münster, nos. 75, 103 and 111 of 22/3/1885, 29/3/1885 and 3/4/1885, and H. Bismarck to Krauel, no. 11 of 4/4/1885; R.Kol.A.2834, A.A. to Münster, no. 103 (draft) of 29/3/1885, with Bismarck minute thereon.

117 Ibid., Krauel to A.A., no. 32 of 2/5/1885; C.O.225/20, paper 7852, Mercer's minute of 5/5/1885 on Thurston's report; ibid., paper 8176, Fuller minute of 7/5/1885 on draft declaration respecting the Pacific Islands.

this brought for both powers.[118] While there was no reason to suppose that Bismarck would suddenly become receptive to Britain's colonial wishes, there was now at least some hope of that fierce and seemingly implacable opposition all over the world which had caused the Gladstone administration so much trouble and embarrassment being abandoned.

This change was apparent in Pacific diplomacy also, where Bismarck's policy of protecting German commerce by means of protectorates had led to a clash with Spain over the Caroline and Palau groups. When he asked Britain to repeat their joint protests of 1875 against Spain's claims to those islands, the Colonial Office was unenthusiastic; 'Let Germany fight her own battles. The Carolines are quite out of our beat', minuted Ashley, the parliamentary under-secretary, a sentiment with which Derby fully concurred.[119] Yet Salisbury, soon after coming into office, assured the German ambassador that Britain 'will be ready to concert with the German government as to the measures to be taken'. To the Colonial Office, which believed that Spain had the better claim, this gesture was 'a little further than we intended' and quite inexplicable, but the prime minister had good reasons for his offer. As he explained to Iddesleigh:

> I have been using the credit I have got with Bismarck in the Caroline Is. and Zanzibar to get help in Russia and Turkey and Egypt. He is rather a Jew, but on the whole I have as yet got my money's worth.[120]

Salisbury approached the Samoan problem in a similar spirit. Like his predecessors in office, he was far more concerned with the larger problems of Ireland, Egypt, the Balkans and the defence of India than with what went on in distant island groups in the Pacific. Unlike them, he was willing to demonstrate openly to Berlin that he wished to be friendly, and he instituted a more positive policy of seeking a solution for the minor problems to the satisfaction of all concerned, if that were at all possible. Soon after coming into office he was made aware of the Samoan problem and given an opportunity to put his ideas into practice. The reports from the group indicated that the chaos was continuing, since Tamasese had now come out in open revolt and was being recognized as king by all the German officials; the latter had also removed

118 Lowe, *Reluctant Imperialists*, 1, pp. 62-63; A. J. P. Taylor, *The Struggle for Mastery in Europe* 1848-1918 (Oxford 1954), pp. 301-303; G. Cecil, *Life of Robert Marquis of Salisbury*, 4 vols. (London, 1921-32), 3, pp. 222-24.

119 C.O.225/20, minutes on papers 4468 and 10321.

120 F.O.58/203, Salisbury to Hatzfeldt, 10/7/1885; C.O.225/21, minutes on papers 13917 and 14323, F.O. letters of 6/8/1885 and 11/8/1885; Cecil, *Life*, 3, p. 230. Salisbury was also persuading the Sultan of Zanzibar not to resist German action in Witu.

themselves from the jurisdiction of the Municipality.[121] By this stage, too, Thurston's report on the delimitation of the respective Pacific interests of the two powers had been communicated to the German government, which was informed that Britain was ready, apart from one or two minor modifications, to accept a settlement along the lines indicated by the commissioner. While generally approving of the demarcation proposals, Bismarck nevertheless declined to accept the scheme for strengthening Malietoa's government and urged that administration by one power, which would naturally be Germany, was the only feasible solution.[122]

With the possibility of establishing some form of joint control over Samoa fading rapidly as Bismarck accepted the arguments of his colonial officials and traders for a single authority for the group, Salisbury offered another suggestion in order to arrange a quick settlement. Berlin was sent a memorandum, originating in the Colonial Office, which argued that the islands could most easily be administered from nearby Fiji, whereas it would cost Germany great expense and many difficulties to rule due to the great distance of Samoa from the other German colonies in the Pacific. The answer was predictable and unchanging; it would be no bother to Germany to administer the islands and due to her predominant position there it was 'well nigh impossible for the German government to give way on this point'.[123]

Having probably anticipated such a reply, the premier was not disappointed; but the uncompromising attitude in Berlin did place the ball back squarely into his court. If Bismarck refused to accept either a joint protectorate or a British administration, there appeared to be only one other solution possible, one which Salisbury's Europe-centred view of foreign policy logically suggested. Yet, although Thurston in Fiji urged that the only feasible and sensible way out was the establishment of a German administration of Samoa in some form, even Salisbury could not bring himself at this stage to agree to a German protectorate 'owing to the state of public feeling in the Colonies'.[124] What he lacked was an adequate loophole through which he could arrange a settlement which

121   F.O.58/201, Churchward to Granville, no. 23 of 28/4/1885; F.O.58/203, Churchward to Salisbury, nos. 31 and 37 of 23/6/1885 and 28/7/1885; R.Kol.A.2837, Stuebel to Bismarck, no. 62 of 22/7/1885.

122   A.A./*A.M.L.B.*/*Allgemeine Kolonialpolitik*, vol. 2, A.A. to Münster, no. 278 of 12/7/1885, with enclosures; F.O.58/203, Scott to Salisbury, no. 289 of 3/7/1885.

123   Ibid., C.O. to F.O., 7/8/1885, and F.O. to Scott, no. 340 of 12/8/1885; F.O.58/204, Malet to Salisbury, no. 500 of 17/10/1885; A.A./*A.M.L.B.*/*Allgemeine Kolonialpolitik*, vol. 2, A.A. to Münster, no. 465 of 19/10/1885.

124   F.O.58/205, Pauncefote's minute on C.O. to F.O., 24/12/1885.

maintained and strengthened friendly relations with Berlin while appeasing to some extent Wellington's indignation at such a deal. Passing on the Colonial Office's reasons why the German scheme could not be accepted, he therefore confidentially told Hatzfeldt, the new German ambassador, that

> in my own personal view the right given to us by the Treaty of insisting on the independence of Samoa was not indispensable to this country; and that in exchange for some adequate consideration I thought it very possible that an arrangement such as Prince Bismarck wished might be arrived at.[125]

This opinion, which would have caused severe alarm in New Zealand, was deliberately not sent to the Colonial Office; but even if they had known of it, they would not have worried for long, for Salisbury's shaky administration collapsed before he could find the 'adequate consideration' he needed for an arrangement with Bismarck. Nevertheless, he had indicated in what direction his mind was moving and what kind of solution he would seek.

125   F.O.58/210, Salisbury to Malet, no. 19 Secret, of 9/1/1886 (cf. his earlier despatch to Malet, no. 5 of 4/1/1886, ibid.); R.Kol.A.3011, Hatzfeldt to A.A., tel. no. 6 of 9/1/1886.

2

'Furor Consularis' and the Establishment of the Tridominium 1885-89

i *Salisbury, Bismarck and the Secret Anglo-German Treaty on Samoa*

In the few years following the 1884-85 Samoan troubles, a dramatic change in the overall situation occurred as Britain, under Salisbury's cautious handling, became less of an obstacle to German hopes while at the same time the United States suddenly emerged as a real threat to them. Despite the memory of the American 'forward' policy in Samoa in the years 1873-78, the idea that Washington might wish to have a say in the political future of the group was not seriously considered in either London or Berlin before 1886, due to the patent lack of interest shown by the United States in the period after the *Lackawanna* peace of 1881. American warships never visited the islands; the Apia Municipality Convention of 1879 was never officially ratified or acknowledged in Washington, although as has been seen the State Department privately recognized its usefulness for the purposes of local government; and, when the U.S. consul expressed concern in 1883 at what the New Zealand agitation and intrigues might mean to America's coaling station rights at Pago-Pago, he was told that these rights were in no way exclusive, an interpretation which was to undergo a complete change by the 1890s. Moreover, when the 1884 crisis in the group arose, Canisius' despatches were merely acknowledged, for the Arthur administration was on the point of being replaced by Cleveland's new government and there was therefore no opportunity to formulate a definite policy.[1]

It was left to the new secretary of state, Thomas F. Bayard, to let the world know that the United States intended to take seriously its treaty rights and obligations in the Samoan Islands. Although the public and commercial interest of America in the Pacific was gradually growing in these years, there is little sign of the imperialist enthusiasm that was to

---

1 Ryden, *U.S. Policy in Samoa*, pp. 261-65, briefly summarizes the U.S. policy in the years 1881-84 with regard to Samoa.

sweep the land in 1898.[2] While her legal position in Samoa
was firmly secured by the 1878 treaty, America's strategic and
trading interest there was in reality very small; the group lay
too far south of the main trans-Pacific routes to the Far East,
and trade between the United States and Australasia was not
large. Despite this, the small but influential group of expansionists, which included Bayard in their number, was looking
to the future and felt that it was important to keep the islands
independent, particularly since so few remained unannexed
by the European powers after 1885.[3] Furthermore, Cleveland's
administration could exploit this apparently altruistic defence
of the poor Samoans for domestic purposes—if only to forestall criticism from their opponents for not maintaining
America's true interests and traditions.[4] Nevertheless, although
the Samoan affair was not lacking what Grenville and Young
have termed 'the baneful influence of politics on American
foreign policy', only the arrogant action of the German
officials in the group and Bismarck's attempts to arrange its
political supervision without much regard for the rights of the
United States can fully explain the strong feelings aroused in
Bayard and his fellow countrymen over Samoa. Salisbury,
preoccupied with the European diplomatic situation and only
too aware of the shortcomings of local colonial officials, might
be able to overlook the German actions; America, proud,
aloof, self-confident and self-righteous, found it impossible.
An understanding of the peculiar American national tempera-
ment and the scorn for old-fashioned secret diplomacy was to
fail most German statesmen, including Bismarck, who
regarded Washington's expostulations as pure hypocrisy and
deviousness.

At first Bayard moved slowly in the matter, digesting
information from the U.S. consul and relying upon Bismarck's
assurances that the German government intended to maintain
the status quo in Samoa. Only on 7 December 1885, when the
German minister Alvensleben told him that Berlin had decided
to assume political control of the group but would not prejudice or erase America's rights, did the secretary of state
speak out, categorically refusing to accept this policy. Instead

2 Though W. LaFeber holds that the expansion of 1898 was 'the natural culmination' of
a gradual trend, which Bayard's Samoan policy of the 1880s illustrates; see his *The New
Empire: An Interpretation of American Expansion* 1860-1898, (New York, 1963), pp. vii-ix,
53-58.
3 H.-U. Wehler, '1889: Wendepunkt der amerikanischen Aussenpolitik. Die Anfänge
des modernen Panamerikanismus—Die Samoakrise' in *Historische Zeitschrift*, 201 (1965),
pp. 86-109.
4 J. S. Grenville and G. B. Young, *Politics, Strategy and American Diplomacy:
Studies in Foreign Policy*, 1873-1917 (London/New Haven, 1966), pp. xvii-xviii, and
especially 39-73.

of observing that the German proposal was bound to affect the most-favoured-nation rights of the United States and therefore made nonsense of the assurances contained in the latter part of Alvensleben's communication, Bayard based his argument squarely upon Article V of the American-Samoan Treaty of 1879, under which Washington's good offices were promised in the event of a dispute between the Samoan government and a third power. By this clause, Bayard exaggerated, 'The United States had assumed the position of a benevolent protector, and the German intervention would mean the virtual displacement of the United States from that preferred status.'[5] In other words, while the United States was not going to annex the group, she was not going to let any other power do so either. This was hardly the answer Bismarck had expected to his message and it was to be a long time before he appreciated that the Americans were really serious in this attitude.

The new foreign secretary in London, Lord Rosebery, had to tread far less heavily than his American counterpart. Nor was he in a position to come forward with any suggestion for a quid pro quo agreement with Berlin, as Salisbury had been inclined to do, since he was less well acquainted with the Samoan question; since his Liberal government had to act even more cautiously towards Germany; and since his chief concern in Pacific affairs was to get the Anglo-German demarcation arrangement concluded as quickly as possible.[6] Although he made enquiries inside the Foreign Office as to Salisbury's suggestion, he told Hatzfeldt in February 1886 that he 'was not in a position to discuss the question of a modification of the arrangements existing in Samoa'.[7] When Malet wrote from Berlin that a solution might be found in allowing the duties of the British consul to be taken over by his German colleague, Rosebery declared this to be 'inadmissable' without even waiting for the Colonial Office to protest against it. Although much more inclined than Salisbury to act touchily and resentfully when diplomatic pressure was being brought to bear, even Rosebery could appreciate that 'we are kept on the stretch by questions other than Samoa'.[8]

5   Ryden, *U.S. Policy in Samoa*, p. 299; C. C. Tansill, *The Foreign Policy of Thomas F. Bayard* 1885-1897 (New York, 1940), pp. 30f.

6   This agreement was finally reached on 6 April 1886. For the details see F.O.64/vols. 1150-52; and R. J. P. Bünemann, 'The Anglo-German "Colonial Marriage" 1885-1894' (Oxford B.Litt. thesis, 1955); The German side of the negotiations can be traced in R.Kol.A.2518-19, 2938.

7   F.O.58/210, Hervey memo of 11/2/1886; F.O.58/211, Rosebery to Malet, no. 110 of 19/2/1886.

8   Ibid., Malet to Rosebery, no. 138 Confidential of 11/3/1886; F.O.343 (Malet Papers)/7, same to same, 13/3/1886; F.O.343/2, Rosebery to Malet, 17/3/1886.

What was worse, all reports from the group suggested that the situation there was going from bad to worse. In his despatches, Stuebel had been continually impressing upon Bismarck the danger of New Zealand intrigues and the clear anti-German attitude taken up by Malietoa, both of which necessitated vigorous counter-measures; he also stressed that Tamasese's revolt was a purely natural and popular development, uninspired by the Germans, who, however, stood to gain from this change in the monarch.[9] Yet the British consul's reports revealed that, far from being impartial, Stuebel was assisting Weber's efforts to oust Malietoa and to bring in their somewhat reluctant protégé, Tamasese. At the turn of the year Weber had the king driven away from Mulinu'u altogether and the Samoan flag hauled down by Stuebel and some sailors from S. M. S. *Albatros*. Bismarck, indeed, was much perturbed at this second landing of marines and promised repeatedly that the independence of the islands would be respected by Germany. While seeking to gain control of Samoa by negotiation, the chancellor always ruled out a coup, which Stuebel, Krauel and Herbert Bismarck favoured: 'Doesn't our treaty run "nothing to be changed without agreement with England and America"?', he scribbled angrily on the consul's despatches.[10] On the other hand, the German government did proceed to ratify the November 1884 treaty and to bombard the Foreign Office in London with complaints about the obstructionism of the British consul in regard to the measures taken to protect German commercial interests in the group. As always in such cases where his own policy was under criticism, Bismarck preferred to take the diplomatic offensive in order to divert attention elsewhere and relieve pressure upon his government's position.

Dismayed by the chancellor's complaints and by the fresh outburst of troubles in Samoa, Rosebery readily embraced the suggestion of his permanent under-secretary, Sir Julian Pauncefote, who on 26 February had minuted:

> I do not see how matters in Samoa can be settled unless Germany and the U.S. will agree with us to send a Delegate in a Man of War to enquire impartially into the state of affairs & to restore peace and good order & secure future good govt. on the footing of the independence of the islands, & the joint Protectorate of Great Britain, the U.S. & Germany.[11]

9 See, for example, the despatch by Stuebel to Bismarck, no. 90 of 14/10/1886, in R.Kol.A.3011.

10 F.O.58/205, Powell to Salisbury, no. 51 of 9/12/1885 and tel., 31/12/1885; F.O.58/210, same to same, no. 1 of 5/1/1886; F.O.58/211, Powell to Rosebery, no. 5 of 3/2/1886; R.Kol.A.3012, Bismarck minutes on Stuebel's despatches, nos. 7 and 26 of 7/1/1886 and 2/2/1886.

11 F.O.58/210, minute of 26/2/1886 on Malietoa to Victoria, 4/1/1886.

Shortly afterwards, Rosebery repeated this idea to Hatzfeldt but it was immediately turned down by Bismarck, who much suspected that the British and American commissioners thus proposed would combine together to out-vote the German; and that such a balance of force would be built into any joint protectorate. He was prepared to send an Anglo-German commission, though, for it might offer a suitable vehicle for obtaining an agreement for a de facto German administration particularly if Thurston was appointed as the British investigator.[12] With the other colonial questions now almost all settled, it was time to bring the uncertain state of Samoan affairs to a close. Indeed, Hatzfeldt hinted that Bismarck was 'very sick of his colonial policy, and only wished to wind up Zanzibar and Samoa', a fact which made Rosebery fear that a German protectorate would soon be demanded 'without any *quid pro quo*'.[13]

During this interchange Bismarck had given the impression that he anticipated no more than nominal protests from the United States at the assumption of a German protectorate over Samoa; but shortly afterwards the news of a further crisis and the beginnings of an American diplomatic 'counter-offensive' forced him to accept Rosebery's idea of a commission in full. A German cruiser squadron had arrived off Apia in April 1886, ignored Malietoa and accorded recognition to Tamasese as monarch; but, as soon as the warships had gone, the U.S. consul Greenebaum impetuously declared a protectorate over the islands. Furthermore, all reports indicated that a native civil war would break out soon.[14] Bayard, repudiating Greenebaum's act as soon as it became known, took the initiative by suggesting that the whole problem be dealt with in conference by him and the British and German ministers in Washington. Though persisting for a few days in his wish to have only an Anglo-German commission, fear of further unilateral action by the United States caused Bismarck to accept Bayard's proposal and to suggest that an American investigator also be sent to Samoa before the Washington conference began. In fact, the Germans were suddenly in a very weak position on Upolu, since they had hauled down their flag and their warships were far away. London was requested to ensure the protection of German subjects if war did break

12 F.O.58/212, Rosebery to Malet, nos. 173 and 188 Most Confidential of 24/3/1886 and 31/3/1886; F.O.58/213, same to same, no. 195 of 2/4/1886, and Malet to Rosebery, nos. 194 and 197 of 23/4/1886 and 27/4/1886.

13 F.O.343/2, Rosebery to Malet, 7/4/1886 and 14/4/1886.

14 F.O.58/214, Powell to Rosebery, no. 16 of 28/5/1886; R. Kol.A.3014, Stuebel to Bismarck, no. 63 of 20/5/1886; BA/MA 625, PG65070, *Die Entsendung von Kriegsschiffen nach den Südsee-Inseln*, vol. 3, A.A. to Adm., Secret, 16/6/1886.

out; and Stuebel even began to look to his British colleague for support, a move which Rosebery thought 'surpasses all that one has ever heard of the lamb and the cockatrice etc.'.[15]

It was at this stage, as the commissioners were preparing to travel their separate routes to Samoa, that Rosebery left the scene and a new Salisbury cabinet came into power in July 1886. Although the quiet and self-effacing Iddesleigh occupied the Foreign Office, the prime minister retained his overall control of Britain's foreign relations, where the prime concern remained the situation in Bulgaria following the forced deposition of Prince Alexander on 20 August, which drove Britain into a more definite anti-Russian posture and greater dependence upon Berlin. As could be seen from the entries in Iddesleigh's diary-style notebooks at this time, Samoa was of little significance compared with the host of problems facing the Foreign Office in the Balkans, Egypt and with France.[16] Salisbury, referring Randolph Churchill to the German irritation over Samoa and Zanzibar, wrote that 'We have no interests in either of those two places—& Germany may do her worst—except so far as we are bound by previous engagements.'[17] A little while earlier, he had written that his policy was to go along with the Germans 'in all matters of secondary importance—indeed in all matters where we have not an imperative interest to the contrary'.[18] Therefore, despite some scruples about the injustice to their own consul, the British agreed that Powell should go upon indefinite leave together with Stuebel, 'who is personally so deeply committed to a policy of disorder that there can be no peace while he is there'.[19]

Bismarck's desired concessions were rather larger, however, than the mere elimination of a local difficulty; he wished for a British acknowledgement of Germany's claim to predominance in the group before he faced the Americans. Moreover, at this stage in Anglo-German relations the chancellor still held the much stronger position in the 'diplomatic duel' which he and Salisbury were beginning to fight: a duel in which the loser was to bind himself to Austria-Hungary over Balkan affairs, thus alienating Russia and thereby losing his freedom of action. Pushed forward by Bismarck, the British lost the

15 F.O. 58/214, Rosebery to Malet, nos. 299, 305 and 316 of 4/6/1886, 5/6/1886 and 15/6/1886; F.O.343/2, same to same, 30/6/1886.
16 British Museum Additional Manuscript (hereafter Addit.Mss.) 50044, Iddesleigh's notebook for the period 6-22 August, 1886.
17 Salisbury Papers (Christchurch College, Oxford), Class D, Salisbury to Randolph Churchill, 19/9/1886.
18 Ibid., A44/17, Salisbury to Malet, 13/6/1886.
19 F.O.58/217, Iddesleigh to Malet, no. 405 of 24/8/1886; Herbert minute on paper 25186 Secret, F.O. to C.O., 24/3/1886, in C.O.537/136.

first round of this struggle by their signing of the Mediterranean agreements of 1887; while at the same time Salisbury remained heavily dependent upon German goodwill with regard to Egypt, a weakness which he accepted but deeply disliked.[20]

Along roughly the same lines as this larger 'duel' over European policy, a smaller one was being fought over Samoa. While uninterested in the group itself, the prime minister wanted compensation for a British withdrawal but, once again, he was in the weaker position and therefore could not avoid Bismarck's demands. With regard to the latter, it is difficult to see how by 1886 motives relating to a diplomatic bid for France's friendship, to a Reichstag election or to 'manipulated social imperialism' can be attached to the chancellor's attempts to obtain Samoa. The European situation had now greatly changed since 1884-85, and one fails to perceive how internal factors were at work when he was so deliberately eschewing the 'grab anything' tactics and the emphasis upon prestige which was to characterize German colonial policy after 1897. During the Pacific demarcation discussions with London, the chancellor had felt that a successful outcome was being pre-judiced by the extensive and often shadowy claims of the German firms in New Guinea, the Solomons and elsewhere; 'we have already more territory there than we can make use of' he minuted. The same was true in Samoa, where he had felt that the claims of the German companies were 'stretched too high'. Bismarck's attitude was always more realistic and sober, and he insisted upon a firm commercial base for any colonial acquisitions; 'Property and trade must first of all be formed privately, then the flag and protection can come in as well', he noted in a minute which summarized his whole view of colonisation.[21] While he had been convinced by the arguments of the *D.H.P.G.* and of his own *Auswärtiges Amt* officials that the predominant German trading interests in Samoa could only flourish if given governmental protection from native and New Zealand threats, he always regarded Stuebel's arguments for action with distaste, feeling that it was 'not a matter of authority and ridicule, but of material commercial interests'. Later reports from the consul only confirmed Bismarck's suspicions of him, and the *Auswärtiges Amt* was told that Stuebel seemed 'dangerous for our peace with other powers'.[22]

20   P. Kluke, 'Bismarck und Salisbury: ein diplomatisches Duell' in *Historische Zeitschrift*, 175 (1953), pp. 292-94; Cecil, *Life*, 4, pp. 28-84; Langer, *Alliances*, pp. 365-410.

21   R.Kol.A.2835, minute on Krauel to Bismarck, no. 24 of 22/4/1885; R.Kol.A.2518, minutes on H. Bismarck reports, nos. 46 and 50 of 2/9/1885 and 6/9/1885.

22   R.Kol.A.3012, minutes on Stuebel to Bismarck, nos. 7 and 26 of 7/1/1886 and 2/2/1886; R.Kol.A.3012, Berchem to Bismarck, no. 8 of 31/5/1886; and minute thereon.

On the other hand, the chancellor's determination to acquire the group had steadily hardened, much to British dismay. Following Weber's urgings and a well-argued memorandum by Krauel, he was gradually brought around to the idea that Malietoa and Tamasese should be treated as equals; and by the end of March 1886 he had virtually agreed to the withdrawal of his recognition of the former on account of the monarch's anti-German attitude.[23] Moreover, consultations were well under way as to the type of administration Germany would create for the islands. In this connection, it is interesting to note that a scheme proposed by Stuebel and involving a $100,000 loan from the German government was disapproved of by Bismarck as the sum would have to be obtained from the Reichstag; but he was more favourable to the idea of this money being lent at interest by the *D.H.P.G.* instead. The chancellor was still at the stage where he believed that colonies could be run on the cheap, either through their own finances or through some form of chartered companies.[24] And now that Salisbury had again replaced the more difficult Liberals, it was time to press the British to give way. As Hatzfeldt pointed out, 'Lord Salisbury is however too clever not to know that the political understanding he seeks also presuppose concessions in colonial regions.' (Bismarck: 'Naturally').[25]

The visit of the special commissioners to Samoa in the latter part of 1886 soon revealed the exact form of the concession which Bismarck demanded, for Thurston reported that his German colleague Travers was pressing him to recommend a German administration, or at least that Germany should hold a predominating influence upon a governing council; Berlin was determined that its predominance in the commercial sphere should be reflected in any political arrangement. The easiest solution would be a straightforward protectorate but in recognition of the British and American governments' susceptibility to public opinion Bismarck was willing in the last resort to accept some form of administration which appeared in theory to be joint while in reality permitting German predominance. More attractive still would be an agreement under which the other two powers allowed Germany to act as mandatory administrator for all three, a concession which could soon be exploited to establish an unchallengeable supremacy.

23 R.Kol.A.3012, Krauel memo of 10/2/1886, and A.A. to Alvensleben, tel. no. 14 of 25/3/1886.

24 R.Kol.A.2947, Stuebel to Bismarck, no. 76 of 16/9/1885, and A.A. to Stuebel, A13 of 1/12/1885.

25 A.A./*England* 69, vol. 31, Hatzfeldt to Bismarck (copy), 26/7/1886, and minute thereon; G.P., 4, nos. 795, 800 and 802.

Asked what compensation Germany would offer for Britain's consent to these schemes, Travers indicated that Berlin might agree to allowing the British to administer Tonga. As this particular quid pro quo had been in Thurston's mind since 1885, he was not averse to the idea, despite his instructions to 'provide for a just recognition of all interests, both native and foreign'.[26] While submitting to the Colonial Office a long and formal report upon the causes of the Samoan troubles and a scheme for the strengthening of the native government through external assistance, he also sent a secret despatch, urging the alternative and pointing out to Stanhope, the colonial secretary, that

> apart from any strategical value the harbour of Pango-Pango may possess, our actual interests in the Samoan Islands are not sufficient to make it worthwhile being on unfriendly terms in respect of them with a neighbouring Power having such intimate relations with us as Germany.

If Pago-Pago could be neutralized by a joint agreement and the Tonga 'deal' arranged, Thurston believed that the Australasian colonies would be satisfied.[27]

At home, much pressure was being brought to bear upon the British government to accede to the German scheme. Krauel was in London once more in November 1886 and urged a settlement, while Hatzfeldt hinted that Bismarck would be very annoyed if little progress was made. They were told that Thurston's report must be received before any decision could be reached, and the Colonial Office still maintained that the German suggestion 'cannot be entertained, as Australia and New Zealand would regard its acceptance with the strongest dissatisfaction'.[28] When Thurston's formal report for the strengthening of the native government arrived, this view was reinforced and Herbert considered that Travers' scheme would entail 'a deliberate betrayal of Colonial Interests —which we are specifically pledged to uphold'.[29]

However, these views were not shared by all members of the British government. Iddesleigh had already informed Malet that they were 'not indisposed' in principle to the German scheme of one mandatory power, but on 27 November his parliamentary under-secretary, Sir James Fergusson,

26   C.O.537/136, paper 84/86, Thurston to Stanhope, 8/10/1886, Secret and Confidential.
27   Ibid., and compare with C.O.225/22, paper 21993, Thurston to Stanhope, 1/10/1886. See also, R.Kol.A.2839, Krauel to A.A., enclosing, Travers (private) letter of 22/10/1886.
28   F.O.58/219, Hervey memo of 3/11/1886, and Pauncefote to Bramston, 5/11/1886; C.O.225/22, Hervert minute of 12/11/1886 on paper 20203.
29   Ibid., minute on paper 21993 (Thurston's report) for draft to F.O.

came out in a very strongly written memorandum for concessions to Berlin, arguing that

> the course to be taken by H.M.Gvt. in the future conduct of the Samoan
> question shd. be settled upon considerations of general policy and too
> much weight shd. not be given to Colonial ideas. The time has gone by
> when G.B. can assert a Monroe Doctrine in every part of the world . . .
> It is absurd to regard a German possession of Samoa as menacing to our
> Australasian or Southern Pacific possessions unless we intend to assert
> a wide predominance which we shd. find very difficult to maintain,
> especially in view of our need of European alliances . . . would it be
> very inexpedient to consent to Germany exercising authority over these
> islands under Convention with the other Powers for a term of years?
> . . . We can secure the fullest equality to British trade & full protection
> to British interests; and at the same time, I apprehend, enlist to a great
> extent in our favour the support of the German Empire when we most
> need it.[30]

Perhaps the most surprising fact relating to this memorandum
was that Fergusson was governor of New Zealand in the early
1870s, and had been considered by some to have favoured
Vogel's expansionism! Times had changed greatly since then,
and there exists no clearer statement of the Foreign Office's
belief that Samoa was merely a pawn on the European
diplomatic chessboard than this document.

This was a viewpoint, naturally enough, which Salisbury
fully shared. A few days earlier, the prime minister had begged
Krauel not to leave for Berlin and had expressed his readiness
to give support at the Washington Conference to the German
proposals for a mandatory supervision of Samoa by the predominant power there for a seven-year period, a new election
for the kingship and a new police organization to protect the
D.H.P.G. plantations. By this form of agreement, the prime
minister believed, Germany would have her wish as regards
single control yet he would be protected from colonial indignation. Salisbury also felt that 'It will be necessary to sit upon
the Colonial Office', since their defiance would adversely affect
Anglo-German relations.[31] After some further consideration,
a seven-point agreement was drafted in the Foreign Office on
21 December 1886, and approved of by Salisbury, Iddesleigh,
Stanhope and Churchill.[32] Shortly afterwards, Thurston's

---

30 F.O.58/219, Fergusson memo of 27/11/1886. See also, F.O.343/2, Iddesleigh to
Malet, 17/11/1886.

31 Salisbury Papers, Class E, Hatzfeldt to Salisbury, 27/11/1886, with enclosure, and the
reply of 29/11/1886; ibid., Class D, Salisbury to Churchill, 17/11/1886, and Salisbury to
Currie, 30/11/1886, from where the quotation comes; R.Kol.A.2875, Hatzfeldt to
Bismarck, no. 220 of 11/11/1886.

32 Salisbury Papers, Class E, Hatzfeldt to Salisbury, 15/12/1886 and 21/12/1886, and
reply of 15/12/1886; F.O.58/219, Hatzfeldt memo of 15/12/1886, and Pauncefote to C.O.,
21/12/1886, enclosing bases of arrangement.

secret despatch arrived in London, together with a private
letter to Herbert stating that 'Samoa is an excessively over-
rated place'; and with this, the Colonial Office's standpoint,
already circumvented by Salisbury, collapsed altogether.[33]

In moving towards his decision to support the German
wishes, the prime minister had been attracted by the clause
which permitted the power with the predominant commercial
interests in the group *at the time* to act on behalf of all three
nations. As he put it to Currie, 'if we make our arrangement
dependent upon preponderance—it is likely as not to be ours
whenever the first turn is over'.[34] It is difficult to see how this
optimism could be justified, however, for there had been no
trade reports since 1884 and Thurston had willingly acknowledged the German commercial predominance in all his reports.
Most likely, it was to be used as an argument with which to
pacify Australasia and Salisbury did not refer to it again after
Thurston's secret report arrived with the suggestion of obtaining Tonga. This notion offered a far more tangible and satisfying quid pro quo by which New Zealand opinion might be
placated and the prime minister, who took over the Foreign
Office once again after Iddesleigh's sudden death, spent the
first four months of 1887 attempting to reach an agreement
along these lines with Germany.

Salisbury's bargaining position, however, was terribly weak,
for he had already signalled his assent to the German scheme
before learning of Thurston's idea of securing Tonga. Moreover, the overall diplomatic situation seems to have been
alarming to him at this time, and in February 1887 he
was worrying about Britain's isolation and the possibility of
the powers joining together to treat the empire as 'divisible
booty', thereby settling their own differences.[35] In vain he
hoped that Bismarck would be too busy with domestic politics
'to devote much of his capacious mind to Samoa and Zanzibar'. Playing the Eastern and Egyptian cards for all they were
worth, the chancellor instructed Hatzfeldt to warn Salisbury
that

> if we are not very shortly fully convinced by the reports of our agents
> in Zanzibar and Samoa that England is loyally supporting our effort
> there, our representatives in the Orient will receive word to become
> friendly with the French.[36]

33   C.O.537/136, paper 84/86, and enclosures.

34   Salisbury Papers, Class D, Salisbury to Currie, 30/11/1886.

35   Cecil, *Life*, 4, pp. 23-24; G. E. Buckle, ed., *The Letters of Queen Victoria*, Third Series,
3 vols. (London, 1930-1932), 1, pp. 261-73.

36   G.P., 4, no. 809. For Salisbury's hopes that Bismarck would not press him at this
juncture, see Salisbury Papers, A64/1, Salisbury to Malet, 19/1/1887.

In certain aspects of the proposed Anglo-German arrangement, the prime minister achieved limited success. Travers'
plan that the power having the largest land claims in Samoa
would provide the chairman of a Land Court was rejected as
being 'a premium on impudence', while after a lengthy
argument Salisbury persuaded the Germans not to debar
Malietoa as a candidate for the new elections for the kingship.
These, though, were minor points, and hard to gain at that;
as he put it to Malet, he could never 'get them to show any
decency in their treatment of the wretched native sovereigns
whom they despise'.[37] On a major point, such as the powers of
veto Britain and the United States would exercise over the
administration of Samoa by a German adviser, Salisbury was
forced to accept Berlin's position.

Most important of all, he found it impossible to secure the
Colonial Office wishes regarding Tonga, where the religious
troubles and the great age of the native king were causing
London to believe that intervention would soon be necessary.
Since such a step would violate Tonga's neutrality as established under the 1886 Anglo-German demarcation treaty, the
Colonial Office hoped to secure German recognition of prior
British claims there at the same time as they reluctantly agreed
to Bismarck's scheme for placing Samoa under the mandatory
supervision of Germany.[38] The German response at first was
that Tonga was most important to them and that their trade
interests in that group were larger than Britain's, but should
this change they would not be averse to an arrangement similar
to the one proposed for Samoa.[39] Salisbury took 'formal note
of this admission' but contested the German assertions of
commercial predominance in Tonga and suggested that a
recognition of British superiority there was necessary to
reconcile the Australasian colonies to German rule in Samoa;
but at this, the German tone became harsher, fresh trading
statistics were handed over to Salisbury and he was told that
Bismarck could hardly agree that Britain was to rule Tonga
undisturbed while Germany had to administer Samoa under a
mandate.[40] Complaining of the 'very hard bargain' that
Bismarck was driving with him, Salisbury therefore gave way

---

37 Ibid., A64/5, same to same, 13/4/1887. (The other native sovereign was the Sultan
of Zanzibar). For the earlier quotation, see his minute in F.O.58/225 on C.O. to F.O.,
Secret, of 21/1/1887.
38 Ibid., Herbert to F.O., 24/1/1887, with enclosure; C.O.537/136, paper 10/87 Secret,
F.O. to C.O., 9/2/1887.
39 F.O.58/225, Salisbury to Malet, no. 78 Secret of 7/2/1887. The German side of these
talks can be followed in A.A./*A.M.L.B./Tonga*, 1886-1887.
40 F.O.58/226, F.O. to Hatzfeldt, 16/3/1887; F.O.58/227, German Embassy memo of
15/4/1887.

drummond wolff

and on 23 April 1887, signed a secret agreement over Samoa with the German chargé d'affaires, Baron von Plessen, without obtaining the 'adequate consideration' he had hoped for in Tonga.[41] Given the British moves to back up Italy and Austria-Hungary in the Mediterranean in 1887 and the crucial state of the Drummond Wolff negotiations in Constantinople, he could do no more; Australasian protests would simply have to be ignored.

The clauses of this treaty reflected the German obsession with the security of the plantations in Samoa; Bismarck's policy here was made clear in a message to the *Auswärtiges Amt*, stating that 'Our need is not mastery but security of our commerce there against the natives and against strife with England and America.'[42] Nevertheless, the scheme obviously gave Germany de facto control of the group. While all sides would benefit from the decision to maintain free trade and navigation and to establish a land court, a new election for the kingship was intended as a device to get rid of Malietoa, since Berlin believed that Tamasese had the majority of the Samoans behind him. Moreover, the Resident, who would act as adviser to the native government and would be appointed by the power having the greatest commercial stake in Samoa to rule for five-year periods, was specifically to

> supervise those measures which are necessary for the *real* (that word inserted by Bismarck) maintenance of peace and order in general, and in particular for the security of the plantations, dwellings and other property of the foreign subjects in Samoa.[43]

The other two consuls were to lose their political role, while only those clauses of existing treaties with the Samoan government which were not inconsistent with this new arrangement were to remain in force.

After a prolonged diplomatic struggle, therefore, Berlin had won London around to the idea of replacing the separate treaties of the three powers with the Samoan government with an autocratically-conceived form of German control, tacitly supported by the other two interested nations. Whether this new scheme really would have brought an end to the unrest and intrigue in the group remained an unanswered question, however, for while Salisbury found it expedient to give way to Bismarck's wishes, Bayard certainly did not. The toughest stage of the negotiations was yet to come.

41   Salisbury Papers, A64/5, Salisbury to Malet, 13/4/1887.
42   R.Kol.A.3017, Rantzau to A.A., tel. no. 37 of 30/10/1886.
43   The text of the treaty can be found in F.O.58/227, F.O. to C.O., 27/4/1887, or in R.Kol.A.2915. The insertion made by Bismarck can be found in R.Kol.A.2842, in the drafts enclosed to Alvensleben, A33 of 13/6/1886.

ii *The Washington Conference and its Aftermath*

Although his diplomatic intervention in the summer of 1886 had temporarily permitted the United States to take the initiative in the Samoan question, there is no evidence that Bayard had any fixed solution for this problem himself. His policy was the much more negative one of reacting to Germany's moves, which was a difficult task when the soothing noises emanating from Berlin were so often contradicted by Stuebel's actions in the islands. Moveover, there were potential dangers in both a too rash and a too cautious policy; a forward policy in the Pacific which led to a confrontation with the mighty Bismarck might arouse strong disapproval from American traditionalists and the powerful German-American voting groups, while a failure to preserve American rights in Samoa might lead to Opposition censures against a 'weak-kneed' acquiescence in further European aggression against independent native states. A polite but firm denial of the German wishes regarding Samoa appeared to be the best course of action until the attitude of the American public became clearer.[44]

Bayard's personal desire to see as many of the remaining unannexed Pacific groups preserving their independence as possible was shared by the American special commissioner, George Bates. Indeed, while the latter hauled down the flag which Greenebaum had hoisted, thus repudiating the idea that the United States might be harbouring annexationist designs, he officially recommended that Washington assume the mandate for administering the Samoan islands on account of her commercial disinterest and neutral position; far from accepting Travers' argument that Berlin should undertake this task due to Germany's predominant interests, Bates held that it was precisely this factor which would prevent an impartial German administration of the group's affairs. During his mission in Samoa, he also slipped over to the Tongan Islands, where he concluded a treaty with King George which, amongst other concessions, gave the United States coaling station rights and caused considerable disquiet in London, both at the time and afterwards.[45]

Even before the Washington Conference had begun, a mutual suspicion and antagonism had developed between American and German foreign offices. Bismarck was furious

---

44 United States policy in the Samoan question before and during the Washington Conference is covered in detail in Ryden, *U.S. Policy in Samoa*, pp. 317-66.

45 Ibid., pp. 320-21; F.O.58/225, Herbert to F.O., 24/1/1887, enclosure, Trotter's (Tonga) letter of 2/11/1886. For the later consequences of the American-Tongan treaty, see P. M. Kennedy, 'Britain and the Tongan Harbours, 1898-1914' in *Historical Studies: Australia and New Zealand*, vol. 15 (April, 1972).

at the support which he believed the United States was giving
to the Hawaiian government's interference in Samoan politics,
which had led to a treaty of friendship between King Kalakaua
and Malietoa on 17 February 1887. In fact, both Bayard and
Salisbury had discouraged the Hawaiian move but the chancellor was unaware of this at first and regarded it as an
impudent threat to Germany's Samoan interests devised by
Kalakaua's American backers. The chancellor's warning that
any further interference would lead to a state of war between
Hawaii and Germany, together with Bayard's reserved attitude, brought about a rapid withdrawal by Kalakaua's
delegates but did nothing to improve German-American
relations.[46] Bayard for his part was annoyed to learn that a
Bavarian adventurer called Brandeis, formerly a *D.H.P.G.*
employee, was giving military instruction to the Tamasese
faction. Support from Salisbury against this new development
was unlikely, however, for the prime minister felt that 'It is
Germany's broth—she may cool it.'[47] Finally, Bayard's repeated
delays in convoking the conference led to much resentment in
Berlin.

There was thus little prospect of agreement when Bayard
met the two ministers, Alvensleben and Sackville West, for the
first session of the Washington Conference on 25 June 1887.
The Secretary of State, while rejecting Bates' idea of an
American supervision, was determined not to accept any
proposal which would turn Samoa into a de facto German
colony; Alvensleben was under instructions from Bismarck to
press for precisely that aim; and Sackville West had been told
by Salisbury in an 'absolutely confidential despatch' to support
his German colleague and to argue that a winding-up of the
disastrous state of Samoan affairs could not be unwelcome to
the United States either. The divergence was revealed as soon
as each party read out its proposals; for, while Bayard submitted a complex plan for a strengthened Samoan government
assisted by white advisers, Alvensleben bluntly, and West more
tactfully, advocated an administration controlled by the power
having the greatest interests.

From that point onwards, the conference was doomed to
failure. Compromise might be, and indeed in several cases was,
reached upon a further election for the kingship, the constitution of a Land Court, customs dues and taxes, but Bayard
could not swallow the German plan 'to make the preponder-
ating interests the beginning, end and middle of the whole

---

46 BA/MA 625, PG65070, *Die Entsendung von Kriegsschiffen nach den Südsee-Inseln*,
vol. 3, A.A. to Adm., Secret, 7/8/1887.
47 F.O.58/227, minute on Symonds to Salisbury, no. 16 of 26/4/1887.

scheme of government'.[48] Yet this was the German *conditio sine qua non*, the very essence of Berlin's calculation, which had evolved from the rather crude concepts of economic imperialism held by Bismarck and still more by the *Auswärtiges Amt* and a very anxious *D.H.P.G.* In addition, the meetings were marred by the personal hostility between Bayard, who was aware that the Republican majority in the Senate was 'incurably hostile' and would reject all concessions to Germany, and Alvensleben, an arrogant and easily irritated man whose temper was completely frayed by Bayard's sharp criticisms and the 'simply awful' heat of Washington in mid-summer.[49] After six formal sessions, the conference was therefore postponed on 26 July.

All this proved most embarrassing for West, who had to implement the British policy of supporting Berlin without, however, provoking Bayard's suspicion of 'appearing to have disposed of their (U.S.) interests before taking them into council'.[50] Noticing that Bayard stiffened visibly every time that Alvensleben mentioned the German predominance, West attempted to modify the manner, if not the reality, of his colleague's proposals but was repeatedly reproached for his 'lukewarm support'. Since the British government itself opposed the German minister's suggestions that the Resident be appointed *before* the kingship election—an 'undisguised attempt to secure the election of Tamasese'—and that the other two powers surrender any rights of veto, West earned few thanks from his German opposite number.[51] His assistant Spring-Rice found this basic dilemma puzzling, explaining:

> If West supports & echoes every word of Alvensleben, then there is no chance of Bayard yielding to an European conspiracy as the Press here would be sure to call it . . . If West acts as mediator (the only chance for a successful issue) the German complains. Which of the two forms of support is required? i.e. does H.M. Gvt. wish to seem to support Germany or does H.M. Gvt. wish for a settlement of the Samoan question?[52]

Salisbury, however, declined to get further involved in what was for him basically a German-American quarrel and felt that 'We have no reason to repine at the course events are taking.' Even at the news that Weber had been advising Alvensleben in Washington throughout the conference and that he would probably be the Resident Berlin was pressing

48 Ryden, *U.S. Policy in Samoa*, p. 364.
49 F.O.58/228, Spring Rice letters of 24/6/1887 and 30/6/1887 (copies).
50 F.O.58/227, Herbert to Pauncefote, 30/3/1887, enclosure draft of the British views.
51 Salisbury Papers, A77/7 and 8, West to Salisbury, 12/7/1887 and 22/7/1887.
52 F.O.58/229, Spring-Rice to Hervey, 12/7/1887.

for, the prime minister's reserve did not break.[53] Samoa was not his concern.

Bayard's firm stand provoked the German government to take more drastic action to deal with the anarchic situation in the islands. The Admiralty had already been asked in June to send their cruiser squadron to the group, to obtain satisfaction for misdeeds committed against German subjects, and to remain a considerable time there

> since it will contribute to strengthen the confidence of the pro-German party of Tamasese and at the same time to prevent an Anglo-American agitation for Malietoa's benefit, breaking the *status quo* and leading to an outbreak of hostilities between the parties.

At the same time the new German consul Becker was told that 'it would be a political failure to let the anti-German intrigues have a free hand'.[54] Following the collapse of the conference, Herbert Bismarck and Krauel pressed for the immediate deposition of the pro-English Malietoa and the erection of a German-controlled administration, thus presenting the other two powers with a fait accompli. Although sharply rejecting these proposals and declaring that 'such acts of force lie outside our colonial tasks if we are not in agreement with the interested civilized powers beforehand', Bismarck was gradually persuaded to adopt a harsher line.[55] The continuous damage to the *D.H.P.G.'s* property, coupled with the resentment felt at a brawl that had earlier broken out at a party on Upolu in honour of the German emperor's birthday, caused Berlin to send further instructions that war was to be declared upon Malietoa if he refused to apologize and also to give compensation for the plantation damages. Any interference from the ambitious Hawaiian government would also cause a state of war to exist.[56]

The German Admiralty itself had little enthusiasm for gunboat diplomacy in distant waters (a trait also shared by the British and American navies) and was particularly worried by the implications of the action requested. What, the *Auswärtiges Amt* was asked, would happen if British or American vessels intervened on Malietoa's behalf? More pertinently,

53   F.O.58/228, minute on Spring-Rice letter of 24/6/1887 (copy); ibid., West to Salisbury, no. 227 Confidential of 3/8/1887.

54   BA/MA 623, PG65060, *Die Entsendung von Kriegsschiffen nach Australien u. den Südsee-Inseln*, vol. 6, A.A. to Adm., 29/6/1887, with enclosure.

55   R.Kol.A.2842, H. Bismarck memo of 3/7/1887; R.Kol.A.2843, Berchem to Bismarck, 23/6/1887, and minute thereon, and same to same, no. 6 of 28/7/1887; R.Kol.A.2846, Rantzau directives (2) of 1/8/1887.

56   BA/MA 625, PG65070, *Die Entsendung von Kriegsschiffen nach den Südsee-Inseln*, vol. 3, A.A. to Adm., Secret, 7/8/1887.

what would happen if a German-Hawaiian war broke out, and how should such a campaign be fought? Should they blockade Honolulu? Where would the ships come from? How were the Germans in Hawaii to be protected? What would the United States do? Faced with these sobering questions, the *Auswärtiges Amt* softened its stand and agreed that friction with the representatives of other nations was to be avoided at all costs and that no action should be taken against Hawaii, although this latter point was to be reserved.[57] The prospect of the other powers intervening to protect Malietoa was considered slight.

The *Auswärtiges Amt* had reasonable grounds for this belief; the mission could be represented as a punitive measure with which the other two nations need not concern themselves. In any case, there were no American warships in Samoan waters then and it was not expected that Salisbury would raise objections. Despite this, the prime minister was not officially informed of the cruiser squadron's mission until 15 August although several hints had been dropped beforehand that Berlin was looking for another way to settle the whole question following the collapse of the Washington Conference. At the same time as he conveyed this news, Hatzfeldt urged that British warships remain clear of Samoa for a while, assuring Salisbury that British life and property would be respected.[58] The possibility of a coup d'état, or at least some violence, was thus very large. In view of his commitment to Germany, however, the prime minister contented himself with warning the British consul that he was to observe 'complete neutrality both in word and action', an order that one indignant Colonial Office clerk interpreted as meaning 'that we are not to look too closely at what is about to go on at Samoa'.[59] But Bayard, reported West, was astonished at the German information, 'for, he said, to talk of the preservation of the neutrality of Samoa when war was to be declared if fines for which there was no money to be had were not paid, appeared to him absurd'.[60]

The four German warships under Commodore Heusner, after waiting a few days until the Sydney mail steamer had left Apia on 23 August and Samoa was cut off from the outside

57 Ibid., Adm. replies of 8/8/1887 and 10/8/1887, and A.A. to Adm., 8/8/1887, 10/8/1887 and 13/8/1887.

58 F.O.58/230, German Embassy copy of H. Bismarck to Hatzfeldt, 7/8/1887 (communicated on 15/8/1887), and Salisbury to Malet, no. 387 Very Confidential of 15/8/1887, copies of which were sent to the queen, cabinet and C.O.

59 C.O.537/136, paper 51 Secret, F.O. to C.O., 23/8/1887, with Fuller minute thereon. See also, G.P., 4, no. 818.

60 F.O.58/231, West to Salisbury, no. 271 Confidential of 19/9/1887; Ryden, *U.S. Policy in Samoa*, pp. 384-87.

world for another three weeks, soon revealed to the excited whites and natives the reason for their presence. The sum of $13,000 was demanded by Becker as reparation for insults and damages and, when Malietoa pleaded for some time to consider this, war was declared upon him and 700 marines with some field guns were landed. Tamasese was then proclaimed king while Malietoa, who had fled into the bush, was ordered to give himself up before much blood was shed; and, when he did this, he was promptly deported in a warship. Martial law was declared, and a curfew imposed upon all Samoans. The British and American consuls protested and declined to recognize Tamasese as king, particularly as Brandeis suddenly emerged as his premier; but they did not encourage any resistance to the German actions, nor did they seek to prevent the chiefs of the various districts in the group from signing under duress a paper by which they recognized the change of monarch and government. Furthermore, the German marines took control of all vantage points and Becker declared the municipal administration of Apia to be in abeyance, blaming the U.S. consul Sewall's non-attendance at the municipal council for this. Samoa had become a de facto German possession.[61]

Although Herbert felt these proceedings to be a 'great cruelty to the king & impertinence to us & to the United States', Salisbury remained unmoved and indeed reprimanded the British consul for protesting against them, thereby breaking his absolute neutrality. Relations with France and Russia were still too bad, and the Egyptian question still too unsettled, for the prime minister to do otherwise. Indeed, Hatzfeldt had called at the Foreign Office and told Pauncefote that 'it had all been arranged with our knowledge & assent. It was a matter of "give & take", and we had agreed to give Germany a free hand in Samoa, just as Germany had agreed to give us a free hand in Egypt.'[62] In view of this reminder, the ambassador's next statement, that Germany was in no way seeking to affect the treaty rights of the other two powers in Samoa, made little sense but the British government resisted pointing this out. They were, however, beginning to get seriously alarmed about the future of Tonga with such a large German naval force in neighbouring waters, and Pauncefote suggested

61 Reports of the German coup are in F.O.58/230, Wilson to Salisbury, nos. 29 and 30 of 1/9/1887, and Mitchell to Salisbury, tel. of 25/8/1887 and no. 28 Consular of 2/9/1887; BA/MA 625, PG65070, *Die Entsendung von Kriegsschiffen nach den Südsee-Inseln*, vol. 3, Heusner to Adm., 8/9/1887; Ryden, *U.S. Policy in Samoa*, pp. 371-84.
62 C.O.225/26, paper 20481, Adm. to C.O., 11/10/1887, with Herbert minute thereon; F.O.58/230, Salisbury note of 10/9/1887, and Pauncefote memo of 8/9/1887.

the immediate despatch of a warship to that group.[63] The religious strife and persecutions in Tonga, which had only a short while earlier been the subject of a lengthy investigation by the high commissioner, added weight to the belief that a supervision of its affairs by a white power would soon be necessary; and London was keeping a watchful eye for possible intervention by the United States, France or even Hawaii as well as Germany. The Colonial Office now became most worried at the latest rumours from the Pacific and felt that 'if anything is done, it should be done quickly. While we are parleying, Germany takes action & the F.O. have no interest in the feeling of the Australian Colonies.'[64]

The criticism was unjust, however, for Salisbury also took a keen interest in obtaining the group as a solatium for the colonies when they discovered that Germany was to administer Samoa; 'It is in Tonga that we must look for compensation for the superior position which their more active trade has given to the Germans in Samoa.'[65] He therefore warned Hatzfeldt at the end of 1887 that 'we could not admit the predominance of any other influence at Tonga'. Despite receiving German assurances that he need not worry himself on that score, Salisbury wished to keep a warship there, even during the hurricane season, and was most annoyed when it was withdrawn against his advice.[66] Having warded off possible action in Tonga by Berlin, though, the prime minister was less disposed than ever to ruffle German feelings with complaints about their actions in Samoa and he contented himself with repeatedly warning the British consul to stay absolutely neutral. The latter was also told that Britain had 'no interest in this controversy' and later instructed to recognize Tamasese as de facto ruler of Samoa for the time being.[67] The press agitation in Australasia against the German measures was completely ignored, and from this time onwards the Colonial Office virtually abandoned any attempt to modify Salisbury's Samoan policy. The only thing the prime minister would not do was join with Berlin in combined representations at Washington, for this might so easily prejudice the course of the important Fisheries Conference there.

63 Ibid.
64 C.O.225/26, paper 18645, Fuller minute of 19/10/1887 on Thurston report of 13/9/1887.
65 F.O.58/232, Salisbury minute on C. in C., Australia, to Adm., 27/11/1887.
66 F.O.58/231, F.O. to C.O., 28/10/1887, and C.O. to F.O., 10/11/1887; F.O.58/232, C.O. to F.O., Pressing, 30/11/1887, with Salisbury minute thereon, and F.O. to Adm., 14/12/1887; F.O.58/238, Adm. to F.O., 9/1/1887, and Salisbury minute thereon; Salisbury Papers, Class D, Salisbury to Holland, Dec. 1887 and 15/12/1887; R.Kol.A.3019, Hatzfeldt to Bismarck, no. 422 of 7/12/1887.
67 F.O.58/231, Salisbury to Wilson, tel. of 31/10/1887, and no. 43 Political of 3/12/1887.

Bayard, for his part, was furious at the news, although he remained uncertain as to whether American treaty rights themselves had been infringed by the German actions. Perhaps the United States cabinet did argue, as Spring-Rice claimed he overheard them do, that opposition to Germany 'would be a grand thing for the election';[68] but the secretary of state's anger was primarily due to what he saw as German duplicity in negotiating at Washington while preparing for a coup in Samoa. Nor did later developments assuage his indignation, since his proposal for an immediate election of a king and vice-king was answered by a German note, declaring that this was unnecessary as the Samoans had already selected Tamasese as their monarch.[69] The *Auswärtiges Amt* was in fact being misled by Becker, who reported that only the actions of the U.S. consul Sewall were causing any unrest to continue, and that the Tamasese-Brandeis régime, assisted by his 'confident advice' and some 'physical force', was running smoothly and welcomed by all except a few Anglo-American recalcitrants.[70] According to the reports of the other two consuls, however, the opposition, both native and white, was much more widespread; in fact, the chiefs had only acknowledged Tamasese as king in the presence of a German warship and marines.

Even Bismarck, who had felt rather guilty over a further landing of marines despite defending this action to British and American diplomats in Berlin, was mollified by Becker's assurances. However, he did cable the consul to make the occupation as short and painless as possible and to avoid conflicts with the Americans, saying 'Our striving was not for an increase of power but for the securing of our commercial interests, and this is now achieved.'[71] Although to the outside world Germany clearly had effected an 'increase of power', Bismarck's attitude *was* different from that of his advisers and the *D.H.P.G.*, who continually pressed for a formal German annexation regardless of the views of the other nations. It would in fact appear that much of Germany's 'forward' policy in Samoa at this time was being formulated by Herbert Bismarck and Krauel, while the chancellor (chiefly absent from Berlin and concerned as ever with European diplomacy and

68   F.O.58/229, Spring-Rice to Hervey (private), 23/7/1887, in which he claimed that, while at a place between the offices of the Navy and War Secretaries, he overheard the U.S. cabinet discussing Samoa!

69   F.O.58/231, Salisbury to Malet, no. 468 of 17/10/1887; ibid., U.S. Legation to Salisbury, 25/10/1887 and especially his minute; Ryden, *U.S. Policy in Samoa*, pp. 388-89.

70   *Stenographische Berichte über die Verhandlungen des Reichstages* (hereafter *Reichstag*) 7. Legislaturperiode, IV Session, vol. 5, section 110, documents 8, 14, 15, 17 and 18.

71   R.Kol.A.2849, Rantzau to A.A., 29/10/1887; ibid., A.A. to Becker, A49 of 8/11/1887.

domestic politics) read 'scarcely one-sixth of the relevant reports'; and that the state secretary saw the whole affair in terms of prestige and of combating the plots of intriguing Americans.[72] Furthermore, so long as these methods appeared to offer the only way of protecting the German commercial interests in the group, Bismarck did little to control his underlings. Aware that he had not infringed the treaty rights of the other powers and unable to conceive that the latter would object to Germany's punishment of Malietoa (which he once likened to the exile of Ceteweyo by the British), the chancellor blandly defended Becker's actions and indeed complained frequently of the obstructionism of local Anglo-American factions to the 'legitimate' rule of Tamasese. As Herbert shrewdly noted, Bismarck

> concerns himself little about these intrigues of his subordinates, who have many interests with the traders; but he will support their views put before him by them & we must be careful that when we have to put our foot down it shall be in a matter of real importance & in an indisputably right cause.[73]

Since Salisbury had no intention of 'putting his foot down' in the Samoan affair, this problem was of little importance on the British side; but it certainly perplexed Bayard, who was uncertain how best to act to preserve the American position in the group. He was also embarrassed by the chronic shortage of American warships in the south-west Pacific and by the non-recognition of the Apia Municipality Convention by his predecessors in office, which prevented him from protesting against the German endeavours to assume control of the town through their puppet native government.[74] The secretary of state therefore contented himself in the closing months of 1887 with the drawing up of a lengthy review of the whole controversy, which pointed out in detail the fallacies and weaknesses in Berlin's arguments and emphasized

> the importance attached by this Government to the maintenance of the rights to which the United States has become entitled in any of the few remaining regions now under independent and autonomous native governments in the Pacific Ocean.

In the final analysis, Bayard concluded, the German-American quarrel was based upon a basic difference of attitude, which he characterized in the following words:

72 Bismarck, Graf Herbert von, *Aus seiner politischen Privatkorrespondenz*, ed. W. Bussmann (Göttingen, 1964), pp. 464-65.
73 C.O.225/27, paper 11886, Herbert minute of 22/6/1887 thereon.
74 Ryden, *U.S. Policy in Samoa*, pp. 386-90.

Owing, doubtless, to her commercial preponderance in the islands, to Germany the primary object has seemed to be the establishment of a stronger government. To the United States, the object first in importance has seemed to be the preservation of native independence and autonomy.[75]

The tone of this long despatch, which was handed over to Herbert Bismarck at the beginning of 1888, left no doubt as to which aim Bayard regarded as being the more defensible.

By that time, however, the armed intervention by the German cruiser squadron had attracted a great deal of attention in the American press, and the west coast newspapers in particular became very critical of Germany's actions, a fact which strengthened Bayard's position not a little. He also had to consider that in an election year (1888) the Opposition would severely censure him for any signs of weakness in his handling of the matter; in fact, both Senate and House requested the president to transmit correspondence upon Samoa and when it was learned that the protocols of the Washington conference would not be published (mainly due to Salisbury's insistence), the Republicans alleged that he had secretly agreed to Bismarck's demands. The stiffening of American resistance was reflected in the despatch of a warship to the islands and in the persistent policy of non-recognition of, and obstruction to, the Tamasese-Brandeis régime by the United States' consular and naval officials.

While the secretary of state seems still to have been very doubtful as to how to proceed, his consul's attitude, together with the refusal of the Anglo-American community to pay taxes to the new Samoan government, meant that Brandeis' position remained very insecure.[76] In contrast to Becker's bland reports, Commodore Heusner warned the Admiralty upon his departure from Apia at the end of 1887 that Tamasese could not stand without the support of *all* the powers and that a civil war would probably occur as soon as his squadron had sailed away.[77] In the first place, the native government, acting for the *D.H.P.G.*, had become involved in a series of land disputes with the traders of other nationalities, including the largest American (H. J. Moors) and British (McArthur & Co.) firms; in the latter case, a house which the firm had leased to Malietoa and now wanted returned was kept, as the Germans explained it, according 'to the laws of war'.[78] Later, the

75 Ibid., pp. 395-402. The total length of this despatch was approximately 9,000 words.

76 Gilson, *Samoa 1830 to 1900*, pp. 382-95, offers new material on the Tamasese rule, based upon certain records kept by Brandeis.

77 BA/MA 623, PG65061, *Die Entsendung von Kriegsschiffen nach Australien u. den Südsee-Inseln*, vol. 7, Heusner to Adm., no. 471 of 26/11/1887.

78 F.O.58/238, Wilson to Salisbury, no. 15 of 24/3/1888.

attempts of the government to sell off the property of a trader
who refused to pay his taxes led to a large protest meeting by
the Anglo-American community, a development which,
among others, caused the *Auswärtiges Amt* to request the return
of two of their warships to Samoa.[79] Nor did the constant
disputes between Becker and Sewall, and the almost unhind-
ered importation of large amounts of arms and ammunition,
augur well for the new régime.

Besides alienating the majority of the whites, Brandeis also
blundered by attempting to levy a capitation tax upon the
Samoans. A large sum from this source had been collected in
1887, despite later protests by three chiefs, who were deported
without trial for their pains; Becker explained away this
disturbance as being the work of paid New Zealand agents,
which was 'allayed' by the 'friendly' intercourse of the German
warships.[80] In March 1888 the acting British consul reported
that another $47,000 was to be raised from the various districts
and that those who could not pay immediately were to mort-
gage their lands to the *D.H.P.G.*, which would give the latter
an extraordinary hold over the Samoans and also the virtual
monopoly of the group's copra production, almost all of which
was now required to pay for the capitation tax. The money
collected by the government was mainly spent on better roads
to the *D.H.P.G.* plantations, while natives who attempted to
pay off earlier debts to other merchants instead of those to the
German firm were imprisoned. Even Thurston and Salisbury,
the two men most tolerant of German policy in Samoa, were
quick to protest at this blatant miscarriage of justice.[81]

Due to these autocratic and unpopular measures, even the
threat of further large-scale intervention by German warships
could not prevent native unrest. As the resentment grew, encouraged by many of the Anglo-American residents, Brandeis was
driven to more extreme steps; by April 1888, he had forbidden all
public assemblies and even cricket matches, which the Germans
generally regarded as a vehicle of English cultural influence.
This prohibition, the announcement of the new capitation tax,
the threat of more deportations and, most important of all,
the rumour that Tamasese was being encouraged by Brandeis
to claim the *Tafa'ifa*, clinched matters. By May the islands

79   Ibid., same to same, no. 11 of 17/2/1888; BA/MA 623, PG65061, *Die Entsendung von Kriegsschiffen nach Australien u. den Südsee-Inseln*, vol. 7, A.A. to Adm., 1/3/1888; Ryden, *U.S. Policy in Samoa*, pp. 406 08.
80   F.O.58/238, Wilson to Salisbury, no. 3 of 19/1/1888; ibid., Verbal Communication of Baron von Plessen of 27/1/1888, enclosing copy of Becker to Bismarck, 30/11/1887.
81   Ibid., Wilson to Salisbury, no. 14 of 1/3/1888, and Thurston to Salisbury, nos. 25 and 26 of 1/6/1888; ibid., Salisbury to Scott, no. 211 of 10/8/1888; Ryden, *U.S. Policy in Samoa*, pp. 410-11; Gilson, *Samoa 1830 to 1900*, pp. 388-90.

were seething with discontent and the *Auswärtiges Amt*
ordered the Admiralty to help Tamasese by handing over the
17,000 rounds of ammunition previously confiscated from
Malietoa's government.[82] In September the powerful chief
Mata'afa, who had been in dispute with Tamasese for the
Malietoan family title, joined a number of 'rebels' already in
the bush and the revolution commenced. Brandeis, not lacking
in courage, then attempted to put his military 'training' of
Tamasese's warriors into effect. Leading a force of about 500,
he sought to crush the rebellion but was surprised to discover
that the enemy was skilled in warfare and leadership and even
more numerous. On the eleventh of the month, the government's forces lost heavily in a large-scale engagement; by the
following day, they were routed from all their hastily-erected
positions and had retreated to Mulinu'u Point, where they
were protected by the gunboat *Adler*.[83] Yet another sudden
change had occurred in Samoan politics and the Tamasese-
Brandeis régime, for all intents and purposes, was at an end.

The German-American quarrel, however, was not yet over;
in fact, with the outbreak of this rebellion and the consequent
German efforts to suppress it, this much more important
dispute was only beginning to come to a climax. Both nations
started to direct more and more of their naval forces to the
islands while the press of both countries, especially in the
United States, began to demand action; a vicious circle was
developing which, if the statesmen and officials concerned
were not careful enough, might quickly get out of control.
The Samoan problem seemed even further away from a
satisfactory solution at the end of 1888 than it had been in
1884, at the time of the first German intervention. As for
Salisbury, he was disgusted. He had told Hatzfeldt in July that,
so far as he was concerned, the situation in Samoa was satisfactory though he did not want to raise another diplomatic
quarrel by passing on to Washington his own proposal that
the United States take Hawaii, Britain Tonga and Germany
Samoa.[84] Now, due to the blunders of the German officials,
this irritating little question had again thrust itself to the fore.
'We have left Prince Bismarck a free hand in Samoa', he complained to Malet, 'and a pretty mess he has made of it.'[85]

82 BA/MA 623, PG65061, *Die Entsendung von Kriegsschiffen nach Australien u. den
Südsee-Inseln*, vol. 7, *Olga* to Adm., nos. 36 and 47 of 25/3/1888 and 23/4/1888; ibid.,
A.A. to Adm., 3/10/1888.
83 F.O.58/240, Coëtlogen to Salisbury, nos. 41 of 10/9/1888 and 44 and 45 of 17/9/1888;
R.Kol.A.2853, Becker to Bismarck, no. 84 of 17/9/1888.
84 A.Vagts, *Deutschland und die Vereinigten Staaten in der Weltpolitik*, 2 vols., (London/
New York, 1935), 1, p. 639.
85 Salisbury Papers, A64/33, Salisbury to Malet, 18/9/1888.

Captain Leary M.S.H. Rear Adm. Fairfa R.

iii *The German-American Confrontation over Samoa*

'We shall probably have some difficulty by & by as events develop themselves', prophesied Pauncefote gloomily, after receiving further details on the outbreak of Mata'afa's rebellion;[86] yet this forecast, although correct in substance, proved to be a gross understatement. In Berlin, the news had been greeted with dismay and annoyance, and with far less willingness to let local events run their course. Alarmed by Becker's reports, the *Auswärtiges Amt* begged the Admiralty to send more warships to Samoa as quickly as possible, for the *Adler* alone could not be expected to guard all German life and property, or to protect Tamasese's followers from the attacks of 3,000 rebels.[87] Although Bismarck was worried lest the American Captain Leary seek to provoke a clash between the naval forces, he was convinced that the troubles had been engineered by a small group of Anglo-American intriguers and he was not prepared to allow an anti-German king in Samoa: 'We must show sharp teeth', he minuted, possibly gaining comfort from Bayard's disapproval of the actions of the American officials. Urged on by an anxious *D.H.P.G.*, the chancellor believed that they might have to declare war on Mata'afa, and he reprimanded Holstein for telling the United States chargé that Germany did not care which 'Nigger Chief' was in charge.[88]

If Bismarck was annoyed at this new development, the German officials were much more so and the *Adler*'s commander reported that it was important to teach the natives that they could do nothing without Germany.[89] Although a cease fire was agreed upon in early October and the British Rear-Admiral Fairfax managed to persuade all sides to respect Apia and its harbour as a neutral zone in any future conflict while paying a fleeting visit to the group, the situation rapidly deteriorated after his departure. Tamasese shifted his headquarters further along the coast to Saluafata because of the hostility shown by Leary and the American Vice-Consul Blacklock following an attack upon a United States citizen. The American and British representatives also protested when the *Adler* violated the neutrality of Apia by firing at some Samoans across the harbour, an action which so aroused the Mata'afans that a full-

86 F.O.58/240, minute on Coëtlogen to Salisbury, no. 47 of 9/10/1888.
87 BA/MA 625, PG65071, *Die Entsendung von Kriegsschiffen nach den Südsee-Inseln*, vol. 4, A.A. to Adm., 17/9/1888 and 3/10/1888.
88 R.Kol.A.2852, Kiliani (Hamburg) to Bismarck, no. 146 Confidential of 29/9/1888 and minute thereon; ibid., Rottenburg to Holstein, 4/10/1888; R.Kol.A.2853, Rottenburg to A.A., 16/11/1888.
89 BA/MA 625, PG65071, *Die Entsendung von Kriegsschiffen nach den Südsee-Inseln*, vol. 4, *Adler* to Adm., no. 157 Secret, 17/9/1888.

scale attack upon the town was feared and all three powers landed marines to protect their property. Existing antagonisms were further provoked when a German armed patrol attempted, but failed, to catch Mata'afa while he was attending mass. Later, the *Adler* left Apia to bombard some rebel villages but abandoned this task when the American and British cruisers sailed with her.[90]

Throughout the final quarter of 1888, the German position steadily worsened. It was clear to all that the Tamasese-Brandeis régime could not regain power 'except by the aid of armed forces landed by the German ships' and its demise was welcomed even by Thurston, who saw at last that the German political predominance meant that 'British trade & commercial rights will be sacrificed to the *D. H. P. G.*'[91] The local troubles thus became a clear-cut struggle between Mata'afa and the Germans, while Tamasese's importance declined and Brandeis disappeared from the scene altogether. In November Becker himself left the islands and was replaced as consul by Dr Knappe, an appointment which soon turned out to be even more disastrous for Germany. By the beginning of December, the Germans had collected sufficient forces and were prepared to disarm the Mata'afans, who were plundering the *D.H.P.G.* plantations. At Knappe's request, a contingent was landed on the eighteenth and set off inland, accompanied by some of the plantation labourers. The result was a disaster. Fearing extermination, the Mata'afans ambushed this force in the bush, killing and wounding over fifty sailors and driving them back to the coast; some of the bodies were later decapitated.[92] It was the first serious defeat of an advanced white power in the Pacific, and a healthy reminder that gunboat diplomacy could only be effectively carried out within the range of a warship's guns.

After this disaster, the German consul completely lost self-control. He and the German naval commander, Fritze, became so excited at the humiliation suffered and at the support which they believed the Anglo-American community was giving the Mata'afans that they proclaimed a state of war on 19 January and later declared that the islands and all nationalities were under martial law; furthermore, they announced that all vessels would be searched for arms and that Germany would take control of the police force. Only if the rebels surrendered,

90   F.O.58/240, Coëtlogen to Salisbury, nos. 47, 49, 50 and 51 of 9/10/1888, 16/10/1888, 5/11/1888 and 3/12/1888; Ryden, *U.S. Policy in Samoa*, pp. 414-17.

91   F.O.58/240, Thurston to Salisbury, 25/10/1888; ibid., C.O. to F.O., 14/12/1888, enclosure Thurston to Knutsford. The high commissioner, however, was less hostile to the idea of a regular German administration.

92   R.Kol.A.2859, Knappe to Bismarck, no. 1 of 4/1/1889.

those chiefs who had been responsible for beheading the German sailors were handed over, and the islands accepted permanent German control would peace be made, the consul
declared. In addition, the *Samoa Times* was closed down for
printing an anti-German article and a British subject was taken
from the steamer *Richmond*, which was itself searched.[93]

Knappe's proclamations and his suggestion of annexation
infuriated an already worried Bismarck and he severely
reprimanded the consul, pointing out 'To defend our property
and to answer force with force is right; but to break treaties
lies outside political possibility'.[94] He was determined to punish
Mata'afa, however, and he ordered plans for a large-scale
operation to be drafted. Salisbury and Bayard were informed
that the German government must now support Tamasese and
regretfully

> exchange our position of mediation, under which His Imperial Majesty's
> Consul in Apia was *endeavouring to reconcile the contending parties*, for
> which purpose he had sought the cooperation of his English and American
> colleagues, for one of hostilities against those who attacked us.[95]

However, the German Admiralty pointed out that it would
cost over one million marks to send two companies of marines
to Samoa, plus a further 500,000 marks for coal, all of which
might have to be requested from a somewhat dubious Reichstag. Moreover, if the naval commander was to be restricted in
his military reprisals out of fear of the Americans, it would
be better for German interests if this idea was abandoned;
but even if he was to be given a carte blanche, regardless of
consequences, the ships at Samoa and the three vessels of the
East African Squadron might not be enough to prevent intervention by an American force, and perhaps the whole fleet
should be mobilized.[96] Consequently, the kaiser decided in an
Immediatvortrag on 22 January 1889, against despatching
further vessels to the islands until more information was
received.[97] This decision marked the beginning of the German
retreat over Samoa.

The real reasons for Bismarck's change of course lay elsewhere, in the state of American feeling and in the worsening
political situation in Europe. Although Bayard had resisted
Vice-Consul Blacklock's appeal for an American protectorate,

93   F.O.58/245, Coëtlogen to Salisbury, no. 7 of 31/1/1889; *Reichstag* 7, IV Session,
vol. 5, section 138, documents 45 and 46.
94   R.Kol.A.2855, Rottenburg to A.A., 6/1/1889.
95   F.O.58/245, German embassy memo of 16/1/1889, with Pauncefote's underlining and
note that this was 'a new kind of "mediation" '.
96   BA/MA 625, PG65071, *Die Entsendung von Kriegsschiffen nach den Südsee-Inseln*,
vol. 4, Chief of Admiralty Staff memos of 8/1/1889 and 20/1/1889.
97   Ibid., minute on memo of 20/1/1889.

he was still angry at the German actions and alarmed at the telegram from Apia which said "Foreigners' lives and property in greatest danger.'[98] Yet his feelings were mild compared with the vociferous complaints uttered by the United States press. While the *Chicago Tribune* and the *New York World* demanded an American protectorate, the *San Francisco Examiner* envied the increases the British government contemplated under the Naval Defence Act, exclaiming that 'if only we had them (the warships) we could reduce Bismarck's armada to a pile of iron filings.' The *New York Herald* of 24 January 1889, had a fierce attack upon 'How American Rights Were Needlessly Surrendered by the State Department —Outrages by German Authorities Unredressed', and Bayard came in for much criticism generally from Republican newspapers for his lack of backbone and his 'collusion' in the affair.[99]

Such views, influential as they were, were less important than the angry opinions expressed in the Senate. As early as 10 December 1888, Senator Frye, in proposing that the Foreign Relations Committee investigate the Samoan affair, made several scathing attacks upon Bayard's unwillingness to preserve the independence of the islands. Sewall, who had abandoned his consular duties in Samoa in order to publicize the German actions in the group, criticized his superiors' weakness also in a series of press interviews. With only the German-American political circles dissenting from the universal condemnation of Bismarck's gunboat diplomacy, the United States government's hand was enormously strengthened. After the news of the ambush reached Washington on 5 January, the Cabinet decided upon firm counter-measures and despatched Rear-Admiral Kimberley, the commander-in-chief of the Pacific squadron, to Samoa with orders to protect American lives and property and to protest against German misdeeds. On the fifteenth, President Cleveland transmitted the relevant correspondence to Congress and invited them to act upon it. The answer was swift and decisive; after Sewall had been interviewed by the Foreign Relations Committee and many extreme anti-German remarks had been made by leading senators, they granted $500,000 for the defence of America's Samoan interests and the execution of her commitments, plus a further $100,000 for the construction of a naval station at

98 Ryden, *U.S. Policy in Samoa*, pp. 418-19.
99 A.A./*U.S.A.* 20, vol. 1, copy of *Chicago Tribune* of 8/4/1889; BA/MA 625, PG65071, *Die Entsendung von Kriegsschiffen nach den Südsee-Inseln*, vol. 4, copy of *New York World* of 31/12/1888; N.A.R.G. 80, File 3931 Samoa, Box 416, copy of *San Francisco Examiner* of 8/3/1889; F.O.58/245, Herbert to Salisbury, no. 23 of 24/1/1889, enclosing copy of *New York Herald* of that date. See also, Arco to Bismarck, nos. 47 and 83 of 28/1/1889 and 15/2/1889 in A.A./*U.S.A.* 2, vol. 1.

Pago-Pago. In addition, they also allowed for a large increase in the naval estimates, which were being discussed at this time.[100]

Was there a danger of a German-American war over Samoa in early 1889? Most probably not, and the British chargé in Washington reported that the chairman of the Foreign Relations Committee, Senator Sherman, had admitted that their appropriations were only a 'bluff'.[101] However, it does seem likely that Bismarck, although very annoyed at being forced to beat a retreat, believed this to be a possibility and could not afford to call their bluff. Less likely, though still feasible, is the notion that the chancellor did not believe that this risk existed but wished to avoid a complete disruption of relations with the United States over such a relatively small matter. The flood of reports on American naval preparations, whether they turned out later to be true or mere rumours, was certainly a cause for concern. Rear-Admiral Kimberley had been despatched with two warships, and another was to follow almost immediately. From Washington the chargé Sternburg reported the despatch of more vessels to Samoa, the existence of fast, dynamite-throwing cruisers and the Americans' ability to move troops in large numbers via San Francisco to the group. (Bismarck: 'What for?'). By February, there were reports of the U. S. Asiatic fleet moving into the Pacific and a squadron leaving the Mediterranean for the islands. In addition to all this, Bismarck learnt that the U. S. S. Nipsic had cleared for action and prepared her torpedoes at the time of the ambush of the German sailors, while Sternburg worriedly cabled that 'every commander of an American warship is authorised to attack if the occasion demands it.' (Bismarck: '!').[102] Warning Fritze under no account to fire the first shot, the chancellor felt that 'It would be inexcusable if in this way 2 Nations, who were friends and had all reason to remain so, came into conflict.' So ominous were these many reports that on 23 February the acting chief of the Admiralty asked for a memorandum upon how a war was to be waged strategically against the United States.[103]

100 Vagts, Weltpolitik, 1, pp. 648-58; Wehler, 1889, pp. 95-100; Ryden, U.S. Policy in Samoa, pp. 421-24.

101 F.O.58/245, Herbert to Salisbury, no. 24 of 24/1/1889, and private letter of 25/1/1889. See also, A. Vagts, 'Hopes and Fears of an American-German war, 1870-1915', part 1, in Political Science Quarterly, 54 (December, 1939), pp. 517-18.

102 A.A./U.S.A. 5a, Vol. 1, Arco to Bismarck, no. 8 of 7/1/1889 and tel. no. 4 of 20/1/1889; Münster to Bismarck, no. 5 of 21/1/1889, and Hatzfeldt to Bismarck (copy), no. 50 of 30/1/1889; Sternburg memos of 1/2/1889, 15/2/1889 and 25/2/1889; Börsen-Courier (copy) of 27/2/1889; Arco to Bismarck, no. 135 of 11/3/1889 and many others.

103 R.Kol.A.2861, Bismarck minute on Adm. to A.A., Secret, of 4/3/1889; H. H. Herwig and D. F. Trask, 'Naval Operations Plans between Germany and the United States of America 1898-1913. A Study of Strategic Planning in the Age of Imperialism', in Militärgeschichtliche Mitteilungen, 1970 (2), p. 6.

eneral Waldersee

Alarm-signals, too, were transmitted from Carl Schurz, the most famous of the German-Americans, who warned Bismarck that war could easily result if his Samoan policy was not abandoned and that in such a situation the United States would immediately seek an alliance with Germany's hereditary foe, France. Although the chancellor warmly disputed Schurz's reasonings, he was clearly rattled by them, especially when General Waldersee confirmed the American's argument; nor did the prediction of the Cincinnati consul that all the German-Americans would fight against their fatherland in any such conflict ease his mind.[104] These warnings were enough to daunt any European statesman familiar enough with the somewhat unpredictable nature of American foreign policy.

Compelling and important though these factors were, the complete German retreat over this affair can, as is usual with Bismarck, only be adequately explained by reference to the overall domestic and European situation; and this, to put it mildly, was bad. His influence in the Reichstag had deteriorated and his internal power position was now much less secure since the accession of the young Kaiser Wilhelm II and the favouring of the growing anti-Russian faction at court. Moreover, while a 'pronounced strain of dissatisfaction' had crept into Germany's relations with Austria, there were also ominous signs that the chancellor could no longer keep Russia and France separated; in October 1888 the first Russian loan was floated in Paris, and in January 1889 the Russians placed a large order for French rifles after pledging that these would never be used against France. Even Bismarck himself had doubts about the continuance of friendly relations with Russia.[105] Most important of all, Boulangism swept to its heights in France, with the election of the ex-general to the Seine *département* on 27 January and the possibility of a future Franco-German war again loomed large. The significance of all these factors can be exaggerated, but it is clear that Bismarck was in an exceedingly difficult position at the beginning of 1888. The hostility of the United States over the affairs of Samoa was therefore to be avoided at all costs.

The position with regard to England was also one which recommended caution over Samoa. In brief, Bismarck was losing his diplomatic 'duel' with Salisbury over European

---

104 A.A./*U.S.A.* 16, vol. 1, Arco to Bismarck, no. 65 of 5/2/1889, and reply, no. 29 of 24/2/1889; ibid., Arco to Bismarck, no. 83 of 15/2/1889, with enclosure; *Waldersee, Denkwürdigkeiten des General-Feldmarschalls Alfred Graf von*, ed. H. O. Meisner, 3 vols. (Stuttgart/Berlin, 1923), 2, pp. 37-38.
105 Langer, *Alliances*, pp. 460-61; Taylor, *Struggle for Mastery*, pp. 325-26; G.P., 6, no. 1221, and minutes thereon.

policy, and he knew it.[106] Britain's very favourable geographical position and her proposed fleet increases gave the prime
minister two strong cards and contrasted sharply with Germany's unenviable location in central Europe and her fixed
alliance obligations; and while Bismarck still sought British
support for Austria-Hungary in the Balkans, he increasingly
desired her naval backing for Italy should the deteriorating
Franco-Italian relations in 1888-89 lead to a war in the
Mediterranean. By January 1889, just as the news of the
Samoan crisis reached Berlin, the chancellor was making his
famous alliance offer to Salisbury. Many historians have
queried the sincerity behind this move and argued that
Bismarck had anticipated in advance that the cautious prime
minister would politely decline;[107] but the fact remains that
Berlin persistently sought to remain friendly to London in this
period. In November 1888, Holstein actually sent word to Salisbury not to be too conciliatory in foreign affairs, lest he
endanger his political position at home; and Bismarck
deliberately 'sat upon' Germany's colonial enthusiasts in order
not to provoke British annoyance. The chancellor's admission
that 'At present we need England, if peace is still to be maintained' was a clear recognition of the altered circumstances
since 1885.[108] The gradual modification in the German attitude
towards Tonga, from refusing to acknowledge the British claim
to predominance at all (April 1887) to agreeing not to interfere
in the group (December 1887) and finally to suggesting that
Britain take Tonga (July 1888) reflects this more general
change.

Salisbury, although still wishing to be on good terms with
Bismarck, was at no stage willing to assume Germany's defence
burdens in either the east or the west and he declined the
alliance offer with the explanation that Britain's internal
political situation and her parliamentary traditions prevented
such a step from being taken.[109] Nor was the prime minister
willing to be drawn into an anti-American posture on account
of German misdeeds in Samoa; he did not respond to Hatzfeldt's hints that the new American naval increases might be
aimed against Britain, and the British chargé in Washington

106 Kluke, *Bismarck und Salisbury, passim.*

107 R. Moller, 'Bismarck's Angebot an England vom Januar 1889' in *Historische
Vierteljahresschrift* (1938), and W. Schüssler's criticisms in his *Deutschland zwischen
England und Russland* (Leipzig, 1940), pp. 62-102; the debate is continued in *Historische
Zeitschrift*, 163 (1941), and makes reference to the older literature by Ritter, Rothfels,
Rachfall et al.

108 F.O.343/10, Malet to Salisbury, 10/11/1888; G.P., 4, note on no. 952; H. Pogge von
Strandmann, 'Domestic Origins of Germany's Colonial Expansion under Bismarck', in
Past and Present, 42 (February, 1969), pp. 152-59.

109 G.P., 4, no. 945.

was told that ostentatious friendship with his German colleague 'would be unwise'.[110] Nevertheless, Bismarck persisted
in pointing out the danger from America and the need for
Britain to have her rear protected from a French attack, at the
same time telling Schurz that his vision of an American-French
alliance 'would almost certainly bring about an Anglo-German
one'.[111] While endeavouring to exploit any British concern at
the expansion of the United States and thus to serve his European aims by drawing London closer to Berlin, the chancellor
was also hoping to check American bellicosity by presenting
Washington with the prospect of an Anglo-German combination. In fact, as soon as the news of the ambush reached Europe
the German chargé in London had asked if London would help
to restore order and stressed that Berlin 'attaches great value
to being in accord with Her Majesty's Government with whom
they have a community of interest in this question'.[112]

It proved impossible to convince Salisbury of this fact,
however. Following the Sackville West affair, Britain's
relations with the United States were worse than usual and in
any case the prime minister disliked Bismarck's suggestion of
another Samoan conference since the Germans were 'apt to be
masterful—and to think themselves ill treated if the other
members of the conference do not vote exactly as they wish'.[113]
Moreover, he swiftly demurred when Bismarck, in his famous
Reichstag speech of 26 January, in which he referred to
England as 'our old and traditional ally', also declared that
the two governments were in perfect agreement over Samoa;
Hatzfeldt was informed that Britain was in no way responsible
for Germany's actions in the group.[114] Little positive support
could be expected from London, therefore, and Salisbury had
only criticism for the German attitude, telling Malet:

> Prince Bismarck's Colonial undertakings are a great nuisance. If they did
> Germany any good I should mind it less—as we are sure to get some
> slice of any commercial opening anywhere. But he has ruined everybody
> else's trade at Samoa and Zanzibar without in the least benefiting his
> own.[115]

If Bismarck desired some friendly reply to his alliance offer,

110 A.A./*U.S.A.* 17, vol. 1, Hatzfeldt to Bismarck, no. 50 of 30/1/1889; Salisbury Papers
A77/23, minute on Herbert to Barrington, 11/1/1889.

111 A.A./*U.S.A. 17*, vol. 1, Bismarck to Hatzfeldt, no. 98 of 1/2/1889; A.A./*U.S.A. 5a*,
vol. 1, A.A. to Hatzfeldt, no. 251 of 17/3/1889; A.A./*U.S.A.* 16, vol. 1, Bismarck to
Arco (for Schurz), 24/3/1889; Vagts, *Weltpolitik*, 1, pp. 668-69.

112 F.O.58/245, Salisbury to Malet, nos. 11 and 12 of 7/1/1889.

113 F.O.58/245, minute on Pauncefote note of 23/1/1889.

114 Ibid., Malet to Salisbury, no. 37 of 28/1/1889 (print copy), and Salisbury to Malet,
no. 30 of 29/1/1889.

115 Cecil, *Life*, 4, p. 126.

which was left unanswered between 11 January and 22 March, then it was hardly likely that he would annoy the prime minister by further actions in Samoa.

In view of the possibility of a conflict with America, of his weakened domestic and European position, of his disillusionment with colonial affairs by 1889, of his delicate relations with Salisbury, and finally of the attacks upon his overseas policy in the Reichstag, it was not surprising that Bismarck's backdown over Samoa, although reluctant, was swift and complete. Malet reported on 17 January that the chancellor had personally visited him to say that he had proposed to the United States government that the conference on Samoa should be resumed (this time in Berlin) and that

> he seemed anxious at the turn which affairs had taken in the island and observed that the consequences of the events which were passing there might be out of all proportion to the interests engaged. Samoa was not worth the evils which might result from a collision between the armed forces of Germany and the United States and he was therefore anxious to come to an understanding on the subject by peaceful negotiations.[116]

At the beginning of the following month, therefore, Bayard officially received this proposal together with assurances that Germany laid no claim to any prior position in Samoa; the idea of each of the powers taking turns to direct the affairs of the group was also suggested. It was 'a signal victory for the United States', which the outgoing Cleveland administration just had time to enjoy, and Bayard had no qualms in agreeing to a conference in Berlin.[117]

Fortunately for Bismarck, the news of Knappe's declaration of war and other excesses gave him a ready scapegoat and the chance of a quick withdrawal from an untenable position. This is not to imply that the chancellor himself was solely responsible for the rash German policy in Samoa; in fact, as mentioned before, his son and Krauel seem to have formulated much of it.[118] But, while regarding the consul's attempts to annex the group as 'absurd', Bismarck had been in favour of taking a harsh line against the Mata'afans and he must therefore share some of the blame which he so readily hoisted upon the shoulders of the German officials in Samoa. Completely reversing his earlier judgement, the chancellor insisted that the declaration of war upon Mata'afa was impossible in international law and Knappe was scolded in long, blistering

116 F.O.58/245, Malet to Salisbury, no. 22 of 19/1/1889.
117 Ibid., Beauclerk to Salisbury, no. 83 of 2/3/1889; Ryden, *U.S. Policy in Samoa*, pp. 424-25.
118 See Münster's sarcastic reference to Krauel and the Samoan blunder in N. Rich and M. H. Fisher (eds.), *The Holstein Papers*, 4 vols. (Cambridge, 1955-63), 3, p. 342.

despatches which were swiftly laid before the Reichstag.[119] So persistently and strenuously did the chancellor attack the unfortunate consul, in these published despatches, in private conversations and at a parliamentary dinner, that the German press quickly recognized all this as being more for foreign than for home consumption—a suspicion confirmed when Herbert Bismarck invited the *New York Herald*'s Berlin correspondent to a friendly interview, during which he declared that Germany would respect all treaties in the group.

Besides, the German government had another card up its sleeve. The unfortunate Malietoa had been sent to the Cameroons in 1887, since it was 'politically undesirable' to take him to Germany and excite public opinion there. By the following year, the king's health had so deteriorated that he was brought to Hamburg and then secretly housed in the naval barracks at Wilhelmshaven before being sent to the Marshall Islands.[120] Despite Holstein's denials to the British chargé of any knowledge of the king's whereabouts, the acting British consul in Hamburg was able to discover that, after being 'saturated with oysters and the best cigars' by the *D.H.P.G.* and the naval authorities, Malietoa was judged to have become so pro-German that his return to Samoa and re-instatement as monarch was being contemplated. Faced with the chaos in the islands by February 1889, Bismarck was pleased to learn that the native chieftain had promised from Jaluit that he would place himself under the Kaiser.[121] Although he did not arrive back to Upolu until the summer, Malietoa was obviously being kept 'in reserve' until then.

The final disincentive to any further unilateral action by Germany in Samoa came on 16 March 1889. Although little trouble occurred in the islands after January, due to the lack of sufficient German force, a certain amount of tension naturally remained; a stalemate existed rather than a definite cease-fire and it might easily have been upset by any false move, though this could hardly have led to war after the German and American governments had agreed to resume talks on the future of the group. Yet the *Auswärtiges Amt* still hoped to take some action against Mata'afa, and even optimistically believed that they might count upon the support of

119   For example, *Reichstag* 7, IV Session, vol. 5, section 138, document 47.
120   BA/MA 625, PG65070, *Die Entsendung von Kriegsschiffen nach den Südsee-Inseln*, vol. 3, Bismarck to A.A. (copy), no. 7 of 5/10/1887, and A.A. to Adm., 7/10/1887; ibid., vol. 4 (PG65071), same to same, 6/8/1888.
121   F.O.58/240, Beauclerk to Salisbury, no. 332 Confidential of 24/10/1888; cf. Holstein's denials in Beauclerk's no. 325 of 19/10/1888, ibid. See also, BA/MA 623, PG65059, *Die Entsendung von Kriegsschiffen nach Australien u. den Südsee-Inseln*, vol. 5, A.A. to Adm., Secret, 13/2/1889.

the other powers in this.[122] By that time, Germany had three warships, the *Adler*, *Olga* and *Eber*, in Samoan waters, watched closely by Kimberley's squadron of three vessels, consisting of the *Trenton*, *Nipsic* and *Vandalia*, with the British cruiser *Calliope* also on the scene.

But on 15 March all their local bickerings and suspicions were promptly forgotten about as a hurricane of monumental proportions bore down upon the islands. The barometer fell to a record low, and winds in excess of 100 m.p.h. buffeted the vessels inside the open and crowded harbour of Apia. During the night the *Eber* was driven under one reef in Apia Bay while the *Adler* was thrown onto another, where its wrecked hull can still be seen today. The *Trenton* and the *Vandalia* were also sunk, and the *Nipsic* and the *Olga* were forced to beach themselves, being refloated months later. Only the *Calliope*, aided by larger engines and the skilful seamanship of Captain Kane, survived by fighting her way out to the open seas.[123] The prospect of military action in Samoa had been literally blown away, and tempers further cooled with the realization that the warships lost were probably worth more than the group itself. This calamity, which Malet prophesied would make Samoa 'a more evil name than ever in German ears', certainly affected Bismarck and increased his wish to settle the affair as swiftly and amicably as possible.[124]

This complete abandonment of his Samoan policy in early 1889 tends to confirm that picture of his attitude toward colonial affairs which the documents of the previous four years revealed. Electoral considerations were totally missing and, while this is not to deny the concept of 'social Imperialism', domestic calculations seem to have played no part in the German policy towards Samoa in the 1880s, a complete contrast with later years.[125] Bismarck always insisted that Germany's interests in the group were 'commercial' and that 'We have no *political* interests in Samoa in the normal sense of the word.'[126] Nor can it be regarded as having been diplomatically motivated either, for Bismarck was as surprised as anyone by Stuebel's first move; and after autumn 1885, there was no reason for him to quarrel with Britain. None of this in itself could be considered as sufficient to demolish fully the theories

122 Ibid., same to same, Secret, 20/2/1889.

123 BA/MA 624, PG65062, *Die Entsendung von Kriegsschiffen nach der Südsee-Station*, vol. 1, has the reports of the German vessels, with full barometric and meteorological details. See also, J. A. C. Gray, *Amerika Samoa* (Annapolis, 1960), pp. 87-91.

124 Salisbury Papers, A62/22, Malet to Salisbury, 30/3/1889.

125 Developed further in P. M. Kennedy, 'German Colonial Expansion: has the "manipulated Social Imperialism" been ante-dated?' in *Past and Present*, 52 (February, 1972).

126 R.Kol.A.3068, Brauer to A.A., 22/11/1889.

that Bismarck's overall bid for colonies was occasioned by domestic or diplomatic motives: nor should it be, for these aspects certainly played a role, at least in 1884. But the chancellor's Samoan policy does confirm the contentions of those who believe that the major determinant of his imperialism was economic and often in a defensive sense at that, that there were long-term local reasons for the apparently sudden annexations in 1884 and 1885, and that the above-mentioned domestic and diplomatic motives were of secondary importance, which were useful on the occasion but which could also be abandoned without the fundamental, commercially-based colonial aims being affected.

The claim for political control to reflect Germany's commercial predominance, and the immediate need to protect the German plantations by unilateral action, were the two threads running through Bismarck's Samoan policy. Both had to be given up in 1889 out of fear of a conflict with the United States, but this should not obscure the fact that the chancellor's colonial policy, in this case at least, was almost exclusively commercially motivated; and, on such a calculation, Samoa was simply not worth the risk of war, especially since Bismarck was aware that he had been misled earlier into believing that he could secure overseas possessions for Germany which would be both cheap to administer and valuable for the nation. If there had been any sign of manipulated social imperialism, based upon a pressing need to preserve the political status quo of the Prusso-German state and to divert public attention outwards, this commercial calculation would have been irrelevant and it might not have been so easy or desirable to effect such a swift 'about-turn' in the Samoan policy. As it was, the documents seem to indicate a clear-cut example of colonization based upon simple economic considerations, and that the chancellor firmly believed in the flag following trade. Unfortunately, it was not in the creating or finding of trade, as often appears to have been the case with imperialism in parts of Africa, that the difficulty lay; it was in the hoisting of the flag.

iv   *The Berlin Conference of* 1889

Although Bayard had accepted on 5 February the German proposal for a conference in Berlin to settle Samoan troubles, he was forced to leave the selection of, and instructions to, the American plenipotentiaries to his successor, James G. Blaine. On 18 March the new president Harrison appointed Messrs

Kasson, Phelps and Bates as his commissioners, and on
11 April they received their instructions to maintain the same
attitude as that defended by Bayard in 1887 and to refuse to
recognize the legality of any changes in the islands since the
Washington Conference. There was clearly no weakening of
the American stance: if anything, its position had hardened
because of public opinion and party rivalries, and it was
stressed to the delegates that

> in any questions involving present or future relations in the Pacific, this
> government cannot accept even temporary subordination, and must
> regard it as inconsistent with that international consideration and dignity
> to which the United States, by continental position and expanding
> interest must always be entitled.[127]

During the conference, Bismarck, forced for once onto the
defensive, automatically turned to Salisbury for help, which
the latter, despite his distaste for the German actions and a
fixed determination to avoid personally clashing with the
United States, was quite willing to give, since he had no faith
in any form of joint control. The prime minister's policy
towards the group, despite the renewed representations of the
Australasian colonies and the urgings of Thurston that
'German commercial policy in the Pacific is hostile and
exclusive', was still very much the same.[128] Wishing to remain
as uninvolved as possible, he rejected Bismarck's suggestion
that the conference meet in London and he declined to
consider a petition by the Mata'afan chiefs for British protection—incidentally, the eighth consecutive refusal by a British
government to consider such an appeal.[129] Salisbury warned
the retiring American minister at London that a tripartite
system would not work, and a Foreign Office memorandum of
20 February stated that Britain's policy was 'to produce
stability of government by permitting one power to advise the
native government in all matters that do not affect the interests
of the other two'.[130] Joint control might have been London's
aim in 1885, when there was a need to secure some footholds
in the Pacific in the wake of the Franco-German colonial
onslaughts, but by 1889 Salisbury could see that this would be

---

127   Ryden, *U.S. Policy in Samoa*, pp. 429-42. John A. Kasson had been Minister both
at Berlin and Vienna; William Walter Phelps at Vienna; and George H. Bates had been
the U.S. Commissioner to Samoa in 1886.

128   F.O.58/247, Thurston to Salisbury, 13/3/1889, and enclosed copy of *New Zealand
Herald*.

129   F.O.58/245, Coëtlogen to Salisbury, no. 3 of 4/1/1889; F.O.58/246, Hertslet memo
of 28/2/1889.

130   F.O.58/247, F.O. memo, Most Confidential, 20/2/1889. See also, F.O.58/245,
Salisbury to Herbert, no. 9 of 30/1/1889.

more trouble than it was worth, especially as the touchy Americans were also to be involved.

Although this same memorandum raised an old hope that Britain would 'before long' have the predominance of commercial interests and thus be that administering power, it is difficult to see this as being a major consideration in Britain's Samoan policy: no trade reports had been received for five years and commerce had virtually dried up because of internal conflicts. Most probably Salisbury intended to use this argument again to appease colonial disquiet, for he promptly disregarded any hopes of predominance in Samoa when he discussed the whole situation with Herbert Bismarck at the end of March.

The chancellor's son had come to London in the hope of talking over the preparations for the kaiser's intended visit to England and, more especially, to learn of Salisbury's answer to the alliance proposal. Although this offer was turned down, there was no waning in the German friendship and the two statesmen talked about the Samoan problem with complete understanding. Malet was later informed that Herbert Bismarck meant

> to throw up the sponge at the conference, and abandon the idea of German predominance at Samoa. He suggested that when the American plenipotentiaries came, you should sound them unofficially, and as from yourself, upon the possibility of arranging the Pacific difficulty by resigning Hawaii to the U.S., Samoa to Germany, and Tonga to this country. But he evidently did not believe that there was any chance of the Americans accepting this offer.[131]

This idea of a three-way 'split', which was probably first put forward by Salisbury himself in an earlier conversation with Hatzfeldt, was most attractive to London and Malet and Herbert Bismarck further discussed it upon the latter's return to Berlin. To sweeten the pill for the United States, Germany was also prepared to offer her the Samoan island of Tutuila in addition to Hawaii, so that the U. S. Navy would not protest against the loss of coaling station rights at Pago-Pago, which they would now be able to enjoy exclusively.

So complete was the German retreat that the U. S. commissioner Bates was received by the kaiser and the chancellor in Berlin, after some initial difficulty, despite the anti-German article which he had recently written for an American magazine; that the idea of obtaining compensation from the Samoans for the loss of German lives and property was dropped; and that it was agreed to hold the conference in

131   Salisbury Papers, A64/47, Salisbury to Malet, 3/4/1889.

English to ease the language difficulties of the American
delegates, the first time ever, it was believed, that such an
international meeting in Europe had adopted this tongue.[132]
The Hawaii-Samoa-Tonga 'deal', however, was immediately
turned down by the United States, as the Germans had
expected. Although the leading delegate, Kasson, listened
attentively to Salisbury and Malet's arguments before the
conference began, he possessed direct instructions to refuse to
receive any schemes other than a regulation of the Samoan
question along the lines of Bayard's original principles and
was therefore forced to decline the British suggestions.[133]

Salisbury intensely disliked the anticipated American plan
of three separate advisers who would decide by majority rule,
seeing in this disunified administration many future quarrels,
and he still believed that 'the fate of the Samoan Islands would
be happiest and the course of commerce would be the least
disturbed' if an adviser nominated by one power was installed.
He predicted that the American scheme would be 'quite value-
less' but since Bismarck 'was ready to accept almost anything,
relying on time to show its impracticality' the prime minister
was forced to do the same: 'we cannot fight alone'.[134] Stressing
that the British interest in the group was commercial and not
political, he ordered his delegates at least to oppose any form
of decision by majority rule in a new administration, fearing
that he would be subjected to pressure by both sides should
the Germans and the Americans disagree in the future; whereas
unanimous decisions would allow Britain to stand aside and
declare that she would adhere to anything her two partners
were agreed upon. Even this might not forestall a local crisis,
however, and he suggested that only by laying a submarine
cable from Auckland to the islands could they get rid 'of the
furor consularis'.[135]

Because of the German abandonment of the 'mandatory'
scheme the fate of the Samoan Islands was clear before the
conference opened: what remained to be done was to settle
its administration and other questions, such as land disputes.
In all these areas the American delegates were not tied to
specific instructions but merely told to work out a solution
which would ensure as large a degree of native autonomy as
practicable. In fact, Blaine did not much care for Bayard's

132 F.O.58/251, Malet to Salisbury, no. 6 Samoa, Very Confidential, 28/4/1889; Ryden,
U.S. Policy in Samoa, pp. 432-33, 455-57, 489-96.
133 Salisbury Papers, A64/49, Salisbury to Malet, 24/4/1889; A62/34, Malet to Salisbury,
27/4/1889; Ryden, *U.S. Policy in Samoa*, p.p. 441, 446-50.
134 F.O.58/248, Salisbury to Malet, no. 127 of 11/4/1889; Salisbury Papers, A64/49,
Salisbury to Malet, 24/4/1889 (partly reproduced in Cecil, *Life*, 4, pp. 127-28).
135 Ibid.; F.O.58/250, Salisbury to the British Commissioners, nos. 2 and 3 of 27/4/1889.

scheme of three advisers, and warned his delegates to avoid involving the United States in an 'entangling alliance' although they could join a watered-down form of tripartite administration if nothing else was possible. This flexibility over practical details was more than matched on the British and German sides, whose delegations were led by Malet and Herbert Bismarck respectively in order to ensure a quick and satisfactory solution.[136] To expedite matters further, a working sub-committee to consider special problems was appointed immediately the conference began, on 29 April. Six weeks later it was concluded, it having taken only nine sessions (two of which were concerned with mere formalities) to settle the many topics under review.

The debates and recommendations may be summarized fairly briefly, since they concerned virtually no changes of policy and included little that was not predictable before the event.[137] The delegates immersed themselves first of all in the land question and swiftly agreed that further land sales by the natives should be prohibited; that a special court under a single judge should be set up to give final decisions upon land disputes, after some preliminary investigations had been carried out by a land commission; and that the Samoans should be represented in this matter by an advocate. Seven smaller and more technical proposals about the settlement of the land disputes were agreed upon by the conference, which also accepted that all areas acquired 'in a customary and regular manner' before 28 August 1879 (the Anglo-Samoan Treaty) must be recognized. This was a definite benefit to the *D.H.P.G.*, virtually ignoring all of Weber's dubious acquisitions in fact, and it was only reluctantly accepted by London when the delegates pointed out that there existed no law by which the proposed Land Court could pronounce as illegal transactions made by Germans and Americans earlier than 1880. As they could not legislate retrospectively, only British acquisitions of land would be subject to forfeiture if this decision was rejected, therefore.[138]

A decision to ban the importation and sale of arms, ammunition and intoxicating liquors—but only for the natives themselves—was also swiftly agreed upon. The sub-committee

136   The other German delegates were Krauel (for his knowledge of colonial affairs) and Holstein (for his knowledge of the U.S.A. and the English language); the other British delegates were C. S. Scott (Minister to Switzerland) and J. A. Crowe (Commercial Attaché for Europe).

137   Details of the conference are in R.Kol.A. vols. 2882-2902; F.O.58/250-52; Ryden, *U.S. Policy in Samoa*, pp. 453-513; and Vagts, *Weltpolitik*, 1, pp. 669-86.

138   F.O.58/251, Malet to Salisbury, no. 9 Samoa, 1/5/1889, with enclosure, and Plenipotentiaries to Salisbury, no. 27 Samoa, 18/5/1889; Ryden, *U.S. Policy in Samoa*, pp. 459-63.

further proposed to raise revenue by a capitation tax of $1 upon adult Samoans, taxes on a sliding scale upon the various professions and tradespeople, and a small ad valorem duty upon all imports and the three major exports of copra, cotton and coffee. It was believed that the Samoan government might thus be able to rely upon an annual revenue of almost $90,000, from which it could pay not only for the salaries of its officials but also for roads, bridges, harbour improvement, etc. The conference also decided that the municipality of Apia should resume its own special administrative functions, of which it had been bereft since the termination of the local government in October 1887; but it was now to be ruled by a council of six members and chaired by a president who was also to have a vote and be the chief executive of the township. Consular jurisdiction remained, however, in all non-municipal regions.[139]

None of these questions presented much difficulty and Malet cheerfully reported after the second session that

> all seems to be going harmoniously and the Americans are much pleased with the general attitude of the German representatives . . . I do not think we can go very wrong as the interests of the three nationalities have now become identical through the surrender by the Germans of claim to preponderance.[140]

The ambassador's optimism was soon tempered as the more critical problems of the kingship and the future form of the Samoan central government were approached; here a great deal of skilful diplomacy was to be required to avoid a breakdown. Mata'afa's candidacy for the kingship was resolutely opposed by Bismarck on account of the death and mutilation of the German sailors: this was virtually the only point in the conference upon which the German government made a firm stand. On the other hand, the Americans were equally opposed to Tamasese, whom they continued to regard as Berlin's puppet; yet their instructions to secure a free election were criticized by experts such as Bates, Sewall and Powell (the latter two being the clerks to the American and British delegations respectively) since experience showed that deciding the monarch by native methods invariably meant civil war. At the fifth session, Malet therefore proposed that the question could most easily be solved, if they all simply agreed to revert to the status quo ante and to inform the Samoan people 'that if they take Malietoa as King, such act on the part of the Samoans

139   F.O.58/251, Malet to Salisbury, no. 18 Samoa, Secret, enclosing Protocols of the second session.
140   Salisbury Papers, A62/37, Malet to Salisbury, 4/5/1889.

shall receive the sanction of the treaty powers'.[141] Such a proposal would also steer the conference from any investigation of the deposition of Malietoa in the first place, which the Americans thought could hardly be ignored but which the Germans would bitterly resent. Malet's suggestion was therefore warmly taken up by Herbert Bismarck, who had arranged the whole issue with the British ambassador beforehand and who now had hopes that Malietoa would prove to be pro-German; and by Kasson, who favoured a return to the pre-1887 situation and who overrode his fellow plenipotentiaries' preference for Mata'afa and suspicion that Malietoa had been indoctrinated during his time in captivity.[142]

The future form of the Samoan government proved to be the thorniest problem of all: what sort of advisers should the monarch have, how were they to be appointed and what would their powers be? On 17 May, at the fourth session, the sub-committee suggested that the post of chief-justice of Samoa be established and that this person be not only the land judge and final appellate judge but also the 'umpire' in the case of future monarchical elections where the natives could not agree upon one candidate: for although the powers selected Malietoa as king, his successors were to be elected 'according to the laws and customs of Samoa'. In addition, the president of the muni-capality of Apia was to control the income and expenditure of the Samoan government, to supervise all measures relating to shipping and the harbour, and to advise the natives 'in all matters that concern foreign interests'.[143] Thus a supreme judicial officer and a chief executive officer would be set up; while the powers themselves, together with the Samoan government and the municipality, would provide legislation at various levels (the powers only to legislate to revise the decisions of the conference itself).

The scheme appeared tolerably effective in theory, but the American government was very wary of possibly losing its influence over the administration of the islands and revived for a short while Bayard's plan of three advisers to the king, or at least two, so that three major posts (one chief justice and two advisers) would exist for the three powers to fill. This Salisbury strongly opposed; if the premier was to have joint control of the group forced upon him, then it was to be as sensible and trouble-free a system of government as possible, and not one

141   F.O.343/3, Holstein to Malet, 21/5/1889; F.O.58/251, Malet to Salisbury, no. 18 Samoa, Secret, 28/5/1889, enclosing Protocols of fifth session; Ryden, *U.S. Policy in Samoa*, pp. 470-75, 493-97.

142   Ibid.

143   F.O.58/251, Plenipotentiaries to Salisbury, nos. 26 and 28 Samoa, Secret, of 18/5/1889 and 22/5/1889.

full of obvious weaknesses from the start. So determined was Salisbury on this matter that the Americans gave way but Harrison and Blaine then insisted, at the very last moment, that the chief justice of Samoa be nominated by the king of Sweden and Norway and be of neutral nationality. Since this officer had to be well versed in English law, the sub-committee had previously recommended that he be appointed by the lord chief justice of England; now the American delegates were forced to withdraw from this proposal with some embarrassment. Salisbury was very willing to allow a neutral designator since he had only with reluctance agreed to appointments being made by the lord chief justice—a system which would have brought Britain more into the centre of Samoan affairs than he wished. However, he revolted at the idea of excluding from the post 'the only lawyers who know anything about the laws and language of the foreigners in Samoa', and Washington thereupon also abandoned its insistence upon a neutral chief justice.[144]

The Germans, while supporting the British arguments, tended to stay in the background over these disputes, another symptom of their withdrawal from the centre of the stage. By this time Bismarck was thoroughly disgusted with colonialism in general and Samoa in particular. Convinced that the whole crisis had been the result of an outbreak of *morbus consularis* he ordered Knappe to return home to be reprimanded. When, in March, the *D.H.P.G.* pleaded once again for single rule of the group by Germany, the chancellor savagely minuted 'the old song!'; and later in the year he willingly forwarded to America the news that the firm would sell out if a suitable offer were made.[145] He had striven for years to protect German commercial interests in the islands and to try to satisfy their demands for German control but his determination in this matter had its limits.

Finally, all was settled and the Final Act of the Berlin Samoan conference was signed by the plenipotentiaries on 14 June 1889. It formed a milestone in Samoan history by creating for the first time, legally and officially, a system of tripartite supervision by the powers over the whole group. It also offers a useful insight into the final years of Bismarck's diplomacy, a period in which he was not only beginning to lose control at home but also one in which he found it increasingly difficult to maintain intact by diplomacy alone Germany's

144　F.O.58/252, same to same, tels. 12, 16, 17 and 18 Samoa, Secret, of 22/5/1889; F.O.58/250, Salisbury to Plenipotentiaries, tels. 24 and 26, Secret, 23/5/1889; Ryden, *U.S. Policy in Samoa*, pp. 508-12.

145　R.Kol.A.2477, D.H.P.G. to Bismarck, 23/3/1889, and minute thereon; ibid., Berchem to Arco (copy), Private, 26/12/1889.

many interests and responsibilities in Europe and overseas. Crowe, one of the British delegates, shrewdly explained the chancellor's foreign and domestic difficulties in a letter to Salisbury on the day after the close of the conference:

> The Samoan question has been decided, as your Lordship knows, with an obvious wish on the part of the German government to propitiate the Americans who are obviously bent on extending their influence. The Chancellor and his officials went half-hearted into the conference on Samoa, they asked for one concession only, and that was the exclusion of King Mata'afa from the kingship, and in doing so silenced the main opposition which was the opposition of the Emperor, and the naval and military commanders. There has not been a time since 1870-1 in which the soldiers and sailors who surround and flatter the military pride of H.I.M. have had more influence than now. The Emperor has more than once, in the presence of persons whom I know, expressed his impatience at the studied peaceful attitude of the Chancellor . . .

> But the Chancellor, I believe, sees war looming in the future and his yielding attitude in the Pacific is no doubt due to the anxiety which the state of affairs in Europe causes. 'We cannot risk any quarrel with the U.S.', Baron Holstein said to me, 'by challenging the Americans in the Pacific. We have enough to do to keep free of encumbrances this side . . .'[146]

The Americans had won a diplomatic victory, it was clear; but they had not emerged with what Washington set out, rather short-sightedly, to obtain. Harrison and Blaine had deliberately avoided recommending Bayard's complete scheme of government to their delegates in the hope that they could reach an arrangement whereby native independence and self-government would be preserved without much interference or support from the powers. The plenipotentiaries themselves soon came to realize how illusory such a hope was when the islands were in a state of chaos, with the white nationalities ranged against each other, the Samoans engaged in civil war, planting and commerce disrupted, and all manner of normal administration lacking. If rule by one nation was excluded, then a form of native government had to be devised which would not only allow for a viable administration but also for the equality of the three powers: a tridominium was the only answer. It may be true, as their press asserted, that this involved them in an entangling alliance which was contrary to the traditions of the United States. But they were, in fact, legally involved in the Samoan dispute since the signing of their 1878 treaty; and they were to learn that, as they expanded into the

---

146   Salisbury Papers, A60/41, J. A. Crowe to Salisbury, 15/6/1889. See also Holstein's comments to Waldersee upon complications with the U.S.A. in *Aus dem Briefwechsel des Generalfeldmarschalls Grafen Waldersee*, ed. H. O. Meisner, (Berlin/Leipzig, 1928), pp. 227-28.

Pacific along with the other great powers, they could no longer rely upon purely commercial, 'informal' influence; and, finally, they could think of no alternative solution to the problem.

Nevertheless, it is difficult to describe the American policy as being purely one of concern for the independent peoples of the Pacific: strategic interests were also at work and the Samoan crisis had offered superb propaganda material for naval enthusiasts and expansionists.[147] With the navy department and the west coast newspapers pressing for a secure foothold in the South Pacific, Blaine went so far as to ask his delegates to 'take every judicious step to obtain if possible full recognition by treaty of our exclusive right to the great harbour (Pago-Pago) the concession of which is already so nearly complete.'[148] The United States, the secretary of state felt, might even pay Samoa up to $20,000 for the securing of this right. However, Kasson argued that it would be injudicious to focus attention upon this question and that it would be better quietly to buy up all the lands surrounding Pago-Pago Bay and thus achieve exclusive control in a more discreet manner. Nevertheless, the American delegates made sure that no import duties were levied by the Samoan government upon coal and naval stores, and that the rights granted in former treaties to the powers were not affected by the Berlin act. Moreover, by preventing 'mandatory' rule they had achieved their instruction of not allowing the naval station to be subordinated to the supervision of another nation.[149]

The Final Act of Berlin, the Americans felt, was the best that could be achieved under the circumstances; but the British and German governments were rather less sanguine about its results. Yet, although Salisbury and Bismarck were doubtless correct in believing that rule by one power made for a better administration than any multi-national form of government, at least the structure they had evolved, as the prime minister put it, 'could hardly be more injurious than the existing state of things'.[150] The proposed new system had solved the immediate problem of Samoa and, seen from this viewpoint, it was a success.

In the long-term, however, it was an unsatisfactory settlement. Despite the first article of this act, which was 'A declaration respecting the independence and neutrality of the islands

147 Vagts, *Weltpolitik*, 1, pp. 653-69; Wehler, 1889, *passim*.
148 Ryden, *U.S. Policy in Samoa*, p. 465.
149 Ibid., pp. 437-38, 465-67.
150 F.O.58/250, Salisbury to Plenipotentiaries, no. 2 of 27/4/1889.

of Samoa',[151] the powers had reduced that independence to nothing. They had kept separate the key township of Apia; they had retained the consular jurisdiction outside the municipality; they had imposed a king of their own choosing upon the Samoans and ignored the fact that by 1889 the majority of them supported Mata'afa; they had given this king a supervisor of revenues and a permanent 'adviser'—controller might be a better word; they had created a Supreme Court to be the final body in all appeals, including contested elections to the kingship which the natives could no longer settle in their customary way; they had, upon insufficient evidence, decreed a tax system for Samoa which was soon to prove to be a gross miscalculation; they had ignored all the dubious land sales before 1879; and they had, by establishing a monarch bereft of all strength—he had to call upon the three powers if he required military aid—made the kingship into a figurehead for the Samoans themselves to scorn. Moreover, the twin rivalries, those between the native factions and those between the various white nationalities, had been in no way eliminated and could indeed flourish in a system which relied for its efficacy upon so many balancing influences and jurisdictions. Finally, no move had been made about laying a cable to the group from New Zealand and it would still take three or four weeks for full reports—or perhaps even the news itself—of any future local crisis to reach the home governments.

Some of these difficulties were appreciated at the time; others emerged only later. But, even when weaknesses were seen at the conference, the delegates either thought them to be the best of a number of bad solutions or were often reluctant to tackle them at all. As Herbert Bismarck remarked during the discussions, the whole thing 'was the result of a series of compromises and that, if he attempted to dislodge a brick, others might do the same and the foundations might be shaken'.[152] It was a fair summary of a conference in which diplomatic relations were paramount and no thought was ever given to what the Samoans themselves might want. The main achievement had been to mend an American-German quarrel, rather than to produce a lasting solution to the Samoan question. Because of this, the Berlin Act was, in effect, a postponement rather than a settlement.

---

151   The text of the Act is in *Accounts and Papers*, 1890 (LXXXI), (C. 5911).
152   F.O.58/252, Plenipotentiaries to Salisbury, tel. no. 15 Samoa, 7/6/1889.

3

Tripartite Rule and International Relations 1889-98

i *The Workings of the Berlin Act*

IF THE delegates to the Berlin Conference felt that their task was complete as they left the *Auswärtiges Amt* after the signing of the Final Act, the work of the consuls in Samoa to carry out the provisions of that document was clearly only just beginning.[1] By June, 1889, the situation in the islands was slowly improving, though an immediate implementation of the act was impossible because nothing could *officially* be done until the United States Senate had discussed and ratified the agreement. In fact, the ratifications were not exchanged until 12 April 1890. Although this prevented an immediate proclamation against the purchase of land and other actions for which American citizens were not yet legally liable, the three governments felt justified in proceeding with the kingship decision. Unwilling to see Mata'afa enjoy the fruits of his victory in Samoa any longer, Germany requested that the consuls be instructed unanimously to recognize Malietoa as king and to announce the decisions of the conference. As soon as the old monarch was restored to power, he should be informed of the clauses concerning land alienation, arms and liquor sales etc. To speed his return, a German naval vessel had already left for the Marshalls to bring the king back to Apia.[2]

It is impossible not to feel some sympathy for Mata'afa at this stage. Being related to both the Malietoa and the Tupua families, he was an ideal candidate to heal the dynastic split which had done so much to retard the group's progress and to prevent the Samoans from presenting a common front to the intrusion of white influence. He was, moreover, a fine military leader and a far more imposing personality than either Malietoa Laupepa or Tamasese. Finally, by throwing off the Brandeis-Tamasese control and defeating the German landing party, he had gained immense prestige and attracted

1 The experimental tripartite rule over Samoa is discussed (critically and at exhausting length) by Vagts, *Weltpolitik*, 1, pp. 681-797, and (more sympathetically and at less length) in R. P. Gilson, *Samoa 1830 to 1900*, pp. 396-424.
2 F.O.58/249, Hatzfeldt memo of 5/7/1889; ibid., Coëtlogen to Salisbury, no. 33 of 15/7/1889; R.Kol.A.2905, memo of 26/6/1889.

the majority of Samoans to his standard: he was their Hereward, their Tell, their William the Silent.

On 11 August 1889, Malietoa was brought back to his family and friends in Upolu by the gunboat *Wolf*. The captivity and journeys had greatly weakened the former ruler and he very willingly resigned the kingship to Mata'afa at a large native assembly, which met in early October. Bismarck, although reprimanding Stuebel for his obsession about Anglo-American backing for this development, nevertheless became very uneasy at it and pressed Salisbury for his support, warning that Mata'afa's succession even to the vice-kingship would 'render it impossible for the German Government to ratify the convention recently agreed to at Berlin'.[3] Since nothing could have annoyed Salisbury more than a revival of the diplomatic squabbles over Samoa, Coëtlogen was instructed to join his fellow consuls in recognizing Malietoa as quickly as possible. Their proclamation to this effect was issued on 9 November. On 5 December, Malietoa hoisted his flag and assumed control of the Samoan government, receiving at the same time the official recognition of the powers.[4] Faced with this unanimous stand by the signatory nations, the Samoans received these decisions quietly and the expected troubles did not occur.

Yet, satisfying though this was for the relations of the powers, it did not greatly help the situation in Samoa. There the very negation of government existed; for while the pre-1889 system had been demolished by the Berlin Act, the new structure had not yet been raised in its place. Moreover, it was to take many months, even years in some cases, before the many specific provisions for the better regulation of affairs in the group were carried out. Had the new structure been immediately set up in all its aspects, there would probably have been a readier acceptance of the scheme of government drawn up in Berlin. Instead, it was constructed piecemeal, which aroused the suspicion of the Samoans and the vitriolic criticism of the group's most famous resident, R. L. Stevenson.[5]

The chief justice, a Swedish judge named Conrad

3   F.O.58/249, Salisbury to Beauclerk, no. 296 Confidential of 5/9/1889; ibid., Sanderson note of 3/9/1889; R.Kol.A.3024, Stuebel to Bismarck, no. 84 of 16/7/1889; ibid., Rottenburg to Berchem, 24/8/1889. Stuebel had been sent back to Samoa after Knappe's recall.

4   F.O.58/249, Salisbury to Coëtlogen, tel. of 16/9/1889; ibid., Coëtlogen to Salisbury nos. 45 and 46 of 8/11/1889 and 6/12/1889; Ryden, *U.S. Policy in Samoa*, pp. 513-14; *Reichstag* 8, I Session, I Anlageband, section 64, nos. 10-12.

5   Following his *A Footnote to History*, Stevenson's criticisms can also be found in his *Vailima Letters* (London, 1895), in his various letters to the *Times*, and in his letter to Rosebery (Rosebery Papers, Box 91, letter of 2/1/1894).

Cedercrantz, was not nominated by the king of Sweden and Norway until 1890; while the appointment of the German candidate for the presidency of the municipality, Baron Senfft von Pilsach, was not settled until December 1890 and he did not arrive in Samoa until May 1891. Until then, the newly-elected municipal council could hardly function. Cedercrantz himself only assumed his post in Apia in January of that year. Moreover, the new British consul, Cusack-Smith, reported that the Samoan government still had neither influence nor money, since the native districts were refusing to pay the capitation tax; and that the court was not yet open and Cedercrantz was asking for an advance of money from the three powers to pay for a Samoan constabulary, without which little could be done.[6]

Matters continued to go from bad to worse throughout 1891. The chief justice quarrelled fiercely with the land commission over the latter's expenses, refused to pay any taxes upon his salary and then left for an eight week tour of Fiji. The president adopted a dictatorial attitude towards the Samoan government, became involved in a quarrel over the use of German currency in the group and, in October, resigned when he learnt that a German member of the municipal council had corresponded with the king without his knowledge. While these petty arguments were developing, Mata'afa moved away to Malie, where he was crowned king by his followers.[7] By the beginning of 1892, therefore, Samoa still lacked any form of peace, order and effective administration.

The governments of all three powers were acutely embarrassed at the continued reappearance of difficulties which they had hoped the Final Act had eradicated. Senfft's resignation was angrily declined by the German government and he was urged to show co-operation, but the squabbles of the officials continued. The chief justice and the land commissioners still argued over their respective powers, while the whole municipality complained when an attempt was made to take away the customs revenues from it and give them to the Samoan government: yet without this move, the native administration would be crippled by a lack of finances. Senfft also clashed with the consuls. Salaries, which consumed $28,520 from the budget, were in arrears and taxes were unpaid. Moreover, action against Mata'afa was repeatedly

---

6   F.O.58/260, Cusack-Smith to Salisbury, no. 35 of 23/5/1891; R.Kol.A.3026 Stuebel to Caprivi, no. 75 of 4/11/1890 and no. 24 of 28/3/1891.

7   On these difficulties, see Cusack-Smith's despatches (Political) nos. 36, 45, 47, 50, 51, 53, 57, 60 and 71, throughout the latter half of 1891 in F.O.58/Vols. 261 and 262; and vice-consul Schmidt's reports, nos, 51, 55, 67, 80 and 95 of the same period in R.Kol.A.3027.

postponed and Malietoa's prestige sank further. Faced with this chaos, the Americans proposed a further conference, which would modify sections of the Final Act and perhaps abolish the post of municipal president altogether. However, the German government opposed this reduction in their influence and preferred instead to replace both the chief justice and the president.[8] As Sanderson wearily noted, 'The United States Government are clearly getting tired of the present arrangement. But I am afraid we must get further into the Slough of Despond before the Germans are convinced'.[9]

The new chief justice Ide did not arrive in Samoa until the November of 1893, while President Schmidt assumed office on the penultimate day of that year. Only in the work of the land commission was an improvement in the situation gradually taking place. Suffering repeated delays due to the illness and absenteeism of the German and American members, the commission's enquiries only really got under way in 1893. Their task was enormous, with some 3,942 claims demanding investigation. Moreover, as the British member, Bazett Haggard, pointed out, the area claimed by the many applicants totalled 1,700,000 acres, which was 'some 900,000 more acres than there is supposed to be acreage in Samoa'.[10] By the end of 1894, after further delays and a great deal of work, the commission had finished its marathon task, which Haggard summed up in the following table:[11]

Nationality	Acreage Claimed	Acreage Confirmed	Percentage Confirmed
German	134,419	75,000	56
British	1,250,270	36,000	3
American	302,746	21,000	7
French	2,307	1,300	57
Various	2,151	2,000	95
Totals	1,691,893	135,300	8

8   F.O.58/265, Senfft von Pilsach to Salisbury, 29/2/1892; Cusack-Smith to Salisbury, nos. 8 and 10 of 1/3/1892 and 10/3/1892; F.O.58/266, same to same, no. 13 of 26/4/1892; F.O.58/267, same to same, nos. 24 and 34 of 3/8/1892 and 11/10/1892; F.O.58/268, Herbert to Rosebery, no. 312 Confidential of 3/11/1892; Sanderson memo of 18/11/1892; Malet to Rosebery, no. 283 of 31/12/1892; Ryden, *U.S. Policy in Samoa*, pp. 530-33; and Vagts, *Weltpolitik*, 1, pp. 713-19.

9   F.O. 58/267 Minute on Cusack-Smith to Rosebery no. 33 of 13/9/1892.

10   F.O.58/262, Haggard to Salisbury, 8/12/1891.

11   F.O.58/287, Haggard to Kimberley, 5/12/1894, reviews the work of the commission. The German side is covered in great detail in R.Kol.A.2918-24. The commission's rejection of extravagant claims by several British subjects, such as a certain Frank Cornwall, who claimed 414,000 acres in Savai'i, accounts for the low percentage of acreage confirmed for this nationality.

From that time onwards, land disputes in Samoa were of very minor significance.

A further development in 1893 was the outbreak of another civil war, followed by the capture and deportation of Mata'afa. Despite the pleas of Malietoa's government, action by naval forces had been continually postponed by the powers throughout 1892 and the advent of the hurricane season again forced its delay until after the April of 1893. None of the signatory nations were at all eager to carry out their pledges to the Samoan government, and the British Admiralty sent a warship to the group 'very reluctantly'.[12] The German Foreign Ministry also warned their vessels that there were to be no landings and that the commanders must wait for the warships of the other powers to join them in disarming the Samoans and forcing Mata'afa to surrender.[13] The Americans, reluctant converts to the project, did not despatch a vessel—from New York—until 24 June. By that time, Mata'afa had unfurled his standard, rejected the warrants of the Supreme Court to come to Apia, and war had been officially declared. His main support now came from the powerful *A'ana* and *Atua* districts, who were traditionally opponents of the Malietoa house and who had turned to Mata'afa after the death of Tamasese in 1891. However, Malietoa's forces managed to defeat the rebels and drive them onto the small island of Manono. At that stage, a British warship arrived on the scene and joined the German vessels in 'persuading' Mata'afa to surrender. The chief was then taken away with some of his main supporters in a German warship to the Union Islands and thence to the Marshalls.[14]

Unrest among the Samoans was not crushed by the deportation of Mata'afa, although the *A'ana* and *Atua* districts were naturally depressed by the loss of their leader and the unanimous support of the treaty powers for Malietoa. The continuation of the troubles again hit the *D.H.P.G.* harder than most, since, as Percy Anderson noted, 'War is fatal to the planter but a matter of indifference, and even an advantage, to the outside importer.'[15] Consequently, it was the Germans who pressed most insistently for disarming the natives and for

---

12   F.O.58/275, Adm. to F.O. 27/3/1893. ' "Very reluctantly" is a bit strong', Rosebery noted caustically.

13   BA/MA 624, PG65062, *Die Entsendung S. M. Schiffe nach der Südsee-Station*, vol. 1, A.A. to R.M.A. (Reichs-Marine-Amt) 23/3/1892; ibid., vol. 2, PG65063, same to same, 14/7/1893; Vagts, *Weltpolitik*, 1, pp. 719-21; Gilson, *Samoa 1830 to 1900*, pp. 421-23.

14   F.O.58/276, Cusack-Smith to Rosebery, nos. 32 and 36 of 10/7/1893 and 18/7/1893; Ryden, *U.S. Policy in Samoa*, pp. 593-94.

15   F.O.58/286, P. Anderson minute on Cusack-Smith to Kimberley, no. 25 Confidential of 14/7/1894.

rigorously enforcing that control over the sale of arms and ammunition for which the Berlin Act had made provision. The scheme was unenthusiastically accepted by the Foreign Office although it was opposed by the British consul and the Admiralty but, in any case, the coming of the hurricane season forced its postponement.[16]

Early in 1894, fresh conflicts between rival Samoan groups occurred and, although Malietoa's forces were successful, this did not put an end to the troubles. By May, war had broken out again in a more formidable manner, for Tamasese's son (also called Tamasese) was now leading the *Atua* people against the Samoan government.[17] The white residents were believed to be threatened, the plantations once more suffered heavily and Malietoa renewed his appeals for assistance, but the British and American governments remained cool to the idea of military action. Consequently, the German Admiralty even began to plan for a pacification of the group by their own forces alone 'after agreement with the other Treaty Powers', and a scheme for the seizure and blockade of Samoa by a force of six cruisers and almost six hundred marines was worked out.[18]

After the 1894/95 hurricane season, German vessels were once more directed to Samoa, since, as the Foreign Ministry noted, the 'previous intervention of the warships has only had a temporary influence upon the political situation.'[19] But a remedy to the troubles remained impossible to achieve while the United States declined the German plan of searching all vessels for arms, and the German Admiralty preferred to act alone in pacifying the islands since they might have to surrender operational control to a British or an American admiral.[20] The high command, for their part, did not like the Samoan burden at all and was particularly opposed to stationing warships there all the year round, insisting that

the expenditure of means for this purpose is far too great. In the current Budget year the activities of both cruisers of the Australia Station, whose

16 F.O.58/277, Malet to Rosebery, no. 210 of 18/9/1893, Currie minute of 20/9/1893; F.O.58/278, Cusack-Smith to Rosebery, no. 67 of 7/11/1893; R.Kol.A. 3032, Biermann to Caprivi, no. 84 of 30/11/1893.

17 F.O.58/284, Cusack-Smith to Rosebery, no. 3 of 2/1/1894 and tel. of 22/3/1894; F.O.58/285, tel. of 17/5/1894, and German Embassy communications of 17/5/1894 and 4/6/1894; BA/MA 5166, 3. 1-4b, *Geheime-R-Angelegenheit Samoa*, Top Secret, vol. 1. Adm. memo of 1/5/1894; R.Kol.A.3033, Biermann to Caprivi, no. 27 of 26/3/1894.

18 BA/MA 7577, Geh. I, *Hauptakten der Australischen Station*, vol. 1, Oberkommando to *Bussard*, Top Secret of 17/5/1894 and 19/5/1894; *Bussard* replies, Secret, of 17/7/1894 and 30/10/1894. On the political implications of this, see the following sub-chapter.

19 BA/MA 5166, 3. 1-4b, *Geheime-R-Angelegenheit Samoa*, Top Secret, vol. 1, A.A. to Adm., 9/7/1895.

20 Ibid., Adm. to A.A., 23/7/1895; Ryden, *U.S. Policy in Samoa*, pp. 543-45.

crew maintenance takes 310 men (therefore almost the crew of a
battleship) and who burden the maintenance funds by 414,000 Marks
have been *completely* absorbed by the rather small and still not very
valuable Samoan Islands.[21]

Moreover, the German commander-in-chief of the Australia
station felt it completely unnatural that his warships should
act in favour of the pro-English Malietoa and that they
were always being summoned to act by the U.S. consul (as
the doyen), while that country never provided any vessels. In
view of all these factors, the German Foreign Ministry was
by 1896 compelled to abandon their attempts to eliminate the
native unrest.[22] Since the Samoan government was not strong
enough to act by itself and Malietoa's health was deteriorating,
the opposition party was left unmolested in the years following.

If the state of the native body politic continued to worsen
after 1893 and payment of the crucial capitation tax was
ignored, there was also little encouragement to be found in
the affairs of the white officials. Schmidt, as a former German
vice-consul in Apia, already had many enemies and quickly
proved himself to be as capable as his predecessor of arguing
with the chief justice.[23] He also provoked many objections,
including those of the United States government, by trying
to take control of the Samoan finances, and early in 1895
Malietoa petitioned for his removal. 'The usual monthly
bulletin of squabbles & paralysis of government in Samoa',
was how one Foreign Office official described their consul's
reports on these matters.[24] Schmidt further annoyed
Washington by assuming the chief justice's powers when
that officer took a vacation. Even the German naval officers
found him impossible to work with, while the white residents
wanted his post abolished entirely. Moreover, Ide himself
clashed with the consuls over his assertion that he could
attend political discussions. The American and German
consuls, Mulligan and Biermann, also quarrelled over legislative matters.[25]

21 BA/MA 2023, PG65988, *Bestimmungen über Immediatberichte u. Vorträge*, vol. 3,
Oberkommando Promemoria of 19/1/1895.

22 BA/MA 624, PG65064, *Die Entsendung S. M. Schiffe nach der Südsee Station*, vol. 3,
Oberkommando to R.M.A., 10/12/1895. enclosure C. in C.'s report; A.A. to R.M.A.,
12/6/1896. The documents concerning the German attempt to stop the sale of arms and
giving the right of search to *all* warships are collected in F.O.58/Vols. 305-307.

23 F.O.58/277, Cusack-Smith to Rosebery, no. 46 of 15/3/1893 and Rosebery minute
thereon; F.O.58/285, Cusack-Smith tel. of 17/5/1894; R.Kol.A.3035, Biermann to Caprivi,
no. 59 of 5/8/1894.

24 F.O.58/297, Dallas minute on Woodford to Kimberley, no. 12 of 25/2/1895; ibid.,
F.O. to Malet, no. 42 of 9/2/1895; Ryden, *U.S. Policy in Samoa*, pp. 543-47.

25 BA/MA 624, PG65064, *Die Entsendung S. M. Schiffe nach der Südsee Station*, vol. 3,
A.A. to R.M.A. 25/10/1894; BA/MA 7577, Geh. I, *Hauptakten der Australischen Station*,
vol. 2, A.A. to Adm. 24/2/1896, enclosing Schmidt-Leda report of 30/12/1895.

By 1896, things were no better and a deadlock existed between the officials on many issues. Schmidt added to his unpopularity by attempting to get everything done in German and the government of the group was almost non-existent: out of an anticipated capitation tax of $30,000 only $10 was collected. The only gleam of hope came with Schmidt's resignation in that year, at which the German government immediately put forward a replacement candidate, having 'just regard for the prevailing German interest in Samoa . . .'[26] No objections being raised to this by the other powers, a Dr Raffel was appointed as the next president. Soon afterwards, Ide also resigned his post and was replaced by another American, William Lea Chambers.

In view of the continuous chaos and unrest in the group, which naturally caused a decline in its trade and planting, all powers manifested great dissatisfaction with the system they had created. For the United States, the Samoan troubles confirmed their worst suspicions of an 'entanglement'. In fact, as early as 1890 Blaine himself was stressing his desire to cut free from the group, and he and his successors at the State Department repeated their complaints upon many occasions. For years Berlin waited, at first suspiciously and then more hopefully, for an American withdrawal. In 1894 Secretary of State Gresham publicly regretted that America had not adhered to

> the wise policy that had previously preserved us from such engagements as those embodied in the general Act of Berlin, which, besides involving us in an entangling alliance, has utterly failed to correct, if indeed it has not aggravated, the very evils which it was designed to prevent.[27]

Indeed, Cleveland declared his administration's discontent in three successive annual messages to Congress, inviting that body's opinion on the possibility of a withdrawal from Samoa. However, they preferred not to act lest America's naval station rights be prejudiced, although little enthusiasm was evinced for the existing arrangement.[28]

The British were also discontented at the situation, although they did not display their feelings in so public a manner. Little official comment was made in the first few years of the tridominium, partly because of Salisbury's close hold over Britain's Samoan policy and partly out of sympathy for the group's teething-troubles. Moreover, there always was the hope that German influence was waning, that 'the trade is

26 F.O.58/302, Hatzfeldt communication of 22/6/1896.
27 Ryden, *U.S. Policy in Samoa*, p. 554, quoting Gresham to the president, 9/5/1894. The repeated private hints by Blaine and Gresham can be found in R.Kol.A.2867-68.
28 Ryden, *U.S. Policy in Samoa*, pp. 555-56.

likely to pass in a few years into British hands' and 'that perhaps Samoa may fall into our lap like a ripe plum, if it is worth picking up'.[29] But, as the troubles in the islands continued and the Liberals came into power in London once again, the criticism grew and by 1893 the colonial secretary, Lord Ripon, felt that 'the present tripartite administration is unworkable and that it is hopeless to expect any good government in Samoa as the result of so absurd a system!'[30] By the end of 1894, he noted that 'The state of things in Samoa is disgraceful' while his parliamentary under-secretary thought that 'This rotten little island gives more trouble than it is worth.'[31]

The feelings of disillusionment in Berlin towards Samoa were not very different. The *D.H.P.G.* had lost 400,000 marks worth of goods and produce in the 1888-89 disturbances and was not in a very healthy position despite the managerial reorganization of 1890. The company operated at a loss in 1889, 1891 and 1892, and the profit of the following two years was solely due to better copra prices in Europe; but by 1895 and 1896 the bottom had dropped out of the market and a much smaller profit was made. The subsidized steamer service, too, lost heavily in the early 1890s and was withdrawn. The *D.H.P.G.* had also definitely surrendered their commercial predominance in Tonga to the British.[32] Moreover, while the consul was worried about the growing influence of the L.M.S. missionaries by 1895, the German naval commander reported that the *D.H.P.G.* was being hard pressed by Australasian commercial rivalry and that English influence, in the form of more teachers, traders and shipping connections, was growing rapidly: as a sure sign of this, he mentioned that cricket had been re-introduced into the islands for the first time since it was banned by Brandeis in 1888! Pointing out that the Reich had in the past twenty years spent in the region of fifteen million marks in naval expenditure, solely for the protection of this now decrepit firm, the commander-in-chief urged that something drastic needed to be done.[33] If these reports are contradicted by some

29   F.O.58/275, Currie minute on Cusack-Smith to Rosebery, no. 20 Confidential of 28/3/1893; F.O.58/284, Dallas minute on letter of C. Lempriere of 8/1/1894.

30   Addit. Mss. 43516 (Ripon Papers), Ripon to Rosebery, Confidential of 22/4/1893.

31   C.O.225/46, Ripon minute on paper 16914, F.O. to C.O., received 25/9/1894; ibid., Buxton minute on paper C.O.2383, F.O. to C.O., 7/2/1894.

32   Staatsarchiv-Hamburg, D. H. P. G. Archiv, *Bericht der Direktion an den Aufsichtsrat*, for the years 1889-96. Vagts, *Weltpolitik*, 1, pp. 686-96, 718.

33   BA/MA 624, PG65064, *Die Entsendung S. M. Schiffen nach der Südsee Station*, vol. 3, Oberkommando to R.M.A. 10/12/1898 including Scheder's report; ibid., Scheder's report of 9/4/1896; R.Kol.A.3038, Schmidt-Leda to the Chancellor, no. 81 Confidential of 6/9/1895.

equally gloomy British accounts, they at least confirm that a general air of despondency and decay lay over Samoa in the 1890s.

An attempt was, in fact, made to buy out the *D.H.P.G.* and therefore the German interest in Samoa at the close of 1894. It was an idea which the New Zealanders, under their vigorous premier, Richard Seddon, had repeatedly urged— without, however, offering the money themselves. But in November a British consortium, Messrs J. Arundel & Co. and Messrs John Morrison & Co., began to make approaches to Hamburg about forming a joint Anglo-German company. The *D.H.P.G.* declined to do anything other than to sell out completely, demanding in return the large sum of £750,000. At this, the negotiations collapsed, for the British companies could not possibly raise this amount without a guarantee from Her Majesty's Government—and this was so dim a prospect under a Liberal government that serious negotiations along this line were never attempted. Besides, the German Foreign Ministry did not look kindly upon these negotiations, seeing in them a threat to their claims to a say in the ad- ministration of Samoa. If the firm fell into British hands, it was realized, Germany's interests in the group would be non-existent. With the abandonment of these talks, the *D.H.P.G.* was therefore compelled to carry on, hoping and pressing for a drastic alteration in Samoa, above all for a German annexation.[34]

The truth of the matter was, that all sides realized that the 1889 settlement had proved to be a failure and that order and prosperity would not return to the islands until some major change occurred. Not only did Samoa's native social and administrative structure possess disintegrating and disunifying tendencies, but the whole concept of a tridominium appeared false to nations who were then so used to straightforward territorial acquisitions and rule by one power. In an age when imperialist agitation in Britain and Germany was steadily rising, fanned by certain press organs and pressure groups in both countries, no government felt strong enough to disentangle itself from the Samoan troubles—even Cleveland was hesitant about that. As Herbert shrewdly put it:

In fact, neither our Parliament here, not any Australasian Parliament, nor the German Parliament and press, can give up any portion of the existing position, even tho' such surrender might be the means of

34 Details of the negotiations are in C.O.537/136, paper 475 Secret, of 1895; St. H., D.H.P.G.Archiv, Abteilung 26, Sitzungs-Protokolle, 20/11/1894 and 10/1/1895; R.Kol. A.2478, Kayser to Meyer-Delius (D.H.P.G.), 26/5/1894, and replies of 30/5/1894 and 28/12/1894.

acquiring solid advantages. We must make the best of the present state of things, as far as the *flags* are concerned, until (if ever) politicians become more reasonable and newspapers less mischievous.[35]

It cannot be denied that the tridominium, despite its drawbacks, had been a distinct improvement in many ways: land disputes were settled, the sale of alcohol to the Samoans was virtually eradicated, some roads were built, litigations were settled in the Supreme Court, and a native civil war was prevented. But the three major weaknesses—the powerlessness of the Samoan monarchy, the deeply-rooted rivalries of the white nationalities, and the lack of a unified executive—were left uncorrected and as strong as ever. Were one power unchallenged in the group, as had been the case in Fiji, matters would have been regulated by annexation long before the late 1890s; but with three nations claiming equality, Samoa had to be given a patched-up, temporary settlement—if only to avoid a repetition of the anarchy and international rivalries of the 1880s. Yet herein lay a further basic weakness: everyone, whether in Samoa or in the offices of the metropolitan governments, was aware that the 1889 Final Act, despite its title, was only a temporary measure.

There was thus little hope of this unique structure of government functioning smoothly when the vast majority of the participants and observers looked forward to its future demise. The angry outburst in 1897 of Beckmann, the manager of the *D.H.P.G.*, that 'there would be a row next year'—he did not now care which Power annexed Samoa, whether America, England, or Germany, but Samoa must be annexed by one of them[36]—reflected the dissatisfaction and frustration felt by all. Something had to be done, and soon, for there was little future left in the tridominium. Of course, the advent of the new Chief Justice Chambers and Municipal President Raffel might serve to postpone the event should these officials prove capable of co-operating in a friendly and impartial manner with each other for the good of the islands; but they might also prove to be the catalysts to a further crisis, leading to the complete breakdown of the 1889 structure.

ii *Samoa and Anglo-German Relations*, 1890-96

The year of the Berlin Samoan conference by no means marked the high point of the so-called Anglo-German 'colonial marriage': that honour was reserved for twelve months

35 C.O. 537/136, paper 475 Secret, Herbert to Meade, 2/1/1895.
36 F.O.58/310, Cusack-Smith to Salisbury, no. 2 of 23/1/1897.

later, when the Heligoland-Zanzibar treaty was signed. These important arrangements have been sufficiently well examined and argued about to make only a brief reference to them necessary here.[37] But hidden among the expressions and symptoms of Anglo-German cordiality at this time lay several disquieting factors. The first of these was the extent to which public opinion and pressure groups on both sides were pushing their respective leaders to dispute the ownership of tropical lands—despite the small value of such territories and the imperative European reasons for avoiding any such quarrels. Although Salisbury's policy in the 1888-92 period in Africa was dictated by his 'strategic defence' of the Nile watershed, there seems little doubt that British public opinion was also forcing him to take a firm stand in areas of east and central Africa which did not possess this significance.[38]

In Germany, various sections of public opinion were similarly interested in imperial expansion and this movement received a powerful if unintended boost at the signing of the Heligoland-Zanzibar treaty. Out of the ashes of German colonial hopes in East Africa arose the bitterly anti-British predecessor of the Pan-German League and the popular tradition that Britain always came out on top in any colonial deal.[39] Bismarck himself suffered many attacks upon his policy of conciliation with Britain in 1888-89, although he was able to brush most of these aside;[40] but whether his successors, lesser mortals who were more sensitive to the charge that they were ignoring Germany's overseas interests, could withstand such pressure was an open question.

The events of 1890 were important for another reason. Whatever his earlier suspicions of Bismarck's foreign policies, Salisbury was aware that by the late 1880s the chancellor was desperately striving to maintain peace in Europe and therefore he felt the change in Berlin to be 'an enormous calamity of which the sinister effects will be felt in every part of Europe.'[41] Although the prime minister assured Bismarck's successor, General Caprivi, that he hoped 'to preserve un-impaired the excellent understanding between England and

37 On this treaty, see G. N. Sanderson, *England, Europe and the Upper Nile*, 1882-1899 (Edinburgh, 1965), pp. 47-66; Bünemann, *Colonial Marriage*, pp. 96-131. W. L. Langer, *The Diplomacy of Imperialism*, 2nd ed., (New York, 1951), pp. 1-20.

38 Sanderson, *Upper Nile*, pp. 49-56; Robinson, Gallagher, Denny, *Africa and the Victorians*, pp. 223-34, 290-300.

39 M. S. Wertheimer, *The Pan-German League*, 1890-1914 (New York, 1924), pp. 25ff; R. Beazley, 'Britain and Germany in the Salisbury-Caprivi Era, 1890-1892' in *Berliner Monatshefte*, 12 (1934); M. Sell, *Die deutsche öffentliche Meinung und das Helgoland-Abkommen im Jahre* 1890 (Berlin/Bonn, 1926).

40 Pogge von Strandmann, *Domestic Origins*, pp. 152-59.

41 Salisbury Papers, A64/62, Salisbury to Malet, private tel. 'not for print', 19/3/1890.

Germany in regard to the main objects of their policy',[42] he was nonetheless more dubious about the reliability and stability of a country now apparently ruled by an impulsive monarch and his military entourage. Moreover, while Salisbury would work closely with Germany he had no wish, nor would British opinion have allowed him, to enter into fixed military arrangements with the Triple Alliance, as Berlin desired. Furthermore, the cutting of Bismarck's 'wire to Russia' was ultimately a severe blow to Germany's favourable diplomatic position and meant the loss of a bargaining counter against Britain. As Bayer points out, 'Every cooling of Russo-German relations gave important trumps into the hands of the English leadership,'[43] for Germany had openly committed herself to the defence of Austria-Hungary, which would force the Russians to turn reluctantly to Paris for support.

Both these factors, the increase of colonial enthusiasm and the alteration in Britain's and Germany's relative diplomatic positions, can be overstressed: the latter in particular was a development which would take some time to blossom out. But there were already signs that the German government would have to tread warily in colonial matters: for example, the idea of abolishing the post of municipal president was strongly opposed by Berlin out of regard for public opinion. Malet was informed that

> in view of the severe attacks in the Reichstag whenever the slightest handle was given to the opposition, it would be impossible to abstain from appointing a President of the municipality because to do so would be held to be weakness and abandonment of German interests.[44]

Nevertheless, the British policy towards affairs in the Pacific in the early 1890s was scarcely one which could annoy the sensitive men of Germany's 'new course'. Salisbury maintained his attitude of staying friendly, although not allied, to the Triple Alliance and of subordinating the minor affairs of tropical regions to the demands of his overall policy. Nowhere could this be more clearly seen than in the establishment of a protectorate over the Gilbert Islands in 1892. This group was, according to the 1886 Anglo-German demarcation treaty, in the British sphere of influence but London had shown no sign of wanting to accept additional responsibilities there. In 1891, however, the German government asked the

---

42 Ibid., A64/63, Salisbury to Caprivi, 12/4/1890. This was in reply to a message of Caprivi's of 4/4/1890.

43 T. A. Bayer, *England und der neue Kurs* (Tübingen, 1955), pp. 2-8. See also, W. Herrmann, *Dreibund, Zweibund England 1890-1895* (Beiträge zur Geschichte d. nachbism. Zeit u.d. Weltkrieges, Heft 6, Stuttgart 1929), *passim*.

44 F.O.58/274, Malet to Rosebery, no. 17 Confidential of 14/1/1893.

British to annex the group in order to protect their labour market for the Samoan plantations from possibly falling into American hands. When the Colonial Office and the Admiralty strongly objected to this request, Salisbury told them that he would have to let the Germans themselves annex the islands. This, as he no doubt anticipated, changed the minds of the Colonial Office immediately.[45] Thus, to please Berlin, the British assumed responsibility and expense for a group of islands sprawled across the mid-Pacific for which they had no interest whatsoever. Meade, at the Colonial Office, put his finger on the real significance of the matter when explaining it to the new colonial secretary, Lord Ripon:

> This is just one of the many effects of our remaining in Egypt. As we encounter everywhere the hostility of France, so we have to purchase support from Germany in regard to Egypt by pliability in other matters. This confronts us in every colonial question, where Germany, France or Italy are in the least concerned.[46]

With regard to Samoa, British policy remained basically one of indifference to the various troubles which beset that group. Neither Salisbury, nor Rosebery who followed him, intended to get involved in the islands at the risk of annoying Germany or to bring upon themselves the criticism of the Australasian colonies if they surrendered their interest altogether. Salisbury moved cautiously between the Scylla of the latter by minuting 'Do nothing with Samoa till there is a row somewhere else, or we shall have trouble with the Australians' and the Charybdis of the former by declaring that 'it is important to avoid all causes of friction with the Germans in Samoa.'[47] Rosebery was even more explicit. 'Our duty in this matter is not primary' he minuted, 'It is for Germany and the U.S. to agree and for us to bless them.'[48] A few weeks later he wrote, 'the main point to make clear is that we wish to stand in the second line in this affair as disinterested friendly observers.'[49]

Rosebery's unwillingness to do anything in Samoa was naturally noticed in Berlin. Public opinion there, which had long shown an interest in the group as the place of Germany's first colonial ventures and been greatly moved, rather than

45   F.O.83/1285, Adm. to F.O., 5/1/1892; C.O.225/37, papers 13791, 14520 and 20920, F.O. to C.O., 6/7/1891, 18/7/1891 and 23/8/1891; C.O.225/41, paper 457, F.O. to C.O., Immediate, 8/1/1892.

46   Meade minute on paper 16569, high commissioner to C.O., 28/6/1892, in C.O.225/ 38.

47   F.O.58/261, minute on Cusack-Smith to Salisbury, no. 51 of 15/8/1891; F.O.83/1285, F.O. to C.O., 23/1/1892.

48   F.O.58/268, minute on Sanderson memo of 18/11/1892.

49   Ibid., minute on Malet to Rosebery, no. 283 of 31/12/1892.

repulsed, by the death of her sailors in the fighting of 1888 and the destruction of her warships in the hurricane of 1889, was now led by a monarch who displayed a similar interest in overseas acquisitions. Pressed by political difficulties at home, the men of the 'new course' would, while avoiding American anger, take any reasonable opportunity to achieve control in Samoa and thereby a diplomatic success to strengthen their internal position.

This policy of waiting for the United States to retire proved to be too negative and slow for the kaiser. Learning in January 1893 of the annexation of Hawaii by the American minister there (temporarily as it turned out) he minuted 'We must just so act in Samoa! It is a good moment.'[50] Hatzfeldt was therefore instructed to sound out Rosebery as to suggesting once again to Washington a Samoa-Tonga-Hawaii 'split'. Reports from the United States indicated that any German action regarding Samoa would be frowned upon and, in any case, Rosebery's policy towards Hawaii 'was to ignore the whole matter'.[51] Marschall, the state secretary, was not displeased at this British answer but sought for an assurance of her future help *should* the Americans one day abandon Samoa. Rosebery first declared himself to be personally for the idea but he was unaware of Salisbury's secret discussions of 1889 on the topic and, on sounding out the Colonial Office about these earlier talks, he discovered that they disapproved of the scheme. Marschall then let the matter drop altogether, fearing that further rumours of such discussions would annoy the United States just at a time when Germany was hoping for some tariff concessions from the incoming administration.[52]

In fact, British reluctance to accept any such three-way partition scheme was much stronger than that represented to Hatzfeldt by Rosebery. The Liberal government of 1892-95 marks the beginning of a *real* change in British awareness of Australasian feelings regarding the Pacific, despite the leadership of Gladstone and the influential positions occupied by Harcourt and the other anti-imperialists. Even Salisbury

50   A.A./*Südsee-Inseln I*, Vol. 1, minute on Bremen to A.A., 29/1/1893.

51   Ibid., A.A. to Hatzfeldt, no. 42 of 30/1/1893, and his reply, no. 14 of same date; A.A. to Washington, tel. no. 2 of 31/1/1893, and reply, tel. no. 5 of 2/2/1893; Hatzfeldt to A.A., no. 16 of 1/2/1893. The quote is from Rosebery's minute on Wodehouse (Hawaii) to F.O., tel. of 5/4/1893 in F.O.58/279. See also M. Tate, 'Great Britain and the Sovereignty of Hawaii' in *Pacific Historical Review*, 31 (November 1962).

52   *A.A./Südsee-Inseln* 1, vol. 1, A.A. to Hatzfeldt, no. 45 of 2/2/1893, and his reply, no. 20 of 6/2/1893; A.A. to Hatzfeldt, tel. no. 23 of 21/2/1893, and Hatzfeldt to the chancellor, no. 159 of 3/3/1893. On the British side, see F.O.343/3, Rosebery to Malet, 8/2/1893; F.O.343/11, Malet to Rosebery, Private and Confidential, 11/2/1893; and F.O.343/13, Malet to Rosebery, 18/2/1893.

seems to have been temporizing about his earlier acquiescence over giving up Samoa for Tonga by the early 1890s[53] and, when he left, the Colonial Office once again rose to take a more influential part in the forming of British policy in this question. Certainly, Rosebery was left in no doubt as to the Colonial Office's views regarding a Samoa-Tonga-Hawaii partition arrangement. They opposed any division of the Samoan group itself, fearing that they would receive the large but rather useless island of Savai'i, and emphasized that

> as regards a partition of Hawaii, Samoa and Tonga between the three Powers it must be borne in mind that as regards the first and third they already practically fall under the full control of the U.S. and G.B. Therefore if the proposal is carried out this country & the U.S. would get only what they had substantially already. But Germany would get the whole of Samoa of which she now has only one third.[54]

Nevertheless, Rosebery at this stage appears to have been still more concerned in co-operating with Germany than in satisfying the demands of the Colonial Office. What changed him were the events of the following year, the prolonged and bitter colonial quarrels with Berlin, and the rise of the Australasian agitation to such a height that Whitehall seems to have been genuinely scared that concessions in the Pacific would lead to the throwing-off of all links with Britain.

In April 1894, American discontent at the tridominium became more open than before and it seemed as if the German dream of gaining Samoa might come true. Their minister at Washington was told by Gresham of America's private wish to withdraw, Cleveland had been critical of the tripartite arrangement in his annual message of December 1893, and members of the Senate were also promising to get the question reviewed. All the signs were, that, while taking over Tutuila, America might well step out of the remainder of the Samoan group.[55] Within a few days, Marschall had suggested a Samoa-Tonga deal to Malet and a week later he ordered Hatzfeldt to do the same at London. 'The object of our policy there is the establishment of a German administration', the state secretary wrote, adding that

> this would not only present a solution satisfying to our considerable local interests there, but it would mean a political triumph at home the

53 R.Kol.A.2867, Hatzfeldt to Caprivi, no. 58 of 7/12/1890; G.P., 8, no. 2039.

54 C.O.225/44, paper 3161, Meade to Currie on 20/2/1893, and other letters therein. See also the C.O. minutes on paper 17241, F.O. to C.O. of 9/10/1893, on rear-admiral. Bowder-Smith's suggestion of giving up the British interest in Samoa, ibid.

55 R.Kol.A.2867, Saurma (Washington) to Caprivi, nos. 136, 141 and 142 of 31/3/1894, 1/4/1794 and 3/4/1894.

effect of which should not be underestimated. As Your Excellency is aware, public opinion in Germany has occupied itself for years over the Samoan question and it would therefore be of great value to the Imperial Government to bring about a final settlement of this affair in a manner according with German wishes.[56]

But to their surprise, the British reply was icy cold. Rosebery minuted: 'The only line we can take with the Germans with regard to Samoa is to say that we intend to adhere strictly to our Treaty engagements. Even if the United States withdraws, these are not invalidated.'[57] Hatzfeldt was sharply told by Kimberley that 'The feeling of the German Colonial Party could not be more acute than that of our colonists, who, especially in New Zealand, would greatly resent the abandonment of Samoa.'[58]

This blank refusal, especially from Rosebery, came as a cold douche upon the German aspirations and led to some mystification in Berlin. Yet the reasons for the change of attitude are not hard to find. First of all those slowly-developing changes in the international position of Britain and Germany were beginning to affect their relationship. The events of 1890 had led directly to the disappearance of the hegemonial diplomatic position Germany had possessed under Bismarck and she could no longer press Britain for colonial concessions by threatening to ally herself permanently with Russia or France, although purely temporary ententes over specific problems were still possible. Moreover, the Egyptian problem, though still tricky, was not so pressing by the early 1890s, while the Eastern Question, too, though still unsolved, was relatively quiescent and both these factors lessened British dependence upon the central powers.

Clearly, the most important development was the creation of the Franco-Russian Alliance. It naturally caused a great deal of worry at the Admiralty, who believed their Mediterranean position to be endangered.[59] It was possibly even more alarming for the Germans, who not only saw themselves 'encircled' but who also had to deal with two very anxious allies, Austria-Hungary and Italy. Great stress was laid in 1893 by Berlin upon obtaining Britain's moral and military support for the weaker members of the Triple Alliance; but, although moral encouragement was freely given, no promises

56 G.P., 8, no. 2024. Marschall's own soundings are recorded in F.O.58/285. Malet to Kimberley, no. 70 Confidential of 21/4/1894.
57 F.O.58/285, Rosebery minute of 5/5/1894.
58 Ibid., Kimberley to Malet, no. 124 of 27/4/1894.
59 A. J. Marder, *The Anatomy of British Sea Power* (Hamden, Conn., 1964 reprint), pp. 144 231.

of military support could be elicited from a reluctant British government. The result of this trend was that on the one hand Germany was tempted into putting pressure upon the British in Africa and the Pacific, not only to gain colonial concessions which would be popular at home but also to force a change in Britain's European policy: on the other hand, the British were less inclined to succumb to German pressure in touchy colonial matters and any 'blackmail', as they called it, increased their determination to escape from dependence upon Germany.

Secondly, from late 1893 onwards, Britain and Germany became involved in a series of ever sharper colonial quarrels. Marschall, already suspicious of London's general attitude, read into a number of minor matters (the procurement of Singapore coolies for the German New Guinea Company's plantations; opposition to Asia Minor railway concessions; Cameroons hinterland, etc.) a deliberate series of affronts to which he responded by ceding to France early in 1894 a place on the Upper Niger—only a few months after the signing of an Anglo-German treaty on that region, by which London had hoped to prevent a French advance to the Nile. This German move had in fact been provoked by resentment at British dealings within their sphere, London did not realize this and considered that Berlin had 'double-crossed' them by dealing with France. Indeed, the British resentment here marks a new, and much greater widening of the gap and this automatically doomed all German hopes regarding Samoa to failure. The British in turn arranged a new treaty, this time with the king of the Belgians, aimed chiefly at keeping the French away from the Upper Nile once again; but as the famous 'corridor' clause of the Anglo-Congolese treaty of 12 April 1894 ignored German reversionary rights to the eastern part of the Free State, it provoked an explosion of annoyance in Berlin, where the government was already under heavy pressure from its critics.[60] The combined Franco-German attack upon the Anglo-Congolese treaty eventually forced the British to withdraw it—but it was a humiliation which Rosebery and Kimberley never forgave.

The third factor in the deterioration of Anglo-German relations was the agitation upon both sides for a firm stand, and if possible an advance, in the colonial field. The catalyst in this press war was, as in 1883, New Zealand. With hopes

---

60 Sanderson, *Upper Nile*, pp. 162-87. I have also used for the above narrative Professor Sanderson's private paper, 'The African Factor in Anglo-German Relations, 1892-1895' given to the Commonwealth and Overseas Seminar at Cambridge, and I am most grateful to him for allowing me to refer to it.

reawakened by noting the 'cracks in the fabric of tripartite
control in Samoa and the obvious impermanence of that
particular settlement', Seddon began pressing London to
arrange a New Zealand administration of the group and this
call was avidly taken up by the local newspapers.[61] It was
received with some sympathy by the *Times* and other English
newspapers, and also by the *Vossische Zeitung* and Eugene
Richter's radical *Freisinnige Zeitung*; but it provoked fearsome
denunciations and violent abuse in the remainder of the
German press, including all the government organs. The
Weser Zeitung, *Kölnische Zeitung* and the official *Norddeutsche
Allgemeine Zeitung* strongly denounced the idea, while the
Börsen-Courier declared that the English press 'by its hypo-
critical and overweening treatment of the Samoa question
will not contribute to lessen the deep distrust which prevails
towards England in Germany'. The *Post* demanded the
despatch of a regiment to Samoa to protect German nationals
and their property, but the *Times* responded by displaying
statistics to show that German interests in the group were
declining. In addition, the colonial pressure groups commenced a large campaign with the Pan-German league at
one extreme and Seddon at the other.[62]

As a consequence, neither Berlin nor London could be
persuaded to yield a foot in the Samoan dispute. Hatzfeldt
was urged to seek a lasting settlement with the British but
Kimberley absolutely turned down any suggestion that
Germany take over Samoa, while Rosebery begged the
ambassador not to press about it.[63] Ripon also urged
Kimberley not to let the Americans withdraw from the
group lest London be 'left with the Germans alone', a worrying
prospect. The colonial secretary would personally be happy to
hand over the group but 'Australasian opinion would not
suffer us to do it.'[64]

Faced with this hostility of the British to their wishes, with
the rumours of further native disturbances, and possible
action by New Zealand, certain circles in Berlin began to
advocate a swift seizure of the group by six cruisers and a
strong landing force. Pan-German and colonial pressure

61 On the New Zealand agitation, see Ross, *Aspirations*, pp. 245-49.

62 BA/MA 5078, *Samoa*, vol. 1, copies of the *Times* (25/4/1894, 27/4/1894 and 14/5/1894),
the *Weser Zeitung* (24/4/1894), the *Kölnische Zeitung* (26/4/1894), *Norddeutsche Allgemeine
Zeitung* (26/4/1894 and 29/4/1894), *Vossische Zeitung* (27/4/1894), *Freisinnige Zeitung*
(29/4/1894), and *New Zealand Herald* (17/4/1894 and 10/5/1894). See also, F.O.58/285,
Gosselin to Kimberley, nos. 83 and 86 of 4/5/1894 and 12/5/1894, and C.O. to F.O. of
26 April and 1, 17, 18, 21 and 31 May 1894; Vagts, *Weltpolitik*, 1, pp. 736-40; Weck,
Deutschlands Politik, pp. 125-34.

63 G.P., 8, nos. 2026, 2027 and 2029.

64 Addit. Mss. 43526, Ripon to Kimberley, 19/4/1894.

groups demanded such an action and the kaiser, influenced by his military advisers and by his wish for an exciting overseas policy, seems to have been attracted by the idea; but Caprivi, who intensely disliked colonial entanglements, was not, and he rejected the plan put forward by Dr Kayser for taking Samoa and presenting Britain with a fait accompli. Nevertheless, the navy continued its planning for operations to take over the group and disarm the natives, insisting that this could only be properly done if the German flag was hoisted, a protectorate declared, important buildings and all arms seized, and the group was blockaded.[65] It is difficult to know whether this was to be done with the consent of the other powers, since it was sometimes stated in the operations documents that there would be no hindrances from Britain and America, and yet the strength of the other two navies in the Pacific was also carefully calculated. Perhaps the idea was to seize the group suddenly and disarm the Samoans in the belief that the British and Americans would, although complaining, see the good side of this action and do nothing about it.[66]

With his opinions challenged by these more aggressive views, Caprivi sought Hatzfeldt's advice.[67] The ambassador replied in a long despatch, suggesting that the best solution might be to seize the opportunity offered by the recent Anglo-Belgian Congo treaty to join up with France in Africa and to make difficulties in Egypt. Hatzfeldt also suggested an alternative solution but this section of his despatch was entirely omitted from the *Grosse Politik*. The ambassador declared that, if German public opinion made action imperative, the cruiser squadron should go ahead and seize Samoa. If the international circumstances were favourable to Germany, the British would probably swallow their pride and accept this as a fait accompli:

> But if they decline to come to an agreement, our task would then be to make it clear to them that we would consider as an unfriendly act any attempt to drive us out again and that, since we are not strong enough at sea, we would answer it by placing our entire influence completely at the disposal of England's foes, both in Europe and elsewhere.[68]

65   R.Kol.A.2868, Caprivi to Hollmann, 5571 of 28/4/1894 ~ '   ~mo of i/5/1894; BA/MA 7577, Geh. I, *Hauptakten der Australische*   vol. I, Oberkommando to *Bussard*, Top Secret, of 17/5/18?! nd 29/5/1894; *Bussard* replies, Secret, of 17/7/1894 and ?!!?

 Ibid., memo on British and American naval strength in the Pacific, 29/5/1894.

67   G.P., 8, no. 2035.

68   A.A./*England* 78 *Secret*, vol. 2, Hatzfeldt to Caprivi (private), Secret, 1/6/1894, and compare with G.P., 8, no. 2039.

Hatzfeldt did not hide from his superiors the fact that public opinion in Britain might push the weak Liberal government into decisive counter-measures and he therefore advocated pressure in Egypt and the Congo as the first tactic, but should this prove fruitless and should internal political considerations make further delay impossible, then there would be nothing left to do but to adopt this more extreme measure.

It should be noted that it was the entire despatch—and not just the first, published, part—which the kaiser found to be 'Excellent. Exactly corresponds with my views and we must arrange our policy as recommended here, and starting with the first way suggested—Egypt.'[69] Planning for the seizure and pacification of Samoa therefore continued into the following year, although the operation was never implemented.[70] The reasons for its postponement and final abandonment are not hard to find. America's attitude to such an action was unpredictable and Washington was making no further steps to withdraw. A British warship remained in the group and undertook some small joint actions with the two German vessels there. Finally, the British gave way over the Congo treaty, though with reluctance, and the tactic of pressure in Africa was therefore preferred to a rash step in the Pacific.

Nevertheless, the discussions indicated how far a German government, split internally and needing to recoup some of its lost popularity, might go should public opinion press it and the obstacles to the success of such a daring venture became less formidable. Indeed, at one stage in the quarrel, Marschall wrote in his diary: 'The Samoan question worries me. The reputation of the New Course depends upon it.'[71] The entire incident also revealed how far apart the two countries had drifted over the Samoan question and foreign affairs in general since the friendlier days of the 'colonial marriage'. Samoa was both a contributory part of this mutual disenchantment, and a mirror of the overall relations. Moreover, the effects of this Niger-Congo-Samoa dispute were felt in the more vital European theatre also, for Rosebery had threatened Vienna that German hostility in Africa would lead to British indifference to the Triple Alliance's requests for support in the Mediterranean.[72]

69 Kaiser's closing minute on ibid.

70 BA/MA 7577, Geh. I, *Hauptakten der Australischen Station*, vol. 1, Oberkommando to *Bussard*, 19/2/1895, replying to the operational proposals enclosure in Scheder *Bussard* to Oberkommando, no. 53, Top Secret, 30/10/1894.

71 H. Pogge von Strandmann, 'The Kolonialrat, its Significance and Influence on German Politics from 1890 to 1906' (D.Phil., Oxford, 1970), p. 293.

72 Sanderson, *Upper Nile*, p. 173.

Thus, the seeds were being sown in Rosebery's administration for a permanent frigidity in Anglo-German relations. Both governments were run by men whose irritability and sensitivity contributed to the split; while that gift, possessed both by Salisbury and Bismarck, of appreciating the other side's point of view, was sadly lacking. Perhaps the most significant factor of the 1894 Samoan dispute was the way in which imperialistic feelings upon both sides had pushed their governments into an open quarrel, which in turn triggered off a further explosion of dissatisfaction from the press and pressure groups. This was not so unpredictable in the case of Germany but it marks a definite advance upon the British side, where even the English newspapers contributed to the fray. The real change of mind appears to have been at London, for the agitation in the antipodes was certainly not more noticeable than in the 1883-85 period. Nevertheless Seddon's despatches had become more important than the *baton égyptien*, and the anxiety felt in Whitehall for an Australasian reaction to any 'back-down' over Samoa had become the guiding motive upon the British side. For example, Sidney Buxton, Ripon's parliamentary under-secretary, urged the Foreign Office not to contemplate

> any deal which would involve giving up our position there. There would be the devil's own row in Australia & New Zealand if we did; and the power & position of the growing party of secessionists there would be enormously strengthened. It would be suicidal.[73]

Similar sentiments were expressed in November 1894, when Marschall complained bitterly of the way in which Britain obstructed Germany in every corner of the globe. The British chargé in Berlin, Martin Gosselin, consequently took it upon himself to urge a Samoa-Tonga deal, with Germany renouncing at the same time any political interest in the much more vital regions of Delagoa Bay and the Transvaal.[74] Rosebery sharply noted that Britain could of course give up Samoa 'but, as I remarked to Count Hatzfeldt, that concession might involve the loss of Australia or New Zealand or both.'[75] Furthermore, Kimberley's regard for Australasian opinion was reinforced by the fixation he had developed about the Germans, who 'thwart us whenever they can all over the world'.[76] Only this can adequately explain his furious

---

73   F.O.800/38 (Grey Papers), Buxton to Grey, 23/12/1894.
74   Gosselin to Kimberley, no. 244 Confidential of 25/11/1894 in F.O.58/287.
75   Rosebery minute on ibid.
76   Addit.Mss.43526, Kimberley to Ripon (private and confidential), 22/10/1894.

marginalia upon Gosselin's suggestions for an Africa-Pacific arrangement.

> We must oppose in every way the attempts of Germany to interfere in the Transvaal. It would have a most disastrous effect in South Africa if she were to get footing there . . . We must be prepared for Germany doing us all the mischief she can in Africa (if not elsewhere).[77]

Indeed, as Samoa and the Congo faded into the background of Anglo-German relations, southern Africa became a new and much more serious cause of conflict. By October 1894, Berlin's claims to having interests there had provoked the reply that Britain would not even 'recoil from the spectre of war' to preserve her supremacy in the region.[78] For the first time ever, the two countries were quarrelling over an interest vital to one of them and if Germany did not withdraw, the chances of a permanent alienation were high. But Germany did not withdraw, despite the return of Salisbury to office in 1895 and despite Malet's warning to the kaiser that south Africa was the *point noir* in Anglo-German relations. Instead, the mutual suspicion and recrimination over the Transvaal grew and grew until it exploded in the crisis of the Jameson Raid and the Kruger Telegram. The kaiser's fantasies about a war—but only on land—in Africa were accompanied by the more realistic British gesture of creating a special flying squadron. This, in its turn, provoked fear and a reaction, and for the first time ever the German navy began to prepare materials for an operation plan against England.[79] It was, no doubt, a defensive measure but it had never been found necessary before then.

Furthermore, although Salisbury told Malet 'We certainly wish to be good friends with Germany; as good friends we were in 1892. That is to say, we wish to lean to the Triple Alliance without belonging to it.' there was in fact, a change and suspicion had replaced the former friendship.[80] That letter, indeed, was a purely tactical bid by Salisbury for German friendship whilst the British moved into the Sudan, which would automatically cause a worsening of relations with France. Nowhere could the suspicion be more clearly

77 F.O.58/287, minutes on Gosselin to Kimberley, no. 244 Confidential of 25/11/1894.
78 L. M. Penson, 'The New Course in British Foreign Policy' in *Transactions of the Royal Historical Society* (hereafter *T. R. Hist. S.*) Fourth series, xxv (1943) pp. 128-34; J. Butler, 'The German Factor in Anglo-Transvaal Relations' in *Britain and Germany in Africa*, pp. 192-201.
79 BA/MA 5587, III I.N.10, *Operationspläne gegen England*, vol. 1, Grapow memo of 15/2/1898. On the Kruger Telegram crisis, see N. Rich, *Friedrich von Holstein*, 2 vols. (Cambridge, 1965), 2, pp. 466-70.
80 Salisbury Papers, A122/6, Salisbury to Malet, 10/3/1896.

seen than in Samoa, where each side watched the other's moves very carefully after June 1894. A British vessel was kept there during the winter season, despite the hurricane threat, and Kimberley also nervously wished to know how things stood 'with regard to the Tonga Islands'.[81] The *Auswärtiges Amt*, too, refused to let their warship leave Samoan waters and ignored the protests of the navy until the kaiser himself was persuaded to agree to their withdrawal.[82]

The mutual suspicion was matched in areas other than Samoa and the Transvaal. While Britain's policy of reserve in the Mediterranean continued to dismay Berlin, Germany's indifference to the Armenian question disappointed London. They had also parted company earlier, over the Sino-Japanese War and its outcome, when Germany joined the Dual Alliance in forcing Japan to reduce her territorial claims while Britain remained an observer. Salisbury's chief concerns proved to be the increase of the fleet, the betterment of his position with France and Russia, consolidation in Egypt and withdrawal from Constantinople. The non-renewal of the Mediterranean agreements was also to further this trend indirectly. While Germany strove to improve her position inside Europe, especially by her courtship of Russia, Britain sought to ease her own problems outside Europe. The overall policy of the two powers was now becoming rather similar: whether it was called 'Splendid Isolation' or 'the Free Hand', both indicated that they meant to work alone, realizing that 'the basic common interest which had been so strong up to 1894 had disappeared.'[83]

This gulf should not be exaggerated out of all bounds, but rather placed in its context. In 1896, and indeed in the years following, Russia and France continued to be regarded as Britain's real foes. Similarly, Germany saw the real threat to her existence in the Franco-Russian Alliance, even though she was upon amicable terms with Russia, and all her war plans (apart from the one naval officer detailed off in 1896 to collect planning materials for a possible war with Britain) were directed towards meeting this two-fronted danger. Nevertheless, a decisive change had occurred and a new pattern had been set. British conciliation to Germany over Samoa became only a memory for Hatzfeldt to wistfully allude to.

81   F.O.58/287, Kimberley query of 11/12/1894.

82   BA/MA 624, PG65063, *Die Entsendung S. M. Schiffe nach der Südsee Station*, vol. 2, A.A. to R.M.A., 20/10/1894; vol. 3, (PG65064), Oberkommando to R.M.A., 21/1/1895, and A.A. to R.M.A., 12/2/1895.

83   Lowe, *Reluctant Imperialists*, 1, p. 116. On British policy in 1895-96, see J. A. S. Grenville, *Lord Salisbury and Foreign Policy* (London, 1964), pp. 1-124.

The chauvinistic feelings of the press and colonial pressure groups rose even faster in the latter half of the 1890s than at any time previously: this was particularly true in Britain and Joseph Chamberlain's deliberate selection of the colonial secretary's post foretold how much the imperial factor in British foreign policy was to be stressed in the years following. In such a climate, colonial concessions were out of the question and the British consul's inopportune suggestion at the end of 1895 that Britain should withdraw from Samoa because of the decline of her trade there was received with abuse in the Colonial Office, which continued to play the important role in formulating overseas policy which it had resumed in 1892 and which Salisbury's return in 1895 did not materially weaken. 'In my opinion, Mr Cusack-Smith is an Ass!', scribbled Chamberlain angrily on the despatch, while one of his officials minuted that 'Such a course is impossible unless we hand over Australia at the same time.'[84]

The previous Anglo-German friendship had been replaced by coolness, the co-operation by working alone, and the confidence by suspicion. As Professor Sanderson points out, the years 1892-95 'seem to mark a very important watershed, if not in British foreign policy itself, at least in the attitudes and assumptions upon which foreign policy was based'.[85] A similar conclusion could well be made about German foreign policy at this time. As the year 1897 approached, therefore, there seemed little prospect of any drastic improvement in their relations being effected in the foreseeable future; and certainly, there seemed little prospect of the Samoan question being arranged in a manner satisfactory to both sides.

iii   *The Early Years of German* Weltpolitik

In 1897, German internal and foreign policy took a decisive turn, the significance of which has perhaps only recently been fully appreciated.[86] For in that year, the men of the *persön-liches Regiment* of Kaiser Wilhelm II manoeuvred themselves into the key positions of state, although this move was partially obscured by the retention of the old and weak Prince Hohenlohe as chancellor. Led by Bülow as foreign

84 C.O.225/51, Chamberlain's minute on paper 3263, F.O. to C.O., received 13/2/1896, and J. Anderson's minute on paper 4081, F.O. to C.O., received 24/2/1896.

85 Sanderson, *The African Factor in Anglo-German Relations*, 1892-1895 (private paper for Commonwealth and Overseas Seminar of Cambridge University), p. 1.

86 See the work of J. C. G. Röhl, *Germany without Bismarck* (London, 1967). Also useful is E. Eyck, *Das Persönliche Regiment Wilhelm II* (Zurich, 1948).

secretary, Tirpitz as navy secretary and Miquel as Prussian minister of finance and vice-president of the Prussian council of ministers, the government turned deliberately towards *Weltpolitik, Flottenpolitik* and the 'Mobilisation of the Masses'. From that time onwards, Wilhelm possessed the politicians he needed to assist his ambition of playing a leading role in world politics, of constructing an enormous battlefleet, and of creating internal unity and a stabilization of the political status quo. The country was directed towards the twin aims of reaction at home and an extravagant, expansionist policy abroad. Yet, although this provided a short-term solution by avoiding the coup d'état contemplated by the kaiser, it merely served to postpone rather than solve the internal problems of post-Bismarckian Germany. Moreover, it created enormous difficulties in the field of naval and foreign policy.

Miquel's tasks were simple to outline, even if they were rather harder to achieve in practice. He had to supervise a government policy of satisfying the demands of the land-owners and the industrialists and of uniting them under the crown, at the same time joining them in a combined effort to arrest the spread of social democracy, liberalism and parliamentary government. Objections to this swing to the right and to the development of a form of 'Caesarism' were of course anticipated, since the kaiser was already the object of much criticism by 1896 as a result of his rash and reactionary utterances; but, on the other hand, an alliance of crown, aristocratic landowners and powerful industrialists would form a strong check against the alarming growth of the social democratic party. Unfortunately for these schemes, the Reichstag elections continued to return a majority of represent-atives from parties who could not be absolutely relied upon. It became the fixed determination of the kaiser's protecting entourage to boost the popularity of their master, to build the nation together and to stifle the opposition by embarking upon an adventurous naval and foreign policy—in other words, they planned to export the internal tensions of the Reich and to capture the support of the masses by a manipul-ated social imperialism. The people's enthusiasm for such a course, it was reckoned, would propel the formal parties in the Reichstag willy-nilly into accepting this development. Not only did they hope to cement the nation by this *Flotten-politik* and *Weltpolitik*, but they would also satisfy Wilhelm's cravings for world glory and renown. However, these decisions led them remorselessly and ineluctably to adopt an anti-British posture.

All these aspects are most clearly revealed in the naval

policy of Wilhelmine Germany. The first Navy Law was recognized by Tirpitz as 'the best possible weapon against educated and ignorant Social Democrats' and by Bülow as benefiting 'the person of our dear Kaiser'.[87] The fleet's historical connections to liberalism and national unity were repeatedly stressed by a superbly-organized, government-supported propaganda campaign. Moreover, and this was most important, it was not to be a navy composed chiefly of overseas cruisers, the natural type of vessel for the protection of Germany's growing foreign trade, but of a large number of battleships based mainly in North Sea anchorages. Why? Not merely because of the kaiser's enthusiasm for, and the general acceptance of, Mahan's views upon the importance of the battlefleet, not merely because these were the most splendid-looking type of warships, and not merely because Germany possessed insufficient overseas bases for the effective adoption of cruiser warfare *but chiefly because it was the only weapon with which Great Britain, who seemed to be always standing in the way of Germany's attempts at colonial expansion, could be neutralized.*[88]

War, of course, was not desired—although if it ever occurred it was hoped that Germany might be able to do something—and the fleet was more important as a way of attracting the masses and of checking Britain's opposition to German expansion. In other words, as Tirpitz himself was to put it, Germany required 'a certain measure of naval force as a political power factor'.[89] The overseas successes required to achieve the *internal* aims of the *persönliches Regiment* would be hard to come by in view of the state of international jealousies and the fact that the larger part of the world had been already acquired by the great powers. Thus the colonies Germany required for her bursting population, as markets for her overproductive industries and sources of vital raw materials, and as symbols of her world power would simply have to be taken from weaker nations, so the pan-Germans asserted publicly and the German government believed secretly. Several small regions could possibly be acquired with London's grudging consent but Salisbury's increasing unwillingness to offer 'compensations' and the

87 Röhl, *Germany without Bismarck*, p. 253; J. Steinberg, *Yesterday's Deterrent* (London, 1965), p. 83, quoting H. Hallmann, *Der Weg zum deutschen Schlachtflottenbau* (Stuttgart, 1933).

88 Steinberg, *Yesterday's Deterrent, passim*; V. R. Berghahn, 'Zu den Zielen des deutschen Flottenbaues unter Wilhelm II' in *Historische Zeitschrift*, 210 (February 1970); and P. M. Kennedy, 'Tirpitz, England and the Second Navy Law of 1900: A Strategical Critique' in *Militärgeschichtliche Mitteilungen*, 1970 (2).

89 Steinberg, *Yesterday's Deterrent*, p. 209.

rise of imperialistic feelings in Britain indicated that little
could be gained in that direction without some leverage.
However, there was hardly any thought of despoiling the
British Empire, the chief concern of the German government
in the years immediately following 1897 being with China and,
more particularly, with the colonial territories of those other
'dying' nations which the British would probably seek to
protect from German occupation i.e., the Portuguese, Spanish,
Danish and Dutch colonies which figure so often in Berlin's
memoranda and calculations in this period.[90] If the British
stood still or fell back before the steady German demand for
fresh markets, trading advantages, colonies and coaling
stations then well and good: if they did not, then some
leverage would have to be applied. Given the delicate balance
of power between Britain and the Dual Alliance, a large fleet
could well swing this against the former, or at least it was
hoped that London would see things that way.

The same internal considerations applied in the formulation
of German foreign policy. It was to be a feature of this
Weltpolitik that any gains, however small, were trumpeted
before the nation as a great addition to the German empire
and an outstanding diplomatic achievement—a case in point
was the acquisition of the Caroline Islands, which the navy
privately thought worthless. Bülow, in contrast, enthusiastically told the kaiser that 'This gain will stimulate people and
navy to follow Your Majesty further along the path which
leads to world power, greatness and eternal glory.'[91] The
apparently determined opposition of the British to Germany's
expansion, however, made the future success of their policy
somewhat doubtful, and thus the fleet was to be constructed
to neutralize Britain's objections, and as a tool which would
ensure those diplomatic successes. This was the long-term
plan, concealed beneath phrases about a defensive force and
the need to protect German commerce.

It was the foreign ministry's task to ensure that Germany
kept on good terms with Britain, at least until the fleet was
strong enough. As a slightly later memorandum put it:

> The task of diplomacy is, so far as honour allows, to avoid every armed
> conflict with England so long as Germany is weak at sea and is not
> alliance-worthy to Russia. The task of the military organs is, however,

90   On these colonial ambitions, see BA/MA 5174a, 3. 1-15, *Ueberseeischen Flottenstütz-
punkte*, vols. 1-3; BA/MA 5166, III. 1-4e, *Geheime-R-Angelegenheiten: Dänische Kolonien*,
vol. 1; A.A./*Deutschland* 167; and A.A./*England* 78 Nr. 1 *Secr.*, vols. 1-14.

91   F. Fischer, *Krieg der Illusion* (Düsseldorf, 1969), p. 93, quoting Bülow to the Kaiser,
25/2/1889; compare with the Navy's unenthusiastic view in A.A./*Südsee-Inseln* 3 *Secr.*,
vol. 2, Oberkommando to A.A., 10/12/1898.

to keep clearly in mind a warlike conflict with England and to consider its possibility.[92]

Consequently, Bülow was brought from the Rome embassy to Berlin to take charge of this delicate policy towards England. It was enormously eased by the fierce antagonism which existed in the late 1890s between Britain and the Dual Alliance, a factor which allowed Germany to straddle between both *blocs* and to take advantage of this position by pressing London to accede to her demands. But it was complicated by the kaiser himself in two ways. Firstly, through his regard for Queen Victoria and general admiration for things English, he could move too closely towards Britain and thus prejudice not only Germany's relations with Russia but also the entire meaning of the *Flottenpolitik*. Secondly, and in direct contrast to this, by pressing impatiently for colonial acquisitions and fleet increases, Wilhelm might cause undue alarm in British government circles. The kaiser's love-hate relationship towards England was to stretch even Bülow's diplomatic abilities.

Bülow was assisted by the constant support he received from Philipp Eulenburg, ambassador in Vienna and the 'organiser' of the 1897 changes, and by Hatzfeldt and Holstein, both of whom did not perhaps realize that German policy towards Britain was undergoing a decisive change. Pressure for colonial concessions was still of course to be exerted upon England, but no longer to show her that she needed to ally herself with Germany, for this would so arouse the Russians that the Reich's entire security would be threatened; and moreover, a Britain allied to Germany would destroy the raison d'être of the fleet. It would also cause tensions within the internal political structure which Miquel was building up, as this included many anglophobe elements.[93] Bülow's policy was that of the 'Free Hand', a line which he was to operate with some skill until the calculations upon which it was based proved to be erroneous. He himself later outlined the dilemma of such a policy:

> We could neither allow a fundamentally anti-English policy to determine the law of our decisions and actions, nor for the sake of England's friendship pass into dependence upon her. Both risks existed and more than once came dangerously near. In our development as a sea power we could reach our desired aim neither as England's satellite nor as her antagonist.[94]

92 BA/MA 5656, VI, 1-3, *Flottenerweiterungsprogramm-Ganz Geheim*, Grapow's draft of 19/1/1900.
93 Fischer, *Krieg der Illusionen*, p. 94. This is a point made repeatedly by Eckart Kehr. e.g., 'Englandhass und Weltpolitik' in *Zeitschrift für Politik*, (1928).
94 B. v. Bülow, *Deutsche Politik* (Berlin, 1916), p. 30.

Much of this also explains Bülow's policy towards Russia. Until the growth of the fear after 1896 that Britain would forcibly stunt Germany's overseas expansion, the sole serious danger to the future existence of the Reich appeared to be the powerful Czarist colossus. Moreover, if Berlin and St Petersburg clashed, this would also bring into the fray a revengeful France, whose hostility to Germany was taken for granted even if her military power was not so greatly feared. The outcome of a two-front war was unknown, but few wished to experience it. Consequently, it became Berlin's fixed policy to establish good relations with Russia and to avoid all points of dispute: to this end the kaiser also worked, attempting through private letters to influence the younger Czar by appeals to monarchial solidarity.[95] The task was greatly eased by the 1897 Austro-Russian agreement to put their Balkan disputes 'upon ice', for this meant that Germany found it no longer necessary to beg London to support the dual monarchy in eastern Europe. It was, furthermore, assisted by Russia's turn to the Far East, a change which Bülow and Wilhelm actively encouraged as a way of easing the pressure upon Germany's eastern borders. Convinced that a future Anglo-Russian war was unavoidable, Berlin elected to sit upon the fence and to await the outcome, conscious of the fact that this policy might not only bring short-term gains but also allow Germany's industrial strength, trade and fleet, to develop undisturbed.[96]

Three pitfalls, however, had to be avoided; Britain and Russia must be kept apart by diplomatic means should they ever show signs of coming together; Germany must not too openly range herself with Russia, for London would then give up all hope of obtaining Berlin's support and refuse to be considerate in colonial questions; yet she must not, on the other hand, move too close to Britain, for reasons already outlined above. Such were the calculations, basically speaking, of the *Auswärtiges Amt* after 1897. Many aspects of this grand design already existed beforehand e.g. placating the public with overseas successes, avoiding disagreement with Russia—but they had never been brought together and formulated as a complete concept until the accession to power of Bülow, Tirpitz and Miquel. It is with some truth, therefore, that Dr Röhl has concluded that 'Not 1890 but 1897 was the decisive year in the early part of Wilhelm II's reign.'[97]

95 For this, see W. Goetz, ed., *Briefe Wilhelms II an den Zaren* 1894-1914, (Berlin, 1920).
96 Langer, *Diplomacy of Imperialism*, pp. 374-75, 500-02, 515-16; *Holstein Papers*, 4, pp. 38-39.
97 Röhl, *Germany without Bismarck*, p. 276.

At first events proved relatively easy to regulate. Nevertheless, Wilhelm's 'pathological activity and restlessness', as
Holstein called it, was soon to lead the country into difficulties
and to give their *Weltpolitik* its first baptism of fire. For some
years the German navy had had its eye upon obtaining a part
of the Chinese coast and in November 1897 at the urgings of
Wilhelm and his influential chief of naval cabinet, Admiral
von Senden-Bibran, steps were taken to secure Kiaochow—
despite the worries of the *Auswärtiges Amt* and the temporary
opposition of Tirpitz himself.[98] Here was a clear example of
a situation in which the kaiser's entourage could not control
their impulsive sovereign, and had to rely upon moderating
his demands and protecting him from criticism. The Russian
government however, took offence at this step and for a while
the prospect of an open clash loomed large. Fearing the
worst, Berlin anxiously turned for some support to London,
although Holstein bitterly remarked that 'The only really
valuable trump against Russia, namely the possibility of
entering into closer relations with England, has been taken out
of our hands by the navy with its continuous agitation against
England.'[99]

Nevertheless, the crisis blew over within a few weeks.
Unable to accept the humiliation of a retreat, Berlin stood
firm and seized Kiaochow while Russia did nothing. The
kaiser enthusiastically telegraphed his congratulations to
Bülow and became even more excited about the possibility of
establishing a large overseas empire. For the *Auswärtiges
Amt*, however, two salutory lessons clearly emerged. Firstly,
they resolved privately never to oppose Russia again in the
Far East lest this trigger off a European war. From that time
onwards, Bülow paid a very high regard towards keeping upon
good terms with St Petersburg. Secondly, Salisbury's refusal
to assist Germany during this crisis and his apparent wish to
see her embroiled with Russia in the Far East deepened
German suspicion of England and furthered their determination to obtain and maintain for themselves a 'Free Hand'
between London and St Petersburg.[100]

It was with these guidelines firmly in mind that Berlin
reacted to the suggestion from London in the spring of 1898
for an alliance with Germany.[101] Chamberlain's motives in

98 Langer, *Diplomacy of Imperialism*, pp. 448-51; Steinberg, *Yesterday's Deterrent*,
pp. 154-55.
99 *Holstein Papers*, 4, p. 50.
100 Langer, *Diplomacy of Imperialism*, pp. 453-54; N. H. Rich, *Friedrich von Holstein*,
2, pp. 561-64.
101 The literature upon these negotiations is enormous: see the rather dated bibliography
in Langer, *Diplomacy of Imperialism*, pp. 532-36B. More recently, see Rich, *Friedrich von*

making these overtures were quite clear: Britain was in deep trouble, in Africa where the French challenged in the west and east, and especially in China, where Russia appeared likely to swallow up regions hitherto dominated by British merchants. Faced with these difficulties, the colonial secretary was willing to arrange an alliance with America, or Japan, or Germany, or in fact anybody. Salisbury, disappointed by his failure to come to an agreement with Russia and no longer enjoying the good health and political predominance he had possessed in earlier cabinets, did not forbid Chamberlain's pourparlers, although he remained sceptical. Had anything concrete emerged, then he would doubtless have made plain some of the reservations he entertained against a fixed alliance and which he outlined on occasions before and after 1898.

Salisbury's pessimism as to German intentions soon proved justified. Although encouraging noises were made for a time, merely to discover how far Britain needed Germany's support, Berlin soon outlined why she would not form an alliance. The reason given, that a later British Parliament might refuse to recognize the treaty, partly obscured the genuine fear of the German leaders that Russia would react to their partnership with England by threatening Germany's borders.[102] Bülow was also appalled by the idea that Germany should become the number one foe of the Dual Alliance, while Britain would slip into the background and watch the continental powers fight it out amongst themselves. Although, as Taylor has pointed out, he flattered himself that Germany could in the future team up with Britain, the foreign minister was already revealing his wish to straddle permanently and exploit the Anglo-Russian antagonism. 'We must hold ourselves independent between the two', Bülow minuted, 'and be the tongue on the balance, not the pendulum oscillating to and fro.'[103] Wilhelm was therefore encouraged to pick his way delicately between the two rival powers, since an inclination in any direction would endanger Germany's future: at the same time, the British were to be encouraged to be conciliatory in specific colonial arrangements and thereby to smooth the way to a more permanent rapprochement. In this respect, German hopes clearly lay with Chamberlain,

Holstein, 2, pp. 567-86; Grenville, *Salisbury and Foreign Policy*, pp. 148-76; and H. W. Koch, 'The Anglo-German Alliance Negotiations. Missed Opportunity or Myth?' in *History*, 54, no. 182 (October, 1969). The best German surveys still remain: F. Meinecke, *Geschichte des Deutsche-Englischen Bündnisproblems* 1890-1901 (Munich, 1927) and G. Ritter, *Die Legende von der verschmähten Englischen Freundschaft* 1898-1901 (Freiburg, 1929).

102   G.P., 14/1, no. 3790, Kaiser's closing minute thereon.

103   Ibid., no. 3785 and minutes on no. 790; Taylor, *Struggle for Mastery*, p. 377.

from whom they expected the many 'considerations' which would appease colonial circles at home. Salisbury was always recognized to be a harder nut to crack and was disliked because of his known wish to reach an understanding with France and Russia, which would nullify Germany's bargaining position. Berlin was extremely enraged, for example, when the prime minister's approach to Russia in the spring of 1898 was made known by the Czar.[104]

It was with this hope of extracting concessions from the British, and the need to appease the clamour of the kaiser and the colonial groups for overseas territories that Germany burst in upon the Anglo-Portuguese discussions of the early summer of 1898.[105] Moreover, the list of 'compensations' for allowing Britain to offer a loan to Lisbon upon the security of her African customs receipts (and implicitly upon the colonies themselves) revealed just how enormous the German colonial demands had become. The story of the negotiations and Salisbury's steady resistance to these claims has been adequately covered in many studies, but it is interesting to note that Bülow really opposed any joint approach by Germany and France to extract concessions, 'not only for our colonial future but also for our entire position in Europe and in the world . . .'[106] In other words, private persuasion at London was better in the long term than throwing themselves into the French camp and permanently alienating the British. However, the prime minister's stubbornness made this difficult to accomplish and provoked the kaiser's violent remark that

> Lord Salisbury's conduct is quite Jesuitical, monstrous and insolent! If he has to have regard for the feelings in the Colonies, then I have to bear in mind the feeling of the German people and that is for me the more decisive. One can see once again how the noble Lord plays with us and shifts around, merely because he does not fear us since we have no fleet —which has been continually refused me in ten years of government by that fool (eseldummen) Reichstag. For the rest I stand fast on my list (of compensations) and make no further concessions, sharing Herr von Bülow's view that it is better to resign ourselves to the unavoidable and to use it for the fleet.[107]

104 G.P., 14/1, nos. 3803-804; Rich, *Friedrich von Holstein*, 2, pp. 582-85.

105 Ibid., pp. 586-87; Grenville, *Salisbury and Foreign Policy*, pp. 177-98; Langer, *Diplomacy of Imperialism*, pp. 520-29; G.P., 14/1, chap. 92; G. P. Gooch and H. Temperley, eds., *British Documents on the Origins of the War*, 11 vols. (London, 1926-38,—hereafter B.D.), 1, chap. 2.

106 A.A./*England 78 Nr. 1 Secr.*, vol. 3, Bülow to A.A., 15/7/1898.

107 Ibid., vol. 4, kaiser's minute on Richthofen to Eulenburg, no. 22 of 20/7/1898, and compare with G.P., 14/1, no. 3835. See also BA (Bundesarchiv, Koblenz), Eulenburg Papers, vol. 51, Eulenburg to Bülow, 23/7/1898.

This minute, omitted in the *Grosse Politik*, captures much of the kaiser's sensitivity to public opinion, dislike of Salisbury, craving for the respect he believed a fleet would give him, and his determination to use diplomatic setbacks as a pretext for further naval increases.

However, Bülow was able to persuade Wilhelm that breaking-off the talks would make Germany more dependent upon France and Russia and reduce her freedom of movement. Fortunately, too, Salisbury went on holiday and abandoned the direction of the talks to his nephew, Arthur Balfour. As a result, an agreement was rushed through and signed on 30 August 1898. It could hardly be said, however, that this boded well for Anglo-German relations. On the one hand, Salisbury regarded the German policy with greater distaste than ever and did all within his power to ensure that the future arrangements regarding the disposal of the Portuguese colonies never came into effect. He later told Hatzfeldt that he would never have signed the document had he been at home then.[108] On the other hand, Berlin did not regard the treaty as being unduly favourable to them and also suffered some embarrassment, since they were bound not to reveal its clauses to the German public who suspected another 'sell-out' to the British.[109] Its sole benefit was the effective withdrawal of German claims to political influence in southern Africa and the Transvaal, but this was something Berlin had been seeking to do—for a price—since 1896.

Bülow continued to keep a protective eye upon the kaiser lest he stray from the fixed lines of the 'Free Hand' policy, for there was always the danger, given his dislike of the French and fear of the Russians, that Wilhelm would one day succumb to Chamberlain's importunacy. Even before the treaty was signed, therefore, arrangements were made to impress upon St Petersburg the fact that this was confined purely to Africa and should not be interpreted as an anti-Russian move. Moreover, immediately after the kaiser's talk with the British ambassador, Lascelles, on 21 August, Bülow hastened to flatter his master with the idea of being *arbiter mundi* and to assure him that he was doing the correct thing by keeping the British at arm's length.[110] Some months later, Eulenburg sent him an even more sycophantic letter, tactfully

108   Grenville, *Salisbury and Foreign Policy*, pp. 197-98, 260-62; P. R. Warhurst, *Anglo-Portuguese Relations in South-Central Africa* 1890-1900 (London, 1962), pp. 144-45; *Holstein Papers*, p. 141; B.D.1, no. 99.

109   A.A./*England* 78 *Nr.* 1 *Secr.*, vol. 9, kaiser's comment on Tattenbach to chancellor, no. 99 of 24/9/1898; ibid., vol. 10, Deutsche Kolonialgesellschaft to chancellor, 3/10/1898, and reply; BA, Richthofen Nachlass, vol. 5, Bülow to Richthofen, 4/10/1898.

110   G.P., 14/1, nos. 3867 & 3868.

pointing out that the British possibly gained encouragement of German support from the kaiser's personal initiative, but 'Thank God your Majesty is smart enough to understand everything that is brewed up there.'[111] For Eulenburg, as for Bülow, the 'Free Hand' policy had a distinct twist in favour of Russia and, for obvious military reasons, pressure for 'considerations' was never brought to bear upon her. Only if they knew that Russia had bound herself to France for other than defensive purposes, Holstein believed, would Germany seek the active alliance of Great Britain.[112]

By the end of 1898, the entourage of the *persönliches Regiment* was aware that Wilhelm was impatiently pressing for more battleships, although it was only six months since the first Navy Law had been passed. For the kaiser, a large fleet had become a sort of elixir, a solution to all of Germany's overseas problems as well as a way of pacifying German public opinion. It was, if his angry marginal comments are to be believed, an implement to command Salisbury's respect, to counter a possible Anglo-American alliance, and to check the aggressiveness of the United States in the Pacific.[113] However, Tirpitz felt that the time was not yet ripe to press the Reichstag for further warships and, moreover, warned that

> all policy hostile to England must be left alone until we have a fleet which is as strong as the English. The alliance with Russia and France would not help us. The Russians cannot come over the mountains to India, they have enough to do to maintain their Far Eastern possessions.[114]

As the year 1899 approached, therefore, the policies dearest to the kaiser's heart were being steadily if cautiously implemented by his followers. At home reaction had set in and a turn was taken against both the Poles and the Social Democrats.[115] A start had been made in the plan to construct an enormous battlefleet and the programme of *Weltpolitik* had been finally launched; while public opinion was being deliberately and systematically directed to ignore domestic problems and to concentrate upon this heady expansionism. Moreover, this was to be continued and enlarged in the

111 BA, Eulenburg Papers, vol. 52, Eulenburg to Wilhelm, 15/11/1898. See also Eulenburg's letter to Bülow of the same date.

112 A.A./*England* 78 *Nr.* 1 *Secr.*, vol. 8, Holstein to Radolin (private), 3/9/1898.

113 Ibid., vol. 3, comment on Holleben to A.A., tel. no. 67, received 13/7/1898, and omitted from G.P., 15, no. 4158; A.A./*U.S.A.* 17, vol. 2, comment on Radowitz to A.A., 19/3/1898.

114 Fürst Chlodwig zu Hohenlohe-Schillingsfürst, *Denkwürdigkeiten der Reichskanzlerzeit*, ed. K. A. von Müller (Stuttgart/Berlin, 1931), p. 464.

115 Röhl, *Germany without Bismarck*, pp. 246-58.

years following, for, in November 1898, Bülow outlined Wilhelm's directives to the government departments and the newspapers and publicists they influenced:

> In discussion of the present world situation, His Majesty desires that over-careless and damaging attacks either against Russia or against England and America be avoided, but on the other hand the following points be placed in the foreground:
> I. How necessary the increase of the fleet has been. No successful overseas policy without a strong fleet. The role of the fleet in the Spanish-American war and during the Fashoda quarrel. Why does Spain lie on the floor? Why does France retreat before England?
> II. So long as we possess insufficient naval forces, their deficiency must be replaced by a unanimous consolidation of the Parties, the Reichstag and the Nation in all great matters of foreign policy. Never would there be more cause to direct the gaze from petty Party disputes and subordinate internal affairs on to the world-shaking and decisive problems of foreign policy.[116]

Unity at home, glory abroad and the growth of the fleet were inextricably connected in the kaiser's blueprint for a greater Germany; and it was with this 'national' programme uppermost in mind that Berlin approached the crisis in Samoa which occurred in 1899.

iv *The American Expansion and the Changing Relations with Britain and Germany*

For almost the entire duration of the nineteenth century, the United States had so faithfully followed the precepts of Washington and Jefferson in maintaining a reserve and aloofness to the activities and disputes of the other nations of the world that this had become not merely a policy but an integral part of America's national tradition and political philosophy. The exceptions which had occurred to interrupt this general rule were the result of the activities of individual pressure groups, enterprises and statesmen rather than the deliberate choice of the American people themselves or their representatives in Washington. Given the widespread acceptance of this tenet by all but a few Americans, therefore, the astonishingly swift expansion of the United States into the Caribbean and especially into the Pacific in the final few years of the nineteenth century appeared to many observers to be nothing less than revolutionary.

In 1897, President McKinley negotiated a new treaty of annexation with Hawaii and laid it before the Senate. There

it was treated circumspectly until the events of the war with
Spain caught up with the Legislature, who voted for the
proposal and thus allowed McKinley to transfer the group
to the United States on 12 August 1898. In the same year,
Wake Island and Guam were taken over by American forces,
as were the much larger and more important islands of the
Philippines, Puerto Rico and Cuba. Only the latter country
was promised its freedom, which, after all, had been the
chief aim of the Spanish-American war: the rest were ceded
to, or legally acquired by, the United States early in 1899.
The congressional and public debates about the extension of
American sovereignty over the Philippines, an act which
Professor Bemis has termed 'The Great Aberration of 1898',
revealed more than anything else the widespread realization
that America's foreign policy was taking a new and radical
course.[117] Moreover, this expansion was paralleled by a
corresponding increase in the size of the United States navy,
by a large rise in American overseas trade, and by a growing
governmental and public concern in the question of the
Chinese Empire and its future. At one blow, or so it seemed,
the United States had emerged from its long period of
introspection and become an important factor upon the scene
of international politics.

Without doubt, the war with Spain was the catalyst for this
sudden outburst of American imperialism, although there
were certain underlying factors during the 1890s which
indicated that the gradual development of United States
power and influence overseas was quite foreseeable. There
are hints that in America, as was the case much more clearly
in Germany, a certain 'manipulated social imperialism' took
place.[118] Populism, bimetallism and agrarian discontent,
widespread strikes and disorders, racial strife, unemployment
and the demagogism of Bryan appeared to have been checked
by the economic recovery after the mid-1890s and by
McKinley's election in 1896.[119] However, these discontents
scared not only the large banks, corporations and industrial

---

117 S. F. Bemis, *A Diplomatic History of the United States*, 85th ed. (New York, 1965)
pp. 463-75.

118 I take the phrase from Dr H.-U. Wehler's paper, 'Industrial Growth and Expansion'
given privately at the Theories of Imperialism Seminar of Oxford University on 28/11/1969.
This view is supported to a certain extent by R. Hofstadter in his article 'Manifest Destiny
and the Phillipines' in *American Imperialism in* 1898, symposium in the *Problems in
American Civilisation* series, selected by Amherst College Department of American Studies
(Boston, 1955), pp. 55-57 and more positively by Lafeber, *The New Empire*, pp. 34-35, and
Vagts, *Weltpolitik*, 2, pp. 1,257-59.

119 There is a good summary of this internal turbulence in S. E. Morison and H. S.
Commager, *The Growth of the American Republic*, 4th ed., 2 vols., (New York, 1950),
2, pp. 236 65.

companies but also leading members of the administration and legislature. Overseas expansion and nationalism would not only serve to effect internal political unity and attract the attention of the newly-literate classes but also to provide fresh markets for American industry; while this prosperity in turn would eradicate the chief cause of social unrest.

The economic motive is more clearly visible, if only because it can be measured in statistics and hard facts rather than half-expressed fears and emotions. The commercial crisis of 1893 was still warm in the memories of financial and business circles, and in industry, whose hoped-for revival had been partially checked by the 1895 Venezuela crisis and the 1896 bimetallist scare. By 1897, however, an enormous export-led revival was under way, leading these circles to believe 'that the United States was on the point of capturing the markets of the world'.[120] Furthermore, the importance of this development was augmented by the belief that America was facing a crisis of over-production and would be unable to maintain her prosperity unless new markets were found. Interest was particularly turning to the apparently vast, untapped markets of the Chinese Empire where American exports had doubled within twelve months. At the end of that year, however, the German seizure of Kiaochow precipitated what appeared to be a scramble for territorial concessions in China which would probably lead to tariff discrimination against American goods. Faced with this threat, even such anti-imperialist papers as the New York *Journal of Commerce* began not only to advocate energetic diplomacy to achieve commercial equality throughout China but also the acquisition of Hawaii. There seems little doubt that the serious state of the Chinese Empire was of crucial importance to the American government and business circles in their decision to acquire such mid-oceanic points as Hawaii, Wake Island and Guam, and even more with regard to the Philippines.[121]

The clinching factor for the annexation of the latter territory came in the sphere of foreign affairs, and in the deterioration in German-American relations. These had not been particularly friendly since the 1889 Samoa crisis and their spiralling tariff war of the 1890s had also caused some mutual discontent but there was no direct and obvious clash of interests until the expansion of both powers into the Pacific and China in

120 J. W. Pratt, 'American Business and the Spanish-American War', in *American Imperialism in 1898*, p. 28.

121 J. A. S. Grenville and G. B. Young, *Politics, Strategy and American Diplomacy: Studies in Foreign Policy, 1873-1917* (New Haven/London, 1966) pp. 267-96; Thomas J. McCormick, *China Market, America's Quest for Informal Empire, 1893-1901* (Chicago, 1967) pp. 109-25.

1897. The American annexation treaty with Hawaii, carried
out to forestall the Japanese and to regulate the affairs of
that group, caused deep discontent among pan-German and
colonial advocates and, as Hohenlohe put it,'aroused a general
wish to use this opportunity to bring about a final settlement
of the unsatisfactory conditions in Samoa'.[122] Hatzfeldt was
asked to persuade Salisbury into agreeing to a joint Anglo-
German approach to Washington, intimating to the United
States that she should either recognize the neutrality of
Hawaii or withdraw from her share in Samoa: if the latter
suggestion was adopted, a Samoa-Tonga split between
Britain and Germany might follow.

Salisbury, however, proved unreceptive. While he did not
favour an American annexation of Hawaii since this would
mean the introduction of restrictive tariff barriers there, he
had already told the Japanese minister in London that he
would not oppose the United States and that keeping quiet
was the best way to defeat this move.[123] Foreign representations, the prime minister reckoned, would almost certainly
provoke the Senate into ratifying the annexation treaty.
Although Salisbury spoke in a friendly manner to Hatzfeldt,
it was later pointed out by Sanderson that an American-
German-British neutralization of Hawaii would perhaps
violate the 1843 Anglo-French agreement upon that group
and the prime minister thereupon became less willing to go
further in the matter. Nor did the idea of an American
withdrawal from Samoa appeal, since, as a Colonial Office
minute remarked, 'It would leave us face to face with the
Germans alone, and would I fear lead to our being rapidly
elbowed out.'[124] Salisbury also resisted the idea of a British
withdrawal from Samoa and the acquisition of Tonga in
compensation, declaring that he would be putting his hand
into 'a wasp's nest' and that only the cession of German
New Guinea would be sufficient to placate Australasia: his
price was evidently much higher now than in 1887 and
Hatzfeldt indignantly rejected such a proposal. The prime
minister's increasing distaste for any joint representations at
Washington ensured the virtual abandonment of these
discussions.[125]

Although the United States knew little or nothing of this,

122   A.A./*Südsee-Inseln* 1, vol. 5, Alldeutscher Verband to Chancellor, 19/6/1897; G.P.,
13, no. 3409.
123   F.O.58/309, minute on Sanderson memo of 11/4/1897.
124   C.O.337/36, J. Anderson minute on paper 743 Secret, F.O. to C.O., 18/8/1897.
125   These Samoa-Hawaii negotiations can be followed in F.O.58/309, particularly
Hatzfeldt's three memos of 31/7/1897, 15/9/1897 and 9/12/1897; in A.A./*Südsee-Inseln* 1,
vols. 5 and 6; in R.Kol.A.2872; in G.P., 12, chap. 84; and in Ross, *Aspirations*, p. 300.

these talks were a portent of the way in which the relations of the three powers were to develop—Britain and Germany remained upon relatively cool terms: the United States and Germany began to drift further apart: and Britain and the United States were gradually moving closer to each other, in the affairs of the Pacific and China at least. This latter development was not only an astonishing one, it was also one of the most important in world history of the past hundred years.[126] It was true that the Irish vote was losing some of its influence in the United States, that memories of Britain's attitude during the Revolutionary and Civil Wars were dying away, that American business interests supported the British attempt to maintain the 'open door' in China, and that the 1890s saw a rapid growth of 'race patriotism' and a belief in the superiority of the Anglo-Saxons. Nevertheless, 'For many Americans Britain was *the* enemy: an implacable vindictive foe ever on the watch for an opportunity to strike down the impertinent republic that had once been British.'[127]

It is to be doubted whether Salisbury ever possessed an affection for, or a deep understanding of, the republic but his determination not to arouse her anger or suspicion played a crucial though negative role in the improvement of Anglo-American relations. A more positive role was played by such warm friends of America as Chamberlain and Balfour and by the British press, which on the whole staunchly supported the United States before and during the Spanish-American War. Doubtless this was also motivated by self-interest, the hope of securing American support in a friendless world and of possible joint action in China. Doubtless, too, there were still many vital differences (Alaskan boundary, Isthmian canal, the fisheries and the seal question) which required much tactful diplomacy for a satisfactory settlement. But it was the open British friendship to the United States during the Spanish-American War which not only caused a change in the feelings of most Americans towards their old enemy but also facilitated a settlement of the remaining differences.

The U. S. navy, more than any other body, benefited from the British attitude during the war. The Hong Kong authorities blatantly ignored the rules governing neutrality and allowed Dewey to cable messages to Washington via the Eastern Telegraph Company's line. All over the globe the Americans

---

126   On this development, see C. S. Campbell, *Anglo-American Understanding* 1898-1903 (Baltimore, 1957); A. E. Campbell, *Great Britain and the United States* 1895-1903 (London, 1960); H. C. Allen, *Great Britain and the United States: A History of Anglo-American Relations* 1783-1952 (London, 1954) pp. 549-629; R. G. Neale, *Britain and American Imperialism* 1898-1900 (Queensland, 1965).

127   C. S. Campbell, *Anglo-American Understanding*, p. 1.

received help with coaling difficulties and much information from British officials. On the other hand, the British authorities at Suez created many obstacles for the Spanish squadron which was seeking to pass through the canal: it was as a direct result of these unneutral steps that Spain attempted to threaten Gibraltar in the months following.[128] People in Europe and the United States believed that a secret Anglo-American alliance existed, that Britain had offered America the use of her warships, that she had prevented a continental coalition from intervening on behalf of Spain, and that the British vessels in Manila Bay had aligned themselves to support Dewey against the German squadron there. Although none of this was true, the effect upon the American people and government was considerable. Moreover, the State Department knew that Britain was encouraging them to take the Philippines, and that officials like Spring-Rice were also privately urging that they annex Hawaii before Germany raised difficulties over the Samoan question.[129]

The German attitude was much less friendly. The German navy in particular pressed for 'compensations' and Tirpitz regretted that the Spanish-American War had come before the German battlefleet was built and thus prevented them from intervening in the affair. This was, he felt, their last chance to seize the Danish West Indies and to create an 'economic market' in South America before American chauvinists took over these areas.[130] Admiral Knorr urged the kaiser that America's embarrassment in the war gave Germany the best chance to expand into the Caribbean, and he forwarded memoranda upon both the Danish and the Dutch West Indies. A few months later, Knorr sent Wilhelm details about 'the ideal fleet base', and upon possible naval stations in the Philippines or Sulus.[131] The kaiser's brother, Heinrich, wrote from the Far East, asking 'What will come out of Spain? Will we have chances for the Philippines and Samoa?' The kaiser himself wished to obtain Samoa, the Carolines, Borneo and one of the Philippine Islands 'if possible', while Hatzfeldt

128 W. R. Braisted, *The United States Navy in the Pacific* 1897-1909 (Austin, Texas, 1958), pp. 32-33; Neale, *Britain and American Imperialism*, pp. 35-81.
129 N.A.R.G.59/M-30, roll 181, Hay to Day, 3/5/1898; C. S. Campbell, *Anglo-American Understanding*, p. 41; S. Gwynn, ed., *The Letters and Friendships of Cecil Spring Rice*, 2 vols. (London, 1929), 1, pp. 246-51.
130 BA, Bülow Papers, vol. 20, Top Secret memo by Klehmet of 16/3/1898 on conversation with Tirpitz. In the margin Bülow himself wrote 'Karolinen. Samoa. Hafen an das Nordküste von Sumatra.' See also Hohenlohe, *Denkwürdigkeiten der Reichskanzlerzeit*, pp. 442-43.
131 BA/MA 3419, PG67346, *Kolonien*, vol. 1, Knorr to Wilhelm, 20/4/1898; A.A./ *Deutschland* 167, vol. 2, Knorr to Wilhelm, 13/7/1898, Top Secret; Vagts, *Weltpolitik*, 2, pp. 1,325-27.

thought that Germany should go ahead and seize the Sulus and the Carolines.[132]

Already on 3 June, the German squadron under Diederichs had been directed to Manila to report upon the situation and twelve days later the Admiralty staff thought the rise of America naval power so disturbing that they decided to prepare plans for operations against the United States.[133] In view of all of these speculations, it is difficult to accept the orthodox view that the large assembly of German warships in the Philippines was purely an administrative measure caused by the changing of the crews.[134] If the newspapers of the time exaggerated Diederichs' activities, there is no doubt that the real motive for his presence at Manila was to be at hand should the Americans decide not to take the Philippines.

Bülow was alarmed by all these urgings and feared that the influence of the navy upon the impressionable kaiser could possibly wreck his 'Free Hand' policy by arousing America's hostility. In March, news that an attack by the United States was planned upon the Philippines was transmitted to the queen of Spain on the orders of Wilhelm, who felt that 'the scoundrels the Yankees want war.' But Bülow then insisted that they dare not openly oppose the Americans or show any signs of partiality for Spain: Germany's naval strength was inadequate and her trade with the United States too large to risk provoking a conflict. Their policy should be to push others to the fore.[135] The consequent friction between Dewey and Diederichs must have caused him considerable anxiety, and he did everything in his power to check the deterioration of German-American relations. Newspapers which pleaded for Germany to take advantage of the war by obtaining compensations in Samoa were warned to keep quiet and the kaiser was also privately restrained, although the latter could not help minuting on one despatch: 'America plunders Spain's colonies and England Portugal's.'[136]

Nevertheless, the aim of the *Auswärtiges Amt* was basically the same: colonial compensations to please the kaiser and public opinion. It merely wished to do this in a more discreet manner, realizing that open provocation and demands would

132 BA, Bülow Papers, vol. 3, Heinrich to Wilhelm (copy), 11/7/1898; *The Holstein Papers*, 4, pp. 79, 89.

133 BA/MA 7537, I.15, *Akten des Kreuzer-Geschwaders. Die Philippinen*, vol. 1, Kaiser to Diederich, 3/6/1898; BA/MA 5174b, III, 1-16, *Vorabeiten zu den Operationspläne gegen die Vereinigten Staaten von Nordamerika*, vol. 1, Admiralstab memo of 15/6/1898.

134 W. Hubatsch, *Die Aera Tirpitz*, (Göttingen, 1955), pp. 35-41.

135 Grenville and Young, *Politics, Strategy and American Diplomacy*, pp. 282-84.

136 A.A./*Deutschland* 122 *nr.* 3, vol. 6, Hamman and Bülow minutes on *Hamburgischer Correspondenz*, 18/4/1898 and *Hannoverscher Courier*, 20/4/1898; A.A./*England* 78 *nr.* 1 *Secret*, vol. 4, Kaiser's minute on Tattenbach to Chancellor no. 113 of 15/7/1898.

enrage the touchy Americans. Richthofen, the assistant state secretary, therefore called upon the United States ambassador in July

> and urged that Germany ought to have some assurances as to territory in the Pacific, stating that Germany does not want large annexations and could not afford to take Philippines if they were offered her, but that she should be left unhampered in Samoa, and should eventually have also, say, the Carolines and a naval station in the Philippines.[137]

White, the ambassador, urged Washington to conciliate the Germans but this viewpoint did not please his superiors. He was told that nothing had been settled about the Philippines but that this matter could be safely left with the United States and that the president 'is much surprised' at the German request. Moreover,

> Questions as to Samoa are not involved in pending controversy and should not be injected into it. The United States has a right to expect the friendly neutrality of Germany in accordance with long established relations of the governments.[138]

In Washington there already existed a deep suspicion of Germany's policy in the Pacific due to the continued presence of Diederichs' squadron at Manila and to the activities of the warship *Irene*. White's reports confirmed that Berlin was apparently seeking to have a say in the disposal of the Spanish empire, and the American reaction was therefore to reinforce Dewey's squadron immediately. They also enquired how long Germany intended to maintain her warships in Manila Bay, a question which Richthofen begged White not to make known lest the kaiser regard it as an affront. The ambassador was amiable enough to be drawn into a further conversation upon territorial compensations, which angered the secretary of state, Day, who informed White that he had 'gone distinctly beyond the attitude of absolute reserve.'[139] Clearly, all that the German suggestions did was to arouse American suspicion and to propel them into taking the Philippines.

The effect of these moves, and of the inflated newspaper rumours, was to cause further suspicion to spring up upon both sides. American newspapers such as the *Morning Oregonian*, violently attacked Germany as 'our bitter, relentless, uncompromising enemy. She is an intense hater of our

---

137 N.A.R.G.59/M-44, roll 85, White to Day, tel. of 12/7/1898; see also, A.A./*England* 78 *nr*. 1 *Secr*., vol. 3, Richthofen memo of 12/7/1898.
138 N.A.R.G.59/M-44, roll 85, White to Day, 13/7/1898; ibid., M-77, roll 71, Day to White, 14/7/1898.
139 N.A.R.G.59/M-77, roll 71, Day to White, 15/8/1898; Braisted, *U.S. Navy*, pp. 39-42.

institutions, and a violent opponent of our scheme of colonial expansion and national progress.' Even the more moderate *Washington Post* declared 'We know by a thousand unmistakable signs and by the experience of years, that in the German Government the United States has a sleepless and insatiable enemy.'[140] Although such expressions were never publicly used in American ruling and diplomatic circles, Germany became an object of mistrust among such influential men as Lodge, Roosevelt, Mahan, Hay and perhaps also McKinley.

On the German side, too, suspicion was rife, and the latent resentment and fear of the kaiser and aristocratic circles for the republic which challenged Germany's commercial and colonial expansion and against which no diplomatic pressure could be employed reached new heights. Wilhelm advocated the construction of a stronger fleet to prevent any future American intervention in Europe and even the old chancellor, Hohenlohe, gloomily predicted that

> when they have built up a strong fleet and a respectable army as a result of the war, the Americans will make themselves very disagreeable in Europe. This prospect will hopefully convince our narrow-minded bourgeois that we need a strong fleet.[141]

Moreover, the violent anti-American utterances of the Agrarians were now joined by those of the colonial pressure groups, and a German-American press war developed, much to Bülow's dismay. Even the kaiser realized the senselessness of alienating a nation as influential as the United States, although with regard to the Agrarian and Bismarckian newspapers he felt that 'We cannot control them and are not responsible for them. Holleben (the German ambassador in Washington) and also America knows that!'[142]

Counter-measures were therefore taken to check this trend. As a defensive and negative step, the Wilhelmstrasse endeavoured to prevent anti-German news reaching the United States and to convince Americans that Germany was friendly. Their annoyance at what appeared to be the attempts of the British press to divide the two nations was partly justified, for most of the newspaper rumours concerning German designs in the Orient emanated from London or Hong Kong. A particularly bad offender was the Associated Press, which

140   A.A./*U.S.A.* 16, vol. 3, copy of *Morning Oregonian*, 18/9/1898; A.A./*U.S.A.* 1, vol. 10, copy of *Washington Post*, 25/11/1898.

141   A.A./*U.S.A.* 16, vol. 2, kaiser's minute on Prussian Minister in Dresden's no. 96 of 6/7/1898; BA, Eulenburg Papers, vol. 52, Hohenlohe to Eulenburg, 22/7/1898.

142   A.A./*U.S.A.* 16, vol. 2, minute on Holleben to chancellor, no. 154 of 18/7/1898.

reported on 1 July 1898 that Germany had landed troops in
the Philippines and two days later declared that Russia,
France and Germany would settle the future of that group.[143]
Since this agency dispersed its news reports throughout the
American continent, the German Foreign Ministry was
understandably perturbed and even threatened the Associated
Press representative in Berlin over the matter.[144] This did not
prevent the flow of anti-German reports, however, and
Holleben found it extremely difficult to combat this trend in
America.

A second and more positive aim, and one for which the
German government was to strive for many years, was to
ensure that an Anglo-American alliance never achieved
reality. It would be no exaggeration to state that Bülow
regarded this as one of his major tasks, since the existence of
such an alliance would severely damage his foreign policy
schemes. Combined together, these two maritime powers
could forestall any German annexations overseas and, with
Japan, could dominate the Far East. Moreover, Salisbury
would then feel even less inclined to accept the German
argument that London required Berlin's support and needed
to purchase that support with colonial concessions. In the
middle of the negotiations over the Portuguese colonies,
when Salisbury was still stubbornly refusing to agree to the
German demands, Bülow worriedly cabled the *Auswärtiges
Amt*:

> The measure of English friendship for us will depend in the first instance
> upon the extent of the American need to lean upon England and secondly
> upon the mood of the Americans toward us. Cannot Holleben do
> something in the American press?[145]

Furthermore, with her rear covered, and the Far East under
control, Britain might be in a position to meet the German
naval challenge in the North Sea.

The key to the problem clearly lay in America: as an
Auswärtiges Amt despatch put it:

> England will only become susceptible to other political combinations
> once again when the present hope of an Anglo-American alliance comes
> to nothing. But to frustrate this hope we will have to begin not in England
> but in America.[146]

143 Ibid., copies of Associated Press reports of 1/7/1898, 3/7/1898 and many others;
ibid., Holleben to chancellor, no. 154 of 18/7/1898; G.P., 15, no. 4148.
144 A.A./*U.S.A.* 16, vol. 2, Mumm memo of 20/8/1898.
145 A.A./*England* 78 *nr.* 1 *Secr.*, vol. 3, Bülow to A.A., 15/7/1898.
146 G.P., 15, no. 4154.

As a result, Richthofen pressed White upon this matter when mentioning the German desire to have Samoa, the Carolines and a naval station in the Philippines. The ambassador reported him as saying that 'close relations and co-operation of United States and Great Britain will certainly result in a continental coalition against United States.'[147] Alas for White and for the German hopes: in the State Department's stiff reply of 14 July, it was pointed out that 'Nothing in the relations of the United States and Great Britain need give any ground for apprehension on the part of the Continental Powers.'[148] In fact no American politician could have possibly dared to secure an alliance with Britain but McKinley's administration had a greater regard for British sympathy and assistance than for German threats, and clearly saw why Berlin was worried at the Anglo-American rapprochement.

Heedless of German opinion, the American expansion continued, led by the navy, as had been the case much of the time. Since the United States had suddenly become a first-class power in the Pacific, the recently-established strategic advisory body known as the Naval War Board advocated in August 1898 the acquisition and fortification of several overseas fleet stations to help maintain their position. Among those mentioned was Pago-Pago, whose situation the board found 'so central, and otherwise so suitable in case of operations in that quarter, that it is recommended to be retained. If possible, political possession of the whole island in which the port is, or at least of ground sufficient for fortifications, is desirable'.[149] Consequently, a certain chief engineer, Frank T. Chambers, was despatched to the group to erect coalsheds and to prepare Pago-Pago as a base. Despite the later protests of Captain Crowninshield of the Bureau of Navigation that the harbour was very unhealthy and that it could only be used by warships steaming from Hawaii to Australia, 'and a naval vessel has not visited that country in 12 years', this work went ahead. The board and the expansionist Bureau of Equipment had a more influential voice, and the head of the latter body, Captain Bradford, strongly advocated a partition of Samoa, with Tutuila falling to the United States.[150]

---

147 N.A.R.G.59/M-44, roll 85, White to Day, 12/7/1898; see also G.P., 15, nos. 4156-57.

148 N.A.R.G.59/M-77, roll 71, Day to White, 14/7/1898.

149 N.A.R.G.45, Entry 371, vol. A (*Naval War Board Letterpress*) pp. 335-54, Sicard, Crowninshield and Mahan to Long, 22/8/1898. See also Grenville and Young, *Politics, Strategy and American Diplomacy*, pp. 294-96.

150 N.A.R.G.80/M-625, roll 321, Crowninshield endorsement of 14/12/1898; ibid., File 3931 (Samoa), Box 415, Bradford to Long, 28/12/1898; Braisted, *U.S. Navy*, pp. 57-58.

Although little comment was made in Britain upon this latest American move into Pago-Pago, the reaction from Germany was bitter. We may close this chapter by citing the viewpoint of the Berlin section of the German Colonial Society, when it learnt of the news.

A favourable opportunity to establish themselves at Samoa has been seized—by the Americans. Not by us Germans, whose interests in these splendid islands are by far the greatest, and whose sailors have shed their blood! We look quietly on, and when America and England share the booty, and perhaps magnanimously give us a crumb or two, we rejoice at the success! Why did we not take advantage of the occasion, as before and during the war it would certainly have been possible to come to an understanding with America and also with England! If we should now approach the matter we would meet with scorn and derision from the supercilious English, and the 'Yankees' who are inflated by their military successes! Is that the position which is due to us in the world? Does no one realise the extent of the humiliations to the great German Empire if we are compelled to recede here where our rights are the greatest?

We cannot bring ourselves to believe this, or to give up the hope that we will eventually claim our rights. But why this delay, why are fears and apprehension allowed to spread, why does no word come from an authoritative source?[151]

It is a fair and not too extreme example of the utterances of the colonial pressure groups in Germany, bursting with national pride and at the same time full of jealousy at Britain and America. Moreover, it was typical of the jeers at their own government's lack of backbone and energy, criticisms which Bülow strove desperately to avoid by seeking the overseas successes which would satiate such groups and protect the kaiser. It was therefore easy to predict that, as the Americans advanced into the Pacific and Berlin came under pressure at home to do something about this, the Samoan question would once again be raised—and this time perhaps, more persistently—by the German government. All that was required was evidence of the complete failure and collapse of the 1889 arrangement—and that was not very far away.

---

151 N.A.R.G.59/M-44, roll 86, Jackson to Day, 14/11/1898, quoting from a *Mitteilungs-blatt* of the Berlin section.

4

The Samoan War
and International Politics 1898-99

i *The Origins and Outbreak of the Samoan Civil War*

At the beginning of 1897, the American consul-general
Churchill felt that 'the present peace of Samoa is but skin
deep'.[1] Malietoa was feebler and more indecisive than ever
and there was a growing campaign by many of the chiefs to
press the king to appeal to the powers for the return of
Mata'afa and his followers from Jaluit. This movement,
Churchill wrote, was inspired by the Germans, who had kept
the exiles under close supervision and who obviously reckoned
that they were now friendly to German aspirations in Samoa.
Feeling that Mata'afa would be 'a pawn in German colonial
policy', he therefore opposed the return. Cusack-Smith, too,
advised the Foreign Office to decline any such appeals, since
they had been instigated by Dr Irmer, the governor of the
Marshall Islands.[2]

Churchill and Cusack-Smith possessed much knowledge
of Samoan affairs and their opinions were accepted by their
respective governments. Unfortunately they were both replaced
around the turn of that year by consuls who lacked experience
of the islands, and this changeover closely followed upon the
arrival of the new chief justice, Chambers, and president,
Raffel. Only the German consul, Rose, remained, and he
advocated the return of the Jaluit exiles. Moreover, in October,
1897, the Mata'afan family and clan joined the native government and the threat of a rebellion receded. But once within
the Malietoan camp, they pressed even more strongly for the
release of their leader until the king himself appealed to the
powers to this effect. Consequently, when the new British
consul, Maxse, reported that this could be 'a source of
strength' to Malietoa's administration, London did not
oppose the idea. The new American consul, Osborn, also
urged the return of Mata'afa, since his support for the
Samoan government would greatly weaken the rebels' cause

---

1 N.A.R.G.84, Apia Consulate despatches (C38-8a), vol. 1, Churchill to S.D., no. 45
of 11/1/1897.
2 Ibid.; F.O.58/310, Cusack-Smith to Salisbury, nos. 1 and 4 of 11/1/1897 and 25/1/1897.

and would perhaps lead to a more effective collection of the head tax.[3]

After some discussions by the home governments, the consuls were told in July 1898 that the return of Mata'afa and his followers had received the assent of the powers and the German warship *Bussard* was despatched to the Marshalls to bring them back. Shortly before the vessel left, however, the king's condition worsened rapidly and he died on 22 August. Possessing no instructions, neither Maxse nor Osborn felt justified in preventing the departure of the *Bussard*, although both appealed for a warship and predicted that there might be trouble since the Samoans were armed in large numbers and there were several possible candidates for the succession. Maxse telegraphed later that Mata'afa's return should be delayed until after the election of a new king. Although the consuls and the municipal president joined together in a proclamation enjoining peace and order, there was therefore some doubt whether this state of tranquillity would endure for more than a few weeks. The only way to avert trouble, the British consul believed, would be a swift and unanimous decision on the kingship by the treaty powers.[4]

That such a decision was not arrived at was solely due to the policy of the United States. Fearing that the possible death of Malietoa could lead to complications, the British government approached Washington on 12 July with the proposal that the powers should consider the arrangements to be made for the selection of a successor. This the State Department declined to do, pointing out that the Berlin Act provided solely for an election by the natives themselves 'according to the laws and customs of Samoa'. Nevertheless, upon learning of the death of the king, the British renewed their attempts to persuade the Americans to agree to keeping Mata'afa away from Samoa and to instruct the consuls to submit suggestions upon the manner of procedure in a Samoan election. The new secretary of state, John Hay, agreed to the former idea but held firm to his predecessor's view that the powers should not interfere in the succession question.[5]

3 F.O.58/311, same to same, nos. 40 and 43 of 5/10/1897 and 1/11/1897; F.O.58/315, Maxse to Salisbury, nos. 3 and 13 of 16/4/1898 and 16/5/1898; ibid., F.O. to Lascelles, no. 119 of 24/5/1898; N.A.R.G.59, T-27, roll 24, Churchill to S.D., nos. 108 and 115 of 29/9/1897 and 28/10/1897; ibid., Osborn to S.D., nos. 21, 36 and 38 of 18/2/1898, 14/4/1898 find 16/5/1898.

4 F.O.58/315, F.O. to Maxse, tel. of 13/7/1898; F.O.58/316, Maxse to Salisbury, nos. 40 and 43 of 24/8/1898 and 1/9/1898; N.A.R.G.59, T-27, roll 24, Osborn to S.D., nos. 50 and 55 of 9/8/1898 and 31/8/1898; *Papers relating to the Foreign Relations of the United States* 1899 (Hereafter F.R. 1899—Washington, 1900), pp. 604-07.

5 F.O.58/316, Villiers memo of 30/8/1898; F.R.1899, pp. 607-13; Ryden, *U.S. Policy in Samoa*, pp. 549-51.

Hay's interpretation of the Berlin Act was undoubtedly the correct one, and his desire to allow the Samoans as much liberty as possible was commendable and in line with the traditional American policy towards the group; but by ignoring the signs of possible trouble and adhering inflexibly to the treaty, the United States let pass what was probably the last chance to prevent an explosion in the islands. Since the monarch created by that act was a virtual figurehead in any case, was there much *practically* wrong in the powers ensuring a smooth succession by unanimously agreeing upon one of the candidates, as the British and German governments were hinting? Washington should at least have been ready to inform their representatives as to the eligibility of the contenders for the kingship and the attitude to be adopted by the consular body. Left without instructions, the white officials in Samoa quickly arrived at varying interpretations of the clauses of the 1889 treaty. Moreover, the State Department reacted too slowly to allow instructions to be sent to prevent Mata'afa's return, which occurred on 19 September.

Since the charge was often made later in British, American and Australasian newspapers that the troubles of 1898-99 were a direct consequence of a cunning German plot to re-introduce Mata'afa as the king and their puppet, it may be worthwhile here to consider whether such charges can be substantiated. First of all, as mentioned in a previous section, the Germans were particularly worried about the rapid decline of their commercial paramountcy in the group.[6] Although the 1898 harvest gave the *D.H.P.G.* the opportunity to pay its first dividend for many years, and although the company was still the greatest landowner and taxpayer in Samoa, it remained beset with labour difficulties and the extent of its land under cultivation had shrunk: the German navy referred to it sarcastically as the 'once promising but now ever decaying company'.[7]

But the chief concern, at least of the German officials in the group, remained the extent of the influence exerted upon the Samoans by the L.M.S. How effective this really was is difficult to judge, but the belief that Malietoa was

6 This decline can be measured in *Accounts and Papers*, 1884 (LXXX), pp. 644-46, Report on Samoan trade for the year 1883; cf. ibid., 1898 (XCIX), pp. 775-83, Report on Samoan trade for the year 1897. These British figures, based upon information from the Apia customs house, conflict violently with those given in Document no. 97, 53rd Congress, 3rd Session, *Correspondence on Samoa* 1889-1895, enclosure 1 (copy in N.A.R.G. 80, File 3931 Box 415). In view of this disparity, all that can safely be said is that the German shipping predominance had disappeared altogether and that their trading predominance was being somewhat challenged.

7 BA/MA 697, *Akten der Kreuzer Division*, vol. 6, Diederichs to Oberkommando, 29/10/1898.

in the hands of the English was a constant thought upon the German side, and one which colonial circles strove to combat. In 1897, representatives of the Catholic missionary society, the Marists, had secretly urged Berlin to press for the release of Mata'afa, who was of their confession, and promised in return that they would influence him to be pro-German. This had then been declined by Marschall and was objected to by the *D.H.P.G.*, which feared the unrest that might follow. However, consul Rose strenuously advocated the return of the Jaluit exiles, since it would strengthen the German position in Samoa and combat the growing influence of the British missionaries. It was an idea which attracted members of the centre party, some of them being friends of Bülow; which appealed to the official dealing with Samoan affairs in the Colonial Division of the Foreign Ministry, Schmidt-Dargitz, who was pressing for financial help for the Marist school to the tune of 12,000 marks from the secret funds; and, finally, which persuaded the *D.H.P.G.* to drop its opposition in 1898.[8] There is, however, little concrete evidence that Berlin was planning anything other than a defensive move, aimed at halting the decline of German influence in the group, rather than a plot leading directly to their exclusive control with Mata'afa as their puppet.

What does seem clear, is that some of the local German officials interpreted their instructions to imply that a positive policy was intended. Rose, whose reports reveal a constant obsession about the preservation of *Deutschtum* in the group, had advocated since 1896 the use of Mata'afa as a 'tool' with which to combat the *Anglisierung* of Samoa and thus automatically he assumed that Berlin had agreed to his scheme. Nor did the *Auswärtiges Amt's* directions dispel such ideas, for the admiralty was requested that Mata'afa and his followers be brought back in a German warship 'for political reasons' and that the magnanimity of the pardon and the sanctity of the oath the exiles must take should be afterwards reinforced by celebrations.[9]

As a result, the officials at Jaluit and the crew of the *Bussard* made much of Mata'afa, stressing also, however, *that his release was solely due to the wish of the kaiser*. Moreover, such celebrations were repeated in Samoa itself and attended by Rose, although the other consuls were absent;

8 A.A./*A.M.-Botschaft Rom*, vol. 1, Bülow (Rome) to Hohenlohe, 12/2/1897, and Marschall to Bülow, 10/3/1897; R.Kol.A.3041, memo of 19/3/1898; Vagts, *Weltpolitik*, 1, pp. 779-83, 797-801.
9 BA/MA 5079, *Samoa*, vol. 2, A.A. to Admiralstab, 19/7/1898. For Rose's urgings, see R.Kol.A.3040, Rose to the chancellor, no. 150 of 29/12/1896; R.Kol.A.3041, same to same, no. 109 Secret of 1/11/1897.

and when the *Bussard* arrived at Apia, the anthropologist and
general intriguer, Dr Krämer, rushed aboard to consult the
exiles, causing much annoyance to the British and American
consuls, who had arranged that Mata'afa should be first
received by all the treaty officials at once. Krämer and several
equally indiscreet colleagues then became active participants
at Tupua assemblies, and thus objects of much suspicion.
It is further worth noting that the same Dr Irmer, who had
charge of the exiles in the Marshalls and was the first German
to press for their recall, later boasted to Saunders, the *Times*
correspondent in Berlin, 'that he had trained Mata'afa, when
a German prisoner, for the role he was afterwards to play in
Samoa'.[10]

The months following Mata'afa's return were full of quarrels,
not so much between the Samoans themselves as between the
treaty officials. From the very outset, the British consul and,
to a lesser extent, his American colleague were suspicious of
German designs. In fact, unable to ascertain the truth of the
rumours that Germany was planning to annex the group and
mindful of what was occurring at that time in the Philippines,
the British quickly sent a warship from Fiji to Samoa upon
the heels of a German vessel.[11] Moreover, the senior officer
in the islands, Commander Sturdee, had been considerably
influenced by the Kruger Telegram and therefore possessed,
to use his own words, 'a firm conviction that the Germans,
instead of being regarded with cousinly affection, must be
looked on as possible potential enemies in the future'.[12] This
suspicion was reciprocated upon the German side and Rose
sent home reports about the attempts of the L.M.S. to secure
a pro-British candidate for the throne.[13]

The treaty officials were divided over other matters also,
especially after Raffel suddenly began to assume an arbitrary
and dictatorial attitude which alarmed the Anglo-American
community. The truth of the matter was that the president
was very ill with malarial fever and, as the other officials
soon discovered, had had several fits of insanity.[14] Although

10 BA/MA 3419, PG67346, *Kolonien*, vol. 1, Knorr to Wilhelm, 8/11/1898; Saunders
Papers (Times Archives, Printing House Square), Saunders to Chirol, 10/11/1899;
F.O.58/316, Maxse to Salisbury no. 47 of 1/10/1898; R.Kol.A.3042, A.A. to Rose, no. 58
Confidential of 26/7/1898; ibid., Rose to the chancellor, nos. 72 and 78 of 6/9/1898 and
27/9/1898.
11 C.O.225/55, paper 17036, Sturdee's report of 1/6/1898, enclosure in Adm. to C.O.,
28/7/1898.
12 Sturdee memo (in the Sturdee Papers), undated, but clearly written after 1914 and
thus his view of Germany in this account seems coloured by a World War I atmosphere.
13 R.Kol.A.3042, Rose to the chancellor, no. 68 of 5/9/1898.
14 F.O.58/317, Maxse to Villiers (private), 1/11/1898; N.A.R.G.59, T-27, roll 24, Osborn
to S.D., no. 59 of 26/9/1898.

Berlin quickly made suggestions about his successor, it would clearly be months before Raffel was replaced and his strange and arbitrary actions continued to annoy Maxse and Chambers, neither of whom possessed large quantities of patience and tolerance. Indeed, the British consul argued that the presidency should be abolished altogether and the duties of that office taken over by the consular board.[15] Rose vigorously supported his countryman's actions and at one stage pressed for the abolition of the Samoan monarchy and its replacement by the president, an idea which the British and Americans bitterly opposed. By the end of the year, Rose was attacking Chambers as 'a corrupt judge and a dishonourable man', and the treaty officials were thus in no position to present a united front to the native discords which were rumbling under the surface.[16]

During that month, the German element in Samoa openly began to back Mata'afa's candidature. The old warrior chief was immensely popular and the clear choice of the majority of the Samoans—but since he was supported by the Tupua clan, he was automatically opposed by the Malietoa districts, who put forward instead the dead king's nineteen-year-old son, Tanu. This party was joined by Tamasese, who resented Mata'afa's great influence. Because of the German agitation for Mata'afa, Tanu immediately secured the affection of the Anglo-American community, although they did no campaigning for him. Both Osborn and Maxse recognized Mata'afa's qualities and believed him to be the best candidate, although they suspected the German backing for him.

Both parties having proclaimed their chief as king, having claimed for him the necessary four titles and having anointed him, the decision as to who really was king of Samoa was referred to a very reluctant chief justice, as the Final Act of Berlin directed. The court hearings by Chambers went ahead in late December, despite threats of action from the well-armed Mata'afan party should the verdict not be favourable to them, and despite the refusal of the Germans to promise to accept the decision. It was gradually becoming apparent that the phrase 'according to the laws and customs of Samoa' was useless when applied to a succession dispute: there were no laws and the customs clearly meant tribal warfare. On New Year's Eve, Chambers gave his ruling—Mata'afa's candidacy was invalid for he had been banned from the kingship at the

---

15 F.O.58/316, Maxse to Salisbury, no. 44 of 6/9/1898, with enclosures.
16 N.A.R.G.59, T-27, roll 25, Osborn to S.D., nos. 66 and 68 of 19/10/1898 and 29/10/1898; R.Kol.A.3042, Rose to the chancellor, no. 68 of 5/9/1898; F.O.58/317, Maxse to Salisbury, no. 70 of 24/12/1898.

special request of Bismarck in 1889, and the agreement on this formed part of the protocols to the Final Act of Berlin: Tanu, being the only other contender, was therefore adjudged to be king.[17]

The Germans and the Mata'afans exploded with rage at this, exclaiming that the protocols to the Final Act did not have the validity of that act; that Mata'afa had the support of the majority of the people; that Tanu did not have the requisite number of titles for the *Tafa'ifa*; and finally that Chambers himself had some months earlier declared that there was no objection to Mata'afa standing for the kingship. The British and American consuls, however, proclaiming that they were bound to accept the chief justice's decision, at least until the powers unanimously decided otherwise, inclined to accept Tanu as king. On the following afternoon the Mata'afans decided to settle the matter by force. Tanu's forces were outnumbered about two to one, and were soon retreating in confusion before their much stronger and better-led opponents. That evening Apia was in chaos, with firing going on continuously, bands of natives fighting in the street, and houses being plundered and burned. Early in the morning, Sturdee had Tanu and his vice-king Tamasese passed out to H.M.S. *Porpoise*. At a meeting of the consular and naval officers on the second, it was agreed that Sturdee would disarm the Tanu natives under his protection, the Germans would persuade the Mata'afans to cease hostilities, and terms of surrender would be arranged for the defeated natives on shore.

On 4 and 5 January, at further meetings of the consuls and naval officers, the British and Americans reluctantly agreed to join their German colleagues in recognizing Mata'afa and twelve of his chiefs as the provisional government with Raffel as their chief executive. However there would be no other changes from the regulations of the Berlin Act. With the followers of Tanu as refugees on board the *Porpoise* and the Mata'afans in absolute control of the island, there was little else that could be done if peace was to be restored.

Flushed with this success, the Germans affixed a notice on the court-house door on 6 January, declaring the building closed until further notice by the provisional government.

17 The chief justice's decision and the events of the turbulent first week of 1899 are covered in Adm. 116/97, Sturdee to Pearson, nos. 47 and 1 of 26/12/1898 and 10/1/1899; F.O.58/317, Maxse to Salisbury, no. 74 of 27/12/1898; F.O.58/326, same to same, tels. of 11/1/1899 and 12/1/1899; N.A.R.G., T-27, roll 25, Osborn to S.D., no. 77 of 23/1/1899; *Staatsarchiv* (1899), pp. 264-87. A more detailed account of the naval actions following can be found in P. M. Kennedy, 'The Royal Navy and the Samoan Civil War, 1898-1899' in *Canadian Journal of History*, vol. 5, no. 3 (March, 1970).

Claiming that Chambers had vacated his office by withdrawing to the British warship, Raffel also announced that he was now the new chief justice. This immediately provoked Chambers into calling upon the armed assistance of the *Porpoise* to help him reopen his court, which Sturdee was quite willing to offer. On the morning of the seventh, he asked for the co-operation of Captain Schoenfelder of the German vessel *Falke* which was moored nearby in Apia harbour, but this was quickly refused. Preparing for the worst, the *Porpoise* secretly loaded her guns in case the German ship should interfere, but in fact the *Falke* remained inactive.[18] The reopening party was led by the two consuls and the chief justice, followed by an armed group of sailors. The protesting German officials were thrust out of the way, the locks which Raffel had just put on the court-house were broken off, and the party entered the building, where it held a short meeting before retiring; their point had been clearly made for all in Samoa to see.

Relatively little happened in the following weeks, both because of the withdrawal of the rebel natives (which allowed the Tanu followers to return to Apia), and because Raffel left for San Francisco in mid-February. By March, however, the British activities in attempting to check Mata'afan depredations and recruitment were provoking those natives into prowling menacingly around Apia once again. This was the situation when, on 6 March, the heavy cruiser U.S.S. *Philadelphia* flying the flag of Rear-Admiral Kautz sailed into Apia harbour. His task was to protect American interests, but he had also been instructed to act in accordance with the views of the majority of the treaty officials if an emergency arose and the consuls were still divided. Kautz was a bluff authoritarian and not inclined to have South Sea islanders disputing his commands. After a few days of enquiries, he gave out his views at a meeting on 11 March of all the consular and naval officers, by declaring that the Berlin Act should be adhered to and that the provisional government should be dissolved; a proclamation to that effect was posted in Apia that day.[19]

There was little likelihood that the well-armed Mata'afans

18 This fact emerges from Sturdee's later account, and also from Beveridge to Thomson, 3/2/1899 in the Archives of the London Missionary Society, South Seas Letters (hereafter L.M.S./S.S.L.), Box 45.
19 The January-March period is covered in Adm. 116/97, Sturdee to Pearson, nos. 3, 6, 9, 14 and 16 of 23/1/1899, 7/2/1899, 20/2/1899, 7/3/1899 and 17/3/1899; F.O.58/326, Maxse to Salisbury, nos. 1-3 of 23/1/1899; F.O.58/328, Maxse to Salisbury, tels. of 7/3/1899 and 20/3/1899; N.A.R.G.59, T-27, roll 25, Osborn to S.D., nos. 77, 84, 86 and 90 of 23/1/1899, 13/2/1899, 18/2/1899 and 22/3/1899; R.Kol.A.3046, Rose to A.A., tel. no. 5 of 16/3/1899.

would accept Kautz's views in any case, but on 13 March the German consul added fuel to the fire by his counter-proclamation, in which he said Kautz's claims were 'absolutely untrue' and that he would continue to acknowledge the provisional government. This action, the rebel natives' disregard for the admiral's messages and, finally, their attempt on the following day to occupy Mulinu'u Point from their war canoes, provoked Kautz into hostilities. *Philadelphia* promptly opened fire on those vessels, forcing them to retreat along the coast; at the same time *Porpoise*, at Kautz's request, weighed anchor and proceeded to bombard several Mata'afan villages in the vicinity. Mata'afa's answer came that same evening with an attack upon the township, particularly upon the Tivoli Hotel. Rushing to their ramparts and other defensive positions, the bluejackets forced the attacking natives to withdraw but not before they had lost three of their own men. On 17 March, both American and British consulates were subjected to another fierce attack by the Mata'afans. Only one American sailor was killed in this action, but the sniping of the next few days wounded several others, and imposed a great strain upon everyone.

The bombardment of the coastal villages became a daily event from 16 March onwards while sorties were repeatedly made by landing parties led by Sturdee. By 23 March, the British and American forces felt strong enough to put into effect what they had been fighting for all this while, i.e., the chief justice's decision that Tanu was king of Samoa. At 2 p.m. on that day they set out along the coast to Mulinu'u, where the young king was crowned, toasts drunk in his honour, the Samoan flag raised, speeches made and gun-salutes fired. On the following day H.M.S. *Tauranga* under Captain Leslie Stuart arrived and he now became senior British naval officer.[20]

As the only immediate way of building up their strength to crush the rebels was to recruit additional friends, the warships were employed in trips to Savai'i and Tutuila from which hundreds of Tanu followers were brought back to Apia in order to be trained. On 30 March, Sturdee led a mixed Anglo-American force of ninety-one bluejackets, plus a hundred natives under Lieutenant Gaunt, in a prolonged sweep along the coastal roads, driving small numbers of rebel warriors before them. On the thirty-first, this tactic was

---

20 It is worth noting that the British government had declined to allow the C. in C. Australia Squadron himself to go to Samoa; it was more convenient for them if the angry Germans knew that an American admiral was directing these operations. See Villiers minute on Adm. to F.O., 31/3/1899, in F.O.58/329.

repeated in greater force. That these relatively small numbers of bluejackets were able to operate with virtual impunity against vastly larger forces was due to the rebel natives' respect for the white man and his better weapons, such as the machine-guns, and to the fact that they were fighting along the coastline and therefore covered by their warships. Yet such was the confidence of the Anglo-American troops that they had no hesitation in pursuing Mata'afan forces *inland* on 1 April when returning to Apia from another of their punitive raids along the coast. The result was a fierce attack upon this contingent by thousands of armed Mata'afans, who were angered by the destruction of their villages and eager to take advantage of the freedom offered by the absence of the warships. The casualties of this expedition, seven killed, were remarkably light considering the circumstances, but they included the three senior officers, and many others in the party were wounded.[21]

This disaster did not put an end to the Anglo-American 'punitive' raids, although later expeditions were always planned with more care: on the contrary, it tightened the resolve of both navies to finish the job. Shellings and sorties continued unabated, and both sides attempted to recruit support from the other islands of the group; but on 21 April H.M.S. *Torch* arrived from Sydney, bringing the news to Maxse and Stuart that the whole matter was to be settled by an international commission which would shortly reach Samoa and that, pending their arrival, a cease-fire should be arranged. This news did not mean the end of the fighting, for the Americans had no instructions to attempt a cease-fire and, in any case, the Mata'afan forces were still very active. Hostilities continued for a further few days. On 25 April, just as the Anglo-American forces with their native allies were preparing another raid, word was brought to Apia that Mata'afa had agreed to withdraw to the cease-fire lines prescribed by the navies. Enforcing the truce proved to be almost as arduous as waging war itself and alarms were common during the days following, but hostilities were virtually at a standstill when the commissioners, transported from San Francisco by U.S.S. *Badger*, finally arrived on 13 May. At this the conflict ceased altogether.[22]

21 The military operations from 11 March—1 April are covered in Adm. 116/97, Sturdee to Stuart, no. 18 and Stuart to Pearson, no. 32, enclosure in Pearson to Adm., no. 138 of 17/4/1899; N.A.R.G.45, Subject File VI, Box 641, *Report of Affairs in Samoa by Rear Admiral Albert Kautz, U.S. Navy, to the Secretary of the Navy—March 6th to May 18th* 1899.

22 Ibid.; Adm. 116/97, Stuart to Pearson, nos. 35, 40, 44, 50 and 53 of 14/4/1899, 26/4/1899, 3/5/1899, 12/5/1899 and 30/5/1899.

The underlying cause of the Samoan civil war of 1899 lay undoubtedly with the faulty phraseology of the Berlin Act, which did not take into account the basically unstable nature of Samoan politics. The future course of the kingship could not be determined by reference to the few trite sentences of the act. If Chambers' decision in favour of Tanu was judicially irrefutable (and this the Germans strongly questioned) it was disastrous politically: Mata'afa was always a far stronger and more impressive candidate than his young rival. His authority was so great that he did not need to engage in the fighting at all. The immediate cause of the war, however, was the split between the treaty officials. The arbitrary actions and open bias of the Germans for Mata'afa in the weeks prior to the judgement, and their refusal to accept—if only temporarily—the decision of the supreme court, enraged the other nationalities. But mistakes were clearly made upon the Anglo-American side also. Sturdee was, to put it bluntly, 'trigger-happy'. Maxse also erred, not only by reporting to London too rosy a picture of Tanu's side, but also by participating in the fighting. Chambers lacked the tact and insensitivity to criticism which his difficult post required. Finally, Kautz's decision to depose the provisional government and to open hostilities against the Mata'afans was as politically rash as the naval actions were militarily pointless. Only Osborn kept his head, although he felt bound to oppose the Germans and Mata'afans after they had disregarded Chambers' decision. But working against his calming influence were a host of petty intriguers and agitators upon both sides, and the period January—April 1899 was consequently as full of political quarrels as it was of military actions. *Furor Consularis* had returned for a second time to the Samoan islands, and it became once again the task of the diplomats to straighten the situation out.

ii *Diplomatic Repercussions of the War*

Of the kaiser's personal wish to see Samoa attached to the German Empire there can be little doubt. This distant island group appeared to him to crystallize many of his own hopes and beliefs about Germany's colonial expansion, her future *Flottenpolitik* and the need to please the public by securing this most popular object of their desires. It was hardly surprising, therefore, that the group should be included in the list of territorial compensations sent to Hatzfeldt in June 1898 and repeatedly mentioned by Berlin during the

Portuguese colonies discussions.[23] It was hardly surprising, too, that Salisbury's refusal to consider a British withdrawal from the islands on account of Australasian opinion infuriated the kaiser. 'The brazen scoundrel!' Wilhelm noted, believing that the prime minister was using 'either the feelings at home or in this or that Cape or Colony, in order to give us the slip!'[24] An appreciation of the British government's difficulties with public opinion was not one of the kaiser's strong points.

No sooner had Samoa been dropped out of these African negotiations than it arose again with the news that the United States intended to erect a coaling station at Pago-Pago. Thereupon, Wilhelm demanded that Washington be queried about this scheme and, if the Americans persisted in it, that Germany should proceed to erect a similar station in her own treaty port of Saluafata; but as Holleben insisted that the former course would sharpen American suspicion and as Richthofen pointed out that the latter would only complicate the situation in Samoa itself, it was decided to sound out Salisbury once again as to Germany and the United States dividing the islands while England withdrew and took Tonga. The news of Malietoa's death and possible complications in Samoa reinforced this decision and Hatzfeldt was instructed to take action accordingly, despite his own doubts.[25]

These doubts soon proved justified. Finding Balfour still in charge of foreign affairs, Hatzfeldt broached the matter with him on 1 and 2 September and laid particular stress upon the fact that Salisbury had been in favour of such a partition scheme ten years previously. But the acting foreign secretary did not dare become involved in this delicate question and contented himself with promising to tell Salisbury of the German proposals. Already the Australasian newspapers were publishing alarmist reports of an intended coup by Berlin, and Hatzfeldt reported that the *Morning Post* had strongly attacked the idea of Germany obtaining Upolu. Nevertheless, Bülow requested the ambassador to persist in his soundings, but his optimism was soon shattered when Salisbury learnt of these talks, for Hatzfeldt was then coldly informed that a partition could not be discussed.[26] Moreover, the prime

23 G.P., 14/1, nos. 3806, 3835 and 3836.

24 A.A./*England* 78 *nr.* 1 *Secr.*, vol. 4, minutes on Richthofen to Eulenburg, tel. no. 22 of 20/7/1898. (These comments were omitted from *Grosse Politik*, see G.P., 14/1, no. 3835.)

25 A.A./*Südsee-Inseln* 5, vol. 1, Holleben to A.A., tels. nos. 81 and 86 of 9/8/1798 and 17/8/1898, with kaiser's comments thereon; ibid., Richthofen to Bülow, no. 20 of 17/8/1898, and Richthofen to the kaiser, 21/8/1898; G.P., 14/2, nos. 4028-30.

26 A.A./*Südsee-Inseln* 5, vol. 1, Hatzfeldt to A.A., tel. no. 242 of 1/9/1898, and Hatzfeldt to the chancellor, no. 607 of 31/8/1898; ibid., Kempermann (Sydney) to the chancellor, no. 194 of 29/7/1898; G.P., 14/2, nos. 4031-34; F.O.58/316, Balfour to Lascelles, no. 198A Confidential of 2/9/1898.

minister did not take too kindly to the ambassador's reminders
of his previous compliance over Samoa. That Samoa-Tonga
deal, he minuted, was made 'in reference to the possibility
of a larger arrangement. It has no application to the circumstances of the present day'.[27] It was a further illustration of
the fact that Salisbury had used the group as a diplomatic
pawn in his bid to obtain Bismarck's friendship in the late
1880s, and also that he regarded Anglo-German relations as
having changed radically since then.

As the Fashoda crisis loomed nearer and the possibility
of a war with France arose, the prime minister had little
time for German pesterings about the islands. 'Samoa must
wait until more important people are served', he ordered.[28]
During the confrontation on the upper Nile, and because
events in the group itself were relatively quiescent while the
Samoans were discussing the candidates for the kingship,
Samoa slipped again onto the backstage. Wilhelm's interest
also swung to the Anglo-French confrontation, which he
firmly believed would lead to a war, during which Germany's
position would be strengthened. On the one hand he told the
Russians that he would stay neutral if the continent went to
war with England, on the other hand he assured Lascelles
that the British could easily beat the French but that Germany
would intervene should London be opposed by Russia also.
Doubtless his wish was to see France weakened militarily,
while perhaps picking up compensations later from London
for his neutrality.[29] The settlement of the Fashoda question
without a war bitterly disappointed the kaiser and he let
these feelings be known when criticizing the Russian foreign
minister, Muraviev, for advising Paris to give way. At the
same time, the German press was instructed to point out to
the French what an unreliable ally Russia had proved to be.[30]

Wilhelm's actions served only to increase suspicion of
Germany in London and to further Salisbury's determination
to avoid armed conflict with France, if that were at all possible.
'The one object of the German Emperor since he has been on
the throne has been to get us into a war with France' he had
told Balfour earlier in 1898.[31] Victoria was also incensed at
the 'systematic and hardly concealed attempts' of the kaiser

27 Ibid., Salisbury's minute on same.
28 Ibid., minute on Gosselin memo of 10/10/1898.
29 G.P., 14/2, chap. 93; L. Bittner, 'Neue Beiträge zur Haltung Kaiser Wilhelm II in
der Faschoda Frage' in *Historische Zeitschrift* 162 (1940); Langer, *Diplomacy of Imperialism*,
pp. 566-70; Sanderson, *Upper Nile*, p. 363; 'Die englisch-deutsch Annäherung im Jahre
1898' in *Berliner Monatshefte*, II (1933) translated from *Krasny Archiv*.
30 *Briefe Wilhelm II an den Zaren*, pp. 63-68; G.P., 14/2, marginal comment on no. 3938.
31 Addit.Mss.49691 (Balfour Papers), Salisbury to Balfour, 9/4/1898.

to set Britain against the Dual Alliance, and both she and Salisbury agreed that Wilhelm, while wishing to keep Anglo-German relations upon a good footing, was never pleased when Britain became friendly with Russia.[32] Upon the German side, it was found 'agreeable' that France had been humiliated and that many Frenchmen appeared to regard Britain instead of Germany as the natural foe, although the boost to British prestige was regretted. Wilhelm also appreciated more than ever that Germany must possess a large fleet if she was going to play an important role in overseas matters and if she hoped to avoid the humiliation which France had been forced to accept.[33]

Neither side was in a particularly trusting mood, therefore, when the first news of the disturbances in Samoa reached Europe in mid-January 1899. After reading Chambers and Maxse's telegrams, which blamed the entire troubles upon German intrigues, Victoria sent Salisbury repeated messages that the 'atrocious' conduct of Rose must be strongly protested against and she remained dissatisfied with the prime minister's calming assurances.[34] At this stage, Berlin's annoyance was much slighter and the sole concern there was to prevent this affair from assuming too large proportions in Anglo-German relations. This desire was possibly strengthened by the German unease at reports of the progress of Anglo-Russian negotiations over China, which could not only restrict the 'Free Hand' policy and Britain's dependence upon Germany but might also make the Yangtse Valley a British sphere of influence.[35]

When the matter was broached with the British ambassador, Lascelles, on 20 January, the German viewpoint was quite mild. If Chambers had made an impolitic decision, then Rose and Raffel had also erred by attempting to replace the chief justice, and the German consul was promptly told of this. Naturally, Berlin could not resist this opportunity of pointing out once again to the British how unworkable the Samoan tridominium was and how necessary a partition appeared to be. This hint, however, fell upon deaf ears. The Colonial Office refused to hear of such a thing; in fact, they were advocating the annexation of Tonga at this time 'so that

32 Salisbury Papers, Class F, Victoria to Salisbury, 29/1/1899 and 1/2/1899; *Letters of Queen Victoria*, Third series, 3, pp. 340-41.
33 BA, Bülow papers, vol. 22, Mumm to Bülow (copy), 10/11/1898; G.P., 14/2, comments on no. 3926.
34 Salisbury Papers, Class F, Victoria to Salisbury, 18/1/1899 and 29/1/1899; ibid., A83/129, Victoria to Salisbury, 19/1/1899; ibid., A84/94, Salisbury to Victoria, 19/1/1899.
35 A.A./*England* 83, vol. 4, Radolin to chancellor, nos. 498 and 505 of 19/12/1898 and 21/12/1898, and kaiser's remarks thereon; A.A./*China 20 nr. I Secr.*, vol. 59, Lichnowsky (private) letter of 24/1/1899 and kaiser's comments thereon.

Germany would no longer be in a position to offer us what was really ours or at any rate none of hers for our interests in Samoa'. Chamberlain himself, feeling that 'We certainly must not do anything to break the present 'entente' between the U.S. and ourselves', disliked the idea of Anglo-German talks just then and he told the Foreign Office that Australasian opinion would not allow Britain to let the strategically-important Samoan group fall into German hands.[36] While the Colonial Office was prepared to give Germany only the rather worthless Gilbert and Ellice Islands if she would withdraw from Samoa, Bülow was secretly considering such a withdrawal —but only if the British handed over New Guinea, the Gilberts and a coaling station in Malaya![37]

A more important reason for the very conciliatory nature of this approach to Britain was Berlin's worry about complications with the United States, where rumours that Germany was secretly helping the Filipino rebels had increased the American press agitation. Moreover, the forthcoming meat inspection bill and fruit controls, which the German agrarians pressed for, was arousing great annoyance in American trading circles, who strongly advocated retaliatory measures. Articles, such as the one headlined 'Is a Clash coming with Germany?', which the New York *Herald* printed on 13 January, were a source of great concern to Bülow, who noted 'We must maintain the Carolines (but) stay far away from the Philippines. The U.S.A. would indeed go to war over the Philippines; over Samoa and the Carolines, only when the bitterness in America against us raises itself to even more incongruous levels.' Some years later he believed that February 1899 had seen the high point of German-American antagonism.[38] Thus, both he and Holstein as well as the kaiser urged the British government to use its supposedly great influence at Washington to secure better German-American relations, arguing that it could hardly be in London's own interests to see her two natural friends quarrelling among themselves. Salisbury's reply to this was non-committal, however, and gave Berlin little hope for his support.[39]

The United States government was indeed annoyed at the

36 C.O.225/57, Anderson and Chamberlain minutes on paper 1480, F.O. to C.O., 18/1/1899; R.Kol.A.3043, Bülow to Rose, tel. no. 1 of 20/1/1899; B.D., 1, nos. 128-30.

37 C.O.225/57, C.O. minutes on paper 1746. F.O. to C.O., 20/1/1899; of Bülow memo of 21/1/1899 in A.A./*Südsee-Inseln* 5, vol. 1.

38 A.A./*U.S.A.* 16, vol. 3, Bülow to Hatzfeldt, no. 37 of 17/1/1899; ibid., vol. 4, copy of *New York Herald* of 13/1/1899, and many others; A.A./*Südsee-Inseln* 5, vol. 1, Bülow memo, 21/1/1899; Bülow, *Deutsche Politik*, p. 47.

39 Salisbury Papers, A122/55, Hatzfeldt to Salisbury, 22/1/1899, and A122/56, Salisbury to Hatzfeldt, 23/1/1899; F.O.64/1469, Lascelles to Salisbury, no. 15 Secret of 20/1/1899; G.P., 14/2, nos. 4035-37.

news, passed on by the British embassy, of the forcible rejection of Chambers' decision by the Mata'afans and the Germans. The *Philadelphia* was ordered to proceed to Apia immediately, and to follow the majority decision of the consuls. Hay informed White that the president felt the troubles had been chiefly caused 'through the ill-considered and officious conduct of Dr Raffel, aided and seconded by the German Consul-General Mr. Rose'. Their actions, the despatch continued, 'were reprehensible and indefensible in the extreme'.[40] However, the ambassador preferred to give this protest verbally and in doing so he considerably toned down Hay's very stiff language. Moreover, Bülow was falsely informed by a private source that the United States was willing to withdraw from the group, which caused hopes to rise in Berlin that Salisbury's obstructive attitude towards a partition could be circumvented.[41] The pliable White was therefore sounded out upon this scheme but even he was shrewd enough to pinpoint for his superiors the real reasons behind the German proposals.

> It is very clear to me that the dearest wish of the Emperor's heart and, of course, of Minister von Bülow who stands nearer to him in such matters than does any other person, is to add to the territories of the Empire in the Pacific, thus widening German commerce and giving a *raison d'être* for a fleet.[42]

Although the German suggestions received no answer and Hay had informed the British that he would not consider them until the local difficulties were solved, Bülow persisted in this course throughout February, raising the scheme on several occasions with White. On the American side, however, communications were restricted to a defence of their consul and the chief justice against the German complaints. Nevertheless, Berlin believed that the high point in German-American bitterness had passed after Bülow's very conciliatory speech to the Reichstag on 11 February, during which he denied that Germany had been anything other than strictly neutral during the Spanish-American war and attacked those who attempted to cause bad blood between Berlin and Washington.[43] It was a theme which government-influenced

40   N.A.R.G.59, M-77, roll 71, Hay to White, 24/1/1899.

41   F.O.58/316, Villiers minute on U.S. Embassy communication of 11/2/1899; G.P., 14/2, no. 4039.

42   N.A.R.G.59, M-44, roll 87, White to S.D., 25/1/1899.

43   Ibid., same to same, 27/1/1899, 9/2/1899 and 20/2/1899; N.A.R.G.59, M-58, Roll T-27, German Embassy memos of 4/2/1899, 15/2/1899 (2) and 18/2/1899; N.A.R.G.59, M-99, roll 33, Hay to Holleben, 7/2/1899 and 8/2/1899. For Hay's view over a partition, see F.O.115/1130, Pauncefote to Salisbury, tel. no. 5 of 21/1/1899. For Bülow's speech, see *Fürst Bülow's Reden*, ed., J. Penzler and D. Hötzsch, 3 vols. (Berlin, 1907-09), 1, pp. 40-51.

papers such as the *Kölnische Zeitung* had already taken up, and fierce attacks were launched upon Reuter and the Associated Press for their biased news coverage. Moreover, a certain Dr Haedicke was appointed to work for the Wolff's Bureau in New York to combat this anti-German propaganda, while Dr Witte, a member of the embassy in Washington, was given a similar task and busied himself with writing to various American newspapers. Although this helped their case somewhat, the greater part of the press still regarded Germany with suspicion and Pauncefote, the British ambassador, sarcastically reported that Holleben was 'making comical efforts to win the U.S. over to the German side in the Samoa complications and has met with nothing but snubs.'[44]

The Germans continued to be disappointed in Salisbury's cool attitude to the whole affair. Like the Americans, he refused to accept Berlin's criticism of the chief justice's decision and their defence of Rose's actions, at least not until fuller reports from Maxse had arrived in London. Hatzfeldt's report that the prime minister had agreed with Bülow that all the treaty officials had erred was promptly and sharply denied. More disheartening still was Salisbury's refusal to consider any British withdrawal from the group. Tonga had no value for England, he declared, and while affairs in Samoa were bad they would have to become much worse before Australia would recognize the necessity for a partition. With the prime minister in this mood and his regard for Australian opinion made very obvious, the ambassador could only repeat the suggestion that the Americans be persuaded to agree to a Samoan partition first of all.[45]

Hatzfeldt approached the subject in a more indirect manner on 23 February, when he attempted to convince the prime minister that all powers of the world were in need of allies. Recognizing this as a German opening bid to discuss London's dependence upon Berlin's friendship, Salisbury stoutly maintained that the time for alliances in general was past. He also added that Britain would only accede to a partition arrangement if she obtained the main island of Upolu. Annoyed at this intransigence, Hatzfeldt recommended that Berlin should try to give the impression that Franco-German friendship was not impossible. To Holstein's naïve questions as to whether the prime minister could be circumvented by other members of the Cabinet or whether Cecil Rhodes

44 A.A./*Europa Gen.* 86 *Secr.*, vol. 9, A.A. to Holleben, nos. 14 and A13 of 25/1/1899 and 31/1/1899; ibid., Holleben to chancellor, A32 of 11/2/1899; Salisbury Papers A140/15, Pauncefote to Salisbury, 17/3/1899.

45 F.O.58/327, Salisbury to Lascelles, tel. no. 14 of 1/2/1899; G.P., 14/2, no. 4040.

could exert his influence in the matter, the ambassador was quite pessimistic.[46]

In the event, his pessimism proved justified. Rhodes was visiting Berlin in March 1899 in order to obtain permission to extend British telegraph and railway lines northwards through German East Africa as part of his Cape-to-Cairo schemes. Since this proposal also promised to further the economic development of the German colony itself and was advocated by governor Liebert, it received the support of the German government. But this cannot adequately explain the enthusiastic reception which the kaiser gave to Rhodes, whom he had considered as little more than a brigand three years earlier. With grandiose utterances about world empires and Germany's future, and especially with a 'judicious use of the blessed word Mesopotamia', this businessman-cum-politician completely won over Wilhelm. By the end of his visit, the telegraph arrangement was secured and the kaiser was openly saying that he wished that Rhodes was his prime minister, a remark which must have irritated Bülow considerably.[47]

However, the hopes of the *Auswärtiges Amt* that Rhodes possessed sufficient influence over the government in London to produce a change of mind in their Samoan policy were misplaced, and it soon became clear that Rhodes had little influence over Chamberlain and none at all over Salisbury. Nor did he succeed in persuading the British government to drop its opposition to the German requests for permission to alter radically its telegraphic cable lines to North America. These requests, which involved an abandonment of the use of British cables by Germany in an attempt to lessen her dependence upon Britain for her communication with the United States, led to years of quarrelling between the two governments and the matter is too complex and voluminous to allow anything other than a brief mention of them at this point, where it became momentarily involved with the Samoan dispute. Sufficient to note that Salisbury rejected Rhodes' pressure, minuting: 'I rather flinch from the idea of selling one British trader (the cables companies) in order to promote the speculations of another' (Rhodes).[48]

---

46 Ibid., nos. 4043-46; B.D., 1, no. 132.
47 A.A./*Afrika Gen.* 13 *nr.* 1, vol. 1, Bülow and Irmer memos of 13/2/1899 and 9/3/1899 respectively; London Embassy records, Bülow to Hatzfeldt (private), 22/3/1899; F.O. 800/6 (Lascelles Papers), Bertie to Lascelles, 1/3/1899; F.O.800/17, Lascelles to Bertie 17/3/1899; F.O.800/170 (Bertie Papers), Lascelles to Bertie, 4/3/1899 and 15/3/1899, and Bertie to Salisbury, 8/3/1899; F.O.244/578, Lascelles to Salisbury, no. 13 Africa, Very Confidential, of 10/3/1899.
48 Minute on Brodrick memo of 17/3/1899 in F.O.64/1516. This volume, and nos. 1517 and 1571 cover the Anglo-German negotiations upon the Atlantic cables in great detail.

Apart from these private negotiations in Berlin, Samoa was hardly discussed during almost the whole of March. Salisbury bent his entire energies towards achieving a final agreement over the Nile watershed and towards preventing the clash over the French attempt to obtain a coaling station at Muscat from reaching serious proportions. He was also seeking to clinch the Anglo-Russian agreement regarding railway spheres in China and since all these matters were much more important to him than the periodic internal troubles of Samoa, he made no move upon the subject.[49] Brodrick, the parliamentary under-secretary, wrote disapprovingly of this negative attitude: 'I cannot get Lord Salisbury to take a strong line about Samoa. I think it will come to partition in some form but this is not favoured here.'[50]

Upon the German side, too, matters were fairly quiet, although Bülow was very keen to get all the officials withdrawn from Samoa. Even if the other powers could not be persuaded to agree to a partition of the group, it was not dissatisfying to Berlin to know that a chief backed by German influence was in charge in Samoa. Germany's general position also appeared to be very satisfactory, and rumours of a lasting Anglo-Russian agreement over China were now discounted. The sole disturbing factors were the disputes with the United States, which Bülow hoped to avoid by an amicable commercial agreement and by avoiding arousing American suspicion with any rash moves in the Philippines and Samoa; and the Anglo-American entente, which existed despite the conflicting policies of those two nations over a variety of issues in the western hemisphere. Germany's task was therefore to avoid clashes with either power, since these drove it closer towards the other. All in all, however, things looked good.[51]

This attitude of complacency and self-satisfaction was rudely shattered by the incoming flood of news about the fighting in Samoa. Already, by 16 March, Berlin had learnt that Kautz had instructions to act according to majority decisions should that prove to be necessary. At this, Bülow clearly feared a further deterioration in German-American relations and warned Hay that an 'incorrect' action by Kautz could bring about 'an unfavourable reaction as regards the more general relations': at London, he begged for Salisbury's support. Worried most of all about the roars of protest which would come from the kaiser and the colonial pressure groups

49 B.D., 1, chaps. 1, 4 and 5; B. C. Busch, *Britain and the Persian Gulf*, 1894-1914 (Berkeley/Los Angeles, 1967), pp. 63-93.
50 Curzon Papers, Vol. 10a, Brodrick to Curzon, 3/3/1899.
51 G.P., 14/1, no. 3778.

if German influence and interests in Samoa were undermined by Anglo-American armed action, Bülow pressed for the immediate despatch to the group of an impartial, all-powerful investigating commission, a suggestion first made by Pauncefote somewhat earlier.[52]

In London, Hatzfeldt sought to obtain Chamberlain's help in the affair, hinting that a rash step by the two navies would so enrage public opinion in Germany that her government 'would be unable to maintain its hitherto friendly attitude towards England'.[53] The colonial minister laid all the blame upon the German consul, however, and emphasized that Britain would never accept a partition which did not give her Upolu; and that all Germany would receive for completely withdrawing would be the Gilbert Islands. Moreover, Salisbury left the Foreign Office for a holiday in the south of France near the end of March without giving an answer to the German suggestion, for he was waiting first to learn of Washington's reaction to it. As Sanderson noted, the prime minister was surveying 'the whole question with the most complete calm': he had, after all, borne German pesterings and proposals about Samoa intermittently for fourteen years and was not inclined to get excited about them now.[54]

On 29 March, with the arrival in Berlin of a Reuter's message about the fighting and shellings, the matter suddenly became more serious. By the following day, many German newspapers were violently criticizing the Anglo-American actions, and the right-wing *Deutsche Tageszeitung* appealed wildly for an alliance with the Boers and with Russia against England. Many of these vitriolic attacks were directed against the German government itself, including one by the *Deutsche Zeitung* on the following day, which stung Bülow to the quick by castigating his foreign policy in comparison with Bismarck's. Fearing great unpopularity at home and complications abroad, Bülow also cabled the press bureau that 'The tone of our official press over Samoa must be firm, calm and clear: otherwise the country will not know what to make of us.' Hammann's efforts, catalogued in a special report to Bülow, deserve quotation:

> Before all else, the main thing is to prevent a useless and damaging raging against America and England and resentful expressions against

52	F.O.58/328, German Embassy memos of 20/3/1899 and 23/3/1899; ibid., Lascelles to Salisbury tel. no. 5 of 22/3/1899; F.O.58/329, Salisbury to Lascelles, no. 57A of 27/3/1899; N.A.R.G.59, M-58, Roll T-28, German Embassy memos of 20/3/1899, 22/3/1899 and 25/3/1899; N.A.R.G.59, M-44, roll 87, White to Hay, tel. of 24/3/1899; R.Kol.A.3046, to A.A., tel. no. 5, received 16/3/1899; ibid., A.A. to Holleben, tel. no. 50 of 24/3/1899.
53	G.P., 14/2, no. 4049.
54	F.O.800/9, Sanderson to Lascelles, 29/3/1899.

this government in the serious press. (Bülow: 'yes') In the evening papers, the *Berliner Neueste Nachrichten*, *National Zeitung* and *Lokal-Anzeiger* already bring calm and moderately-held commentary. ('very good') Today these have been joined by the *Kölnische Zeitung*, *Hannoverscher Kurier*, *Vossische Zeitung* and *Frankfurter Zeitung* (herein enclosed). The *Kölnische Zeitung* article was drafted by me and will be cabled today to London and New York. The memory of Kiautchou is once again recalled in the *Hannoverscher Korrespondent*. ('good') Today's morning paper, the *Hamburger Korrespondent*, will have received from America a hopefully good article, which has not yet been given out here ('yes'); it should equally refer to Kiautchou, and should point to the new Chinese expedition as a justification of our lack of ships at Apia. ('good') This will be also done in the *Kölnische Volkszeitung* and through reports about violence against Germans in Shantung given out in the meantime . . . In further handling of the press, once the difficulties of the Samoan situation are correctly appreciated, the inadequacy of our sea power should above all be brought to attention even more.[55]

Despite these endeavours of his press bureau, Bülow realized that the matter demanded immediate diplomatic attention also. The kaiser was incensed at the news, calling it 'entirely unheard of'. Ships of the Royal Navy, of which service he was a proud admiral of the fleet, had joined those insolent 'Yankees' in shooting at German property and damaging her consulate! Doubtless his currently painful lumbago, and the fact that he was at this time much in the company of Tirpitz and other naval officers, did not alleviate his irritation with the British.[56] Bülow therefore ordered that London be informed 'that the further behaviour of England precisely in the Samoa matter will be of decisive and far-reaching importance for the political relations between England and Germany.'[57]

On 31 March, Berlin received news of McKinley's 'surprise and deep regret' at the reported collision and his assent to the German proposition to send a commission to Samoa. With America apparently eager to placate Berlin, German anger at the British government redoubled: in Holstein's words, London was regarded as 'the centre of the Samoan evil'. Bülow considered that in the fighting England had driven and the United States been driven, and that Salisbury was trying to cause trouble between the governments of Washington and Berlin in the hope of becoming the *tertius gaudens*—a place Germany reserved for herself. If satisfaction was not achieved, then the kaiser should withdraw Hatzfeldt from

55   These press articles and the angry marginalia of Bülow upon them are in A.A./ *Südsee-Inseln* 5, vol. 2, Hammann memo for Bülow, 31/3/1899, with enclosures.
56   Ibid., Richthofen to Bülow, tel. no. 5 of 31/3/1899; R.Kol.A.3047, Wilhelm's minutes on A.A. to the kaiser, 30/3/1899.
57   Ibid., Bülow to A.A., tel. no. 1 of 29/3/1899; of G.P., 14/2, no. 4052; B.D., 1, no.134.

London. Once again, the need for a powerful navy had been shown. (Wilhelm: 'What I have been continually preaching to those oxen in the Reichstag for ten years.') Moreover, the German press was to avoid attacks upon the United States and to focus instead upon Britain's intransigence, while Holleben was to attempt to wean the Americans away from the British.[58]

Perceiving the way matters were going in Berlin, Lascelles appealed for conciliation to be shown in London and perhaps also for an expression of regret similar to McKinley's, pointing out 'that the extreme importance which the emperor and the German public attach to Samoa did not appear to be fully realised in England'. Wilhelm, he reported, was 'highly incensed' at the whole question, while Bülow might be forced to adopt a policy less friendly to Britain.[59] The ambassador's urgings were, however, ignored. Being on holiday, Salisbury failed to grasp the urgency of the situation and he was in any case resentful of the German pressure. Feeling that German officials had provoked the entire troubles and that McKinley had only apologized because it was a faulty shell from U.S.S. *Philadelphia* that had struck the German consulate, the prime minister declined to cable any expressions of regret. Moreover, he would only agree to a commission which would make majority decisions and he opposed the idea of a joint and unanimous report, since it would 'enable the Germans to prevent a free and full expression of opinion either as to the past or the future on the part of the other two.' And when Lascelles reported on 3 April that Bülow had declared that many in Germany believed that Britain and America were seeking to drive her out of Samoa, Salisbury replied with a very stiff note which sharply criticized the German consul.[60]

Although the kaiser became infuriated and believed that Hatzfeldt should be immediately sent on holiday as a sign that Germany regarded full diplomatic relations with Britain as being useless and unnecessary, Bülow preferred instead to increase the pressure upon Salisbury, particularly by drawing the Americans upon their side. It proved to be a fierce struggle of wills. The state secretary dared not relax his demands, since the arrival of further reports in Berlin about the crowning of Tanu, the shell damage to the German consulate and the

58 Holstein Papers, vol. 5, Holstein to Hatzfeldt, 1/4/1899; A.A./*Südsee-Inseln* 5, vol. 2, Bülow to A.A., 3/4/1898; R.Kol.A.3047, A.A. to Holleben, tel. no. 64 of 3/4/1899; G.P., 14/2, nos. 4053-54.
59 Salisbury Papers, A121/24, Lascelles to Salisbury, 31/3/1899; B.D., 1, nos. 135 and 136.
60 Salisbury Papers, Class E, Salisbury to Sanderson, tel. of 2/4/1899; F.O.800/9, Sanderson to Lascelles, 4/4/1899; F.O.58/329, Lascelles to F.O., tel. no. 10 of 3/4/1899; B.D., 1, no. 137.

arrest of several Germans upon suspicion of helping the Mata'afans had enraged all of the press. The false rumour that Kautz had threatened the German cruiser *Falke* unless it moved out of Apia harbour so worried the naval authorities in Berlin that an enquiry was called for; and, if Bülow's account is to be believed, Tirpitz at that time thought that Britain and America were trying to cripple the German navy before it could emerge as a threat to them.[61] For twelve days, therefore, the German government pressed the British to agree to a commission which could only act by unanimous decision: anything less would have made them too open to the criticism that they were allowing themselves to be outvoted. Yet the prime minister continued to raise objections and alterations to the proposed outline of the commission's tasks and declined to be hurried. By 12 April, Bülow felt that he could stand it no more: Hatzfeldt was told that he was temporarily to break off relations with Britain if he judged that Salisbury would not accede to their wishes.[62] Almost immediately afterwards, however, Lascelles informed the *Auswärtiges Amt* that the prime minister had regretfully agreed to unanimous decision, the result of which he felt would be 'of little value': and Holstein rushed off a telegram to the ambassador in London, instructing him not to deliver the ultimatum.[63] The crisis was over, at least momentarily, although Salisbury was very bitter, cabling testily afterwards that

> the tone of menace adopted by Count Hatzfeldt and the German M.F.A. (Bülow) seem to me very much out of place. We have as much right as any other power to consider carefully the results of our words and actions in a position of serious difficulty.[64]

Salisbury's attitude to the German worries had been certainly very lackadaisical, not to say derogatory. Although his absence from London partly explains this, there were perhaps other reasons for his unconcern. Brodrick privately felt that 'He thought he could get U.S. and Germany to

61 BA/MA 233, PG93995, *Pressangelegenheiten*, vol. 1, Admiralstab to R.M.A., 19/4/1899 and 8/5/1899; BA, Bülow Papers, vol. 154, Zettelnotizen; see also B. v. Bülow, *Denkwürdigkeiten*, 4 Vols. (Berlin 1930), 1, p. 283.

62 On this, see especially F.O.83/1907, F.O. tels. nos. 5-37 to Salisbury, 30/3/1899-15/4/1899; F.O.58/329 in its entirety; F.O.800/9, Villiers to Lascelles, 5/4/1899 and 12/4/1899; F.O.800/17, Lascelles to Sanderson, 7/4/1899, and Lascelles to Villiers, 8/4/1899; A.A./*Südsee-Inseln* 5, vol. 2, Hatzfeldt to A.A., tel. no. 60 of 1/4/1899 with kaiser's angry marginalia (missing from G.P., 14/2, no. 4055); ibid., Hatzfeldt to A.A., tels. nos. 69 and 77 of 6/4/1899 and 12/4/1899; G.P., 14/2, nos. 4055-64; B.D., 1, no. 138.

63 F.O.244/583, Lascelles to Bülow, 12/4/1899; London Embassy records, Holstein to Hatzfeldt (private), 12/4/1899.

64 Salisbury Papers, Class E, Salisbury to Sanderson, 13/4/1899.

knock their heads together and keep us out of the line of fire'[65]—a view Berlin also took. Such an interpretation is possible, but Sanderson was probably nearer the mark when he wrote: 'Hatzfeldt is constantly asking why Lord S. does not move quicker. The real answer which however it is rather difficult to give is that Lord S. always declined to regard the question as having any serious importance or requiring any great hurry.'[66] The staff of the Foreign Office, pestered daily by a near-frantic ambassador and unable themselves to comprehend many of the prime minister's stylistic modifications, were also glad to see the matter of the commission settled. No one, however, thought that it meant the end of the affair. As the French ambassador in Berlin shrewdly noted, 'England has given way; but with enough bad grace as it seems, and perhaps the last word is not yet said.'[67]

iii   *Relations with America and the Work of the Samoan Commission*

The immediate task of the Samoan commission was to undertake the provisional government of the islands. To effect this, it was to exercise supreme authority over all the treaty officials, consuls and naval officers, each commissioner being responsible for his own nationals. Each action taken had to be unanimously agreed upon, and they also had to 'consider the provisions which they may think necessary for the future Government of the islands or for the modification of final Act of Berlin'.[68]

These few sentences, simple in appearance, were, as mentioned previously, the result of some twelve days of argument between Salisbury and the German government: for it was not merely upon the question of unanimity, but upon many smaller technical and legal details, that the prime minister raised objections. He firmly refused to forbid further military actions should the naval commanders deem such to be necessary for defensive purposes, and he declined the German suggestion of disarming the natives since he believed that this would only benefit the rebels. Moreover although Bülow was very eager to replace all five officials in Samoa and urged this upon the British government many

65 Curzon Papers, Box 10a, Brodrick to Curzon, 14/4/1899: see also B.D., 3, pp. 423ff.
66 F.O.800/9, Sanderson to Lascelles, 12/4/1899. See also his letter of 29/4/1899, ibid.
67 *Documents diplomatiques francais* 1871-1914 (Paris, 1929 et seq.), First series, Tome XV, no. 142.
68 G.P., 14/2 no. 4066.

times, Salisbury always turned the proposal down: 'I am averse to treating Maxse and Rose upon the same footing...', he minuted, and regarded it as a great concession to Berlin that the British commissioner would control the consul.[69]

In fact, Salisbury appears to have been much readier to accept without question all of Maxse's complaints against the Germans—perhaps because the British consul was a distant relation of his—than the permanent officials, many of whom questioned the chief justice's decision and the necessity for the shellings.[70] He also declined to let the consuls draft their own cease-fire proclamations lest it be ambiguous — 'the Germans will lay hold of any slip of that kind', — and he disliked the idea of the commissioners meeting before they reached Samoa, remembering perhaps the German attempts to 'arrange' matters with Thurston in 1886.[71] His hopes that the commissioners would be able to arrange a final settlement of the Samoan question cannot have been very great, therefore.

It is doubtful, in fact, whether any side expected that the commission would solve the roots of the crisis. Nevertheless, much faith was placed by all three governments in their respective commissioners to bring about at least temporarily a restoration of peace and harmony. All were adjured to work closely with their colleagues and to take steps in unison to prevent a further recurrence of the troubles.[72] Certainly, the choice of Baron Speck von Sternburg (counsellor of the German embassy at Washington), Mr C.N.B. Eliot (second secretary of the British embassy there) and Mr Bartlett Tripp (a former U.S. minister at Vienna) as the three commissioners was calculated to ensure as little friction as possible: all were chosen because of their unbiased and conciliatory natures.

The instructions to the German commissioner deserve special attention. Despairing of ever persuading Salisbury to agree to a partition of Samoa and wishing to calm German public opinion, Bülow informed Sternburg that their aim was 'to find an honourable way out of the difficulties without encroachment upon our rights and interests and to restore peace in the sense of the still valid Samoa Act'. To achieve this aim, the commissioner was advised upon how to deal with

69 F.O.58/329, Salisbury minute on Villiers memo of 27/3/1899; Salisbury papers, Class E, Salisbury to Sanderson, 14/4/1899, 15/4/1899 and 16/4/1899; B.D., 1, no. 139.

70 See, for example, his own minute 'This seems all right', after Villiers' nervous minute on Maxse to Salisbury, 23/3/1899, and their contrasting minutes on German Embassy communication of 9/3/1899, both in F.O.58/328.

71 F.O.58/330, Salisbury to F.O., tel. of 15/4/1899; F.O.58/329, Salisbury minute on Villiers' memo of 9/4/1899.

72 The instructions to Tripp are in F.R.1899, pp. 615-16; those to Eliot are in *Accounts and Papers*, 1899 (CX), Samoa No. 1 (C.9506), document 1.

the many important individual questions. But he was also instructed to forestall possible future attempts of the British to call into question the unanimity principle by endeavouring to work with the American commissioner. By suggesting that Tripp, because of his age, should be the chairman of the commission, he should be able to win him over to the German side.[73]

These few sentences were, in fact, a small part of a persistent campaign to detach the United States from Britain, particularly over Samoa. London, Bülow felt, would never agree to a partition of Samoa unless Washington was persuaded first: then Salisbury's obstructionism would be exposed and the prime minister would no longer be able to hide behind the objections of the United States. In March, Berlin attempted to persuade the State Department to instruct their consul to act with Rose against Maxse but this the anglophile Hay declined to do, although Osborn was warned to take 'no inconsiderate step'.[74]

In the same way, the German government seized upon McKinley's expressions of regret with great delight and attempted many times to point out to Washington that Salisbury alone was preventing a satisfactory arrangement about a commission—Wilhelm even summoned White personally to tell him this, while Bülow insinuated that Germany 'was even more desirous of working hand in hand with America in this matter than with Great Britain.'[75] Moreover, Holleben was instructed to get in touch with Kasson, the U.S. delegate to the Berlin conference, whom Bülow believed was sympathetic to Germany's position, and to ask him to use his influence to effect a German-American arrangement over Samoa. Encouraged by Holleben's reports that Kasson was indeed sympathetic, the foreign minister urged that he be appointed the American commissioner, upon which he would also be the chairman and possess the power to decide all unsettled questions.[76] Although Kasson was not in fact appointed, the Germans hoped to use Tripp to a similar extent.

73 London Embassy records, A.A. to Hatzfeldt, no. 50 of 13/5/1899, enclosing instructions to Sternburg.

74 N.A.R.G.59, M-58, T-28, German Embassy memo of 11/3/1899; N.A.R.G.84, Apia Consulate records (C38-8c), vol. 2, S.D. to Osborn, 13/3/1899; N.A.R.G.59, M-99, roll 33, S.D. to German Embassy, 13/3/1899; F.O.115/1114, Pauncefote to Salisbury, no. 97 Confidential of 17/3/1899.

75 N.A.R.G.59, M-44, roll 87, White to Hay, 22/3/1899, 4/4/1899, 6/4/1899, 7/4/1899.

76 A.A./*Südsee-Inseln* 5, vol. 1, Bülow to Holleben, no. 52 of 25/3/1899; ibid., vol. 2, Bülow to A.A., tel. no. 1 of 29/3/1899; ibid., A.A. to Holleben, tel. no. 71, additional note to, of 5/4/1899; ibid., Holleben to A.A., tels. nos. 55, 59 and 68 of 27/3/1899, 31/3/1899 and 5/4/1899.

Berlin's attempts to influence the American press provide further evidence of this policy. When the *German-American Review* first started up in 1899, Bülow ensured that it was helped financially by ordering a large number of copies; and Tirpitz was encouraged to lend his support with a letter and a photograph. Holleben managed to get an article in the *Washington Post*, which called for Chambers' withdrawal if the German officials went, and he later persuaded the New York *Tribune* to publish an inspired article which attacked Kautz's actions. Particularly helpful was a magazine called *Uncle Sam's American Eagle*, which regularly called for good relations with Germany: for his pains the writer, together with the press attaché and *Norddeutsche* representative, Dr Witte, received large fees from the 10,000 marks available to Holleben for this purpose. The German consuls throughout the United States were all encouraged to influence the newspapers, and the consul in Chicago succeeded in persuading the great German-American meeting there in June to petition McKinley for good relations with Germany and a satisfactory solution of the Samoan difficulties (kaiser: 'Bravo!'). When joined by the Irish-Americans also, such assemblies became purely anti-British focal points.[77]

How successful these endeavours were, it is difficult to say. Later in the year, the anti-British agitations of the German-Americans and Irish-Americans were to give some worry to McKinley's administration, which had its eye upon the impending elections. Yet the American policy certainly remained firm upon the main points in the Samoan controversy. Although secretary of the navy Long felt that Kautz had acted far too rashly, and a number of highly critical despatches from Osborn later shared this view,[78] Hay's attitude never wavered. While he questioned many of Chambers' actions, the secretary of state maintained that 'the conduct of Raffel has been that of a madman' and he felt that Rose's had been little better. There was no intention upon his part of re-establishing the provisional government.[79] Moreover the savage attack upon the United States of the pan-German, Dr Lehr, and his call in the Reichstag debate of 14 April for commercial reprisals in return for the Samoa

77   BA/MA 2262, PG94160, *Beiträge zur Schriften u. Werken*, vol. 1, A.A. to R.M.A., 23/2/1899; A.A./*U.S.A.* 2, vol. 3, Bülow to the kaiser, 2/5/1899; A.A./*U.S.A.* 16, vol. 6, Holleben to the chancellor, no. 130 of 10/6/1899; and especially all of Holleben's despatches in A.A./*Europa Gen.* 86 *Secr.*, vol. 9; E. Witte, *Revelations of a German Attaché: Ten Years of German-American Diplomacy* (New York, 1916) pp. 43-64.

78   John D. Long Papers, Journal 1899, Vol. 1, Long to his daughter, 14/4/1899; N.A.R.G. 59, T-27, roll 25, Osborn to S.D., nos. 94, 95 and 99 of 19/4/1899, 28/4/1899 and 17/5/1899.

79   Hay Papers, (Library of Congress) Box 26, Letterbook 1, Hay to White, 19/4/1899, Confidential, 'Not for your file'.

humiliation, tended to blot out the good impression which
Bülow attempted to make with his soothing and conciliatory
words upon all sides. Finally, although sympathetic to the
German request for Chambers' dismissal, Hay confided to
McKinley that 'The hyphenated Germans are so frantically
unjust towards us that nothing we could do would have any
effect upon their howling, so that I think we will have to
decide the matter without much reference to them.'[80] This
was hardly the language of one being tempted into the
pro-German camp, while Hay's invitation to the British to
supply the next chief justice indicated how much Washington
now trusted London in comparison to 1889.

The Samoan disputes came most fortuitously for Anglo-
American relations. In February, the Cabinet had reluctantly
agreed to defer the negotiations over the Alaskan boundary
begun with Washington in August 1898, and with this
Salisbury also declined to discuss an abandonment of British
rights regarding a Central American canal which the 1850
Clayton-Bulwer treaty gave to her.[81] Although both governments were eager for a settlement, and both saw the Canadian
attitude as being the chief obstacle, matters were less promising
than in 1898 and Hay confessed that 'these troubles, although
intrinsically insignificant, are likely at any moment to embitter
the relations between our two countries'.[82] Nevertheless,
discussions for a modus vivendi were taken up during the
summer of 1899 and were to achieve success in October;
clearly, neither side wanted to see the good relations disappear.
West coast newspapers, however, were hardly so tolerant
but, luckily, their attention was now switched elsewhere.
As Professor Campbell puts it:

> Who could fail to be moved by the dramatic news a month after the
> collapse of the Canadian negotiations that Americans and Englishmen
> fighting side by side were meeting death at the hands of a common enemy
> on a distant South Sea island? Whatever bitterness may have arisen in
> February was mitigated by the fraternisation in March. And every German
> step served only to enhance the general impression of British-American
> solidarity.[83]

Small wonder, then, that Bülow deplored the Samoan troubles,
attempted to minimize their importance upon the American

80   A.A./*Südsee-Inseln* 5, vol. 2, Holleben to A.A., tel. no. 83 of 17/4/1899; Hay Papers,
Box 26, Letterbook 1, Hay to McKinley, 26/6/1899.

81   Cab. 41/25/no. 3, synopsis of 13/2/1899 discussion; C. S. Campbell, *Anglo-American
Understanding*, pp. 112-19, 124-25, 130-37; A. E. Campbell, *Great Britain and the United
States*, pp. 51-53, 91-95.

82   Hay Papers, Box 26, Letterbook 1, Hay to Henry White, 28/4/1899.

83   C. S. Campbell, *Anglo-American Understanding*, p. 156. On McKinley's eagerness to
avoid a complete breakdown upon all topics, see F.O.115/1109, F.O. to Tower, no. 194
of 4/5/1899.

side, and endeavoured to entice the United States away from Britain. In the work of the commission, he was to believe that he had partially succeeded.

Despite Salisbury's fears, the commissioners travelled together to Samoa, since the United States government had offered the services of a vessel to assist their work. Leaving San Francisco on 26 April and sailing via Hawaii, they arrived off Apia on the morning of 13 May.[84] The three men set to work immediately, commencing with the tricky problem of disarming the natives, although all experience and the advice of those with a knowledge of Samoan affairs indicated that this would be virtually impossible. Receiving Tanu on 19 May and Mata'afa on the following day, the commissioners pleaded with both sides to give up their rifles. Doubtless the offer to compensate fairly for each weapon surrendered was the decisive factor, although neither chief seemed inclined to continue the fighting. Eventually, some 3,631 guns were handed over—a fair comment upon the effectiveness of the ban imposed under the Berlin Act—and a total of $41,245 was promised in return. The rifles which the British had given to Tanu's warriors were also withdrawn, although 100 remained with the native police force, which came under the control of the commissioners and was the only armed body allowed on Upolu.[85] By these moves alone, much of the future peace of the islands was secured.

The commission then turned to the crux of the dispute— the kingship question. Both Eliot and Tripp found themselves 'unable to see upon what grounds the decision of the chief justice can be overturned even though the reasoning by which he came to the conclusion may be open to objection'.[86] Since the Berlin Act gave the final decision in a contested election to the Supreme Court, enjoined all treaty officers to obey the court judgement, and specified that there was no right of appeal to the powers on this, Tanu was clearly the legal king and the action of the Germans and the Mata'afans was equally clearly rebellious. The so-called 'laws and customs of Samoa' only applied when they were not in conflict with the act. As Eliot explained to Salisbury:

> This, in fact, is the root of the matter. All the German criticisms on the decision assume that other parties have the ri̧ ht to pass judgement on it and determine whether it is or is not conformable to the laws and

84 The activities of the commission are covered in F.O.58/323-324; in F.R. 1899, various reports of Tripp and the commissioners, pp. 616-63; and in R.Kol.A.3051-54.

85 F.O.58/323, Eliot to Salisbury, nos. 8 and 19 of 11/6/1899 and 16/7/1899; F.R. 1899, pp. 621-24.

86 Ibid., p. 617.

customs of Samoa and the Act of Berlin. But no-one has such a right, as long as the decision professes to conform to the conditions described it is absolute, final and irreversible.[87]

Confronted with this impeccable legal logic, neither Sternburg nor Dr Solf, the newly-arrived president of the municipality, could make any reply. Tanu was the legal monarch of Samoa.

This was, however, a victory without practical consequences. Investigation by the commission soon revealed that the powers of the monarchy were very few indeed. It was, according to Tripp, 'at best a mere bauble, of value only as a prize for competition'. This was hardly true, but the commissioners could only arrive at decisions based upon information given to them locally and apparently all the white residents had declared that the kingship should be abolished. Moreover, both Tanu and Mata'afa had expressed their willingness to abandon any claim to the post. Finally, Sternburg declared that his government's instructions 'precluded him from allowing Tanu to exercise even nominal authority as King'. Although Eliot and Tripp had hoped this would be temporarily permitted, in order to emphasize the legality of Chambers' decision, they gave way upon the point in reply to the German commissioner's greater concession. Summoning the nineteen-year-old youth before them, they asked him to give up his title, to which he readily assented in return for a promise of a formal education in New Zealand.[88]

Smaller disputes were eliminated, usually with a great deal of give and take upon both sides. Kautz sailed away abruptly, despite the commission's fear that disturbances might follow. Rose left also, and was accompanied by Maxse. The latter was fairly ill and therefore quite willing to give up his post to ease the exit of the German consul. Some bitterness was caused, however, at the resignation of the chief justice: for, while Eliot acknowledged that Chambers' departure would also contribute to the peace, he found Sternburg's demand for this to take place immediately to be 'monstrous'.[89] In fact, the German commissioner had been ordered by his government to insist upon the removal of the chief justice and this was paralleled by formal requests from Bülow to London and Washington. The *Wilhelmstrasse*, sensitive to press criticism of the commission's decision upon the kingship and to attacks upon Chambers, was striving for his departure.

According to the British commissioner, Sternburg then became less pleasant as a result of a reproof from Berlin, and

87 F.O.58/323, Eliot to Salisbury, no. 7, Confidential of 9/6/1899; F.R.1899, pp. 651-53; R.Kol.A.3053, Sternburg to the chancellor, no. 6 of 15/6/1899.
88 F.O.58/323, Eliot to Salisbury, no. 8 Confidential of 11/6/1899; F.R.1899, p. 625.

made objections to the appointment of the acting British consul, Hunter, as 'Native Commissioner'. Eliot, with Tripp assenting, consequently declined the German proposal that Dr Solf assume the posts of native commissioner, acting chief justice and municipal president. Eventually, therefore, the American consul Osborn assumed the post of acting chief justice, while Solf took the remaining offices. On other smaller matters, too, such as the position of the Malietoans and an old quarrel over the true boundaries of the municipality, the British and German commissioners tended to differ. Sternburg reported that the former was completely in the hands of Maxse and the L.M.S. missionaries and by 9 June Richthofen was complaining of Eliot's attitude. A month later, Holleben attempted to persuade Hay to join the German government in asking Salisbury to caution his commissioner. This the secretary of state refused to do until he had heard from Tripp and, when a despatch from the latter arrived on 5 July and contained no criticism of Eliot, he turned down the German request finally.[90] Moreover, when Hatzfeldt raised the matter with Salisbury himself, the prime minister noted sarcastically that if Eliot was out of step with his colleagues, this 'justified the course, which I had earnestly, though in vain, pressed upon the German Government, of allowing the decision of the Commission to be decided by a majority'.[91] He also refused to send any messages to Eliot.

When the British commissioner later learnt of the German complaints, he put them in a better perspective. Since there were few American citizens in Apia, the smaller rivalries there had chiefly been Anglo-German and had consequently caused their respective commissioners to have more to discuss. Furthermore, Tripp had openly declared that America's interest was really concentrated in the harbour of Pago-Pago and had therefore kept out of most of the quarrels, 'although either his instructions or personal political bias led him to generally take the German side'.[92] Doubtless little note would have been made of all this had not the Germans, in their anxiety to detach the United States from Britain, exaggerated the matter out of all proportion, so that Hay himself later noted:

89   F.O.58/324, Eliot to Salisbury, no. 30, Very Confidential of 26/7/1899. For the elimination of the smaller disputes, see his reports nos. 10, 11, 12, 15 and 16, all in F.O.58/323.

90   N.A.R.G.59, M-58, roll T-28, S.D. memo of 6/7/1899; F.O.58/331, Lascelles to Salisbury, no. 171 of 9/6/1899.

91   F.O.58/331, Salisbury to Lascelles, no. 123 of 24/6/1899; Salisbury Papers, A122/62, Hatzfeldt to Salisbury, 8/6/1899; Vagts, *Weltpolitik*, 1, p. 885.

92   F.O.58/324, Eliot to Salisbury, no. 31 Confidential of 26/7/1899.

We are on the best of terms about Samoa. Sternburg backed up Tripp in
everything. So that, to our amazement, Germany and we arranged
everything perfectly harmoniously. It was rather the English Commissioner
who was offish. The Emperor is nervously anxious to be on good terms
with us—on his *own* terms, bien entendu.[93]

In fact, Hay had been somewhat misled. The various
arrangements made by the commission had been agreed upon
by all three members, working harmoniously together, for
the most part. While socially very friendly to this German
colleague, Tripp had supported Eliot as many times as he had
Sternburg, particularly over major issues such as the holding
of the various offices after the commission left. Upon the
most important question of all, the validity of Chambers'
decision and Tanu's claim to the kingship, agreement had
only been reached because the German commissioner gave
way to the Anglo-American arguments. In any case, Tripp's
reports confirmed Hay in his opinion that the German and
Mata'afan refusal to accept the judgement of the chief justice
had been the main cause of the troubles. There was never any
real possibility of a German-American coalition over Samoa
to the detriment of Britain, and Hay's 'amazement' at the
Tripp-Sternburg co-operation in some way indicates this.

By the middle of July, as the commissioners were drafting
a joint report and preparing to leave the islands, they set
about establishing a provisional form of government until
their final recommendations had been agreed upon by the
treaty powers. With some misgivings, the commission vested
power in the Consular Board, which would be assisted by the
municipal president. To prevent 'the troubles of last winter',
the three consuls would be able to act by a majority except
in cases where the Berlin Act expressly required unanimity;
and solemn oaths to keep the peace were taken from both
Samoan factions before the commission left. Nevertheless,
the members pressed their governments to implement their
new scheme of administration as quickly as possible in order
to replace this provisional arrangement.[94]

The new scheme of the commission was only, as they
themselves declared in the first sentence of their joint report,
'a modified and amended version of the act of Berlin'. In the
place of the monarchy, a system of native government upon
the Fijian model was proposed:—each district would be ruled
by a chief and these would meet together annually to decide

93 Hay Papers, Box 26, Letterbook 1, Hay to Henry White, 9/9/1899. For Tripp's
praise of Sternburg, see F.R.1899, p. 634.
94 F.O.58/324, Eliot to Salisbury, no. 30 Very Confidential of 26/7/1899; F.R.1899,
pp. 659 60.

larger matters. Samoan affairs were to be left to the Samoans as far as possible. To centralize and unify the islands, an administrator chosen by a neutral government would be appointed to work with three delegates of the treaty powers. Together they would form a legislative council, while the three national members would take over whatever consular functions were necessary in Samoa—but the administrator would have 'a large measure of authority'. To eradicate the lawless nature of the islands, the powers of the chief justice were to be enlarged to cover cases between natives and foreigners. More important still, the extraterritorial jurisdiction of the consular courts was to be abolished and all such cases transferred to the Supreme Court in an attempt to reduce the rivalries and bitterness among the various white communities.[95]

The commission admitted that their scheme was a compromise, forced upon them by the need to prevent one power from gaining political predominance in the group. Despairing of ever being able to solve fully the national rivalries, they bluntly declared 'that the only natural and normal form of government for these islands, and the only system which can assure prosperity and tranquility, is a government by one power'.[96] In their private reports, the commissioners repeated this point. While Eliot blamed the inopportune return of Mata'afa and the German refusal to recognize Tanu as the immediate causes of the crisis, he pointed out that 'The curse of Samoa is the rivalry existing between the subjects of the three Powers, whether they are officials or private persons', and advocated annexation by one nation if that were possible.[97] Tripp felt that the United States should endeavour to make known the fact that her interests were focussed entirely upon Tutuila and should welcome any chance to free herself from the affairs of the rest of the group.[98]

The commission had been sent to Samoa to restore order, to report upon the troubles and to suggest ways for the better government of the group. This they had done. They had upheld the decision of the chief justice, and condemned the efforts of those who had opposed that judgement. Legally, it had been a defeat for the German point of view: politically, it had been nothing of the sort. The abolition of the kingship, the harmony between Tripp and Sternburg, and also a general reservation about the necessity for the military actions of the two navies had obscured this German reverse. Most important

95   Ibid., pp. 636 48.
96   Ibid., p. 638.
97   F.O.58/324, Eliot to Salisbury, no. 18 Confidential of 9/7/1899; B.D., 1, no. 145.
98   F.R.1899, pp. 648-63.

of all, however, the commission had confirmed the opinion of Berlin that rule by one nation was urgent and necessary. All three governments knew this already, of course, and it was only out of regard for Australasia that London had preferred to continue with the tripartite rule. But now that their position was even more exposed, their excuses made even weaker and their cover torn away by the open and unanimous recommendations of the commissioners, the British could expect further heavy pressure for a settlement of the entire question from an impatient German government.

iv *Salisbury, Wilhelm and the Samoan Question*

While many politicians, newspapers and even Cabinet ministers believed the British Empire at the end of the nineteenth century to be in a position so precarious that she would one day be forced to align herself with some of the other great powers, it is clear that her prime minister felt otherwise.[99] Salisbury never wavered in his belief that, given patience and coolness upon both sides, every problem in world affairs could be met with and surmounted without Britain ever needing to assume the burdensome obligations of specific alliances. Despite his famous 'dying nations' speech of 1898, he did not view the world through the Darwinist-tinted spectacles which affected the political thought of Tirpitz, Chamberlain and others, and he was free from that sense of urgency which influenced the actions of many statesmen of this period. Through steady and undramatic negotiations, he hoped to be able to reach an agreement with France over Africa, with Russia over Asia, and with the United States over various western hemisphere questions. But having no direct conflict of vital interests with Germany, he was never possessed of the same need to settle any problems which arose with her. Nor, for that matter, did he ever believe that Berlin would endanger her eastern borders by assisting Britain in China, the only area where her help was really sought.

Believing an alliance with Germany to be neither necessary nor possible, he consequently declined to further its prospects by making territorial sacrifices in overseas matters. Every colonial dispute had to be settled upon terms fair to both sides, and in this he differed from the view held by Berlin and also by Chamberlain, who felt in principle moved to purchase Germany's alliance by some such concessions although he

99 G. Monger, *The End of Isolation* (London, 1963), pp. 14-20, 37; Grenville, *Salisbury and Foreign Policy, passim.*

found it very hard to do it in practice. This basic position explains his attitude towards the German proposals regarding Samoa, although it cannot be denied that he was extremely unsympathetic to Berlin's pleas that the question required a definite settlement and was also, perhaps, too careless about his treatment of the touchy Wilhelm.

A further factor was Salisbury's self-confidence in the first eight months of 1899 i.e., during the time of the agreements with France and Russia, and before the Boer War was seen to be inevitable. Brodrick reported in mid-March that 'He is in splendid spirits just now & thinks he has done first rate business with Cambon & Fr(ench) agreement. Also the Russian thing is going through, though slowly.'[100] Moreover, in the middle of the crisis over the unanimity of the commission, Salisbury sent a private letter to Curzon in which he argued that France and Russia would only act together in a war against Germany. Holding such a view, and hoping to achieve a 'mutual temper of apathetic tolerance' with the French, he was in no desperate mood to acknowledge any need for Germany's friendship. A few months later, refusing to worry about the negotiations in Madrid for an anti-British coalition, Salisbury noted 'The German Emperor is looking round for allies, but he cannot get any on what he considers to be reasonable terms.'[101]

Much of this, too, explains the kaiser's dislike of him. Wilhelm naturally shared the belief of all those directing German policy that Salisbury's chief aim, as revealed in the Turkish question of 1895 and the Cretan affair of 1897, was to embroil the continental powers with each other; but this suspicion was augmented by a fierce antipathy and disgust when the prime minister continually endeavoured to come to better terms with France and Russia, repeatedly obstructed the securing of overseas territories so necessary to please the German public, and declined to recognize the importance of Germany in world affairs. This last factor was the most important of all to the kaiser and his complaint in March, 1899, that he was being treated as a '*quantité négligeable*' was an all-too-common utterance for English ears.[102] They found it hard to understand that this strutting, bombastic, excitable, immature emperor of the Germans secretly yearned for the respect of England, the country he most admired.

---

100   Curzon Papers, vol. 10a, Brodrick to Curzon, 20/3/1899.

101   Ibid., vol. 221, Salisbury to Curzon, 8/4/1899; Salisbury Papers, A134/29, Wolff to Salisbury, Private and Confidential, 3/7/1899, and the latter's reply, A134/104, of 17/7/1899.

102   F.O.64/1469, Lascelles to Salisbury, nos. 76 and 78 Very Confidential, both of 10/3/1899. The kaiser's outburst was occasioned by the belief that the British ambassador at the Porte was obstructing the construction of a German harbour at Haidar Pacha.

They also did not realize the sensitivity behind his bombast, nor the deep personal feeling of humiliation when he believed that he was being ignored.

The most sensitive aspect of all was Wilhelm's relationship to the English royal family. To visit Britain, to participate in the Cowes Regatta, to talk with his revered grandmother, all these things possessed a great attraction for him and he deeply regretted that the coolness between the two countries following the Kruger telegram had forced him to forego these joys. Nevertheless, he persistently sought to be invited there or, if that proved impossible, to invite Victoria to call upon him during her annual trip to the Riviera; but these efforts, too, proved unsuccessful.[103] However, his hopes arose again at the end of 1898 over the possibility of attending Victoria's eightieth birthday celebrations in the following May. This the queen refused to permit, although she relented sufficiently to invite the kaiser to visit her later in the year. In vain Bülow attempted to cool Wilhelm's eagerness but on 11 March Lascelles reported that the kaiser even nourished the idea of arriving unannounced in England a few days before Victoria's birthday.[104]

More annoying still to Wilhelm was the way in which he was treated over the Saxe-Coburg-Gotha succession, when the Duke of Connaught became heir to the duchy after the death of the young prince in February 1899. The news that the English royal family had decided that the title should go to Connaught's son but that it was not yet agreed whether he should be educated in Germany provoked an angry reaction in the German press. Wilhelm was amazed that the matter had been settled outside the country most concerned and was furious when Connaught issued a proclamation to the people of Coburg without consulting him. Throughout April the German newspapers increased their demands that foreign princes should be legally excluded from inheriting such titles and an explanation from the Gotha minister of state of the negotiations he had conducted with Connaught received a barrage of contradiction and abuse from the kaiser. Bülow explained to Hatzfeldt that 'His Majesty could hardly have spoken otherwise in view of the present feeling in Germany caused by the unexpected and equally unmotivated action of England against us in Samoa.'[105] There was little doubt that

---

103 On this, see A.A./*Preussen* 1 *nr.* 1 *nr.* 40, vol. 4, envelope marked 'only high officials to open', dealing with such endeavours in April 1898; G.P., 14/2, footnote on p. 618.

104 Salisbury Papers, A121/21, Lascelles to Salisbury, 11/3/1899; F.O.800/17, Lascelles to Victoria, 24/12/1898.

105 A.A./*Sachsen-Coburg-Gotha* 3, vol. 1, Bülow to Hatzfeldt, no. 262 of 23/4/1899. This series has all the documentation and press clippings upon the affair. See also, *Letters of Queen Victoria*, Third series, 3, pp. 355-56.

the two crises reacted upon each other and in a later letter Bülow anxiously wondered if the proposed anti-foreign law would annoy Victoria and British opinion, thus intensifying the Samoan dispute.[106] Here was another matter in which the kaiser believed he was being treated as a *quantité négligeable.*

Using his own peculiar logic, Wilhelm blamed everything upon Salisbury. Although he had given way over the unanimity question, the prime minister's later conduct in the Samoan affair did not restore him to favour. When Hatzfeldt reported that the Foreign Office itself had also not understood Salisbury's tactics and that Britain had probably only given way because America had not stood with her, Wilhelm noted: 'Excellently written: And strengthens me in my opinion that I cannot henceforth think of going to England, at least so long as Salisbury is in office.'[107] The prime minister's cheery chaffing to Hatzfeldt at the end of April that he could not understand why the German public became so excited over Samoa did not go down well in Berlin. Nor could the Germans seriously entertain his idea that the treaty powers cast lots for the three major islands in the group: for what would happen if Upolu did not fall to Germany? In fact, Salisbury told Chamberlain that it would be 'undignified' to carry out this scheme. Yet, to the Germans, this joking seemed to show that he refused to take them and Samoa seriously. Hatzfeldt could only suppose that the diplomatic victory over the French and the security engendered by the great naval increases of 1898 and 1899 had led to the prime minister's 'unbounded arrogance', at which Wilhelm noted: '(That) will only fall when we increase our fleet again.'[108] For the kaiser, the British recalcitrance over Samoa and elsewhere was becoming inextricably connected with Germany's need for a larger navy.

Wilhelm naturally found it impossible to conceal this irritation from the British. The military attaché in Berlin, Colonel Grierson, reported that he had been subjected to 'some rather unpleasant chaff about Samoa' in the full hearing of many Germans during the army manoeuvres on 14 April. With the Coburg affair becoming more serious and Salisbury showing little repentance about Samoa, the kaiser returned

106   A.A./*Sachsen-Coburg-Gotha* 3, vol. 1, Bülow to Hatzfeldt, no. 102 of 30/4/1899.

107   A.A./*Südsee-Inseln* 5, vol. 2, Hatzfeldt to Holstein, 15/4/1899. The marginal comment, with many others, was omitted from G.P., 14/2, no. 4067.

108   Chamberlain Papers, JC5/67/111, Salisbury to Chamberlain, 23/4/1899; A.A./*Südsee-Inseln* 5, vol. 2, Hatzfeldt to Holstein, tel. of 26/4/1899; G.P., 14/2, no. 4071 and minute thereon.

to the topic on 1 May, subjecting Grierson to a long tirade over British ingratitude and complaining that

> for years he had been the one true friend to Great Britain on the continent of Europe, and had done everything to help her policy and to assist her and that he had received nothing in return but ingratitude culminating in the Samoan affair . . . Some day, when it was too late, we would regret it . . . His consistent enemy throughout had been Lord Salisbury, and and while the latter remained Prime Minister, it would be impossible for him to come to England.[109]

Lascelles, in his covering letter to this extraordinary report, hit the nail upon the head when he suggested that Wilhelm's pique was caused by a combination of the Coburg controversy, the Samoan events and the queen's refusal to allow him to attend her birthday celebrations. As for the prime minister, he repudiated these charges, privately informing Lascelles that 'My feelings towards him (the Kaiser) have never been very acute in any direction'. Moreover, his own suspicions had now been raised:

> So groundless is the charge that I cannot help fearing that it indicates a consciousness on the part of His Majesty that he cherishes some design which is bound to make me his enemy—and that he looks forward to the satisfaction of saying I told you so!
> It is a great nuisance that one of the main factors in the European calculation should be so ultra human. He is as jealous as a woman because he does not think the Queen pays him enough attention.[110]

The chances of the kaiser regretting his hasty utterances were then completely wrecked by the news that the Grand-Duke of Hesse was travelling to England for the queen's birthday.[111] With his 'Free Hand' policy somewhat deranged by these personal quarrels, Bülow strove to conciliate, at the same time believing that only a quick settlement of the Samoan question could soothe Wilhelm's hurt pride. He was therefore interested to hear that Chamberlain had been talking about an Anglo-German alliance again, and he urged Hatzfeldt to maintain close contact with the colonial secretary since 'as a result of his outstanding cleverness he is more susceptible to rational arguments than many other English statesmen.'[112] He should thus appreciate that as the word Samoa implied for all Germans 'the beginning and starting-point of our colonial

---

109 F.O.800/17, Lascelles to Sanderson, 14/4/1899; *Letters of Queen Victoria*, Third series, 3, pp. 357-60.
110 Salisbury Papers, A122/15, Salisbury to Lascelles, 10/5/1899.
111 Wilhelm's minute on Prussian Legation (Hesse) to chancellor, 8/5/1899, in A.A./ *England* 81 *nr.* 1, vol. 6.
112 G.P., 14/2, no. 4072.

strivings' while it meant very little to the British, it should not be difficult for London to relinquish her claims to the group. Once again, Chamberlain was to be encouraged to prepare the path for an alliance by offering colonial concessions —but even if he did this, of course, no alliance would be concluded. Just before he sent instructions to Hatzfeldt, Bülow had minuted that 'If England shows herself prepared for a fair settlement of the Samoan affair, we will be able to pursue our present independent policy *du juste milieu.*'[113] If she did not, however, Germany would be forced 'to draw closer to Russia and even to France', for the feelings of the kaiser and the public towards Samoa were so high that it had become decisive for Anglo-German relations.

Whether Chamberlain would have responded to these urgings seems doubtful but in any case Anglo-German relations were further disturbed by monarchical differences. On 20 May, Wilhelm received a prim letter from his grand-mother, indicating her annoyance that people in Germany were apparently speculating wildly upon the fact that he had not been invited to Cowes that summer, a rumour she held to be a complete untruth. Believing Victoria's letter to have been caused by 'evil intrigues' or an error on the part of her secretary, the kaiser became very excited. Most annoying of all, he told Bülow, was the fact that while the queen 'speaks to me *for the first time in my life* about Germany's public opinion, to which she apparently attaches great value, she makes no mention of the Samoan affair, which has become so enormously exciting and offensive for our public'.[114]

Two days later, the kaiser despatched his reply, adding fuel to an already blazing fire with some very tactless remarks. After dismissing Victoria's comments upon rumours in Germany upon the Cowes visit as mistaken, he launched straight into a fierce diatribe upon Salisbury's incomprehensible policy towards Germany in the Samoan affair, concluding that

> this way of treating Germany's feelings and interests has come upon the people like an electric shock, and has evoked the impression that Lord Salisbury cares for us no more than for Portugal, Chile, or the Patagonians ... and all that on account of a stupid island which is a hairpin to England compared to the thousands of square miles she is annexing right and left every year.[115]

Of course, the letter was outrageous and exaggerated, and its only possible effect could have been to provoke the annoyance

113   *Holstein Papers*, 4, footnote on p. 118.
114   A.A./*Preussen* 1 nr. 1 nr. 40, vol. 4, Wilhelm to Bülow, 20/5/1899; G.P., 14/2, footnote on pp. 615-16.
115   *Letters of Queen Victoria*, Third series, 3, pp. 375-79.

of the queen and her minister further; but the most astonishing thing about it, as Professor Eyck points out, is that Bülow was consulted before it was sent. The desire to avoid annoying his master and the German public was too great, and the chance of exploiting the antagonism against Britain for further fleet increases too tempting, for Bülow to employ some honeyed words and persuade Wilhelm to abandon his insulting letter.[116]

Two days after sending this letter, Wilhelm burst forth again, and this time to Lascelles at a banquet in Berlin to mark the queen's birthday. A continuous barrage of criticism of the British government's Samoan policy, from an attack upon Sturdee to an accusation that they were bribing the American press to be anti-German, was directed towards the unfortunate ambassador; and when the latter attempted to pass on Salisbury's reply that he could hardly be considered an 'enemy' the kaiser merely sniffed. Bülow and Tirpitz would have been horrified to hear him warn that

> he knew that England was powerful and Germany weak at sea, and therefore the former could act with impunity, but the time would come when even England would have to consider the German fleet as an important factor, and he only hoped that it would not then be too late, and that Germany would not by that time have formed other combinations which would certainly not be agreeable to England . . .[117]

The mutual bad feeling continued into June and any chance of Wilhelm visiting England for the Cowes Regatta collapsed in these recriminations. The queen sent a very sharp and reproving letter to her grandson, obviously intended to put him in his place: in contrast, Salisbury's letter was very formal, coldly refuting point by point every exaggerated accusation of the kaiser and concluding with the opinion that 'it is quite unintelligible to him on what grounds the Emperor can maintain that British action in regard to Samoa has been in any sense unfriendly to the German Government.'[118] The prime minister's refusal to caution Eliot was also regarded in Berlin as a further proof of hostility. Worse still, whenever Hatzfeldt attempted to sound out Salisbury regarding a possible agreement upon the partition of Morocco, he met with a stolid resistance. Britain preferred to keep the status quo in that land, the prime minister declared, and disliked the idea of prearranged colonial 'deals'.[119]

---

116 Eyck, *Das persönliche Regiment*, p. 234.
117 B.D., 1, no. 141; Salisbury Papers, Class E, Lascelles to Salisbury, 26/5/1899.
118 *Letters of Queen Victoria*, Third series, 3, pp. 379-82.
119 F.O.64/1468, Salisbury to Lascelles, no. 109 of 7/6/1899: *Holstein Papers*, 4, pp. 112-22, 137-38.

After the middle of June, however, matters began to change upon both sides and the high point of the antagonism had clearly passed. A little earlier, the Coburg succession had been settled in a manner satisfactory to German feelings, and Victoria had written to Wilhelm, renewing her invitation for him to visit her later in the year. Both these gestures had been made before the British replies to the kaiser's letter but only now did they have effect. Salisbury, too, attempted to restore better relations with Berlin by having his private secretary write a letter to Paul Metternich, the kaiser's friend, assuring him that the prime minister was in no way hostile to Wilhelm and had in fact often expressed 'the warmest admiration for H.I.M.'s talent and industry'.[120] Furthermore, the relative peace which prevailed within Samoa during the visit of the commission naturally caused the German press to become less excited about this problem and to turn their attention to the internal struggles over the Hard Labour Bill and the Prussian Canal Bill. Upon the British side, the breakdown of the Bloemfontein Conference on 5 June switched all attention to South Africa and outlined the need to subordinate smaller matters to this increasingly threatening point.

Another important factor in the restoration of better relations was Salisbury's agreement to allow claims for damages incurred during the naval actions in Samoa to be submitted for arbitration to the king of Sweden and Norway. He had naturally emphasized that 'a corresponding obligation attaches to the German Government' and seemed fairly convinced that an objective examination of the facts would justify the Anglo-American forces—but it was a useful concession, in view of the German concern over the damage their nationals had suffered. Since Salisbury had also not opposed the recall of Chambers and had expressed the hope that he and Wilhelm would be able to remove their differences through a personal meeting, Bülow felt justified in regarding these as healthy signs of British repentance. He hurriedly cabled the kaiser that 'I see a new success for Your Majesty by this declaration', and ordered the newspapers which the government influenced to emphasize very fully the great achievement secured by German diplomacy in this matter.[121]

---

120   A.A./*Sachsen-Coburg-Gotha* 3, vol. 1, Wilhelm to Bülow, no. 6 of 27/5/1899; ibid., vol. 2, Victoria to Wilhelm, 25/5/1899; Salisbury Papers, Class G, McDonnell to Metternich (draft countersigned by Salisbury), 2/6/1899, and the reply of 6/6/1899.

121   London Embassy records, Hatzfeldt to Holstein, 20/6/1899 and reply of 21/6/1899; A.A./*Südsee-Inseln* 5, vol. 3, Bülow to A.A., tel. no. 11 of 18/7/1899; G.P., 14/2, nos. 4077-78; B.D., 1, nos. 143-44.

Bülow's great relief at these signs of British friendship
was not solely due to his regard for the kaiser and public
opinion: equally important was the rise of an alarming series
of differences between Berlin and St Petersburg in the spring
and summer of 1899. These quarrels enraged the kaiser, who
never possessed so high a regard for Russia as either Bülow
or Eulenburg, and they threatened to embitter the good
relations between the two countries for which the *Wilhelmstrasse* so earnestly strove. Wilhelm had a dislike of the
Russian foreign minister which possibly exceeded his feelings
towards Salisbury and when he learned that Muraviev had
been talking of a continental coalition against Britain, he
scornfully rejected it. Nevertheless, Berlin listened carefully
when Muraviev made diplomatic soundings as to a Russo-
German agreement upon the Turkish Empire. These talks
were swiftly exploited by Bülow to strengthen his hand in the
Samoan negotiations—Rothschild and other political figures
supposed to have an influence upon the prime minister were
warned that if the British drove Germany out of Samoa,
Berlin would respond by joining Russia.[122] For a short
while at the beginning of April, perhaps, Bülow actually
believed that what he was saying might turn out to be true.

As the meaning of the Russian proposals became clearer,
Berlin's tone altered. Muraviev's sole wish appeared to be
to prevent the German economic penetration of Asia Minor,
since Russia found it understandably hard to believe that the
Bagdad railway and other projects would not give Germany
a great political influence at Constantinople. However, the
Wilhelmstrasse also had to bear in mind that any major
agreement with Russia would alarm Austria-Hungary and
so annoy the British that no further colonial concessions
could be expected from them. It is nevertheless interesting to
see how Bülow, while threatening London that he would
join Russia, was at the same time informing St Petersburg
that Germany had to act carefully to avoid provoking the
British into hostility and was emphatically denying that there
was any parallel between Fashoda and Samoa.[123] In Berlin's
view, the only possibility of a Russo-German alliance lay
in a permanent mutual guarantee of the existing boundaries
of Germany, Russia and France, which would dissolve at
one blow the danger of the French *revanche* and a two-front
war. At this, the Russians backed away, protesting that France
would not permit such an agreement. At the same time, their

122 A.A./*Südsee-Inseln* 5, vol. 2, Hatzfeldt to A.A., tels. nos. 69 and 77 of 6/4/1899 and
12/4/1899; G.P., 14/2, nos. 4069-70.
123 Ibid., no. 4017.

warships were sent to Beirut, provoking Wilhelm to minute, 'Under no circumstances will I allow us to be pushed out of Syria (Palestine is the same to me) by Russia or at all hindered in our work.'[124] The kaiser was infuriated that the grandiose schemes dreamt up during his Palestine journey and the talks with Rhodes were being opposed by the Russians, who even threatened to come to an agreement with Britain, 'Muraviev is a completely brazen rascal!', he scribbled on one despatch.[125]

At this time, the Russian press violently attacked Berlin for sending a scientific expedition to Bear Island. Although the German government quickly denied any wish to annex the place, such criticisms riled the kaiser, who was also annoyed at the Russians for the way the peace conference at the Hague was developing. Most infuriating of all was the suggestion that Russia would not only stop Germany from moving into the Turkish Empire but also prevent her from taking over Austria-Hungary if that state should collapse. For such a 'Napoleonic' policy, Wilhelm minuted, Russia might receive the same fate as Napoleon III's Second Empire. With his imperial master upon such bad terms with both Britain and Russia, Bülow must have doubted if the 'Free Hand' was such a glorious policy after all, and Eulenburg wondered whether 'it is finally better to run after Russia and England than to anger both of them'.[126]

Nevertheless, they did not lose their nerve. It was agreed to handle Muraviev's soundings very dilatorily while proceeding silently with their schemes for Asia Minor. Meanwhile, Eulenburg engineered a spectacular gesture towards better Franco-German relations when he persuaded the kaiser to visit the French Schoolship-cruiser *Iphigenie*, which they met on their Norwegian cruise, to decorate its captain and to send a friendly telegram to President Loubet. For some weeks afterwards the press of Europe speculated upon a new rapprochement, which Eulenburg regarded as rather exaggerated, since the chief aim had been to improve Germany's standing with both Britain and Russia. At the same time, he strove to prevent a similar gesture being made to the Royal Navy schoolship in those waters. He need not have worried: still angered by the letters of Victoria and

---

124   A.A./*Deutschland* 131 *nr. 3 Secr.*, vol. 1, minute on Beirut Consul to chancellor, no. 993 of 18/5/1899; G.P., 14/2, nos. 4081-21.

125   A.A./*Deutschland* 131 *nr. 3 Secr.*, vol. 1, minute on Radolin to chancellor, no. 361 of 30/7/1899, omitted from G.P., 14/2, no. 4027. See also nos. 4022 and 4025.

126   BA, Eulenburg Papers, vol. 53, Eulenburg to Bülow, 10/7/1899; G.P., 13, no. 3539.

Salisbury, the kaiser treated the bewildered English com-modore to a fierce denunciation of the events in Samoa.[127]

Shortly afterwards, the news of Salisbury's conciliatory moves and of the queen's second invitation to the kaiser reached them. Wilhelm, furious at Muraviev's obstructive attitude, suddenly but not unpredictably reversed course. His hopes once again rose that he might after all be able to visit England, while Bülow felt that this could help to restore his 'Free Hand': 'The main point remains that the relations between our all-highest Master and Lord Salisbury be divested of their previous bitterness, which is so disadvant-ageous for our relations with England and so very crippling for our overall policy.'[128] Although the prime minister was still regarded with deep suspicion, Bülow pressed for better relations with him since 'to our enemies on the Neva and Seine, Tiber and Danube, scarcely anything less desirable could happen.'[129] A visit by the kaiser to Windsor was therefore tentatively agreed upon.

Faced with a number of disputes with Russia, which Bülow naturally tried to keep secret, the German anger at Britain's inconsiderate policy towards them had substantially modified. Their suspicion was further erased by the settlement of the Coburg affair, the departure of Chambers from Samoa, Salisbury's agreement to refer damages claims to arbitration and the prospect of Wilhelm's future visit to England. On the British side, too, it was realized that bad relations with Germany were a handicap to the overall policy. For positive and negative reasons, therefore, the bitterness was slowly dissolving. Only one major obstacle to the restoration of friendly relations remained: a satisfactory and final solution of the Samoan question.

127 BA, Eulenburg Papers, vol. 54, same to same, 6/7/1899 and 11/7/1899; ibid., vol. 53, same to same, 5/7/1899; F.O.800/9, enclosure in Sanderson to Lascelles, 2/8/1899.
128 London Embassy records, Bülow to Hatzfeldt, 13/7/1899 and 17/7/1899; BA, Eulenburg Papers, vol. 54, Eulenburg to Bülow, 15/7/1899.
129 A.A./*Preussen* 1 *nr.* 1 *nr.* 40, vol. 5, Bülow to A.A., no. 13 of 18/7/1899.

5

The Partition of the Islands 1899

i *The German Pressure is Renewed*

The restoration of better Anglo-German relations following
the bitterness between April and June was clearly motivated
by political expediency and in no way indicated a real change
of heart upon either side. British statesmen were well aware
that if events deteriorated in South Africa, 'the Emperor &
others will certainly give us a stab somewhere . . .'[1] Moreover,
a future meeting between Salisbury and Wilhelm hardly
promised any great improvement, since the prime minister
had warned Hatzfeldt that, although he would regard this
as an honour, he could not agree with the ambassador's
view 'as to the political advantage it would bring with it'.
For Salisbury, the differences between the two countries were
political and not personal, and stemmed from the fact that
they were rival colonial powers, which made their relations
'more liable to disturbance than would be the case in regard
to countries which had no colonial competition between
them'.[2]

The prime minister's deep suspicion of all things German
was in fact becoming disproportionate. When Eliot and
Sternburg sent identical telegrams from Samoa over one
particular problem, Salisbury's chief worry was that the
Germans would thus be able to break the diplomatic code.
Moreover, he insisted that British warships should not leave
Samoan waters until all German vessels were gone.[3] More
pointed still were the British attempts to ensure that the
secret agreement over the Portuguese colonies was not
activated. Lisbon was encouraged in her attempts to remain
solvent and assured that Britain would not allow any undue
pressure to be brought against her; and when it was learnt
that a powerful German squadron was to visit the Portuguese
capital, a still larger force of British battleships purposely
arrived there a day earlier and took all the berths.[4] This was
hardly the way in which Berlin had interpreted the 1898

1 Curzon Papers, vol. 10a, Brodrick to Curzon, 7/7/1899.
2 F.O.64/1468, Salisbury to Hatzfeldt, no. 131A of 19/7/1899.
3 F.O.58/325, Salisbury minute on Eliot to Salisbury, tel. no. 1 of 16/5/1899; F.O.58/332,
Villiers minute on Adm. to F.O., 4/9/1899.
4 Salisbury Papers, Class E, Goschen to Salisbury, 7/5/1899; B.D., 1, no. 109.

arrangement, for Bülow had sent Tattenbach 10,000 marks with instructions to use it secretly to pay for Portuguese newspaper articles which would favour a colonial transaction (i.e., withdrawal) to improve the country's financial state.[5]

Furthermore, Salisbury's attitude to the entire Samoan affair remained unchanged. He accepted in full Eliot's conclusion that the return of Mata'afa and the agitation of the Germans had been the main causes for the troubles— without perhaps considering that the instructions given to the British commissioner had already pointed along those lines. Nor did the prime minister criticize Maxse for his too ardent efforts to crush the 'rebels': rather, he recommended that the consul receive a C.M.G. for services rendered, a gesture which provoked annoyed comments in Germany and caused the kaiser to decorate Rose as a reply.[6] In addition, Salisbury steadfastly ignored all German suggestions that an agreement be reached upon the future of Morocco and when Hatzfeldt hinted that this was necessary to restore relations damaged by the Samoan affair he was told rather bitterly: 'You want to please your Kaiser and I am to help you.' The British fleet was sent to Morocco as a strong hint to Berlin that no interference would be tolerated.[7] Finally, the Germans soon learnt that the prime minister had different ideas to theirs as to the meaning of the damages agreement and it was not until 24 August that this matter was completely settled.[8]

On the German side, distrust of Salisbury was still rife and the worst possible motives were attributed to his every move. In the damages question, Hatzfeldt was instructed to ensure that Salisbury did not 'entrench himself behind a possible American opposition, in order to cut loose from the arbitration proposal once again'.[9] Nevertheless, Bülow was clearly anxious to prevent a further deterioration in Anglo-German relations, for reasons already outlined. Throughout July and early August, the kaiser was absolutely furious with the Russians and Eulenburg nervously advised the foreign minister against suggesting anything anti-Russian lest Wilhelm go too far with the idea. From the other side, Holstein warned Bülow not to adopt a too anti-British policy since the kaiser

5 A.A./*England 78 nr.* 1 *Secr.*, vol. 12, Bülow to Tattenbach, no. 22 of 21/3/1899.

6 F.O.58/321, Salisbury note of 15/8/1899; F.O.58/332, Gough to Salisbury. no. 218 of 26/8/1899; Vagts, *Weltpolitik*, 1, p. 896.

7 *Holstein Papers*, 4, p. 141; A. J. P. Taylor, 'British Policy in Morocco, 1886-1902' in *English Historical Review*, 66 (1951), p. 364.

8 F.O.58/332, Salisbury to Gough, no. 136 of 25/7/1899; ibid., bases of agreement, 23/8/1899.

9 London Embassy records, Holstein to Hatzfeldt, 30/6/1899 and 22/7/1899.

would not follow it for very long.[10] Of course, Bülow himself
also realized the dangers to his 'Free Hand', and particularly
to his naval policy, which bad relations with Britain could
cause. As he put it confidentially to Richthofen:

> A so heated personal relationship, which has existed for four months
> between His Majesty on the one side and the English royal family and
> Lord Salisbury on the other side, cannot last very long without creating
> serious complications for us and in any case hurting the freedom of
> action of our policy. The dynastic relations between Berlin and London
> should at least be as friendly as those between St. Petersburg and London
> . . . If the personal relations of the All-Highest to the English statesmen
> could again be brought upon normal lines through a visit of our Kaiser in
> Windsor, then or overall policy would be thereby greatly eased *and that*
> *exactly at a time when, in view of our naval inferiority, we must operate*
> *so carefully, like the caterpillar before it has grown into the butterfly.*[11]

At the same time, however, this was not going to be a hasty
retreat into the arms of the British. Both Bülow and Eulenburg
insisted that a satisfactory Samoan settlement was 'the first
and most essential precondition for a normal relationship
with England'. Moreover, and this decision was to be the
cause of much later worry and calculation, it had to be
arranged *before* the kaiser visited England: if it was not, then
he would not go. While the two statesmen were probably
the originators of this condition, Wilhelm himself found their
proposal to be 'self-evident'. The idea of going to Windsor
greatly attracted the kaiser, Eulenburg reported, yet his bitter
criticisms of England continued.[12] Whether all three fully
realized the risk such an inflexible decision involved when it
was formulated at the end of August, is hard to say. To put
such pressure upon Salisbury, whose habit of carefully and
minutely examining every proposal was well known, was a
policy which hardly appeared to have much chance of success.
It was, indeed, to provoke his resentment still further and,
according to Eckardstein, to occasion the prime minister's
famous retort that he was not going to be dictated to from
Berlin with a stop-watch in the hand.[13] Yet for the Germans
to cancel the visit to Windsor at short notice would enrage
the queen and annoy the British public, and all this at a
time when Germany's relations with Russia were very poor
indeed.

10 BA, Eulenburg Papers, vol. 54, Eulenburg to Bülow, 27/7/1899; *Holstein Papers*,
4, pp. 142-44.

11 BA, Richthofen Papers, vol. 5, Bülow to Richthofen, Secret, 26/7/1899. (my stress).

12 Ibid.; see also vol. 16, Eulenburg to Richthofen, Very Confidential 26/7/1899; BA,
Eulenburg Papers, vol. 54, Eulenburg to Bülow, 26/7/1899 and 27/7/1899; G.P., 14/2,
no. 4079.

13 Hermann v. Eckardstein, *Lebenserinnerungen und Politische Denkwürdigkeiten*, 2
vols. (Leipzig, 1920), 2, p. 14.

Incidentally, while Bülow welcomed the idea that the kaiser would be able to visit England, he foresaw dangers to his policy if Wilhelm was either too irritated or too forward during his stay. He therefore suggested to Richthofen that any such 'personal misunderstandings' would be avoided if Lascelles was privately asked to secure an invitation for the foreign minister also.[14] This was duly arranged.

Bülow and the kaiser did not press London at once regarding Samoa, and Hatzfeldt's instructions during August chiefly concerned a final solution of the arbitration agreement. Possibly they were awaiting the report of the commissioners upon the future of Samoa and did not wish to move until this had been received and digested. Whatever the cause, it seemed to prove to be a fortunate waiting-period, since the overall situation appeared far brighter to Berlin by the end of that month and Bülow's confidence in his 'Free Hand' policy returned. Both the German and Russian governments preferred to forget about an arrangement over the Straits for the moment, although Muraviev and the Czar retained their deep suspicions of the kaiser's policy in Turkey. Bülow, however, found it easy or convenient to forget such disputes, and to persuade himself that his relations with Russia were fully restored.

Not even the news that the French foreign minister, Delcassé, was travelling to St Petersburg for important discussions could prick his bubble of confidence. Both he and Holstein thought that this trip boded ill for Britain, and Hatzfeldt was instructed to impress this fact upon Rothschild and other contacts.[15] In fact, although these Franco-Russian talks did lead to the decision that the two nations must co-operate more fully against Britain than had been the case at Fashoda, Delcassé's great concern at the time was that Germany would seize Austria-Hungary (and therefore a port on the Mediterranean) should the Dual Monarchy suddenly collapse after the death of Francis Joseph. To prevent such an *Anschluss*, the French and Russian governments re-wrote the terms of the Dual Alliance so as to include within its aims the preservation of the European balance of power. While Delcassé and Muraviev had a natural anxiety about their many quarrels with Britain, they had an equal or even greater fear of German ambition in central Europe and Asia Minor.[16]

---

14 BA, Richthofen Papers, vol. 5, Bülow to Richthofen, 3/8/1899.
15 Ibid., London Embassy records, Holstein to Hatzfeldt, 3/8/1899.
16 C. Andrew, *Théophile Delcassé and the Making of the Entente Cordiale* (London, 1968) pp. 119-35.

To Berlin, the political map of the world read rather differently. At the beginning of July, Bülow repeated his view that Germany's neutrality during a future Anglo-Russian war would automatically restrain France from joining such a conflict, and that every sensible English politician should realize this and treat Germany more considerately.[17] Moreover, German-American relations seemed to be improving rapidly and, in the middle of the following month, the special envoy in Washington, Mumm von Schwarzenstein, reported jubilantly that

> according to what I can discover here up 'til now, the peak of the crisis in our relations to the United States appears to have passed. The temperate and waiting attitude of our policy concerning Samoa, the clever inspiring of the German press from Berlin, Sternburg's good relationship to Tripp and the personal and journalistic action of the Embassy upon public opinion here have all contributed their own part to open the Americans' eyes about the continuous English agitations (against us).[18]

Finally, the growing possibility of a war in South Africa seemed to give a further trump into the hands of the Germans. Only after the breakdown of the Bloemfontein Conference in early June was this matter given serious consideration by Berlin and a neutral position decided upon. While this was clearly in line with the spirit of the Portuguese colonies arrangement, Holstein pointed out further reasons why they should remain impartial and refuse to mediate for either side.

> If we demand concessions from the Transvaal which would cause bad blood there, then we have difficulties with German public opinion. If we advise the English not to lay claim any longer to their hegemonial position i.e. as Suzerain, then we will arouse acute mistrust from England.[19]

Believing that Kruger would back down, the *Auswärtiges Amt* did not expect a war, and thus Bülow was content to let Richthofen and Hatzfeldt attempt to arrange a partition of Samoa with Salisbury.

By the end of August, the German viewpoint had altered. The tenor of the commissioners' joint report was known by then, and this strengthened their belief that further tripartite rule was unsound. In particular, several of the clauses in the new administrative scheme were rejected out of hand, despite Sternburg's pleadings. The members of the Colonial Division

17 A.A./*England* 78, vol. 12, Bülow to Minister at Tehran, no. 9 of 1/7/1899.
18 A.A./*Südsee-Inseln* 5, vol. 4, Mumm to A.A., 20/8/1899; Germany's favourable diplomatic position was also stressed in A.A./*Deutschland* 137 *Secr.*, vol. 3, Top Secret memo of 15/8/1899.
19 G.P., 15, no. 4362.

of the *Auswärtiges Amt* opposed the abolition of consular jurisdiction because it would weaken *Deutschtum* in Samoa, while the *D.H.P.G.* pleaded against this proposal lest it give the Supreme Court the power to hear the complaints of the plantation labourers. The Germans also disliked the idea of abolishing the presidency, and opposed the alteration of the Apia municipal boundaries. Having no desire to see the commissioners' scheme implemented, therefore, Berlin wished for a final partition settlement.[20]

More decisive still were the despatches received from Hatzfeldt. On 17 August, he pointed out that only a Franco-Russian intervention on behalf of the Transvaal would cause the British to make great offers for Germany's friendship. On the twenty-sixth, he reported that in his opinion even Chamberlain would 'deal like a Jew' and not offer much for a German withdrawal from Samoa, while Salisbury would oppose any concessions over Morocco. By the following day, however, he reported that the South African situation had worsened again after the Transvaal's bold attempt to offer concessions to the Uitlanders in return for the abolition of all suzerainty. Although Salisbury denied that war was in sight and contested Hatzfeldt's view that the Dual Alliance would take advantage of Britain's embarrassment, Wilhelm welcomed the South African news. The prime minister, he noted, had forgotten that Russia would move towards India and Persia during such a war, 'and then our declaration of friendship will begin to rise high in the market, especially in London!'[21]

On the basis of this information, German policy was formulated. While attention was focussed upon Delcassé's talks in St Petersburg upon the one hand and the looming prospects of a South African war upon the other, Berlin would increase its pressure upon London for a quick settlement of the Samoan question; and to turn the screw still tighter, Hatzfeldt was told that a settlement before the kaiser's visit was an 'absolute necessity'. Nevertheless, the German terms did not appear to be excessive, for while Germany took Upolu and America Tutuila, Britain would be compensated with Savai'i, the Tongan group and the rather insignificant

20 R.Kol.A.2912, Sternburg to the chancellor, no. 20 of 18/7/1899, followed by Irmer and Rose memos. Although this report did not reach Berlin until 7/9/1899, its contents were known and disapproved of before then: see Meyer-Delius (D.H.P.G.) to Bülow, 29/8/1899, and the various marginal comments on the *Münchener Neueste Nachrichten* (17/8/1899), *Magdeburgischer Zeitung* (19/8/1899) and *Kölnische Zeitung* (14/8/1899 and 22/8/1899), ibid.

21 BA, Bülow Papers, vol. 23, Hatzfeldt to Holstein (copy), 17/8/1899; London Embassy records, Hatzfeldt to Holstein, 26/8/1899; G.P., 15, no. 4374.

Savage Island. If, however, the British insisted that they must have Upolu and Savai'i, Germany would withdraw for something of equal value, such as Zanzibar or the English part of New Guinea or the Solomons. Clearly, Bülow had little *personal* attachment to Upolu, and his chief concern was to maintain the 'Free Hand' and to satisfy public opinion.[22]

Berlin's view of the situation in Britain was basically the correct one, although the Germans tended to exaggerate the differences between Salisbury and Chamberlain over South African policy. Certainly, as Brodrick himself noted, 'all minds are on the Transvaal' and the Cabinet was meeting almost weekly to consider the grave development in South Africa.[23] But it was not correct, and this Professor Grenville has clearly demonstrated, to portray Chamberlain as the war-monger and Salisbury as the statesman preferring peace at almost any price. Nor was it really true to imagine that only Salisbury had his eye upon the overall diplomatic scene, although this clearly was in line with his normal practice of considering the wider implications of any action. Other members of the government, but more particularly Goschen, Balfour, Chamberlain, Devonshire and Brodrick, were anxiously watching the diplomatic manoeuvres of the European powers at this stage. The chief difference was that they all believed in principle that the kaiser should be wooed into friendship as a way of forestalling any continental coalition: Salisbury, much more sceptical about the chances of any such combination being formed, did not. His views on this were shared by the permanent staff: while Goschen found the Delcassé-Muraviev talks 'not pleasant reading', Sanderson referred Lascelles to the rumours of a hostile coalition and added, 'I scarcely think that it sounds likely.'[24]

The prime minister was obviously not eager to enter into lengthy and probably heated discussions with the Germans at this crucial moment. In addition to the impending war, his wife had been seriously ill since July and this was gravely affecting his spirits. Hamilton, the secretary for India found him 'very low & depressed: he has now a very heavy load of responsibilities'.[25] Consequently, when Salisbury discussed the Samoan commissioners' report at the end of August with Hatzfeldt, he declared that it would be better to wait until

22 G.P., 14/2, no. 4081.
23 F.O.800/9, Brodrick to Lascelles, 1/9/1899. For the British policy towards the Transvaal, see Grenville, *Salisbury and Foreign Policy*, pp. 235-64; Robinson, Gallagher, Denny, *Africa and the Victorians*, pp. 449-61.
24 Salisbury Papers, Class E, Goschen to Salisbury, 23/8/1899; F.O.800/9, Sanderson to Lascelles, 2/8/1899.
25 Curzon Papers, vol. 144, Hamilton to Curzon, 6/9/1899.

he met Bülow during the imperial visit later in the year. He would then propose that the two powers should decide by lot which one should receive both Upolu and Savai'i, with Tutuila automatically falling to the United States. Since the latter island was some distance from the other two, it could be governed separately without much difficulty.

Dismayed by these ideas, the ambassador believed a success to be 'extraordinarily doubtful' when he received his instructions a few days later to press for a quick solution. He had much preferred to leave it to Bülow and Salisbury, and pointed out privately that the prime minister would argue that Savai'i and Tonga had been frequently offered to Britain and always turned down as being inadequate. Moreover, if Berlin asked for something as valuable as Zanzibar or New Guinea for its withdrawal, Salisbury would claim an equal compensation for a British retreat from the group. Stressing that the prime minister was probably serious when he suggested tossing up for Samoa, Hatzfeldt could only propose that Germany remain cool to Britain and render no friendly services to her.[26]

Anticipating stiff resistance from the prime minister, Hatzfeldt hoped to sound out Chamberlain as soon as the latter came into London.[27] If the colonial secretary could be persuaded to agree, then he could use his influence upon Salisbury; if not, then Hatzfeldt would resume his more direct talks. It was no novel course the ambassador was suggesting. Often believing the two statesmen to be equally powerful, the Germans made a habit of switching from one to the other upon a number of questions; and because of Chamberlain's openly-expressed wish for a close understanding with Germany and Salisbury's known desire to settle things with Russia and France, the colonial secretary was often secretly sought out in such a way. Interestingly enough, if these two-tiered manoeuvres failed completely, then the prime minister was adjudged to be the more influential; if they succeeded, then it was due to Chamberlain's influence. Thus the German dislike of the 'French' Salisbury, as Bülow called him,[28] was always linked to the results of any particular request to the British government.

Chamberlain, however, was not to be contacted and in the meantime Holstein came up with the idea that the partition problem itself should be submitted to arbitration. On 8 September, despite his own doubts, Hatzfeldt therefore

---

26 London Embassy records, Hatzfeldt to Holstein, 26/8/1899 and 30/8/1899; *Holstein Papers*, 4, pp. 152-55.
27 London Embassy records, Hatzfeldt to Holstein, 1/9/1899 and 2/9/1899.
28 G.P., 15, no. 4385.

broached the topic with the prime minister. The occasion was hardly suitable, for that day the Cabinet had decided to send 10,000 troops from England and India to South Africa in view of the possibility of a Boer attack upon Natal, and thus the British were too busy to bother with Samoa. Nevertheless, Salisbury did not altogether reject the idea of an arbitration and listened carefully when the ambassador explained that by such a method neither government could be blamed by its public opinion for losing Upolu if a neutral judge decided against them. While asking for a written précis of these suggestions, he promised that he would consult his Cabinet colleagues. The chances of an early settlement, Hatzfeldt felt, were therefore not too gloomy.[29]

Three days later, the ambassador's hopes were shattered by a twin assault. After receiving the written précis, Salisbury passed it on to the Colonial Office, apparently with a favourable minute. Wingfield, the permanent under-secretary, felt that they still ought to object to a partition of Samoa, to which Chamberlain replied: 'I agree. We should discourage any idea of partition as it is obvious that the German plan would take the oyster, leaving us the shell.'[30] Their fear clearly was that Upolu would be given to Germany. On 12 September, therefore, the prime minister informed Hatzfeldt that he could not enter into any arbitration arrangement unless he knew in advance by what principles the judge would be guided in deciding which nation should be given that particular island, since, according to the German idea, this was all that was to be settled and the losing nation would automatically and without appeal take the other islands named.[31]

At almost exactly the same time, Bülow had cabled to the *Auswärtiges Amt* that the kaiser could not accept any scheme whereby Upolu might not become German. Public opinion was too fixed upon the island where most of the German trade was concentrated, and where German sailors had lost their lives, to allow it to fall into British hands, particularly after the events of that spring. While his fears were chiefly occasioned by the belief that only Upolu and Savai'i were to go to arbitration and a few days later he seemed readier to accept the scheme which involved the Tongan group and Savage Island, Wilhelm had revealed yet again his acute

29   London Embassy records, Holstein to Hatzfeldt, 5/9/1899 and 7/9/1899, and Hatzfeldt to Holstein, 6/9/1899 and 8/9/1899; G.P., 14/2, no. 4082. On the cabinet meeting, see Salisbury Papers, Class F, Salisbury to the Queen, 8/9/1899, and Cab. 41/25/18.

30   Chamberlain Papers, JC7/2/2A/29, minutes of 11/9/1899. The précis, and Hatzfeldt's covering letter of 8/9/1899, can be found in the Salisbury Papers, A122/67 and 68.

31   Salisbury Papers, A122/69, Salisbury to Hatzfeldt, 12/9/1899; G.P., 14/2, no. 4084; B.D., 1, no. 146.

awareness of what Upolu meant to German colonial circles.
If he convinced himself of its necessity, then his entourage
and diplomats could do nothing against his demand and
would have to strive for Upolu, even if the alternatives seemed
more attractive to them. At any rate, Hatzfeldt was left in
no doubt that Wilhelm 'looks on this question as the acid
test for our attitude towards England'.[32]

It was then, late on 13 September, that Berlin received
the news of the prime minister's caution over the arbitration
principles and that he seemed to be attempting to postpone
the question. Nor were Salisbury's own proposals very
attractive, since he suggested either a plebiscite by the Samoans
themselves, or that the nation receiving Savai'i should also
receive a sum of money with which to build a harbour, thus
making it as attractive as Upolu. He also had the nerve to
suggest that both islands should be split down the midde
and divided between them. Hatzfeldt reported privately that
'Salisbury is turning and twisting like an eel' and that he was
clearly waiting to see how events in South Africa would
develop before committing himself. This opinion both
Richthofen and, later, Bülow fully shared, while the kaiser
made several angry minutes upon the ambassador's despatch.[33]

At this point, Holstein appears to have made a grave decision
by himself, for Bülow was away and Richthofen rarely acted
upon his own initiative: Hatzfeldt was privately told to
'Chance it now for bend or break, applying all means of
pressure.'[34] On this very day, 14 September, the ambassador
had just discovered that his job was perhaps in jeopardy as
a result of his failure to extract concessions from Salisbury.
This, Hatzfeldt pointed out, was very unfair, and the rumour
seems to have been a false one. However, it cannot but
have affected the letter he wrote to Salisbury, warning him
that 'an absolutely trustworthy source' had let him know
that unless the kaiser was satisfied in the Samoan question
there would be a complete change in Germany's general
policy ('un changement complet de notre politique generale')
and that he would be withdrawn from London.[35] The threat
had been made, openly and clearly; and the only question
that remained was how the prime minister would respond to
it.

32 London Embassy records, Hatzfeldt to Holstein, 12/9/1899, and reply of 13/9/1899;
G.P., 14/2, no. 4083; *Holstein Papers*, 4, p. 155.

33 Ibid., p. 156; G.P., 14/2, no. 4085-87.

34 London Embassy records, Holstein to Hatzfeldt, 14/9/1899.

35 Salisbury Papers, A122/70, Hatzfeldt to Salisbury, Private and Confidential 14/9/1899;
Holstein Papers, 4, p. 156-57; Grenville, *Salisbury and Foreign Policy*, pp. 275-77.

On the following day, Salisbury replied, apparently without having consulted anyone on this matter. He would deeply regret the ambassador's withdrawal, he wrote, 'but no fear of consequences . . . could justify me in accepting terms that would not adequately express our rights'. A humiliating bargain would arouse great feeling both in England and Australia, and this, not any personal caprice, was the reason for his policy. In his next few lines, he attempted to impress upon Hatzfeldt the plain fact that the idea, so firmly fixed in Berlin's mind, of Britain being especially dependent upon Germany was absolutely wrong.

> I have always earnestly desired a good understanding between England and Germany, because I believe it to be of great value to both countries and to Europe generally. But I cannot admit that it has had a special value for England separately. As a matter of fact, I cannot remember that, except as to the vote of the Caisse three years ago, we have ever made any proposals we wished Germany to accept, but Germany had made two or three proposals which she wished England to accept. We are generally satisfied with the status quo, and have no occasion to ask the assistance of others to get that status quo changed.[36]

This was, in a nutshell, Salisbury's German policy, and had been so ever since he had wriggled away from diplomatic dependence upon Bismarck. By this blunt refusal to acknowledge Berlin's arguments or to succumb to their pressure, the prime minister had called their bluff, albeit in a most sorrowful and polite manner. The next move was up to the Germans. They, however, were already in action, for on the previous day, after a week of patient waiting and hoping, contact had been established with Chamberlain.

ii   *Samoa and the Coming of the Boer War*

On 12 September 1899, Baron von Eckardstein wrote to Chamberlain and requested an interview with him. The Baron explained to the colonial secretary that he had recently returned from Berlin, where people were hoping for a satisfactory elimination of the points which separated the two governments. This was a rosy description of the feelings at the *Wilhelmstrasse*, where, if Eckardstein's memoirs can be believed, Holstein was contemplating those blunt threats which he was in fact to order Hatzfeldt to issue a few days later. Nevertheless, since the knowledge of Salisbury's procrastinations had not reached Berlin before Eckardstein left, he was given instructions to attempt to reach an unofficial

36   Salisbury Papers, A122/71, Salisbury to Hatzfeldt (prior draft), 15/9/1899.

arrangement on Samoa with his acquaintance Chamberlain should the ambassador's efforts with Salisbury prove fruitless. As it happened, this second negotiator fortuitously entered the scene just when the formal discussions appeared to have completely broken down. Only on the sixteenth did Bülow and the kaiser learn of Hatzfeldt's private letter to Salisbury, and they accepted without demur the explanation that since the prime minister remained stubborn it would be better to circumvent him.[37] It was, after all, the only alternative, apart from the complete breakdown which nobody wanted, to long and protracted discussions with Salisbury.

The Anglo-German dispute over Samoa placed the colonial secretary in an ambivalent position. Although his expectations of an alliance with Berlin had been somewhat subdued since the previous year and he had informed Eckardstein in April that 'now it is too late', he still firmly believed that a good understanding with Germany would assist the manifold problems of the British empire; and that, if such an understanding could be attained by disposing of the minor controversies between them, an alliance might yet be possible. In the early summer of 1898, when jotting down ideas for a seven-year defensive arrangement between the two powers, he had noted that Samoa was one of the smaller matters which should be settled within this overall scheme.[38] Moreover, since he was particularly concerned with the South African question, it was natural that he should place it above all others as the situation there worsened. On the other hand, Chamberlain was well aware of his duties to the Australasian Colonies. As Hatzfeldt explained;

> This minister is the leading representative of the widely-spread imperialistic ideas here, which have especially in view the gathering together of the independent English colonies to the assistance of the motherland and which therefore carefully avoid everything that could provoke their annoyance. Hence for a great part the otherwise inexplicable fact that people here have had fewer doubts about exposing themselves to a, so they hope, temporary annoyance in Germany regarding Samoa, than about vexing the unjustifiable wishes of Australia by a withdrawal from the group.[39]

Nevertheless, throughout 1899 Chamberlain was considering a settlement which might satisfy both sides. In May, when it had become apparent that Germany would not accept the Gilberts as the price of her withdrawal, the colonial minister

37 Chamberlain Papers, JC7/2/2B/4, Eckardstein to Chamberlain, 12/9/1899; London Embassy records, Hatzfeldt to Holstein, 14/9/1899, and Holstein to Hatzfeldt, 16/9/1899; Eckardstein, *Lebenserinnerungen*, 2, pp. 33-35.
38 Chamberlain Papers, JC7/2/2A/25, note of June(?), 1898.
39 A.A./*Südsee-Inseln* 5, vol. 3, Hatzfeldt to chancellor, no. 414 of 25/5/1899.

wondered if Berlin would be satisfied with the British Solomon Islands and Savage Island in return for London's assumption of control in Upolu, Savai'i and the Tongan group. He also had in mind some final partition of the neutral area in West Africa lying between Togoland and the Gold Coast, which had been a growing source of trouble to both sides for many years.[40] Yet, although Chamberlain was clearly in favour of a far-reaching agreement with Germany, it was he, and not Salisbury, who had prevented the German suggestion for an arbitration of the Samoan affair from taking place. The colonial secretary's views were succinctly stated in a note of 15 September.

> My personal opinion is that Samoa is of little value to us. The question is obviously a Colonial one and it is only from this point of view that one has to consider it.
>   Put in this connection it is very important and it is certain that Australia and to a much greater extent New Zealand would be bitterly offended if an arrangement was made which they consider unsatisfactory . . . I do not think they would object to a division between U.S.A. and G.B. but they would certainly dislike the proprietorship of any part of the group by any European Power. Still, in place of the Condominium now existing, they could not reasonably complain if a fair division were made but they would certainly resent the acquisition of Upolu by Germany. I do not think it can safely go to arbitration which would almost certainly end in this result . . . & I believe that we must make the best of the present joint arrangement.[41]

While he willingly agreed to meet Eckardstein, therefore, his chief concern was to get Germany out of Upolu at least.

By 18 September, this determination had somewhat altered. On the same day as Chamberlain's above note (i.e., the fifteenth), Richthofen had hinted that Germany would probably reject parts of the commissioners' report, that the kaiser's trip to Windsor might be affected and that Berlin might wish to raise the question of German rights in Tonga, where Britain had recently concluded a treaty with the king. Obviously, none of this made pleasant reading for the British, who were now made aware of the many consequences of refusing to agree upon a partition arrangement. On that same day, Salisbury had outlined the state of the negotiations to Lascelles, concluding somewhat sarcastically that Hatzfeldt's anxiety on the topic appeared to arise neither from the value of the islands nor the feelings of the German public but from the fact 'that it is a question on which the emperor himself has fixed his heart, and is pursuing his own solution with his

---

40 Chamberlain Papers, JC7/4/2/19, notes of 16/5/1899; ibid., JC7/2/2A/27, Chamberlain query of 12/8/1899 and C.O. replies.
41 Ibid., JC7/2/2A/15, note of 15/9/1899.

well-known inflexible tenacity'.[42] Since this despatch was sent on the same day as his firm reply to Hatzfeldt's private letter, the prime minister appeared to be unmoved by the German threats. Three days later, upon receipt of Lascelles' own report, he was rather more worried and confided to Chamberlain: 'I do not see my way "out" quite clearly—and am doubtful what to recommend. Both the German Emperor and New Zealand are quite unreasonable and it is difficult to steer between the two.' Forwarding Hatzfeldt's warning of the fourteenth to him, he pointed out how 'Samoa and the Transvaal are not wholly disconnected, at least in the mind of the German Emperor.'[43]

It was knowledge of this particular letter which occasioned the colonial secretary's famous remark that 'The policy of the German Empire since Bismarck has always been one of undisguised blackmail!' Yet despite his apparently greater indignation, Chamberlain's reaction was quite different to Salisbury's. Believing that 'at the present time the Transvaal question is of much greater importance than any other', he was willing to pay the price for German support 'and we must face the colonial indignation as best we can'. It is also interesting to note, with regard to later developments, that the prime minister was openly told of the planned meeting with Eckardstein and that this letter concluded with the words: 'In any case, I will follow your lead and accept your decision.'[44] When a copy of Salisbury's despatch of 15 September to Lascelles reached the Colonial Office a few days later, the idea of withdrawing from Samoa was vigorously attacked by all the officials there but Chamberlain meaningfully noted: 'I am in communication with Lord Salisbury on this matter which is complicated by other Imperial considerations.'[45] As Bülow had predicted, the looming war with the Transvaal and the rumours of intervention by the European powers were beginning to influence the colonial secretary's mind.

There was absolutely no intention upon the German government's part of joining an anti-British coalition, however, and they hoped that merely the threat posed by this eventuality would be enough to convince London to give way over Samoa. More they would not do, for several reasons. Firstly, the kaiser was furious with Muraviev and did not wish to listen to his 'ingratiating phrases'. Wilhelm thought that this was a

42 B.D., 1, nos. 146-47.
43 Chamberlain Papers, JC5/67/123, Salisbury to Chamberlain, 18/9/1899.
44 Ibid., JC11/30/184, Chamberlain to Salisbury, 18/9/1899.
45 C.O.225/58, minutes on paper 24959, F.O. to C.O., received 18/9/1899.

Russian device to throw the western nations against each other while she expanded elsewhere, i.e., that the Russians believed 'that things will start up in the Transvaal and then they wish to go to work in Asia, Persia, etc. and need us to cover their backs. *Conte de fil blanc*'.[46] If a continental coalition opposed Britain, the vast trade and the colonial territories of the Germans would be seized while Russia suffered virtually nothing. Furthermore, the German policy was specifically aimed at avoiding any risk of conflict with Britain, at least until a much larger fleet had been constructed.

Finally, Berlin did not trust the Dual Alliance. Only if Germany's territorial integrity, and this included Alsace-Lorraine, was guaranteed by treaty, would Berlin even contemplate such an idea. While this condition was not discussed until the spring of 1900, and then abandoned in anger by both sides, it was always the *conditio sine qua non* for the Germans. While they made encouraging noises to the French during the early stages of the conflict in South Africa, they quickly backed away as soon as the Samoan arrangement had been secured. Even had they recalled Hatzfeldt from London because of Salisbury's intransigence, it is scarcely likely that they would have opposed Britain: they might, however, have given the Dual Alliance more encouragement to intervene. It was they, and not the French, who were the chief obstacles to a continental alliance during the Boer War.[47]

The only matter upon which the Germans would stand firm against London was in the question of the Portuguese colonies, although here also no war was contemplated. But if Britain even temporarily took control of Delagoa Bay, Wilhelm and Bülow were determined to seize Tiger Bay, in Portuguese Angola, to obtain compensation and to stem the roar of protest which would inevitably come from German colonial circles. Lisbon's feelings on the subject were, of course, to be ignored. The decision was kept secret even from Hatzfeldt, although he may have suggested the move in the first place, and three German warships were ordered to patrol near Tiger Bay. Only on 16 October, when a British occupation of southern Mozambique appeared to be less likely, was this order rescinded.[48] In view of London's firm

---

46 A.A./*Frankreich* 102, vol. 21, minute on Radolin to the chancellor, no. 382 of 26/8/1899; G.P., 15, no. 4212.

47 G.P., 15, chap. 103; Langer, *Diplomacy of Imperialism*, pp. 651-72; C. Andrew, *Delcassé*, pp. 158-79; Grenville, *Salisbury and Foreign Policy*, pp. 269-90.

48 A.A./*England* 78 *nr.* 1 *Secr.*, vol. 13, Richthofen to Bülow, no. 39 of 10/9/1899, and reply of same, no. 104, Top Secret, of 11/9/1899; Holstein note on Derenthall memo of 16/10/1899. For Hatzfeldt's earlier suggestion of this course, see *Holstein Papers*, 4, p.154.

commitment to protect Portugal's territory, which was given in the treaty Salisbury was negotiating with Soveral at this very time, it was indeed fortunate for Anglo-German relations that the British desisted from taking control of Delagoa Bay.

Part of the German 'bluff' to make Britain more eager to bow to their wishes over Samoa lay in the attempts to persuade the Czar to call in at Potsdam in early November upon his journey from Copenhagen and Darmstadt to St Petersburg. Holstein had advocated such a meeting in July in the hope of improving Russo-German relations which the dispute over the Straits had disturbed. However, the Czar turned down the invitation, explaining that he would not have the time, which provoked Wilhelm to write angrily about the Russian ruler's 'laziness and passivity'. Worried about this development, Bülow persuaded the kaiser that their efforts should continue 'both in the interests of the monarchical order and our *Weltpolitik*'. As he explained to the *Wilhelmstrasse*, 'In view of our position towards England it is necessary that our relations with Russia experience no darkening. The better we stand with Russia, the more regard the English will pay us.'[49] After much earnest pleading by the Germans, Nicholas reluctantly gave way and agreed to pay a short visit on 8 November. Once more, Bülow would be able to demonstrate to the British that Germany stood well with Russia; and, in the shorter term, this meeting would provoke further rumours of negotiations for a continental alliance and further nervousness in the British camp.

While the Germans approached the Samoan talks of September and October in an apparently strong diplomatic position, the British one was clearly very weak. By 19 September, as his note to Chamberlain reveals, even Salisbury appeared to be uncertain as to what should be done. In contrast, Bülow cabled to the *Auswärtiges Amt* that they would be blamed for lack of skill if the worsening crisis in South Africa was not used to obtain a satisfactory settlement of several questions outstanding with England 'especially that of Samoa'. At the same time, he declared that it must not seem as if Germany desired to exploit Britain's difficulties and Holstein several times urged Hatzfeldt to say that it was Salisbury's tergiversations alone which had postponed the negotiations until this time.[50]

49 Hatzfeldt Papers, Holstein to Hatzfeldt, 22/7/1899; A.A./*Preussen* 1 *nr.* 1 *nr.* 4*b*, vol. 12, Bülow to A.A., no. 119 of 13/9/1899, and Wilhelm to A.A., no. 130 of 14/9/1899; ibid., Bülow to Wilhelm, no. 4 of 16/9/1899, and Bülow to A.A., no. 140 of 21/9/1899; G.P., 13, nos. 3540-43.
50 London Embassy records, Holstein to Hatzfeldt, 17/9/1899 and 22/9/1899; G.P., 15, footnote on p. 396.

Chamberlain made his suspicions about the 'opportunism' very clear in his first talk with Eckardstein on 20 September. He nevertheless recognized the force of the German insinuations and sought to arrive at a quick solution of the problem by proposing that Germany should receive the very fertile British-owned Volta Triangle while the Neutral Zone fell to Britain. Because of this great offer by London, the colonial minister claimed Upolu and offered Savai'i to Berlin, while the Tongan group and Savage Island should be divided equally. This latter point, due to the Baron's query, was left open to further discussion but a promising start had been made provided that the Germans would agree to giving up Upolu. Interestingly enough, Chamberlain assured Eckardstein that these were his own ideas, put forward without prior consultation with other ministers. Yet they were almost exactly the same as the suggestions Salisbury had made to him on the previous day. By this scheme, the prime minister had written, they would sacrifice the Manchester and Liverpool merchants in the Volta but it was preferred since the latter, unlike the Australasians, 'will certainly *never* seek their independence.'[51]

Hatzfeldt pointed out to his superiors that these discussions were clearly useful if they could agree to the British demand for Upolu. This Berlin was ready to do, although they preferred to drop the Volta Delta out of the talks, to partition the Neutral Zone and to take Savai'i, Tonga and Savage Island in return for that island. They also wished to see the German firms on Upolu bought out by Britain if they so wished. The prospects further increased on the twenty-second, when the ambassador reported that Salisbury, after attempting in vain to persuade him to give up all Samoa and the Neutral Zone for the Volta, seemed inclined to consider these ideas, agreeing also that the matter should go for official arbitration to alleviate public criticism on either side, although everything would be secretly settled in advance. Bülow optimistically telegraphed the kaiser that a solution was near, and even the more cautious Hatzfeldt thought that it was only a week or so away.[52]

By 25 September, Berlin was reconsidering its demands. The pressure of events in South Africa, the importance of the kaiser's visit to England, and Germany's better relations with America were all favourable factors: 'We must strike while the iron is hot', Bülow declared. Were Germany to give up

51 Chamberlain Papers, JC5/67/124, Salisbury to Chamberlain, 19/9/1899; G.P., 14/2, no. 4089.
52 London Embassy records, Hatzfeldt to Holstein, 20/9/1899, 22/9/1899 and 23/9/1899; A,A./*Südsee-Inseln* 5, vol. 4, Bülow to A.A., no. 147 of 22/9/1899; G.P., 14/2, nos. 4090-93; B.D., 1, no. 148.

Upolu (and this was now to be decided *objectively* by the king of Sweden and Norway), then she must receive in return Savai'i, the Tongan group, Savage Island and the Gilberts. In addition, she would be given the Volta Triangle and would receive the Yendi part of the Neutral Zone, Britain taking the rest. Although the Gilberts were felt to be 'completely worthless' and Yendi slightly less so, and these places were asked for solely to appease German public opinion, the overall terms were much stiffer. There was also the likely chance that Germany would take Upolu *and* the Volta under this scheme, whereas the British had only brought the latter territory into the talks in an effort to get Germany out of Upolu and even out of the entire Samoan group. A further reason for these extra claims was probably to be found in the fact that, as Holstein reported, the navy was urging the kaiser to keep Upolu 'since German blood has flowed there'.[53]

Hatzfeldt did not object to these increases but pointed out that the British would apparently only negotiate if they were certain of getting Upolu. He was therefore given full discretion in this matter and proceeded to prepare instructions for Eckardstein's talk with Chamberlain on the twenty-eighth, which would be followed by his own on the following day. The first of these meetings developed quite promisingly and Chamberlain appeared willing to agree to the West African settlement and to buying out the *D.H.P.G.* provided that this procedure was also adopted for British firms in the Volta Delta. Differences over whether Britain could keep both sides of the Volta river near the mouth and how many of the smaller island groups in the Pacific would fall to Germany were left rather vague, according to Eckardstein's account. The colonial secretary was openly in favour of a quick and comprehensive settlement and had in fact told his parliamentary under-secretary, Selborne, that 'it could certainly be a great advantage if we could clean the slate of all matters of controversy at the same time', much as he disliked the German habit of taking advantage of the British difficulties.[54]

Salisbury proved rather less conciliatory, despite the fact that at the Cabinet meeting of that morning (the twenty-ninth) it had been decided to recall Parliament and to call out the reserves since the Orange Free State intended to ally with the

53   London Embassy records, Holstein to Hatzfeldt, 25/9/1899; G.P., 14/2, no. 4094.
54   Chamberlain Papers, JC7/2/2A/3C, Chamberlain to Selborne, 25/9/1899; ibid., JC7/2/2A/16, heads of agreement, 28/9/1899; London Embassy records, Hatzfeldt to Holstein, 25/9/1899, 26/9/1899 and 29/9/1899, and Holstein to Hatzfeldt, 27/9/1899; G.P., 14/2, no. 4095; Eckardstein, *Lebenserinnerungen*, 2, pp. 49-54.

Transvaal and the Boers remained 'obstinate'.[55] He had
talked with Chamberlain and agreed upon the mutual buying-
out of firms, but on the two issues which the colonial minister
had rather glided over the prime minister was very firm. The
Volta was worth much more than the Neutral Zone and
there could thus be no separate arrangement in West Africa:
the advantages the British were giving away there should be
compensated by Germany in the Pacific. Moreover, Salisbury
absolutely refused to give up Tonga, and instead made
queries about Berlin withdrawing from her extraterritorial
rights in Zanzibar, an idea that had been touched upon
previously. His attitude confirmed all the old German suspicions of him and it was resolved to continue working with
Chamberlain behind his back. The colonial secretary was also
to be told that these obstructionist tactics regarding Tonga
were threatening to upset the agreement he was striving
for.[56]

Here again, however, the gap between Salisbury and
Chamberlain was greatly over-estimated in Berlin. The
colonial secretary's heads of agreement, of which the prime
minister had received a copy as early as the twenty-eighth,
showed that Britain was to get Tonga and both sides of the
Volta river mouth. Either Chamberlain had not made this
clear enough or, more likely, Eckardstein had read into his
remarks a meaning more favourable than there actually was.
The two ministers also agreed on the day following that
Hatzfeldt's claim for Tonga was a 'try-on'. Consequently
when Eckardstein again appealed for an interview, he was
given a discouraging answer. Perhaps Chamberlain, as he
explained in his letter, was genuinely worried that Salisbury
would take offence at these private pourparlers but it seems
equally clear that he wished to abandon the talks with the
Baron since he could think of no way of satisfying both the
British and German claims. Only reluctantly, therefore, did
he agree to resume discussions with Eckardstein the next time
he came to town, although warning that his remarks upon
Tonga had been misunderstood.[57]

In Berlin, the South African situation was being watched
with almost as great a concern as that shown in London.
Using the latest military reports, Bülow calculated on 29

55 Salisbury Papers, Class E, Salisbury to the queen, 29/9/1899.

56 A.A./*Südsee-Inseln* 5, Hatzfeldt to Holstein, 30/9/1899; London Embassy records,
Holstein to Hatzfeldt, 30/9/1899 (2); G.P., 14/2, no. 4096.

57 Chamberlain Papers, JC5/67/126, Salisbury to Chamberlain, 29/9/1899: ibid.,
JC11/30/18, Chamberlain to Salisbury, 29/9/1899; ibid., JC7/2/2B/5, Eckardstein to
Chamberlain, 30/9/1899; London Embassy records, Chamberlain to Eckardstein (copy),
1/10/1899.

September that if Salisbury managed to hold off a war until December, the Boers would be defeated by the vast influx of imperial troops, British prestige would rise and Germany would be given the cold shoulder. Only if the Boers struck soon would concessions be given in Samoa and on the Volta, and Hatzfeldt was pestered daily for the latest news from South Africa. When, on 30 September, the ambassador reported that the prime minister still maintained that war was not necessary, the kaiser angrily wrote: 'Swindle!'[58] Fearing that Chamberlain would become enraged at the criticisms of the German press, the colonial secretary was assured that the German government would remain absolutely neutral. On the other hand, for internal reasons, Bülow dared not accede to the British request that the German consul in Pretoria take charge of Britain's interests in the Transvaal should war break out. Furthermore, it was his policy to offer no favours to London *until* the Samoan matter was settled. For three days, the pros and cons of the British request were argued about in the *Wilhelmstrasse* until it was decided to await the outcome of Hatzfeldt's next talk with Salisbury, explaining this delay away by pointing out that both Wilhelm and Bülow were on holiday.[59]

The meeting of 6 October hardly had much chance of success. The German government insisted that it must have the Tongan group if Britain took Upolu: it also claimed the Gilberts, Ellice, Phoenix and Union groups, and Savage Island. At this, the prime minister declared that far too much was being demanded by Berlin. If Tonga went to Britain and Germany's rights at Zanzibar were given up, a settlement might be possible but in any case more time was needed to consult the experts about all these territories. Under severe pressure himself to achieve an arrangement and desperately in need of a rest, Hatzfeldt urged haste upon Salisbury 'with extraordinary vehemence' and warned again that Germany's future friendship was involved. His efforts were fruitless. The prime minister refused to consider the proposals 'from such a point of view': in other words, it was to be a settlement based solely upon a fair division of the territories in question and he declined again to acknowledge any special reason for buying Germany's friendship. The matter was not pressing, he declared, although he hoped to consult the ambassador

58 A.A./*Südsee-Inseln* 5, vol. 4, Bülow to A.A., no. 160 of 29/9/1899; London Embassy records, Holstein to Hatzfeldt, 30/9/1899 (3); A.A./*Afrika Gen.* 13, vol. 39, minute on Hatzfeldt to A.A., no. 111 of 30/9/1899.
59 A.A./*Südsee-Inseln* 5, vol. 4, Hatzfeldt to Holstein, 4/10/1899 (2), and Holstein to Bülow, 5/10/1899; Derenthall to Bülow, *via* Vienna, no. 157 of 5/10/1899 and reply, no. 179 of 5/10/1899; G.P., 14/2, nos. 4097-100; *Holstein Papers*, 4, pp. 158-59.

within a fortnight or so. After leaving the Foreign Office, a rather desperate Hatzfeldt wrote to persuade Salisbury to forget about an African settlement and merely to arrange by arbitration which country should have Upolu and which Savai'i. A full four days later, he received the short reply that although the terms of the talks were open to criticism, 'this is not the opportunity for examining them'.[60]

It may be wondered if the German government ever forgave the prime minister for this icy rejection of all their arguments and his absolute indifference to their haste. Holstein in particular was amazed at his intransigence and believed that Salisbury's hatred of the kaiser was affecting his entire outlook. A few hours later, he anxiously wondered whether the prime minister secretly felt that Germany was working with the Transvaal, and Bülow thought that the planned German railway from the Transvaal to the Atlantic could have given rise to this suspicion. Hatzfeldt felt that Salisbury was seeking an arrangement with the Russians and would therefore give Berlin nothing. No one could believe that he was being obstinate merely because he did not regard the terms as fair in the circumstances. The kaiser furiously decided that it would be better, in view of public opinion, to be pushed out of Samoa by force than to accept an unsatisfactory treaty. His visit to England, and the whole future course of German policy, were in the balance.

Despite Hatzfeldt's pleas that they should wait until Chamberlain had been sounded out, the British request for representation in the Transvaal was refused, the excuse being given that the German consul in Pretoria was very inexperienced. In reality, fear of criticism at home and anger at Salisbury dictated this decision, and Hatzfeldt was instructed to inform the other Cabinet members privately of the real reason for the refusal and the possibility of the kaiser cancelling his trip. He was also to use Rothschild to work upon Goschen, Lansdowne, Balfour and others, and to stir them up against their chief. Perhaps the queen, or the Prince of Wales, or the foreign editor of the *Times*, or Rhodes could be brought in to compel the prime minister to give way, Holstein wildly suggested. If war did break out, perhaps the newspapers could point out that Salisbury was solely responsible for the lack of armaments on the British side? Perhaps Chamberlain could be told that a *Times* article criticising any concessions to Germany had been directly inspired by the Foreign Office?

60 A.A./*Südsee Inseln* 5, vol. 4, Derenthall to Hatzfeldt, no. 246 of 2/10/1899; G.P., 14/2, no. 4102; B.D., 1, no. 149. On the later exchange of letters, see Salisbury Papers A122/77, Hatzfeldt to Salisbury, 6/10/1899, and the reply, A122/78, of 10/10/1899.

Anything was worth a try, to weaken the prime minister's position and to force him to give way.[61]

While some indications of these manoeuvres did reach Salisbury, it is difficult to believe that he was influenced by them at all: if anything, his suspicions of Germany increased. Brodrick, who also resented the kaiser's 'pistolling us about Samoa', reported him as being 'very well & in a very impertinent mood. No yield anywhere I'm glad to say.'[62] In fact, the prime minister had decided to ignore the German protests and to turn to more important matters. His wife was slowly dying and he wished to spend all of this time out at Hatfield, though he was forced to pay swift visits to London to deal with the South African crisis. In particular, he was very busy with Soveral, the Portuguese minister, in re-negotiating the old treaties of alliance with Lisbon so as to prevent further arms supplies reaching the Boers. The two men were corresponding daily and meeting very frequently: indeed, Soveral visited the prime minister shortly after Hatzfeldt had left on 6 October. Despite his doubts that the Portuguese were playing 'fast and loose', Salisbury reached an agreement on 14 October, when a secret Anglo-Portuguese treaty was signed in London. It did not legally contradict the arrangement with Germany of the previous year and Berlin could have been under no doubt that Britain was not eager to see the Portuguese Empire collapse. Nevertheless, the prime minister must have felt satisfied that he had nullified even further the German *assumptions* regarding their August 1898 treaty and in some way paid them back for their pressure over Samoa.[63]

Throughout this period, Chamberlain had remained at Birmingham, where he received several anxious letters from Eckardstein. After Hatzfeldt's fruitless talks of the following day, all Germans hopes were pinned upon him: with war apparently only a few days away, there was still some hope and Hatzfeldt optimistically reported that the other members of the Cabinet had also promised to help. Chamberlain himself had agreed to meet Eckardstein on the ninth and his letter revealed some concern at the personal questions and 'underlying prejudices' which prevented friendship between the two countries, although he also believed that Germany's need for this was greater than Britain's.[64] On the day appointed,

61 A.A./*Südsee-Inseln* 5, vol. 4, Hatzfeldt to Holstein, 6/10/1899 and 7/10/1899 (2); London Embassy records, Holstein to Hatzfeldt, 7/10/1899 (2) and 8/10/1899, and Hatzfeldt to Holstein, 8/10/1899; G.P., 14/2, nos. 4103-04; *Holstein Papers*, 4, pp. 158 61.
62 Curzon Papers, vol. 10a, Brodrick to Curzon, 13/10/1899.
63 On the Anglo-Portuguese negotiations, see especially F.O.2/vols. 227 and 229; B.D., 1, nos. 117-18; Grenville, *Salisbury and Foreign Policy*, pp. 260-63.
64 Holstein Papers, vol. 6, Chamberlain to Eckardstein (copy), 5/10/1899; Chamberlain

the Baron called at the Colonial Office and the discussions were resumed. Little was decided, since Chamberlain was rather uncertain about several of the matters discussed and required at least another day to go into them. Nevertheless, after some preliminary diplomatic sparring with Eckardstein, he put forward the idea of Germany receiving the English Solomon Islands, the entire Volta Triangle and Savage Island while Britain took the Neutral Zone, the Tongan group, and both Savai'i and Upolu. Since this introduced a new basis for discussions, the Baron also needed to refer back for instructions.[65]

Both sides came away from this talk in a rather uncertain manner, though still with a fair amount of optimism regarding a settlement. On the same day, the German position seemed immeasurably strengthened by the Transvaal's action in issuing an ultimatum which the British would be bound to reject. War was inevitable, therefore, and Chamberlain's desire for a speedy arrangement would surely increase. On the evening of the ninth, however, a further factor entered the scene and assumed great significance upon the British side. For the first time in the entire Samoan dispute, astonishingly enough, the Admiralty had been requested to give a strategic appreciation of that group and of the other Pacific territories under discussion. Its answers, which Chamberlain had just received, offered him the chance of arriving at a quick solution. Guided by this information, he was able to propose a settlement which would eliminate the Anglo-German points of dispute in the Pacific and West Africa and, so he hoped, would lead to the alliance he still desired; which would more than satisfy the sceptical and stubborn Salisbury; and which would delight the kaiser and the German public.

iii   *Naval Memoranda and Political Considerations*

Shortly after his fruitless meeting with Hatzfeldt on 6 October, Salisbury sent his assistant under-secretary, Villiers, round to the Admiralty to ask for a strategic appreciation of the various island groups which had been the subject of that day's discussion. The naval viewpoint was summarized in a private letter by Goschen, the first lord, who wrote:

> Roughly I may tell you that from the strictly naval point of view we care little for the Samoan group, as the Americans have got the only good harbour for a coaling station.

Papers, JC7/2/2B/nos. 6-8, Eckardstein to Chamberlain, 4/10/1899, 5/10/1899 and 7/10/1899; A.A./*Südsee-Inseln* 5, vol. 4, Hatzfeldt to Holstein, 5/10/1899.

65 A.A./*Südsee-Inseln* 5, vol. 4, Hatzfeldt to the chancellor, no. 824 of 14/10/1899; G.P., 14/2, no. 4105; Eckardstein, *Lebenserinnerungen*, 2, pp. 54-57.

> But having no harbour in that group, and content that G.B. should part with it, we hold that Tonga is very important. It has a good harbour, and moreover is so close to Fiji that it would not be agreeable that it should be in the hands of another Power.
>
> As to some of the other groups, some of which have recently been annexed, their value only consists in being possible landing places for the Pacific cable.[66]

Thus the group which had been the object of two decades of diplomatic wranglings, which had been extolled by colonial enthusiasts as a focal point in the Pacific, and over which the Australasians had displayed the greatest interest in case a foreign power be established there, was regarded as worthless for naval purposes—at least, insofar as Upolu and Savai'i were concerned. Yet these were the only islands which could be considered, since the American claims to Tutuila had been recognized by all since 1889. No one disputed the physical advantages which Pago-Pago possessed as a harbour, although its strategical value was also not greatly valued by the Admiralty.

The official reply to Villiers' queries merely expanded the above. The American harbour of Pago-Pago was 'the only place of much importance' in Samoa; Upolu's harbours were unsafe and Savai'i 'would be totally useless by itself'. The Tongan group earned a much higher recommendation, for it possessed 'several excellent harbours that may be of use in the future . . . Its position near Fiji makes it undesirable that it should fall into European hands other than Great Britain's'. In an additional note, which was probably taking account of neutrality problems during war, the Admiralty pointed out that 'If Great Britain is not to be paramount in Samoa it is preferable that the group should be in the hands of one other power. Should this be arranged it is essential that the Kingdom of Tonga should be secured to Great Britain either as a protectorate or otherwise.'[67] It was these considerations which were to give Chamberlain the basis for his sought-after breakthrough.

Nevertheless, if Tonga was suddenly raised to a place of some importance in late 1899, it must be admitted that it had always formed part of the British calculation in the southwest Pacific. Though unwilling to assume control of the group so long as its internal affairs remained regular, the British much

66 Salisbury Papers, Class E, Goschen to Salisbury, 7/10/1899.

67 F.O.83/1781, MacGregor to Villiers, 7/10/1899, Confidential, with 2 enclosures. (These documents were mistakenly filed in the 'Great Britain and General' series and bound in a volume entitled 'Guano and other islands, questions of sovereignty'! Its reproduction in *British Documents* might have altered the orthodox interpretation of why Britain abandoned Samoa in 1899.)

disliked the prospect of another power gaining influence there; it was far too close to Fiji, their most important possession in the southwest Pacific. Because many of Fiji's inhabitants were in fact Tongans or maintained close links with Tonga, there was always the possibility that a foreign power which controlled the latter might also have an indirect influence upon Fiji. Thus Tonga like Samoa was placed in a 'neutral' zone by the Anglo-German demarcation agreement of April 1886, and Salisbury constantly looked to it as a bargaining-counter to appease New Zealand feelings when he ceded British rights in Samoa to Bismarck. In the 1890s, however, the British government recognized that Wellington would fiercely resent such a transaction; and, in any case, London came to believe that because of the growing British trading predominance in Tonga that the group was virtually theirs and therefore no compensation at all for withdrawing from Samoa. British policy towards Tonga was basically negative and little thought was given to strategic considerations until 1898.

In that year the incursion of the powers into the Far East and the Pacific caused the Foreign Office and Admiralty to examine all harbours which might be useful to another nation as a coaling station. Here too, although acknowledging that Pago-Pago provided an excellent anchorage and that Vavau in the Tongan group 'was an almost perfect war harbour', their lordships insisted that the Pacific islands were 'off most trade routes, and not strategically placed so as to be useful to Foreign Powers except the United States in the future'. Persuaded by the Admiralty that only potential bases on the route to the Far East were of import, the Foreign Office ignored the Pacific; indeed, the specific replies to Villiers' queries in October 1899 were clearly based upon this earlier correspondence, which the Foreign Office had forgotten about. Nevertheless, the Admiralty had been a little perturbed at signs of a reviving German interest in Tonga at the end of 1898, and had suggested a loan to the king in return for a promise not to alienate his land to another power. Chamberlain, however, dismissed such fears, claiming that the establishment of second-rate naval powers in islands only made them 'hostages given to fortune'; and the pledges secured from the king of Tonga in March 1899 further stemmed any worries. The primary motive of the Colonial Office was to preserve the group's autonomy, not to keep out the warships of other nations.[68]

68 On the British policy towards Tonga in those years, see P. M. Kennedy, *Britain and the Tongan Harbours*, 1898-1914, *passim*.

It seems evident, therefore, that Tonga was not entirely ignored in these years, even though it took second place to Samoa and the Colonial Office insisted that there would be 'no question of our accepting Tonga as an equivalent for our interests in Samoa'.[69] It is also clear that the information contained in the Admiralty memorandum of 7 October should not have been treated as something absolutely new. Nevertheless, it was received as such, particularly by Chamberlain. This can partly be explained by the fact that the 1898 correspondence upon strategic coaling stations was never sent to the Colonial Office. But the key fact seems to be that here, for the first time, was an authoritative comparison of the two groups from a strategic standpoint and that the Admiralty's advice was that Samoa was useless and Tonga 'very important'. Given the Colonial Office's awareness that the Australasian fears of foreign intrusion in the Pacific, even though exaggerated, were also strategically based, it is not surprising that this information should have caused Chamberlain to reconsider his opinions and to call to mind the apparent German designs upon Tonga earlier in the year and Richthofen's hint of action on 15 September. Moreover, it was a matter which would affect Salisbury's outlook, too. Despite his scepticism about military experts, the prime minister's entire foreign policy reveals that he always gave priority to strategic considerations; and this was particularly so in the Pacific, where maritime communications and the need of coaling stations were of great importance; the Admiralty's strategic assessments had caused alterations in the government's policy during the 1886 Anglo-German demarcation talks, and had also influenced Salisbury's attitude towards the American acquisition of exclusive rights to Pearl Harbour in 1887.[70]

A consciousness of the importance of strategic factors was therefore very strong upon the British side. Upon receiving the Admiralty advice, Chamberlain promptly forgot about his 'hostages given to fortune' theory and concentrated upon securing Tonga for the British Empire—a marked contrast to 20 September, when he had apparently considered the idea of partitioning that group with Germany. Doubtless the wish to solve this entire matter quickly and to get upon better terms with Berlin was the underlying motive of the colonial secretary; but only when he learnt of the true priorities for British policy in the Pacific was he able to pursue his larger

---

69 J. Anderson minute on paper 23395, F.O. to C.O., 17/10/1898, in C.O. 225/56; and on paper 1480, F.O. to C.O., received 18/1/1899, in C.O. 225/57.
70 Kennedy, *Britain and the Tongan Harbours*, 1898-1914, p. 257-58.

aim, smoothly and confidently. By 9 October he knew that the Tongan group possessed 'the best harbour in the Pacific' and began to think out a new solution, though his jottings indicate that this information only reached him *after* his inconclusive talk with Eckardstein, since there is a remark on the same piece of notepaper, 'Contest between Herbert Bismarck & Count Bülow for Chancellorship.'[71] During the evening, therefore, the colonial minister worked upon his new proposals and he returned to the task on the following morning, assisted by Herbert and Anderson. He also telegraphed Eckardstein that 'a new situation has arisen' and that he was 'hopeful of a real settlement'. This new development Hatzfeldt naturally took to be the outbreak of the war, which was to his mind 'advantageous for us and it is very good that we have waited so long'.[72] In point of fact, it is much more likely that Chamberlain was referring to his information about Tonga rather than the Boer War, although the latter could be a useful excuse for a re-framing of the settlement he had discussed with Eckardstein only twenty-four hours earlier.

On the afternoon of the tenth, the Baron called at the Colonial Office to learn of the 'new situation'. There Chamberlain confidently outlined a definite settlement, under which Germany would take the Volta triangle including the left bank at the mouth, Savage Island and all of the British-owned Solomon Islands. If the latter seemed unsatisfactory, they could instead have the middle three islands of the Solomon group only and take the Gilberts, leaving Britain with the three southern islands of the Solomons. In return London would take the Tongan Islands, Upolu and Savai'i, and the Neutral Zone apart from the Yendi region. Germany would abandon her extraterritorial rights in Zanzibar, and both countries would buy out the firms of the other's nationals in the territories they took over. On Anderson's prompting, Chamberlain laid great stress upon the fact that Germany was only giving up her share of joint rights in neutral regions whereas Britain was actually making concessions from her own empire. The Volta Triangle was as valuable as the whole of Togoland while the Neutral Zone was 'a white elephant'.

71   Chamberlain Papers, JC7/2/2A/18, notes of 9/10/1899. (Although the Baron obviously did not report this aspect of the conversation to Berlin, the possible rivalry for the chancellorship seems to have occupied his attention in October 1899 and it is not unlikely that he had attempted to urge a quick and satisfactory solution upon Chamberlain by pointing to the prospect of an anti-English Herbert Bismarck assuming power should the talks fail. See Eckardstein, *Lebenserinnerungen*, 2, pp. 42, 116-19.)

72   London Embassy records, Hatzfeldt to Holstein, 10/10/1899(2); Chamberlain Papers, JC7/2/2B/9, Eckardstein to Chamberlain, 9/10/1899; ibid., JC7/2/2A/31, J. Anderson to Chamberlain, 10/10/1899.

This was his idea of a perfect settlement, it would dispose of all points of dispute between them and it would be a great gain for Germany. Moreover, Salisbury had already given his consent to it and the matter could therefore be arranged swiftly.

Chamberlain also offered, somewhat deprecatingly, a second proposal, whereby Germany would obtain Upolu and Savai'i. For this, however, she would have to hand over the German Solomon Islands, at the same time allowing Britain to take over Tonga and all of the Neutral Zone apart from Yendi. In other words, Germany would give up parts of *her* territory while Britain only surrendered joint rights to neutral lands. This latter proposal Salisbury was unaware of and would probably strongly oppose. It might fall through; it would certainly take longer to arrange. It was very disadvantageous for Germany's real interests but if they were 'stupid enough' to choose it, then the colonial secretary would try to effect a settlement along such lines. But Germany should ask for nothing more with the second scheme, for it would be promptly refused. Nor did he want Upolu and Savai'i to be separated, as they were too close to each other to permit a divided control.[73]

Chamberlain's plan now becomes very clear. He and Herbert agreed that 'politically it would suit us "so far as Australia is concerned" to get the Germans out of Samoa.'[74] Therefore Berlin was offered the utmost inducement, in the form of the much more valuable British-owned Volta triangle and the Solomon Islands, to agree to this scheme. The *D.H.P.G.* would also be bought out and this would free Bülow from the criticism that German trading interests had been ignored. Despite its manifold attractions, however, Chamberlain sensed that public sentiment in Germany might force its rulers to insist upon remaining in Samoa; if so, it would be paid for in full, Berlin losing all of Chamberlain's tempting offers and instead surrendering the 8,000 square miles of the German Solomons for the 700 square miles of Samoa. But the most interesting feature of all, which the colonial minister took care to glide over in his conversation with Eckardstein, *was that Tonga should fall to Britain whatever happened.* Having satisfied the Admiralty about the strategic considerations and relieved Fiji and New Zealand of any worry about foreign naval bases in the southwest Pacific (unless the Germans

73 Ibid.; also JC7/2/2A/20, Chamberlain's heads of proposals, 10/101899; London Embassy records, Hatzfeldt to Holstein, 10/10/1899(2); A.A./*Südsee-Inseln* 5, vol. 4, Hatzfeldt to A.A., tel. no. 315 of 10/10/1899; G.P., 14/2, no. 4106; *Holstein Papers*, 4, pp. 160 62; Eckardstein, *Lebenserinnerungen*, 2, pp. 37-38.
74 Chamberlain Papers, JC7/2/2A/31, J. Anderson to Chamberlain, 10/10/1899.

were silly enough to attempt to convert Saluafata or Apia
into one), having given the Australians the northern Solomons
and New Zealand Tonga, and having avoided the loss of any
territory in West Africa, this second proposal was equally
favourable to Chamberlain and he was quietly confident
that he could persuade others upon the British side to accept
it, although he did not say so to Eckardstein. If possible,
he wanted both Tonga and Samoa; if this was not possible,
then he would take Tonga in any case, together with far
larger compensations. Either way, so he calculated, he would
win.

Chamberlain's confidence also affected Eckardstein and his
crony, Alfred Rothschild. Salisbury was informed by his
secretary, McDonnell, that they were 'in great feather and
highly mysterious last night: and I fear this means a settlement
for their unauthorised diplomacy'. The prime minister was
unperturbed, however, for he had spoken to Chamberlain
on the tenth and learnt of his scheme or, at least, of the first
proposal. Salisbury, who had only briefly discussed this and
erroneously believed that the proposals came from Eckardstein
himself, found the idea that the Germans would give up all
Samoa *and* Tonga 'impossible' but he planned to raise the
matter with Hatzfeldt.[75] If the prime minister was still unaware
of his colleague's deeper plan—probably he was not told of it
until slightly later—then it is clear that there was no sign of
the antagonism which Berlin believed to exist between the
two men. On the following day, Salisbury attempted to
contact the ambassador but was told that the latter was ill.
While this was indeed true, the real reason for this polite
refusal was the German suspicion that the prime minister was
planning an unsatisfactory counter-offer and that it would be
better to deal solely with Chamberlain. If an agreement was
reached privately, then they would use the colonial secretary
and the rest of the cabinet to force the agreement upon
Salisbury.[76]

Despite the attractiveness of Chamberlain's first offer,
Bülow had decided by 11 October that only the second one
could be discussed. Here, too, the advice of naval experts was
decisive. As soon as Hatzfeldt's telegraphic account of the
Chamberlain-Eckardstein meeting of 9 October had been
received in Berlin, both Tirpitz (Reich Navy Office) and
Bendemann (Admiralty Staff) were asked whether the colonial
secretary's proposed compensations 'for giving up our hitherto

75 Salisbury Papers, Class E, McDonnell note of 11/10/1899, and Salisbury minute
thereon.
76 London Embassy records, Hatzfeldt to Bülow, 12/10/1899; *Holstein Papers*, 4, p. 160.

existing position in Samoa seem of full value, particularly in view of the requirements of the navy in that eastern part of the Pacific Ocean'. If they were not and the navy required a good harbour, say, in Tonga, then the *Auswärtiges Amt* would strive to achieve this.[77]

Bendemann, replying on the following day, declared that the British offers were inadequate compensation for a German withdrawal from both Samoa and Tonga, since neither the Volta triangle nor the southern Solomons possessed any strategic value, however great their economic potential. If political reasons demanded that Germany should give up her interests in the two island groups, then she should be offered another station, such as the Chagos Islands in the Indian Ocean.[78] Tirpitz's reply of 11 October contained much the same advice. If anything, he placed greater emphasis upon the importance of Samoa as a naval base and a landing-place for their future world cable, and he believed that even Tonga, should it be acquired, was no equivalent. Moving away from the purely naval aspects, Tirpitz also stressed the national and commercial considerations involved in Samoa: only Zanzibar or Walfisch Bay could be considered as adequate compensation for a withdrawal. Since he had many times pointed out to Bülow that the Samoan dispute must not lead to war with Britain, he also advised that, if neither Samoa could be retained by Germany nor sufficiently valuable territory obtained from the British, then it would be better

> under formal preservation of our rights to give way and entirely to refuse these apparently inadequate compensations, since the acceptance of such could only further increase the impression of wrong and of Germany's naval weakness.[79]

In view of this final remark, it is scarcely surprising that Tirpitz's policy has been seen as a deliberate attempt to prolong the Samoan quarrel for the purposes of naval propaganda.[80] In fact, he sent a further letter to the *Auswärtiges Amt* two days later but the contents of this can only serve to confirm the above suspicion. If adequate compensations such as Zanzibar could not be obtained and if some other territories must be accepted for their withdrawal for political reasons, the admiral wrote, then Germany should ask for *all* of the following: Vavau Island in the Tongan group, Walfisch Bay,

77 A.A./*Südsee-Inseln* 5, vol. 4, A.A. to R.M.A. and Admiralstab, Top Secret, Immediate, 10/10/1899.

78 Ibid., Admiralstab to A.A., Top Secret, 11/10/1899.

79 G.P., 14/2, no. 4107.

80 J. Meyer 'Die Propaganda der Deutschen Flottenbewegung 1897-1900' (Phil. diss., Bern, 1967), p. 103.

the British Solomon Islands, the Gilbert Islands and the Chagos Islands. Of these, Vavau was the most valuable object.[81] Since Tirpitz must have been aware that such a list of demands would outrage even Chamberlain (particularly in asking for Walfisch Bay just after the Boer War had commenced), it would appear that a prolongation of the Samoan dispute, with its effects upon the kaiser and German public opinion, would not have been unwelcome to him. Moreover, if Germany did obtain Samoa or the many compensations listed he could exploit the resultant increase in the government's popularity to point out the need for more warships to protect the new colonies. He would benefit all ways.

Bülow, too, was thinking along the same lines. In a private letter to Tirpitz on 14 October, he declared that the admiral's two memoranda had strengthened his view that they dare not freely leave Samoa. It meant too much to the German people, and his own prestige was also involved after his firm assurances on their rights in the group to the Reichstag. He had told Wilhelm of this, and the latter fully agreed.[82] Possibly Bülow's worry that Tirpitz might become the next chancellor moved him to avoid taking any action which could forfeit his popularity with the kaiser.[83] But apart from this personal motive, he was never a man to place better relations with other powers, especially Britain, before his desire to please his master and to gain overseas successes which would strengthen the establishment at home.

Samoa, in fact, was part of a much bigger policy which was being secretly developed in Berlin at this time. At an *Immediatvortrag* held on 28 September, Tirpitz had presented Wilhelm with his plan for a vast increase of the German fleet. Although he had assured the Reichstag earlier that year that no new proposals would be introduced before the First Navy Law had run its course, the government had been privately considering a more forward policy throughout 1899. With the newspapers and public excited over the Samoan affair and now beginning to turn their attention to the crisis in South Africa, the time had come to strike. Tirpitz carefully outlined his scheme for a fleet of forty-five battleships, which would be achieved in two stages, the first possibly being put into effect in 1901 and the second some years

81 A.A./*Südsee-Inseln* 5, vol. 4, R.M.A. to A.A., Top Secret, 13/10/1899.

82 BA/MA, Tirpitz Papers, vol. 16, Bülow to Tirpitz, Secret, 14/10/1899.

83 Eckardstein, *Lebenserinnerungen*, 2, p. 42. (In 1898, Eulenburg had told Bülow that he was working to get him the chancellorship. See BA, Eulenburg Papers, vol. 52, Eulenburg to Bülow, 29/7/1898.)

later. The kaiser would thus possess a force that was second
only in size to the Royal Navy.

> But we have an undoubtedly good chance against England also through
> geographical situation, weapon system, mobilisation, torpedo-boats,
> tactical training, methodically-organised structure and the unified
> leadership through the Monarch.
>
> Apart from this ratio for fighting, which would certainly not be without
> prospects for us, then out of overall political grounds and from the
> purely sensible viewpoint of the business man England will have lost
> every inclination to attack us and as a result concede to Your Majesty
> such a measure of naval mastery and enable Your Majesty to carry out
> a great overseas policy.[84]

Having this clearly-defined aim, Tirpitz then proceeded to
explain the reasons behind his proposed measure. He accepted
in the most extreme form the Darwinistic concepts of national
rivalries, quoting Salisbury's 'dying empires' speech with
approval and declaring that 'the creation of an effective fleet
is an unconditional necessity for Germany without which
she would be faced with ruin.' She was swiftly and inevitably
becoming a world industrial and commercial power, and
this was leading to points of conflict with other nations:
'therefore power (sea power) is essential if Germany will not
quickly go under'.[85] With this philosophy the kaiser was in
full agreement. To be given an instrument with which to
neutralize possible British objections to German overseas
expansion (for this is what Tirpitz was proposing) was of
great importance to Wilhelm and it would be well worth
waiting a number of years until this aim was achieved.

Tirpitz's arguments in his letter to the *Auswärtiges Amt*
upon Chamberlain's proposals were obviously wrong from
the strategic viewpoint. Yet it would be unfair and naïve to
say that only the British Admiralty could place these Pacific
islands in the right perspective and that Tirpitz was gravely
led astray in predicting a glorious future for Samoa as a
naval station. The real reasons for writing that letter have been
given above. Moreover, he was also aware of the group's
comparative insignificance; it was Tirpitz who, as chief of
staff in the High Command, had written that long protest in
1895 against wasting the whole Australian division upon the
Samoan Islands throughout the year.[86] It is unlikely that his
views had changed much since then, particularly when the
Germans knew that only Upolu and Savai'i came into the
question and that neither island possessed a decent harbour.

84 BA/MA 2044, PG66074, Tirpitz memo of 28/9/1899 *Immediatvortrag* (copy).
85 Ibid.
86 See above, pp. 103-4, footnote 21.

Apia and Saluafata, whose limitations had been revealed frequently since the 1889 hurricane, contradicted every principle of the 'ideal fleet base' which Knorr had laid down for the kaiser in the previous year.

But the most telling criticism of all is that any emphasis upon the value of Samoa from the naval point of view directly contradicted Tirpitz's basic policy—to create a large battlefleet, based in the North Sea, to be used as a lever against England. In 1899, he was engaged in a fierce battle for the kaiser's ear with the retired vice-admiral, Valois, who published a book which attempted to show how sea mastery could be wrested from the Royal Navy by use of hordes of fast armoured cruisers. This was strongly disapproved of by the authorities, since it might arouse suspicion in England. But Tirpitz had an even stronger reason for opposing such views. As he explained to his assistant, Büchsel

> Valois says one must attack England where she is weak. In fact he makes England's seven overseas squadrons ready against us, while on account of her foreign commitments she can only utilise a very small part of these ships in the North Sea. England's weak point is therefore the North Sea, for here we can concentrate our entire force.[87]

None of these criticisms of Tirpitz exclude the fact that the acquisition of Samoa would have been welcomed by the German navy. After the events of 1888-89, Upolu possessed an incalculable sentimental attraction for them too, even though its positive value was often derided. Moreover, the government would be widely praised if it succeeded in securing the group, and this was urgently needed to boost their popularity, which had shown signs of flagging: everyone was aware of the strength of the attacks upon the government from the colonial pressure groups as a result of this lack of success. Finally, as mentioned above, the possession of further overseas colonies would give the navy the chance to point out the necessity for an increased fleet to defend such places. None of these reasons, however, had anything to do with the physical and maritime benefits which Tirpitz claimed he foresaw the Samoan Islands per se would confer upon the German navy. His letter of 11 October upon the importance of the group was motivated by political rather than strategical reasons. His concern was not with the southwest Pacific; it was with Berlin, Wilhelmshaven and the North Sea.

For Bülow, this naval advice clinched matters. He was

87 BA/MA, Büchsel Papers, vol. 11, Tirpitz to Büchsel, 29/7/1899. (Valois' book, *Seemacht, Seegeltung, Seeherrschaft* (Berlin, 1899) earned a rebuke from the kaiser. See BA/MA 3388, PG67159, *Bücher u. Schriften,* vol. 2, Wilhelm to Valois, 16/8/1899).

aware that public opinion would resent any withdrawal from Samoa, and that Wilhelm was determined to have the islands or to call off his visit to England. Nevertheless, Bülow did not immediately accept Chamberlain's second offer; he desired something else, such as the Gilberts, for withdrawing from the Solomons. He also hoped to separate the African settlement from the Pacific one and to keep it for later. Holstein for his part was most suspicious and believed that the second proposal was 'an English trap'. With both opinions Hatzfeldt was forced to disagree: Chamberlain was neither planning a trap nor would he make any more concessions although an attempt would be made by Eckardstein for the Gilberts.[88]

Firmly believing Chamberlain's view that it would be almost impossible to persuade Salisbury to accept the second scheme, Hatzfeldt also urged that the first one be taken up by Berlin. The colonial secretary had agreed to the delay asked for by the Germans on the twelfth, but he emphasized once again that they should accept his first scheme and even suggested that Hatzfeldt might have to fight out the second one with the prime minister himself. The majority of the Cabinet also only favoured a scheme which involved a German withdrawal from Samoa. Finally, he stressed that he would not concede 'a comma more'.

The ambassador urged upon Berlin the fact that the British territories offered 'almost inestimable advantages with which the purely sentimental value of Samoa just cannot be compared at all'. Holstein, too, opposed the views of Tirptiz and the 'sentimentalists' and wrote 'We must protest, however, ever protest and wait.' He was not very optimistic, though, and thought that they were approaching the verge of a chasm. He and Buchka, the head of the colonial division and someone who could appreciate the comparative value of Chamberlain's two offers, were probably instrumental in arranging a meeting of the *Kolonialrat* to discuss the entire question.[89] This consultative body of colonial experts and those representing Germany's overseas commercial interests would surely be able to point out where the country's real interests lay, and thus to stave off a crisis with the British. It was possibly Holstein, too, who secured an invitation to this conference for Eckardstein. There were still some hopes of defeating the naval agitation, he felt, since Bülow was going to bring in some expert officials from the colonial division of the

88   London Embassy records, Bülow to Hatzfeldt and reply, 11/10/1899; ibid., Holstein to Hatzfeldt and reply, 13/10/1899; G.P., 14/2, no. 4108.

89   A.A./*Südsee-Inseln* 5, vol. 4, Hatzfeldt to A.A., no. 320 of 12/10/1899; London Embassy records, Holstein to Hatzfeldt, 12/10/1899; *Holstein Papers*, 4, pp. 161-62.

Auswärtiges Amt to speak in favour of an exchange on the lines of the first proposal.[90]

In this, however, Holstein was greatly misled—or he was misleading Hatzfeldt, which seems far less likely. Bülow was not the person to oppose the combined wishes of the kaiser, the navy and the colonial pressure groups, and on the fourteenth showed some 'vehemence' to Lascelles on the question. The ambassador correctly interpreted this as being

> no doubt due to his knowledge that the Emperor takes great interest in the matter and indeed looks upon it as a personal question, and there may be a good deal in Derenthall's remark, which I have repeated officially, that Bülow's position would become very difficult *vis-à-vis* the Reichstag if he gave up Upolu without obtaining very evident compensation.[91]

Bülow's private letter to Tirpitz and the fact that on the twelfth he had a discussion with Woermann, a Hamburg merchant and member of the *Kolonialrat* who favoured keeping Samoa, all confirm this view.[92]

This also emerges from the meeting of the *Kolonialrat* on 16 October, over which Bülow presided. In a long paper, prepared two days earlier by Irmer, he outlined the pros and cons of Chamberlain's two proposals. The Volta triangle was much more valuable than Samoa and would give life to the ailing Togoland colony, the partition of the Neutral Zone was to be welcomed and the extra-territorial rights in Zanzibar had only two years to run in any case. Savage Island was nothing but the Solomons were the best labour recruiting grounds for the German plantations in the South Seas and, without them, they would have to turn to Chinese labour. Both the southern Solomons and the Gilberts would be desirable possessions. Upolu and Savai'i were not of great importance commercially and German trade was declining there. Tonga had better harbours but British influence predominated in that group. On the other hand, the navy valued Samoa for several reasons, although Apia and Saluafata were not safe harbours. Most important of all, however, it had become an 'imponderable' factor in view of its place in the public mind. 'Under these circumstances', Bülow had written across Irmer's draft and also later declared to the

---

90 A.A.90 A.A./*Südsee-Inseln* 5, vol. 4, Holstein to Hatzfeldt, 13/10/1899. On the activities of the *Kolonialrat*, see the authoritative dissertation by Dr H. Pogge von Strandmann.

91 F.O.800/17, Lascelles to Sanderson, 14/10/1899.

92 A.A./*Südsee-Inseln* 5, vol. 4, Bülow to Metternich (Hamburg), tel. no. 22 of 11/10/1899, and reply, tel. no. 24 of same date.

conference, 'I cannot advise His Majesty the Kaiser to withdraw from Samoa . . .'[93]

The matter was then taken up by the forty-four other people present, among them being Eckardstein, Buchka, Rose, Sternburg, Irmer and Meyer-Delius (of the *D.H.P.G.*) Quickly the various factions were revealed. Eckardstein and Seitz, a former governor of Kamerun, urged the acceptance of the 'extraordinarily advantageous' first scheme. On the other hand, nationalists and pan-Germans such as Vohsen, Staudinger, Heydt and Tucher argued that the retention of Samoa was vital for prestige and on idealistic grounds, and Bülow also urged that a solution should correspond to the 'national feelings'. A third group, consisting of Rose, Hansemann, Schmidt-Dargitz and others with experience in Pacific affairs, pointed out that Samoa would be economically useless without the labour-recruiting fields of the Solomons. After several indecisive motions and votings and a small pause, the meeting resumed and eventually accepted a motion declaring that the acquisition of the Volta triangle and Yendi should be accepted provided that Samoa *together with the northern Solomons* could not be acquired. In other words, Bülow was to try to obtain Samoa and to preserve its economic future; only if this proved impossible would the more valuable first offer be reluctantly taken up. The most noticeable fact emerging from the *Kolonialrat* conference was that, while almost everyone acknowledged the first proposal to be by far the best materially, few were ready to leave Samoa to secure these advantages. Bülow had more correctly gauged their feelings than Holstein, even though newspaper rumours and Eckardstein's faulty memoirs distorted the meaning of their vote.[94] It was not surprising, therefore, that a Post Office report a day later that the laying of a German cable to Samoa would be physically most dubious and would cost far in excess of its worth did not sway Bülow's mind.[95] For him the group was always regarded as an offering to please the kaiser and public; the economic and territorial considerations involved were of much less importance. Strengthened by the *Kolonialrat* decision, he could now renew his pressure in London.

93 A.A./*Südsee-Inseln* 5, vol. 4, Irmer memo of 14/10/1899, Secret, and minute.

94 H. Pogge von Strandmann, *The Kolonialrat*, pp. 296-310. (I am also grateful to Dr Pogge von Strandmann for allowing me to see his transcripts of the A.A./Kolonial-Abteilung, *Akta betreffend Verhandlungen des Kolonialraths*, vol. 19, conference of 16/10/1899). See also Eckardstein, *Lebenserinnerungen*, 2, pp. 39-41.

95 A.A./*Südsee-Inseln* 5, vol. 4, A.A. to Reichs-Post-Amt, Top Secret, Immediate, and reply of 17/10/1899.

iv   *Bülow's 'Free Hand' and the Settlement with Britain*

On 18 October, Bülow instructed Hatzfeldt and Eckardstein to approach Chamberlain once again. They were to persuade the colonial secretary to relent over the northern Solomons or at least Bougainville in his second set of proposals, offering instead Savage Island and the Zanzibar extraterritoriality, and certain concessions regarding Rhodes' railway schemes; but warning that if no settlement was reached their navy would set about constructing a harbour at Vavau in accordance with treaty rights. At the same time, and to avoid annoying Chamberlain, Bülow warned the Boers' representative, Dr Leyds, that he would not be officially received if he came to Berlin.[96]

Neither Hatzfeldt nor Eckardstein believed that these new proposals would be accepted. Nevertheless, it seemed imperative to do something before the kaiser completely surrendered to the wave of anglophobia and to the influence of his irresponsible military advisers. Although the Baron's memoirs have to be treated with care, the descriptions of the anglophobic generals, and of Tirpitz's promise of a more energetic policy against America and Britain when the fleet was larger, do ring true.[97] Lascelles, too, found Wilhelm very angry at the Boer War and saying that his visit to Windsor still depended upon the successful outcome of the Samoan talks.[98] By 18 October, the kaiser could contain himself no longer and, following the launching of his latest battleship at Hamburg, he made a public call for a bigger navy in his 'Bitter need we have of a strong German fleet' speech. Tirpitz had warned Bülow some days earlier that the kaiser must be restrained, but now the cat was out of the bag. Without consulting either the chancellor, the *Auswärtiges Amt* or Tirpitz, Wilhelm had announced his government's intention and his ministers must fulfil this demand as fast as they could.[99]

Why the kaiser made this appeal in such a dramatic way is uncertain. Perhaps, as has been suggested, he had been influenced by the very anti-English Senden, who usually helped him with his speeches.[100] Probably also it was one more repercussion of the Samoan dispute. One of the incidents in the spring of 1899 which had greatly excited Wilhelm and

96   A.A./*Südsee-Inseln* 5, vol. 4, Bülow to Hatzfeldt, no. 269 of 18/10/1899 (cancelled draft); cf. G.P., 14/2, no. 4109; G.P., 15, no. 4393.

97   Eckardstein, *Lebenserinnerungen*, 2, pp. 40-46.

98   F.O.800/17, Lascelles to Sanderson, 14/10/1899.

99   Alfred von Tirpitz, *Erinnerungen* (Leipzig, 1919,) p. 104.

100   Hubatsch, *Die Aera Tirpitz*, p. 69.

German opinion had been the allegedly threatening attitudes of the Anglo-American naval forces to the small cruiser *Falke*, which due to its size had been forced to swallow these insults. In September the kaiser suddenly ordered the ship, which was making its leisurely way home, to be in Hamburg for the launching if at all possible. On the day of the ceremony, he spent a full hour on board the cruiser, talking with the men and listening to their tales. With his usual impetuousness, he decorated four of them and then swept away the ship's commander, Schoenfelder, to accompany him at the launching, which immediately followed. It is probable that the memory of the Samoan incidents and Germany's weakness at sea pushed Wilhelm into his celebrated speech, for he told the *Falke's* crew:

> Let us hope that the day may not be distant when Germany will have larger, more powerful ships and more of them to send out to the far seas for the protection of her interests, and that all other nations will respect her just wishes.[101]

Fortunately for Berlin, its bargaining position vis-à-vis Britain was improving considerably in view of the South African War. Furthermore, the British cabinet had occupied itself on the seventeenth with the question of defending the British Isles from a possible continental coalition, and had decided to call up the militia and to commission some reserve warships. While Salisbury was still unruffled by the rumours of a coalition, believing that the most that would happen would be a Russian move towards the Straits, his colleagues would likely be more alarmed.[102] This factor, and the German mention of their rights in Tonga, probably accounted for Chamberlain's amiability when Eckardstein called on 20 October to say that Berlin accepted the second scheme but wished to have at least Bougainville in the northern Solomons and the right to recruit labourers from the other islands in that group which they were giving up. The colonial secretary agreed to this, although he would cede nothing more, and he advised Hatzfeldt to send a written draft of proposals to Salisbury so that the cabinet could discuss them. He, in turn, would consult Australasia upon the matter.[103]

For Chamberlain, the battle was already over. The mention

101 BA/MA 3410, PG67314, *Stapellauf von Schiffen*, vol. 2, kaiser's note on Admiralstab to Wilhelm, 8/9/1899; Marine-Kabinett no. 3925 (draft) of 10/10/1899; Wilhelm (on board *Falke*) to C. in C., Naval Station, Baltic, 18/10/1899, and accompanying note of 19/10/1899; *New York Times*, 22/10/1899.

102 Cab. 41/25/23 of 17/10/1899; and especially, P.R.O. 30/67 (Midleton Papers)/4, Salisbury to the queen, 30/10/1899, on the 'European Coalition'.

103 G.P., 14/2, no. 4110; Eckardstein, *Lebenserinnerungen*, 2, pp. 62-64.

of German coaling rights in Tonga had worried him enough to ask Anderson for a memorandum on them after his talk with the Baron. But it was now clearly a case of waiting for a formal German approach to Salisbury, who had probably been told by the colonial secretary after the cabinet meeting of the twentieth to expect such a communication. With an arrangement almost in sight, the Colonial Office was beginning to regard it in its fullness; and to like what it saw. Anderson pointed out that as well as the great differences in their harbours, Tonga's commerce exceeded Samoa's. The Solomon islands which they would receive contained less trade at present but they were far larger than the Samoan group and to his mind intrinsically more valuable. Britain would also take Savage Island, while the German request to recruit labourers in the northern Solomons was not regarded as important. A few days later, on learning for the first time that no British cession of the Volta triangle was involved, he wrote:

> If that is so, the arrangement is of course really much more to our advantage than I thought, as even in the Pacific, whatever Australia may say, we would have the best of the deal, and of course the settlement of the Zanzibar and Neutral Zone questions is a further consideration from an Imperial point of view.[104]

The prospect of withdrawing from Samoa, which the Colonial Office had fought against for over fifteen years, was now greeted, not so much with concern, but with relief at escaping from the entanglement. The deal seemed so favourable that little opposition was expected, even from New Zealand.

If the British were satisfied, the Germans were not. Bülow immediately cabled back to Hatzfeldt that he should attempt to gain Choiseul and Isabel Islands in the northern Solomons. Fearing that German colonial circles, and those members of the *Kolonialrat* who had advocated a settlement along these lines, would be greatly annoyed if Britain obtained an economic hold over Samoa through her control of the labour supply, he pressed for concessions in this crucial matter. He also hoped to avoid Chamberlain's proposals regarding a tariff settlement between the Gold Coast and Togoland, and to persuade the British to keep the Zanzibar extraterritoriality question a secret. The talks could still break down, he warned.[105] However, Eckardstein found it impossible to weaken the colonial secretary's position any further. Chamberlain agreed to the German requests concerning West Africa

104 Chamberlain Papers, JC7/2/2A/32 and 33, Anderson notes of 20/10/1899 and 25/10/1899.
105 A.A./*Südsee-Inseln* 5, vol. 5, A.A. to Hatzfeldt, tel. no. 279 of 22/10/1899; G.P., 14/2, no. 4111.

and Zanzibar but at the same time said that Britain should have Savage Island in view of Australasian opinion. Most important of all, he refused to retreat from his claim to Choiseul and Isabel.[106]

This news caused consternation in Berlin. While it is difficult to believe Holstein's note to Eckardstein that the German government would not last long if the Samoan negotiations broke down,[107] Bülow was clearly in a very serious position. Europe was looking towards Germany for some gesture in favour of a continental alliance and the Russian press was making meaningful hints about the silence at the *Wilhelm-strasse*. Throughout the country, a fierce outburst of anglo-phobia was severely worrying the government, and Herbert Bismarck and many of Bülow's enemies were campaigning for an anti-British policy. Holstein fearfully reported that the English journey was under strong attack and that even the kaiser was taking notice of this. Chamberlain *had* to make these small concessions, or the scheme had at least to be dressed up to look better. Hatzfeldt for his part felt that the failure of the talks and the visit would divide the two countries permanently and tempt the British to reject the Portuguese colonies settlement. The only power which could profit from this would be Russia, a prospect both Holstein and Hatzfeldt acutely disliked.[108]

Bülow was possibly even more worried. What Wilhelm would say or do if the Samoan arrangement and the Windsor visit fell through, he hardly dared to guess. On the other hand, if the anti-British press campaign became any stronger, they would have to bend. He would not risk the popularity of the monarchy, nor his own position, by defying the public. Hatzfeldt was privately informed that the visit would depend, not upon the settlement of Samoa itself, *but solely upon its favourable reception by the German people*. Everything hung upon a treaty which revealed as many apparent points in Germany's favour as possible. It was imperative, he wrote, to obtain at least the Shortland and Fauro groups, minute and obscure islands lying just off Bougainville. For the same reason, Hatzfeldt should try once again to secure Choiseul, offering in exchange Savage Island and also Manua Island in the Samoan group, provided that the latter was not claimed by the Americans. The most welcome development of all

106 Ibid., no. 4112.

107 Eckardstein, *Lebenserinnerungen*, 2, p. 61.

108 London Embassy records, Holstein to Hatzfeldt, 22/10/1899; A.A./*Südsee-Inseln* 5, vol. 5, A.A. to Hatzfeldt, tel. no. 278, Urgent, 22/10/1899; A.A./*England* 78 *nr.* 1 *Secr.*, vol. 14, Hatzfeldt to A.A., no. 344 of 22/10/1899.

would be a temporary British defeat in South Africa, which would hurry Chamberlain into an agreement; if this did occur, it might be possible to extort more from London.[109]

In vain Eckardstein attempted to seek out Chamberlain and to persuade him to give more, but the colonial secretary would not even see him and merely sent a note, testily declaring that there would be no more concessions in the Solomons. He seems, in fact, to have been annoyed with these constant pleadings, particularly when he had already assured Salisbury that Hatzfeldt would be getting in touch with him. After waiting for a few days, the prime minister directed his secretary to sound out the German embassy on 25 October as to whether any proposals were contemplated, and Hatzfeldt was again forced to answer that he was too ill to come. On the following day, Salisbury tried once more and Hatzfeldt reported that he could not be held off much longer. On hearing this, Bülow felt that further delay would be dangerous and he instructed the ambassador to get in touch with Salisbury. With eyes still fixed upon public opinion, however, he directed that the treaty should contain the words that Germany would keep 'the islands lying to the east and south-east of Bougainville' *even though this would not be so*; and that she should only give up her rights in Zanzibar when other powers did the same.[110]

On 27 October, therefore, Hatzfeldt addressed a letter to Salisbury, enclosing a seven-point draft of a treaty and carefully explaining the need to use the phraseology therein. At the same time, Eckardstein met Chamberlain and gave him similar details. He found the colonial secretary more self-assured than ever and demanding the formal cession of Savage Island, which was missing from the draft.[111] This was quickly agreed to, but Bülow was appalled to learn that the cabinet ministers were preparing to leave town for a while after their further meetings on the state of the war and he peremptorily minuted: 'All that matters is that we now quickly settle things. The ministers must without fail be immediately recalled for the decision.' The news that they had already left London and that a cabinet could not be

109 A.A./*Südsee-Inseln* 5, vol. 5, Bülow to Hatzfeldt, tel. no. 279 of 22/10/1899, tel. nos. 280 and 282 of 23/10/1899, and 3 tels. (n.n.), Urgent, of 24/10/1899.
110 Chamberlain Papers, JC7/2/2B/11, Eckardstein to Chamberlain, 24/10/1899, and JC5/67/130, Salisbury to Chamberlain, 26/10/1899; Salisbury Papers, Class E, Chamberlain to Salisbury, 26/10/1899; ibid., A122/79-80, Barrington to Pückler and reply, both of 25/10/1899; A.A./*Südsee-Inseln* 5, vol. 5, Hatzfeldt to Bülow, 25/10/1899 and 26/10/1899, to Holstein, 26/10/1899; ibid., Bülow to Hatzfeldt, Urgent, tel. nos. 289 and 297, 26/10/1899; G.P., 14/2, nos. 4113-14.
111 Ibid., no. 4115; B.D., 1, nos. 151-52; A.A./*Südsee-Inseln* 5, vol. 5, Hatzfeldt to A.A., tel. no. 353 of 27/10/1899.

called until 1 November therefore greatly pained him, and he wondered whether their consent could not be secured in writing or whether even this was needed at all. Poor Hatzfeldt was requested to enquire urgently about this but at the same time not to reveal that Berlin was in any kind of hurry! He was also repeatedly warned that the whole Samoan question was to be kept 'absolutely secret' lest the anti-British circles in Germany attempt to shipwreck the settlement;[112] yet this was only a short while after he had been instructed to lobby every person who could possibly influence Salisbury in the matter. It was hardly surprising that the ailing ambassador was confessing privately to Holstein that he was in urgent need of a rest from this demanding work.

All seemed to depend upon whether Salisbury or Chamberlain controlled the Cabinet, therefore, and in this respect Berlin was reasonably hopeful. The colonial secretary and Rothschild assured Eckardstein that the majority of its members were in favour of a swift settlement with Germany, and that all would be well. If Bülow and Holstein were more nervous, it was due to their deeper suspicion of the prime minister and to the fact that they regarded the question in a much more serious light. Nevertheless, they were reconciled to the terms stipulated, albeit reluctantly. Bülow informed Holstein that

> it would be so useful for opinion in Germany and His Majesty's journey to England if England did not maintain its odious demand for the Shortland and Fauro Islands. However, we will make no new step in this direction. But of course any further concessions to England are completely impossible for us.[113]

The prospects seemed good, for on the day of the Cabinet meeting Hatzfeldt had an interview with Salisbury, during which the latter appeared to accept the settlement on the whole although there were 'small editorial modifications' to be made in the final draft and he declined to sign the seven-point scheme immediately. As he was later completing this despatch, the ambassador learnt that the Cabinet had unanimously accepted the proposed settlement and that all that was required by Chamberlain was a closer definition of the Neutral Zone partition line so as to avoid future difficulties. Hatzfeldt therefore proposed to send Salisbury a draft convention for his comment and signature on the following day. The end seemed at last in sight.

112   Ibid.; and tel. no. 358 of 28/10/1899, with Bülow notes to Holstein thereon; A.A. to Hatzfeldt, tel. no. 301 of 29/10/1899. Bülow to Hatzfeldt, tel. no. 289 of 26/10/1899 and minute to Holstein of 31/10/1899.
113   Ibid., further note of 31/10/1899.

This picture is confirmed by a reading of the *Grosse Politik* section on Samoa, for this is the final document therein and the editors give details of the final treaty in a footnote, remarking that 'The remaining negotiations dragged on for a while, without having great importance.'[114] Nothing, in fact, could have been further from the truth, and while little concerning Samoa itself was lost by this omission, the crisis in Berlin and important sidelights upon the 'Free Hand' policy, the influencing of the press, and Bülow's attitude to Britain and Russia have been hidden.

The crisis was caused partly by the steadily rising anglophobia in Germany, and partly by Bülow himself. As to the formidable nature of the first factor, there can be little doubt: sufficient analyses of public opinion at this time confirm the depth of the bitterness against the British actions in the Transvaal, exceptions being those newspapers which followed the government line.[115] This trend frightened Bülow for two reasons. Firstly, that the British would notice it and come to regard Germany as a hostile nation; and secondly, that it would become so strong as to force the German government to abandon its neutral stance. At the news of the Ladysmith disaster, therefore, Bülow sent out special directives to the press.

A cool and calm language is recommended for our press towards the English defeat at Ladysmith. A too clearly prominent *Schadenfreude* and open jubilation would only turn the bitterness of the English against us, whom we are not yet strong enough at sea to meet, and simultaneously nourish the hopes of the French and the Russians that we would be ready to let ourselves be directed alone against England.[116]

Furthermore, Berlin appears to have been very worried at Russian attempts to cause the British to note the anglophobia in Germany. On 25 October, Wilhelm himself wrote to Lascelles, then in England, warning him that a 'swarm of Russian agents' was being sent from Paris and St Petersburg to London to foment bad feeling against Germany and to foil his visit.

Please warn the Govt. and the papers! especially the latter as to the news about Germany which are (sic) being brought to them! There is danger so

114 G.P., 14/2, no. 4117 and footnote; Vagts, *Weltpolitik*, 1, pp. 916-20 applies a corrective.

115 W. Treue, 'Presse und Politik in Deutschland und England während des Burenkrieges' in *Berliner Monatshefte*, vol. 11 (1933); P. R. Anderson, *The Background of Anti-English Feeling in Germany*, 1890-1902 (Washington, 1939); O. J. Hale, *Publicity and Diplomacy with Special Reference to England and Germany*, 1890-1902 (London/New York, 1940); Meyer, *Die Propaganda*, pp. 108-35.

116 G.P., 15, footnote on pp. 414-15.

look out! Both countries are in a perfect frenzie (sic) at the prospect of my visit to England! Beware.[117]

Only a few days later he took further alarm when he learnt that the Russian Telegraph Agency was seeking information for its Foreign Ministry about German opinion towards Britain, and he angrily ordered 'Double watchfulness in the press and every insolent article against England to be immediately cut off at the head . . .'[118]

Probably the strength of the anglophobia and the influence of the Russian newspaper intrigue were exaggerated by Wilhelm and Bülow, both of whom were extraordinarily sensitive to press criticisms of their policy, yet these factors help to explain their extreme worries of the few days following. The news that Upolu and Savai'i would fall to Germany would, it was hoped, take much of the wind out of the sails of the government's critics; it would silence the Russian efforts, and at the same time revive Chamberlain's hopes; it would allow the kaiser to go to England; and finally, it would enable Bülow to maintain his foreign policy.

The latter injected a further note of urgency into the affair by his insistence that the Samoan question must be settled before the Czar called upon Wilhelm at Potsdam on 8 November. The positive reason for this is clear: he wished to bring off a great coup for his 'Free Hand' policy by demonstrating to the world that he could arrange a wide-ranging colonial treaty with Britain at the same time as he entertained the Russian leader. The negative reason, which was explained by Holstein in a telegram to Hatzfeldt on 2 November, was that Bülow had been informed that Muraviev would accompany the Czar and would raise the question of a special Russo-German treaty, probably over the Straits but perhaps over a more general entente. While Berlin wished to avoid this if at all possible, because it might restrict their Bagdad Railway schemes and alienate Britain and Austria-Hungary, they could not contemplate a definite rebuff to the Russians unless their relations with London were apparently friendly and normal.

Hence Bülow's instructions to Hatzfeldt that they must know their position on Samoa before the following Tuesday (7 November) and hence Holstein's telegram that the Russian visit would be as fruitless as usual if the Samoan affair was settled but quite different if the negotiations in London

117 Salisbury Papers, Class E (Lascelles), Wilhelm to Lascelles, 25/10/1899.
118 A.A./*England* 78, vol. 12, minute on Tschirschky's no. 195 of 27/10/1899.

broke down.[119] The cancellation of the Windsor trip and the consequent bitterness in Britain, the impossibility of cooling the anglophobia and internal criticism should a Samoan treaty fall through, the Russian pressure for an agreement, all three factors disturbed the men of the *Wilhelmstrasse*. Only a quick and successful settlement of the Samoan problem could stave off these converging threats. Instead of merely being the elimination of a distant squabble, therefore, it had become a matter upon which, so they believed, their entire existing policy depended.

Thus Salisbury's small modifications and his refusal to sign the seven-point agreement provisionally were not greeted with the calmness the editors of the *Grosse Politik* would have us believe. 'What significance has that? How would it be received in our colonial circles?' Bülow scribbled anxiously alongside the section concerning the altered boundary in the Neutral Zone. 'How would that work out for us commercially?', he wrote against Salisbury's proposals on future most-favoured-nation rights for all three powers in the Samoan and Tongan groups. Moreover, while he shared the prime minister's wish that the United States should participate fully in the treaty, he ordered that this should not 'under any circumstances' delay its conclusion. Chamberlain, Rothschild, and 'whoever else has influence' should be used to prevent Salisbury from stalling. The affair had to be finalized immediately.[120]

Holstein elaborated this in his instructions of 2 November. Berlin could not understand the boundary proposals in the Neutral Zone but was so eager for an agreement that an 'elastic formula', which could be worked out in more detail by experts afterwards, was to be put forward. It being clear that 'we have absolutely nothing to expect from Salisbury's goodwill', Chamberlain must be pushed forward to fight the prime minister's delaying tactics. Particularly worrying was Salisbury's reference to careful consultations with America, for that might delay matters some weeks. Fearing that the prime minister meant to use this as an excuse for further procrastination, Berlin hoped to circumvent him by appealing to Hay directly, by asking Balfour and Chamberlain to exercise their influence at Washington, and by persuading the American ambassador in London, Choate, to help also. Mumm was instructed to

119 A.A./*Südsee-Inseln* 5, vol. 6, Holstein to Hatzfeldt, 2/11/1899; G.P., 14/2, no. 4116. The German distaste for a treaty with Russia is clearly shown in Holstein's memo of 7/11/1899 in BA, Bülow Papers, vol. 91.

120 A.A./*Südsee-Inseln* 5, vol. 6, Hatzfeldt to A.A., tel. no. 365 of 1/11/1899, and cf. G.P., 14/2, no. 4117, in which the minutes are omitted.

tell the State Department that Germany attached 'extra-ordinarily great' value to a swift understanding.[121]

By the following day, matters were even worse. Hatzfeldt reported that Choate and Salisbury had agreed that the United States must fully participate in the settlement, but added that the American ambassador thought Tutuila might not be considered as a sufficient compensation (Bülow: '!') when it was learnt that Germany was to have the two large islands in the Samoan group. It would be difficult to say, Choate had declared, how long the president would need to examine the proposed treaty. (Bülow: '!') These statements caused consternation in Berlin, where it was naturally assumed that Salisbury had encouraged these new demands. 'The Kaiser's visit will be in the grave', Holstein feared, describing Choate's speech as 'Napoleonic' and seeing in it 'a real danger'. Chamberlain must be told that his whole policy of working with Germany would be defeated if this American aspect was not quickly cleared up. Bülow was even more explicit, minuting:

> Salisbury—and especially Chamberlain, the other ministers, Rothschild, and even the Court—ought not to be left in any doubt that if England does not truly and emphatically work for America's swift agreement, then this will not only exclude the Kaiser's visit to England but would be of deep significance for the *entire course* of our policy also.[122]

Without Samoa, he added, 'internal political' reasons would dictate a cancellation of the Windsor trip. As for Wilhelm, he reacted to a friendly letter from Lascelles, which expressed the hope that the English visit would lead to better relations between the two countries, by curtly minuting: 'And Samoa?'[123]

The relief in Berlin on the following day when it was learnt that Hay was ready to agree to the Anglo-German arrangement provided that America received Manua and the smaller islands near Tutuila was therefore immense. The great fear had been that Washington would ask for one of the Caroline or Marshall islands and this, Bülow felt, could 'under no circumstances' be acceded to. Nevertheless, Salisbury's irritating small points still threatened the whole course of the talks. 'The difficulty lies not in these matters', Holstein cabled,' but in the *time-factor*.' With only four days to go before the Czar's visit,

121 A.A./*Südsee-Inseln* 5, vol. 6, Hatzfeldt to Bülow, 2/11/1899 and 3/11/1899; Holstein to Hatzfeldt, 2/11/1899, and A.A. to Hatzfeldt, tel. no. 365 of 2/11/1899; A.A. to Mumm, tel. no. 163 of 2/11/1899; London Embassy records, Holstein to Hatzfeldt, 2/11/1899.

122 Ibid., same to same, 3/11/1899; A.A./*Südsee-Inseln* 5, vol. 6, Hatzfeldt to Bülow and reply, 3/11/1899, and Holstein to Hatzfeldt, 3/11/1899; Hay Papers, Box 19, Choate to Hay, 3/11/1899.

123 London Embassy records, Bülow to Hatzfeldt, Very Confidential of 3/11/1899.

Bülow was becoming really worried: 'Tuesday is the very latest time when we should round the corner and not take up a different course'. Most infuriating of all was the fact that the sense of urgency was missing on the other side and nearly all the ministers, Salisbury and Chamberlain included, were in the country. Perhaps Eckardstein could be sent to Birmingham to press the matter upon the colonial secretary, Holstein pleaded. Bülow felt the same way: 'All details are irrelevant but it is of the highest importance to sign provisionally on Monday. Can this not be arranged via Chamberlain or by a letter to Salisbury? We endure the matter no longer.'[124]

On 5 November, their irritation against the prime minister reached its peak. He had written from Hatfield on the previous day that there were still some modifications required in the text which had been submitted by Hatzfeldt before he could sign the agreement. He mentioned again the dividing line in the Neutral Zone and also felt that the consuls of both countries should not be permanently abolished in Samoa and Tonga. The latter request infuriated Irmer, who foresaw the return of consular friction and a British meddling in the conditions of the labourers on the *D.H.P.G.* plantations. The kaiser viewed things in a broader light. On 6 November, he burst out to Grierson against the 'two-headed' government in London, and threatened the cancellation of his visit. Salisbury's procrastinations were intolerable and had placed the German government in great difficulties. Wilhelm concluded by warning: 'I cannot go sitting on a safety-valve for ever. Does England not want my friendship, about the only one left her on the Continent? Some day when she is in trouble she will find that German patience has been tried too long.'[125]

Despite the bitterness felt against Salisbury, however, the Germans dared not openly lose their temper. In fact, the *Wilhelmstrasse* was now so scared that matters would not be arranged before their self-appointed deadline that they were willing to agree to every little point which the prime minister raised. Hatzfeldt was frantically urging Sanderson and Lascelles to take messages out to Hatfield, and Eckardstein was told to be ready to travel to Birmingham. A compromise was proposed regarding the retention of consuls (no more political activities, only trade and navigation), and Berlin

124 Ibid., Holstein to Hatzfeldt, 4/11/1899(2); A.A./*Südsee-Inseln* 5, vol. 6, Hatzfeldt to A.A., tel. no. 373 of 4/11/1899, and Bülow minute thereon; Hatzfeldt to Holstein, 4/11/1899, and Bülow minutes thereon; Holstein to Hatzfeldt, 4/11/1899; A.A. to Hatzfeldt, tel. nos. 313 and 316 of 4/11/1899 and 5/11/1899.
125 Ibid., Hatzfeldt to A.A., tel. no. 377 of 5/11/1899, and Irmer's minute thereon; B.D., 1, nos. 153 and 154.

agreed to the Colonial Office's wishes over the West African boundary. It was to be made plain to London that they did not really care about the niggling British worries. What mattered, as Hatzfeldt put it, was to get an agreement before Tuesday 'in any form at all'. Yet even if these points were settled, a further danger loomed; Salisbury was still waiting for word from Australasia.[126]

Berlin was by then reckoning the hours to the breakdown. 'I think we are now on the brink' were the opening words of Holstein's telegram to Hatzfeldt on 6 November. The ambassador for his part confessed himself to be 'exhausted' at the strain.

> What was humanly possible has been done to overcome all difficulties and to reach a decision at last. All the same, I cannot as yet tell you with any degree of certainty whether I will be able to report a definite result to you on Tuesday evening.[127]

Hatzfeldt once again urged that they work until the very last moment to avoid a break, for the cancellation of the kaiser's visit would cause 'a tremendous sensation' and would serve 'as a direct notice of the ending of our friendly relations'.

On the afternoon of the sixth, however, affairs rapidly changed for the better. Sanderson and Lascelles co-operated fully with Hatzfeldt in drafting and re-drafting a treaty which would suit both Bülow and Salisbury. Sanderson himself travelled out at once to Hatfield and a special courier was sent there later to obtain the prime minister's views. It was also decided to wait no longer for an answer from the Australasians. On the following day, Salisbury himself came to London and discussed the final draft with Hatzfeldt, but still had four minor technical alterations regarding the American position, the West African boundary line, free trade and navigation in the Pacific, and the inclusion of the small Howe Island within the British sphere. He then initialled the draft under the proviso that his amendments in red ink were accepted by the German government. 'Failing that, acceptance by Her Majesty's Government was to be considered as of no effect.' Finding his protests against this disregarded, Hatzfeldt appealed for instructions.[128]

---

126 A.A./*Südsee-Inseln* 5, vol. 6, Hatzfeldt to A.A., 5/11/1899, and Bülow's minute thereon; A.A. to Hatzfeldt, tel. no. 318 of 5/11/1899.

127 Ibid., Holstein to Hatzfeldt, 6/11/1899; *Holstein Papers*, 4, pp. 164-65.

128 F.O.58/334, Salisbury to Gough, Secret, no. 212 of 8/11/1899; A.A./*Südsee-Inseln* 5, vol. 6, Hatzfeldt to Bülow, 6/11/1899, and Hatzfeldt to A.A., tel. nos. 382 and 383 of 6/11/1899 and 7/11/1899.

But Bülow was in no spirit for further wranglings. Early on 8 November, a few hours before he was due to meet the Czar at Potsdam, he instructed the ambassador to tell Salisbury that they agreed to his latest stipulations. He did not understand the British requests over Howe Island and the West African boundary, nor, for that matter, did he care. At this stage, Hatzfeldt was disputing with Sanderson the correct interpretation of Germany's previous rights to recruit labourers in the Solomons. This, as mentioned above, was most important to the future of the German plantations in Samoa: yet Bülow ignored it. At the same time as his telegram to Hatzfeldt, the news of the agreement was published in Berlin. By the narrowest of margins, he had achieved his aim of a Samoan settlement before the Czar's visit.[129]

Hatzfeldt was not aware of this and, although he gave the German government's assent to Salisbury's stipulations, was still arguing that morning about the labour recruitment question and warning that it was a matter 'much less of Samoa than a political question of the highest importance'. He also allowed himself to explain openly that the treaty was needed urgently to strengthen Bülow's hand against attacks upon his pro-British policy; to assist the kaiser, who faced formidable opposition to his English journey; and to neutralize the Russian efforts, which could be seen in the Czar's visit. Salisbury, reported Hatzfeldt, understood all that had been said but still asked whether Berlin would accept his conditions. Even to the last, he seemed reluctant to help. But the ambassador need not have worried. His news that he had handed over Berlin's consent was answered with the kaiser's award of 'the Diamonds to my high Order of the Black Eagle' and Bülow's fervent congratulations.[130]

One of the ambassador's last telegrams on that hectic day was to report the Foreign Office's 'amazement' that the treaty, which was supposedly to be kept secret for a while, had been given out to the press in Berlin.[131] While this had chiefly been done to demonstrate to Muraviev that Germany could maintain good relations with Britain, there was also a second reason. On 2 November, Bülow had minuted that the publication of the treaty should not be given out first in either Britain or the United States, and he had therefore taken alarm when he later learnt that Salisbury was planning to announce the settlement at the lord mayor's banquet on 9 November: 'We must certainly have it settled before then. We dare not

---

129   Ibid., A.A. to Hatzfeldt, tel. nos. 322 and 323, Immediate, of 8/11/1899.
130   Ibid., Hatzfeldt to A.A., 8/11/1899, and tel. no. 384 of 8/11/1899.
131   Ibid., same to same, tel. no. 387 of 8/11/1899.

leave it to Lord Salisbury to announce the agreement first and
in his own manner *urbi et orbi* as a success for the English
government.'[132] The Samoan settlement had to be presented
as an achievement for German diplomacy, and Bülow greatly
feared that a deprecating after-dinner speech by the prime
minister would hurt the pride of the colonial circles and
perhaps prejudice their acceptance of the deal. Salisbury
would obviously point out the advantages Britain had gained
from it; it was Bülow's aim to forestall this by stressing the
advantages to Germany in a prior announcement. His later
excuse that publication had 'much to their regret' been
necessary, since details were leaking to the press and diplomatic
circles, was therefore a blatant travesty of the truth.[133]

The 'Free Hand' had been saved, and even enhanced, by
this last-minute settlement of the Samoan question. The host
of congratulatory messages showered upon Bülow served
only to convince him of the correctness of his policy. The
Czar, too, politely commented upon the treaty during his
talks and declared that he wished for good relations with
Germany. All the same, both he and Muraviev gently reminded
Berlin of the Russian concern over German plans for Turkey
and the Near East, and suggested that these be submitted
first to St Petersburg to avoid future controversies; but a
direct answer to this was carefully concealed by Bülow in a
cloud of fervent wishes for good mutual relations. In fact, no
mention was made of a treaty over the Straits, nor of better
Franco-German relations, although a firm answer had been
prepared by Holstein should these points have been raised.

> One must therefore tell Count Muraviev that we will be ready for various
> special arrangements *at the moment when Russia and France are ready
> to sign a pacte conservatoire with us, guaranteeing the respective territories*
> of the three great powers.[134]

Since this was at present impossible, Holstein continued, the
Russians would be unable to say anything and Germany's
relations with Britain, Austria-Hungary and Italy would
thereby be unimpaired. Berlin would remain in the middle,
enjoying her position as *tertius gaudens*.

On 14 November, Hatzfeldt and Salisbury signed the
formal agreement, under which Britain renounced her rights
in Savai'i and Upolu while Germany renounced hers in the

---

132 Ibid., Bülow minutes on Hatzfeldt to A.A., tel. no. 365 of 1/11/1899, and on
Hatzfeldt to Bülow, 2/11/1899.
133 Ibid., vol. 7, A.A. to Hatzfeldt, tel. no. 327 of 9/11/1899.
134 BA, Bülow Papers, vol. 91, Holstein memo of 7/11/1899; G.P., 13, nos. 3547-48.

Tongan group.[135] Germany also withdrew from those Solomon islands to the east and south-east of Bougainville—although, in fact, the British allowed them to keep the very small islands immediately offshore. The respective consuls in Samoa and Tonga were only provisionally recalled, and the existing arrangements for German labour-recruiting in the southern Solomons were extended to those islands newly acquired by Britain. Both these clauses were rather vague, and were to lead to further disputes in the future. The Neutral Zone boundary was specified to be the river Daka up to 9°N and it would then be fixed by a mixed commission to continue northwards, allowing Gambaga and the Mamprusi territories to fall to Britain while Yendi and the Chakosi territories fell to Germany.[136] Berlin promised to consider favourably British requests concerning reciprocal tariffs between Togoland and the Gold Coast, although it was privately determined to restrict this development as far as possible. Finally, while it renounced its extraterritorial rights in Zanzibar, this renunciation would only take place when other powers' rights there were also abolished. The Anglo-German tussle over Samoa and smaller colonial matters had at last been settled, in a tidy package deal which seemed to satisfy both sides; and the end of the tridominium was only weeks away.

135   The text is in *Accounts and Papers* (1900), vol. 105.
136   Sir E. Hertslet, *The Map of Africa by Treaty*, 3rd ed., (London, 1967 reprint), vol. 3, pp. 919-21, 927-30, 935-37. A map of these regions faces p. 936.

6

The Aftermath

i *The Diplomatic Aftermath*

THE Anglo-German agreement on Samoa allowed Wilhelm to fulfil his wish of going to England. Even during the fierce negotiations of late October, he had hoped that the visit would take place and had regarded a petition by 3,000 Hamburg citizens against it as 'impudent arrogance'.[1] Now that it could be announced that Germany would obtain Samoa and Eulenburg had quickly assured both him and Bülow that the press attacks had consequently moderated, Wilhelm looked forward to the journey with his usual enthusiasm. Tirpitz reported that 'The Kaiser travels to England on Saturday in a very pleased mood. The settlement of the Samoan affair has worked quite beneficially for this matter.'[2]

Yet if the kaiser was highly satisfied, there was a widespread realization amongst his entourage that the treaty was unfavourable to Germany from the material point of view. To most of the statesmen and diplomats concerned the fact was perhaps rather irrelevant, since their chief aim had been to satisfy public opinion whilst maintaining friendly relations with Britain. Yet if they were satisfied at the political aspect, it is important to see the distinction, for it reveals a great deal about German policy at this time. Bülow expressly told the Americans that 'the entire Samoan question has absolutely no material, but an ideal and patriotic interest for us'.[3] The *Kolonialrat* meeting of 16 October had also pivoted upon the ideal or the real interests involved and came down in favour of the former, to the bewilderment of several officials. A member of the admiralty staff was annoyed to learn afterwards that Chamberlain's proposals had meant that 'in each case the Tongan Islands should be English!'; and further noted that the Solomons were 'ten times as big as Samoa'.[4] Rose, despite his personal interest, felt that Samoa was of 'negative value' while Schmidt-Dargitz admitted to a friend that it had

1 A.A./*Preussen* 1 *nr.* 1 *nr.* 40, vol. 5, minute on petition of 24/10/1899.
2 A.A., Eisendecker Papers, vol. 3, part 2, Tirpitz to Eisendecker, 21/11/1899; BA, Eulenburg Papers, Eulenburg to Bülow, 12/11/1899, and to Wilhelm, 15/11/1899.
3 A.A./*Südsee-Inseln* 5, vol. 6, A.A. to Mumm, tel. no. 167 of 5/11/1899.
4 BA/MA 5079, *Samoa*, vol. 2, Winckler minute on *Kölnische Zeitung* article of 8/11/1899.

been 'simply a prestige victory' (*Ehrenerfolg*).[5] Hatzfeldt and
Holstein also thought that Germany had made a poor bargain,
and Richthofen bluntly admitted to the American chargé that
since the United States had taken Pago-Pago and Britain
Tonga, which possessed 'the best harbour in the South Seas',
the German government had had 'the worst of the bargain'.[6]

Having ensured by the acquisition of Samoa that the
kaiser's English visit would take place, Holstein and Bülow
immediately gave careful consideration to its political aspects.
Already, on 9 November, the *Vortragender Rat* had drawn
some preliminary conclusions from the Samoan dispute and
in particular the idea that no important questions should be
negotiated with Salisbury, since matters could be equally
settled without him. At the same time, it was recognized that
Chamberlain only gave generously when he was in a hurry
and that Berlin should wait to see how he reacted to developments in Morocco or the Portuguese colonies. Time was
against Britain, Holstein felt, and she would become even
more anxious for German support.[7] On the following day,
he advised Wilhelm to say nothing about politics, especially
to Salisbury, and to listen politely but coolly to any suggestions
from Chamberlain for an anti-Russian move. Much of this
was repeated in a later memorandum, which explicitly stated
that Berlin 'will not accept an arrangement which is visibly
directed against Russia'. Since Germany faces 'no visible
danger of war from any direction', Britain would have to pay
well to tempt her out of this strong neutrality. Finally, Holstein
in a fourth document warned that Wilhelm should not ask
for 'a few colonial morsels', since this would raise suspicions
in London. A friendly but reserved policy was all that was
necessary; by it, Germany would profit without running any
risks. Hatzfeldt and Bülow, too, believed that all they needed
to do was to sit still.[8]

In the event, they need not have worried about the visit,
which went off smoothly and without incident. Possibly the
absence of Salisbury, whose wife finally died on 20 November,
assisted this but Wilhelm heeded the words of his advisers
and adopted a very restrained manner. Chamberlain's soundings about a future alliance were handled circumspectly

5 R.Kol.A.3054, Mumm to Hohenlohe, A168 of 22/7/1899 (re. Rose); Schmidt-Dargitz
to Schnee, 12/11/1899, in Geheimes Staatsarchiv, Berlin-Dahlem, Heinrich-Schnee-Archiv,
Nr 52:62 (kindly supplied by Mr. S. G. Firth).
6 Hay Papers, Box 19, Choate to Hay, 3/11/1899; N.A.R.G.59, M-44, roll 89, Jackson
(Berlin) to S.D., 22/11/1899.
7 *Holstein Papers*, 4, pp. 165-67.
8 Ibid.; BA, Bülow Papers, vol. 91, Holstein memo of 10/11/1899, and Holstein to
Bülow, 22/11/1899; G.P., 15, nos. 4396-97.

though at one point he was blankly told that Germany did not need England. No colonial favours were asked for, but both Balfour and Chamberlain were requested to use their influence to secure the recall of Saunders from Berlin. Bülow privately considered the *Times* correspondent and his foreign editor, Chirol, to be 'the most dangerous Englishmen for us', because they brought home to the British people the extent of the anglophobia in Germany and these revelations could alter London's attitude. Nevertheless, Bülow remained, as ever, confident for the future:

> I see the future taks of the German government as being, in possession of a strong fleet and under preservation of good relations with both Russia and England, to await calmly and collectedly the future development of elemental events.[9]

This calculation was naturally kept secret during the Windsor talks, and upon all sides there were expressions of friendliness and hopes of continual good relations between the two powers. Both Wilhelm and Bülow did their best to explain away the feelings of their countrymen, although the former could not resist pointing out that much of the anglophobia had been provoked by the Samoan affair:

> We Germans are full of sentiment for which the English make no allowance —a great deal of the intensity of feeling with regard to Samoa was sentiment—you did not care about the question and therefore couldn't understand our being keenly interested in it; for upwards of nine months we waited in vain for a settlement until the country became exasperated.[10]

Despite the references to old wounds and the worry about public opinion, however, the visit was adjudged to be a great success. The secretary for India, Hamilton, reported that the kaiser 'has gone away delighted both with his social and political reception', and Wilhelm himself told Metternich that 'The visit to England went off excellently in every respect.' Chamberlain was most impressed by his talks with Bülow and the kaiser, while Balfour and Brodrick also felt very satisfied at these events. Only Bertie, perhaps already suspicious of Germany because of his experience in the exchanges over China, the Portuguese colonies and the Atlantic cables, recognized that behind Bülow's bland and assuring countenance there lurked 'a great humbug'.[11]

9   Ibid., no. 4398.
10 Salisbury Papers, A85/89, Bigge memo of talk with Wilhelm, Secret, 20/11/1899.
11 Curzon Papers, vol. 144, Hamilton to Curzon, 1/12/1899; Addit.Mss.49691 (Balfour Papers), Balfour to Salisbury, 28/11/1899; F.O.800/170, Bertie to Bigge, 28/11/1899; A.A./*Afrika Gen.* 13 nr. 2, vol. 7, Wilhelm to Metternich, 2/12/1899; Grenville, *Salisbury and Foreign Policy*, pp. 277-81.

Temporarily, therefore, the kaiser's trip to England had pleased both governments. London especially could regard the journey in a warm light; with most of Europe bitterly critical of the Boer War and the air full of rumours of a continental coalition, the visit was gratefully received by the British press and politicians as an open declaration of German friendship. Upon the German side, Wilhelm had thoroughly enjoyed himself while Bülow was content to see his 'Free Hand' restored and to obtain further confirmation of the British desire to work with Germany. Clearly, little had changed for him and his priorities remained unaltered. Events were soon to show that, despite Chamberlain's deep hopes, German policy was far more concerned with the construction of a great navy and the placating of public opinion than with the establishment of closer relations with Britain.

The attitude of British statesmen and officials to the Samoan partition crisis was less united than on the German side, although all agreed at least that British policy towards Samoa was a negative one, dictated by consideration for Australasian opinion rather than by an intrinsic interest in the group itself. Even such an ardent imperialist as Sir John Anderson could minute:

> The internal politics of Samoa are no particular concern of this dept. The only thing we have always resisted in deference to Australia & New Zealand sentiment has been any suggestion to let Germany have the free control of the group.[12]

This consideration was repeatedly mentioned by the Colonial Office in early 1899, and Salisbury was made well aware of the importance of Australasian opinion. As a consequence, both he and Chamberlain stressed this during their many talks with the Germans and declined to accept any settlement which would not give Samoa—or at least the greater part of it—to Britain. In the spring crisis, one of the Colonial Office staff felt that 'The whole question of Samoa and of our future in the Pacific is at stake';[13] and later in the year Anderson reacted strongly to the partition talks with Berlin by emphasizing:

> Any partition of the Islands will be a grave mistake from the point of view of Imperial policy. The Australians & New Zealanders will never forgive us, if we take money for giving up claims on Upolu. If they would give us the northern Solomons we might think of it, but the position of

12   C.O.225/57, minute on paper 1480, F.O. to C.O., received 18/1/1899.
13   C.O.225/57, Cox minute on paper 6305, F.O. to C.O., received 14/3/1899.

Samoa as a station on the direct route followed by steamers between America & Australia gives it an importance far in excess of its value as a producer of markets.[14]

While it was at this stage that Chamberlain learnt of the German pressure upon Salisbury and found the Samoan question to be complicated by 'other Imperial considerations', it cannot be assumed that the permanent staff of the Colonial Office abandoned their previously-held concepts as quickly as their chief, merely for the sake of pleasing Germany. Not being active supporters of Chamberlain's alliance projects, they adhered firmly to the line of acting 'as trustees for the future of Australia'.[15] For the Colonial Office staff, therefore, the crucial factor was the information contained in the Admiralty memorandum of 7 October; thereafter, their objections to Berlin's acquisition of Samoa disappeared and they greeted with delight the bargain which Chamberlain was extracting. Naturally, they would have preferred to obtain that group as well but the significant fact now was, that possession of Upolu was no longer regarded as a virtual *conditio sine qua non*. Moreover, as a result of their belief that they were doing the right thing in securing Tonga to the empire, these officials became less fearful of an Australasian reaction to the withdrawal from Samoa: 'even in the Pacific, whatever Australia may say, we would have the best of the deal', Anderson wrote.[16] At the news of the Anglo-German arrangement, Herbert, who for fifteen or more years had opposed German aspirations in Samoa, minuted:

> I consider the Convention an extraordinarily advantageous one for the British Empire, & especially for Australia whose trustees we are in this matter. The Solomons Is. will make a splendid British possession, and I should say that we have got the German Solomons for nothing; as the Friendly Islands (Tonga), with the very fine harbour at Vavau, are alone worth more than the whole of Samoa.[17]

This opinion was echoed on the same minute-sheet by Anderson, Selborne and Chamberlain, the latter privately telling Devonshire also that

> The agreement is an excellent one for us & we are not likely to find the Germans in such an accommodating humour again. It appears that popular sentiment about Samoa—which I believe to be a worthless

---

14 C.O.225/58, minute on paper 24959 Confidential, F.O. to C.O., received 18/9/1899.

15 Chamberlain Papers, JC7/2/2A/32, Anderson note of 20/10/1899.

16 Ibid., JC7/2/2A/33, Anderson note of 20/10/1899.

17 C.O.225/58, minutes on paper 30930, F.O. to C.O., 8/11/1899. (Herbert had returned to head the office for a few months, following Wingfield's retirement).

possession—is so strong that Count Bülow is willing to pay anything for it.[18]

At the Admiralty, too, the officials were pleased with the arrangement, one of them minuting: 'It is well worth while to give up rights in Samoa to make certain of Tonga Is., which will be secured to England', and Samoa's strategic insignificance was also stressed by the government spokesman in the House of Lords.[19] Throughout the Samoan talks, the attitude of the senior members of the Cabinet had been rather more equivocal. Statesmen such as Devonshire, Balfour and Goschen realized the need to pay attention to Australasian feelings and made no effort to influence British policy in favour of Germany whilst the Foreign and Colonial Offices held firm. At the same time, they were aware of Britain's precarious world position and of the need to maintain good relations with Germany. Thus, when forwarding to Salisbury the Admiralty's information upon the relative importance of Tonga and Samoa, Goschen also wrote: 'I wish to goodness we could arrange something with that hot-headed German Emperor; for it is not pleasant to contemplate the trouble he might give us just now.'[20] After the outbreak of the Boer War, the Cabinet became increasingly worried about the flood of reports concerning a continental coalition against Britain. Possibly, too, the rumours of Salisbury's intransigence, which Hatzfeldt and Eckardstein were privately spreading, were having their effect. Most important of all was the fact that the Colonial Office now appeared to favour the deal. This news Balfour swiftly passed on to the Foreign Office in order to speed matters up and to avoid 'that most cumbrous of all processes'—interdepartmental correspondence.[21]

All the same, Hatzfeldt was clearly in error in reporting to Berlin that Salisbury was being put under tremendous pressure from the rest of the Cabinet. The letters of both Goschen and Balfour were as polite as usual and contained no veiled threats; while Devonshire's note to Salisbury on 1 November about the German anxiety at the supposed Franco-Russian intrigues was a model of deference.[22] If Chamberlain privately thought that the prime minister 'does not quite like Eckardstein's (and perhaps my) intrusion into

18 Devonshire Papers, Chatsworth, Chamberlain to Devonshire, 5/11/1899.
19 Adm.1/7412, minute on Z107, F.O. to Adm., 21/11/1899; *Hansard*, Fourth series, LXXVIII, pp. 11, 14.
20 Salisbury Papers, Class E, Goschen to Salisbury, 7/10/1899.
21 Addit.Mss. 49739 (Balfour Papers), Balfour to Sanderson, 27/10/1899.
22 Salisbury Papers, Class E, Devonshire to Salisbury, 1/11/1899.

Foreign Office business', he was quite content to leave the final stages of the Anglo-German arrangement to Salisbury and was scornful of the Baron's 'blood-curdling reports'.[23] In fact, the strongest suggestion of all was a mild hint from the queen, who 'thinks it would be such a good thing if we could settle this with Germany, as it would put them in a better humour'.[24]

It is still more difficult to discover where Salisbury and Chamberlain differed in this matter: in other words, to find the 'two-headed government'. The prime minister was in favour of the partition arrangement by 20 October, and probably a few days earlier than that. If the Cabinet of 1 November resolved to accept it 'after a good deal of discussion',[25] this obviously refers to a detailed consideration of the many points in question rather than to any disagreement; their decision was unanimous, Hatzfeldt learnt later. Moreover, when Brodrick wondered how the news of a British withdrawal from Samoa could best be presented to the public and how their policy was to be justified, the prime minister noted: 'The overwhelming case on our side is that Tonga has a good harbour: and the only thing that is of any value to us in those seas is a harbour.'[26] For Salisbury, as for the Colonial Office staff, the Admiralty's memorandum had provided the key and allowed a withdrawal from a group that was now regarded as worthless. A distaste for the methods of German diplomacy did not altogether blind him to the material advantages offered, nor to the necessity of making it appear to the outside world as if Berlin and London were old friends.

More important still, the many small modifications which Salisbury put forward in the last two weeks of the talks were nearly all based upon suggestions from the Colonial Office. It was due to Chamberlain's insistence that the Australasian colonies were consulted, and he also recognized the necessity of apprising Washington of the preliminary, Anglo-German settlement. The Colonial Office strongly opposed the complete recall of the respective consuls in Samoa and Tonga, since they wished British traders and British-protected labourers to have some form of representation in Apia. Finally, the repeated delays over the West African boundary settlement were solely due to the Colonial Office desire to draft the terms as exactly as possible so as to avoid the quarrels which had

23   Devonshire Papers, Chamberlain to Devonshire, 5/11/1899.
24   Salisbury Papers, Class F, Victoria to Salisbury, 30/10/1899; see also, A83/138, same to same, 8/11/1899.
25   Ibid., Class F, Salisbury to Victoria, 1/11/1899.
26   P.R.O.30/67/4, Brodick memo of 28/10/1899, with Salisbury minute.

followed from a rather similar delimitation in 1887-88.[27] Since it was left to Salisbury to clear up these points, however, he alone incurred the wrath of the *Wilhelmstrasse* and the vituperative outpourings of the kaiser.

Nevertheless, this does not fully explain the German belief that the British government was run by two masters. The key here is Chamberlain's own devious manner throughout the talks; it is his conduct, rather than Salisbury's, which requires explanation. During his discussions with Eckardstein, he had apparently spoken scornfully of the prime minister, referred to him as a *'quantité négligeable'*, and promised that he and his cabinet friends would be able to force through a Samoan agreement. He also warned, in contrast, that Salisbury might oppose and shipwreck the partition scheme unless they were careful. How much of this was true, it is hard to say; Hatzfeldt merely saw all these utterances as a confirmation of his belief in the basic antagonism between the two ministers, a belief he had already exaggerated in his reports to Berlin.[28] Moreover, Eckardstein, the sole witness to these remarks of Chamberlain, was often guilty himself of the grossest exaggeration and of reporting what he wished to believe. Yet enough remains to suggest that the colonial secretary had played up his points of difference with Salisbury, not merely to curb Berlin's demands by warning of the prime minister's opposition but also to create the impression that German aspirations were being favourably regarded by others in London. On either count, Chamberlain reckoned, he would obtain a fair Samoan settlement and German gratitude for the future; and these were worth a few falsehoods. Hence, for example, his feigned astonishment on 3 November at the news of Salisbury's various modifications to the German draft—modifications which, it might be noted, had originated in the Colonial Office on the previous day![29]

Yet if the two statesmen acted far more in harmony over Samoa than the Germans ever realized, their basic attitudes towards Germany were very wide apart. Salisbury's policy here remained completely negative: to be on friendly terms with Berlin without acknowledging any undue dependence upon her or indebtedness to her. It was, one could say, his fundamental policy towards any foreign state and Germany was no exception. For Chamberlain, though, the settlement

27 F.O.58/334, C.O. to F.O., Secret and Immediate, 2/11/1899; C.O.225/58, minutes and drafts on paper 30494.

28 A.A./*Südsee-Inseln* 5, vol. 4, Hatzfeldt to Holstein, 13/10/1899, and Hatzfeldt to Hohenlohe, no. 824 of 14/10/1899; ibid., vol. 5, same to same, no. 865 of 30/10/1899; ibid., vol. 6, Holstein to Hatzfeldt, 2/11/1899, and Hatzfeldt to Bülow, 2/11/1899.

29 Ibid., Hatzfeldt to A.A., tel. no. 371 of 3/11/1899.

of the Samoan question was but a means to an end: closer Anglo-German relations throughout the globe. In his talks with Eckardstein, he had stressed his wish 'to maintain the friendliest relations possible with Germany for the future' and also apparently touched upon the idea of an alliance. Furthermore, Chamberlain was prepared to come to an agreement with Berlin over Morocco, something Salisbury constantly refused to do throughout 1899; and only Bülow's eagerness to achieve an immediate Samoan settlement forced the postponement of these discussions. The colonial secretary's real aim in the Samoan talks was made abundantly clear when he continually breached the idea of an Anglo-German alliance during the kaiser's visit to England.[30] Here, indeed, he was poles apart from the prime minister.

Finally, it may be asked, why did the British really decide to withdraw from Samoa? 'Of course, without the Boers it would not have come off', wrote Holleben, and the majority of later accounts, basing themselves squarely upon the *Grosse Politik*, also reached the conclusion that only the outbreak of the Boer War and the threatening European situation forced Salisbury to give way.[31] Brodrick, anxious about possible Russian and French moves, felt the same way.

> This is reckoned a good 'deal', Tonga having so good a harbour—but the main point is it squares Germany—very necessary just now. The European position is very unsatisfactory—the Press universally unfriendly to us—France & Russia are undoubtedly looking out for an opportunity; the German people would join in—the Emperor & Govt. are our only standby . . . A broken reed, you will say—but useful for the nonce.[32]

This was, no doubt, an important consideration, although Brodrick was one of those who were obsessively worried at the prospect of a continental coalition and did not appreciate the obstacles to such a development. It is worth noting that during his Guildhall speech of 9 November, in which he scornfully dismissed that possibility, Salisbury was careful to stress the advantages for Britain as well as the benefit to Anglo-German relations of the treaty:[33] the South African connection was clearly only one side of the story. Furthermore, the subsequent care which he and Chamberlain took to ensure that they secured the Tongan harbours suggests that the primary motive for the British withdrawal from Samoa is

30 Ibid., vol. 5, Hatzfeldt to Hohenlohe, no. 865 of 30/10/1899; Eckardstein, *Lebenserinnerungen* 2, pp. 96-101; G.P., 16, no. 5153.

31 Eisendecker Papers, vol. 2, section 4, Holleben to Eisendecker, 11/11/1899; Langer, *Diplomacy of Imperialism*, p. 624; Rich, *Friedrich von Holstein*, 2, p. 597.

32 Curzon Papers, vol. 10a, Brodrick to Curzon, 3/11/1899.

33 Full text of the speech is in the *Standard*, 10/11/1899.

not to be seen in the South African situation per se but in the fact that they believed that they were getting an incredibly good bargain.

Until the Admiralty memorandum was received, the British were adamant that Tonga (even with the German Solomons) was no substitute for Samoa, and that they should maintain their claims to Upolu. Yet this stubbornness, which Chamberlain shared, would surely have led to a breakdown in the talks, and perhaps in their overall relations; for the Germans, unable to persuade the British to leave Upolu, would have followed Tirpitz's advice and demanded Zanzibar or Walfisch Bay as compensation for their withdrawal. And such extensive claims, particularly at the beginning of the war in South Africa, would have been indignantly rejected by London. If Chamberlain and Salisbury desired to remain upon good terms with Berlin, there is little indication that either of them wished to pay dearly for this. Fortunately for the negotiations, the information about Tonga, which reached the colonial secretary on the same day as the Boers despatched their ultimatum and has thus obscured the British motivation for their withdrawal, provided the key to the breaking of the deadlock.

Throughout the intensive Anglo-German negotiations, the United States had remained well in the background, for reasons which are not hard to discover. After the events of March and April, public excitement over Samoa died down and the administration, concerned with the forthcoming elections, was in no way eager to give undue prominence to the affair. America still regarded its obligations to the group as an 'entangling alliance', and Hay confided to McKinley that 'I think it will be an excellent thing if we can get out of Upolu on satisfactory terms. There will be nothing but trouble so long as the condominium lasts.'[34] Moreover, as the other two powers were apparently willing to recognize that Tutuila should fall to the United States in any partition treaty, it seemed reasonable to let London and Berlin arrange a settlement between themselves.

This policy of abstention from the diplomatic wranglings was also advisable in view of the navy's growing attachment to Pago-Pago. Throughout the summer, work had been quietly proceeding upon the construction of the coalsheds there and the Americans had been endeavouring to buy up as much of the waterfront as possible. In his final report to the State Department, Tripp had urged that the United

34   McKinley Papers, series 1, vol. 37, Hay to McKinley, 11/9/1899.

States should concentrate its entire efforts upon securing Tutuila and withdraw from the rest of the group.[35] This point was also stressed by Austin, the chief of the Bureau of Statistics, to McKinley's personal secretary, while the expansionist-minded Bradford assured his chief, Long, that Pago-Pago was 'one of the finest harbours in the world'.[36] Most important of all, the navy was aware that its right to Pago-Pago was not as absolute and inviolable as it would have the other powers believe. Hay's assistant secretary, Cridler, had earlier pointed out that the United States—Samoan treaty of 1878 could be terminated upon six months' notice by either party and that, although the native government would not think of doing such a thing, a German-controlled Samoan administration would be quick to take action in this direction. Raffel and Rose, he had felt, should be firmly opposed in their endeavours 'to incite strife and discord'. If Britain and America stood firm in defence of the Berlin Act, then Washington's treaty rights to Pago-Pago would remain undisturbed.[37] Clearly, the best policy in 1899 was to say little about a partition, apart from indicating that the United States would be satisfied to receive Tutuila as its share. When Bradford proposed that they should also ask for one of the Caroline Islands, therefore, the State Department ignored this idea; to enter into heated talks with the Germans was the last thing it wanted to do.[38]

In the damages question, too, Hay walked very warily. An open admission that Kautz's actions had been unjustified would not only alienate the navy but also infuriate Congress. When approached by the British and German governments in mid-September to adhere to their agreement of 23 August to refer to arbitration all claims arising from 'unjustifiable military action' by the naval forces, the American answer was at first non-committal. Privately, Hay was not opposed to the suggestion and thought that it would not involve more than $60,000.[39] On the other hand, he had a powerful fear of the Senate's zenophobic attitude towards foreign affairs, and loathed their irrational decisions over treaty matters. This had become something of an obsession with Hay by late 1899 and he therefore hoped to settle the damages question by an exchange of notes, for which only a simple majority

35 F.R.1899, pp. 648-63.

36 McKinley Papers, series 1, vol. 38, O. P. Austin to G. B. Cortelyou, 14/9/1899; N.A.R.G. 80, General Correspondence, 5257/21, Bradford to Long, 29/9/1899.

37 N.A.R.G.59, M-179, roll 1022, Navy Department to S.D., 30/12/1898, and Cridler memo of 18/1/1899.

38 Ibid., roll 1052, Navy Dept. to S.D., 24/10/1899; Braisted, *U.S. Navy*, p. 62.

39 Hay Papers, Box 23, Hay to Adee, 23/9/1899; F.R.1899, pp. 669-71.

in Senate would be necessary. He privately urged Senator Davis, the chairman of the Foreign Relations Committee, to accept this scheme, for in view of the importance of conciliating the German vote for the elections the administration did not wish to give the Germanophobe press and senators a chance to repeat their attacks upon Raffel and Rose, and to worsen relations with Berlin. Davis, however, declined the suggestion, pointing out that the Senate would be furious at any attempt to circumvent its powers.[40]

Hay was thus forced to tell the rather impatient Mumm that a formal treaty would have to be signed, and this he did not submit to the embassies until the end of October. Tactful insertions, such as the words 'if this be shown to have occurred' after the phrase about 'unwarranted military action', were made by Hay to appease the feelings of Senate. The proposed treaty, which allowed the consuls to collect the claims of their respective nationals for final arbitration by the king of Sweden and Norway, was eventually signed at Washington on 7 November. The news of the Anglo-German partition arrangement and the fact that America was to receive Tutuila tended to obscure this act, and the senatorial criticism Hay had feared did not occur. After receiving the approval of the Senate, it was ratified by McKinley on 5 March 1900, and the ratifications were exchanged two days later.[41]

Hay also adopted a very cautious and negative pose in the negotiations for the partition of the islands. Encouraged by the news that German-American relations were gradually improving, Bülow instructed Mumm to secure Washington's support for a settlement, 'which is so important from the point of view of our general policy and in which His Majesty is especially interested'.[42] But Berlin was soon warned that imperialistic feelings still held sway in the United States, and that matters must be handled carefully. Furthermore, Mumm pointed out, Hay would not do anything 'at England's cost'. Attempts to work up American opinion for a Samoan settlement favourable to Germany would be 'pointless'.[43] The emissary's news that there was a widespread discontent in American commercial circles against the German ban upon

40 Hay Papers (Brown University Library), Hay to C. K. Davies, 23/10/1899, and reply of 25/10/1899; W. S. Holt, *Treaties defeated by the Senate* (Baltimore, 1933), pp. 191-92, for Hay's fears of the Senate.

41 Hay Papers, Box 26, Letterbook 1, Hay to Mumm, 27/10/1899; N.A.R.G.59, M-30, roll 53, S.D. to Tower, 31/10/1899; F.O.58/334, Tower to Salisbury, tel. of 7/11/1899; F.R.1899, pp. 671-73.

42 A.A./U.S.A. 16, vol. 7, Bülow to Mumm, 2/9/1899.

43 Holstein Papers, vol. 12, Mumm to Holstein, 6/8/1899, 22/8/1899 and 5/9/1899; Hatzfeldt Papers, Holstein to Hatzfeldt, 4/9/1899; R.Kol.A.3055, Mumm to A.A., tels. 181 and 184 of 31/8/1899 and 2/9/1899.

swine imports caused the *Auswärtiges Amt* to instruct Mumm to withhold Berlin's reply on this question lest it prejudice the Samoan partition scheme.

> The great weight of the material interests involved for us in this commercial matter ought not to let escape the special importance which the Samoan question has attained for German national feelings. I beg you, during the commercial negotiations, to keep in mind continually this viewpoint, which makes the coming about of the quickest and least unpleasant settlement of the Samoan matter an absolute duty for the Imperial government.[44]

In fact, Mumm was to wait another month before he thought it wise to hand over the German note upon commercial relations, and he was immensely relieved to find that it did not seem to have affected the State Department's outlook towards the Samoan question after all. Hay, he reported, still was eager to maintain good relations with Germany.[45]

Hay's pleasantness was only skin deep, however, and he privately confessed to Henry White that the Germans 'are acting badly about our meats, and cannot help bullying and swaggering. It is their nature.'[46] Moreover, while he asked Choate to find out Salisbury's attitude to the idea of partition, he was cold to the view that London should be pressed into any arrangement. On 20 September, he had received a communication from the German Embassy, which pointed out that America should receive Tutuila while

> according to the interests of Germany and England now prevailing in Samoa, Upolu would justly fall to the lot of Germany and Savai'i to England. America would act in her own interests and would render Germany a real service if America would prevail with its whole powerful influence on England for the realisation of such a just partition of the Samoan Islands.[47]

Hay's attitude here can be gleaned from another long letter to Henry White, in which he pointed out that the Sternburg-Tripp liaison

> had nothing to do with our views of partition. I came to the conclusion a good while ago that the Berlin Treaty could not permanently endure. The Tripartite business has given nothing but trouble and annoyance to us and England from the beginning. Cleveland, as you know, was most anxious to get out of Samoa altogether. I think *that* was a great mistake—

44 BA, Reichsschatzamt II R2/1618, vol. 2, Mumm to A.A., 23/9/1899; A.A./*Südsee-Inseln* 5, vol. 4, A.A. to Mumm, no. A82, Secret, 20/9/1899.

45 Ibid., Mumm to Hohenlohe, no. 267 of 6/10/1899; ibid., vol. 5, Mumm to A.A., tel. no. 231 of 23/10/1899, and A.A. reply, tel. no. 155 of 24/10/1899.

46 Hay Papers, Box 26, Letterbook 1, Hay to Henry White, 9/9/1899.

47 N.A.R.G.59, M-58, roll T-28, German Embassy to S.D., 20/9/1899.

we must keep our foothold there in the interest of our Pacific work. But if we could get out of the Tripartite business and keep Tutuila, I should be very glad. Germany, of course, wants us to do it in the manner most offensive to England. This we have declined to do, and for this reason I wanted Choate to sound Lord Salisbury discreetly as the way England would regard the proposition before it is actually made . . . But of course if England refuses, that ends the matter. There can be no compulsion.[48]

Throughout October and early November, Hay was kept in touch with the developments in London and Berlin, despite some later grumbles as to the lack of details. Believing a settlement to be in sight, he cabled Choate to let Salisbury know officially that America would be content with the part of the group east of 171°W meridian. He also responded quickly when he learnt on 4 November from Mumm that Coate had cast doubt upon America's willingness to allow the other two to arrange a preliminary agreement.[49] The immense relief which Hay's agreement to this scheme gave to Berlin has been described above, but the secretary of state was possibly even more overjoyed. Much under the influence of Tripp's recommendations, he was delighted to secure for the U.S. navy 'the Gibraltar of the South Pacific', as he called Pago-Pago, and to escape from the Samoan entanglement. He informed Choate that

> our interests in the Archipelago were very meagre, always excepting our interest in Pago-Pago, which was of the most importance. It is the finest harbour in the Pacific and absolutely indispensable to us. The general impression in the country was that we already owned the harbour, but this, as you know, was not true. We had a lease terminable at the pleasure of the Samoan Government, however that might be defined. I had always looked forward to the possibility of a partition, and when the chance came I was more than ready to embrace it . . . Our Navy Dept. has for a long time been anxious for this consummation and, of course, they are delighted with it. I myself have no doubt whatever that we are the party which has derived most advantage from the arrangement . . . My own opinion is that Germany has the least valuable bargain of the 3, and that she was led by her sentimental eagerness into a bad trade.[50]

When Hay formally received the text of the Anglo-German agreement on 27 November, therefore, he had little comment to make upon it. The only difficulty occurred with the request for a formal American renunciation of their rights in Tonga

48 Hay Papers, Box 26, Letterbook 1, Hay to Henry White, 24/9/1899.

49 Ibid., Box 19, Choate to Hay, 1/11/1899; ibid., Box 4, Mumm to Hay, n.d. (4/11/1899?); N.A.R.G. 59, M-44, roll 89, A. D. White to Hay, 24/10/1899; ibid., M-30, roll 186, Choate to Hay, 25/10/1899; A.A./*Südsee-Inseln* 5, vol. 6, A.A. to Mumm, tel. no. 165, Urgent, 3/11/1899; W. R. Thayer, *The Life and Letters of John Hay*, 2 vols. (Boston/New York, 1915), 1, pp. 281-83; F. R. 1899, pp. 663-65.

50 Hay Papers, Box 26, Letterbook 1, Hay to Choate, 13/11/1899; ibid., Box 4, Tripp to Hay, 13/11/1899; N.A.R.G.59, M-77, roll 155, Hay to Tripp, 24/11/1899.

but this, which is dealt with more fully in a later section, was soon settled. On 2 December, Hay, Pauncefote and Holleben signed a tripartite treaty on behalf of their respective governments. Much simpler in form than the Anglo-German arrangement, it cancelled British and German rights in Tutuila, and American rights in Upolu and Savai'i. While freedom of trade for all nations was maintained, all other treaties and conventions concerning Samoa, including the Berlin Act itself, were annulled. After the Senate had advised its ratification on 16 January 1900, the ratifications were exchanged and proclaimed on 16 February.[51] Hay had achieved all that he had wished.

ii   *The Samoan Crisis and Public Opinion*

Chronicling the developments and bases of foreign policy is perhaps not so difficult a task, given the historian's ability to obtain access to the official documents and private letters of the past. Analysing and charting public opinion of an earlier age is far more difficult, particularly when no opinion polls existed. Nevertheless, an attempt has to be made, for the growth of widespread literacy and of 'popular' journalism at the close of the nineteenth century appeared to make public opinion more measurable and undoubtedly had an effect upon government policy, vague and varied though this often was. One can only concur with the view of a past master in this field.

> Rarely is it possible to say of a statesman or a diplomat that a given cause determined his decisions; the situation is invariably far less simple than that. In the usual complex of causes, public opinion is one of those intangibles whose influence may be important even if it cannot be proved by documentary evidence . . . for it is impossible to escape the conclusion that the men who guided . . . destinies, although they often spoke of the press and public opinion with contempt, were affected by the broad currents of popular opinion and emotion.[52]

Even on the American side, little exists of the feelings of the 'common man' over the Samoan issue, no doubt because foreign affairs are usually the concern of a small minority. The only illumination emerges from some letters in the papers of the navy secretary, Long, which were written a few days after the news of the shellings of early April 1899. However, two of these are for the American gunboat action and two

51 F.R.1899, pp. 665-69.
52 E. M. Carroll, *Germany and the Great Powers* 1866-1914: *A Study in Public Opinion and Foreign Policy* (New York, 1938), p. 8.

against; and such a method of analysis is quite artificial since
it may well be wondered how far such isolated comments
reflected opinion as a whole. The views of eccentrics or
extroverts serve only to confuse the issue, and they possibly
all had personal motives for their attitudes; one of the critics,
for example, was a friend of Rose's wife.[53] It is far safer,
therefore, to fall back upon an analysis of the newspaper
comments upon the Samoan affair. Not only do they positively
record their own influential opinions, but they may also be
said to reflect the general views of the readers or to form
readers' views, it being assumed that Democrats normally
read a Democratic paper, etc.

Yet however concrete such a format for the analysis of
public opinion appears in theory, it quickly breaks down
when applying it in practice to the American newspapers'
attitude to the Samoan question. This was partly due to the
diversity of the regions and interests which the various
journals represented, but was caused primarily by an ignorance
of the topic. Certainly, Samoa never received the coverage in
the press which such places as Cuba, China or the Philippines
secured—which is hardly surprising, in view of what was
involved in each case. As the *New York Post* put it, 'Frank and
blank ignorance about the Samoan Islands and their government was the confessed state of mind of Americans when the
news came that sailors and marines of ours had been killed
near Apia.'[54]

Generally speaking, the American press tended to regard
the first news of the ambush and the fact that a German had
been arrested on suspicion of assisting the Mata'afans in this
action as a further confirmation of the events of Manila Bay.
Many papers pointed to and welcomed this further example of
Britons and Americans standing together against the Teuton,
and were quite bitter in their condemnation of the German
intrigue. The *New York Daily Tribune* (13 April 1899) rather
dramatically declared that 'Since the destruction of the
Maine no greater calamity has come to the navy than the
savage butchery of two popular officers and two enlisted men
on April 1, near Apia', and reported that Senator Stewart
had warned: 'Does Germany want to fight? If so, she may
be accommodated.' Representative Hull, the chairman of the
House Committee on Military Affairs, gave a somewhat

53 John D. Long Papers, Box 47, letters from Dobler, Blossom, Conway and Gaffey in
April 1899.
54 *New York Post*, 16/5/1899. The quotations used in this section are taken from the
large collection of clippings upon Samoa contained in Box 241 of the J. B. Moore Papers;
and in N.A.R.G.43, Entry no. 303, Newspaper clippings and photographs relating to
Samoa and the Commission 1898-99, 2 Boxes.

similar warning, although other members of Congress were more reserved. The anti-imperialist press denounced the shellings as inhuman and contrary to the country's traditional policy.[55] Many papers recorded the facts but offered little comment upon them, which is perhaps a further proof of their uncertainty upon the issues involved.

By the middle of 1899, however, the anti-German trend in the newspapers had become less distinct. This was partly due to a general improvement in German-American press relations, signalized by the swift newspaper denunciations of both Dewey's declaration that the next war would be with Germany and of Captain Coghlan's speech against Wilhelm. Moreover, the navy received further criticism when a letter from Kautz to a relation, in which he called himself the 'Boss of the Ranch' in Samoa, was published. More important still were the opinions of so-called Samoa experts, which every newspaper eagerly sought to obtain. This itself was an indication of the lack of knowledge about the group; anyone who received a letter from the islands could be guaranteed instant publication by editors eager for information. H. J. Moors, the biggest American businessman in Apia and an enthusiastic supporter of Mata'afa, gained a great deal of attention through his many interviews and letters, all of which were very critical of Kautz and the British. Stevenson's widow spoke out against the shelling, which had damaged the author's former residence at Vailima; and his stepson, Lloyd Osborne, provoked much comment in the American and German press by his article in the London *Truth* magazine, which alleged that Chambers was under the influence of the L.M.S. and had therefore opposed the candidacy of the Catholic Mata'afa. Former U.S. consul Mulligan also criticized the Anglo-American actions, while former chief justice Ide attacked Chambers' decision in an article in the *North American Review*.[56] Only Sewall was found to condemn the German position fully.

In view of these opinions, and of further reports from the group, certain papers such as the *Chicago Chronicle* (22 April 1899) took up party lines and felt that 'We are beginning to hear things in regard to this wretched Samoan business which are far from creditable to the Washington administration.' The special correspondent of the *San Francisco Call*, W.E. Williams, sent back many critical accounts of the joint naval actions and this German-influenced paper later published a

55 J. W. Ellison, 'The Partition of Samoa: A Study in Imperialism and Diplomacy', in *Pacific Historical Review*, 8 (1938), pp. 267-68.

56 Henry C. Ide, 'The Imbroglio in Samoa', in *North American Review* (June, 1899).

lengthy article under the broad headlines: 'American and German commissioners to Samoa act in Harmony.'[57] It was taken up with loud cry by the German-American press and whatever papers the German embassy in Washington could influence. Secretly-subsidized magazines, such as the *German-American Review*, decried the fuss over Samoa and felt that 'the game is not worth a candle to either nation'. All this coincided with the growth of the agitation by the Irish-American groups against any alliance with Britain, a cry taken up by the Democrats to embarrass McKinley's party and to attract the German vote in the impending elections. By September, it had grown so great that Hay wrote an open letter to the Ohio Republicans, denying the existence of any secret arrangement. That this was purely an electoral gesture rather than any change of heart upon his part can be seen in his firm assurances to the British that the dementi meant nothing, in his continuous support of London's position during the Boer War, and especially in his private letter to Henry White:

> I simply refute the Democratic platform's charge that we have made 'a secret alliance with England'. This charge was having a serious effect on the Germans and it had to be denied. The fact is a treaty of alliance is impossible. It would never get through the Senate. As long as I stay here no action shall be taken contrary to my conviction that the one indispensable feature of our foreign policy should be a friendly understanding with England. But an alliance must remain in the present state of things an unobtainable dream.[58]

Most of the expansionist, Republican and east coast newspapers maintained a friendly tone towards Britain also, comparing the Boer War to their own efforts in the Philippines.

Nevertheless, the general wish of the American press was to see an end to the tripartite control and a retraction of Washington's commitments to Samoa—always provided it received Tutuila. Isolationism was still the dominant trend, and the news of the Anglo-German partition arrangement was therefore received with general approbation. A great deal was made of the strategic importance of Samoa and the splendid qualities of Tutuila. Chambers was reported by many journals to be delighted with the settlement. The *Mail and Express* would have preferred to have Britain as the neighbouring power in the islands, since Germany had behaved so badly over the tridominium, and the *Washington Post* also welcomed

57 On the German influence behind the *Call*, see Witte, *Revelations*, pp. 56-57.

58 Hay Papers, Box 26, Letterbook 1, Hay to Henry White, 24/9/1899; F.O.5/2392, Tower to Salisbury, no. 292 Confidential of 18/10/1899; H. C. Allen, *Great Britain and the United States*, pp. 586-96.

the chance to create 'relations of the strictest formality with the German Government'. Some, such as the *New York Sun*, declared that America should receive more since she already virtually possessed Tutuila—an argument Hay strongly disapproved of, tartly remarking that 'an acre of land at the corner of Broad and Wall Streets is worth something like a million acres in Nevada.'[59] Only a few Democratic papers protested against the annexation and entered a plea for the native Samoans, reminding readers of America's original principles. These, however, were drowned in the murmurs of approval, for the American press too had lost its previous objections to empire. In its way, the Samoan question had provided a perfect example of this change of heart towards colonization.

No such qualms about abandoning older principles was to be found on the British side, of course; but the Colonial Office was aware that their own very good reasons for abandoning Samoa might be obscured by sentiment, which played a large part in the Australasian attitude towards that group. As Herbert put it, the colonies were 'sadly ignorant and liable not to see straight'. Selborne, too, felt a little uneasy: 'It is a very satisfactory arrangement. If New Zealand or an Australian colony do not like it, it can only be by misapprehension and we should spare no money in telegraphing to them the fullest explanations.'[60] In fact, a lengthy telegram had been drafted by Anderson as early as 26 October. In it he stressed the importance of Tonga, 'which the Admiralty considers as greatly preferable for strategic purposes to Samoa', the fact that the Germans would not withdraw from the latter group at any price, and the 'great riches' of the German Solomons. Australia, when federated, was promised control of the Solomons while New Zealand was told that she could administer the Tongan group provided that the Royal Navy obtained whatever ground for coaling stations it required there.[61]

This message was sent on 2 November but did not elicit the immediate response which the Colonial Office asked for. Seddon, the energetic prime minister of New Zealand, was on holiday and without his leadership the Australian states were rather uncertain as to how they should react. After waiting for a few days, therefore, Chamberlain noted: 'I am sorry not to have Australian reply but we gave them the

---

59 Hay Papers, Box 26, Letterbook 1, Hay to Choate, 13/11/1899; A.A./*Südsee-Inseln* 5, vol. 8, Holleben to Hohenlohe, no. 314 of 18/11/1899.

60 C.O.225/58, minutes on paper 30930, F.O. to C.O., 8/11/1899.

61 Ibid., C.O. to Australasian governments, 1/11/1899, following paper 30494.

chance & must tell them that we were compelled to decide to save the agreement.' On 8 November the colonies were told that 'for important reasons of policy it was decided to conclude the agreement at once. I am glad to announce so satisfactory a result.'[62]

This eventual disregard can only be explained by Chamberlain's appreciation that the treaty had to be initialled before the Czar's visit to Potsdam, and still more by the Colonial Office belief that the satisfactory nature of the agreement would be self-evident to most people in the antipodes; for the colonies, especially New Zealand, had left London in no doubt as to their concern in this matter. Many appeals for the 'conservation of British interests in Samoa' reached the Colonial Office in the spring; the colonial press strongly attacked the German actions in the islands; and New Zealand offered troops to assist in the fighting as well as a government steamer to carry messages. Nevertheless, one wonders how great this agitation would have been without Auckland's particular commercial interest in the Pacific islands and without the fiery zeal of Seddon. When South Australia joined in the appeals in April, for example, the governor pointed out that their action was the result of a request from New Zealand, 'which is more particularly interested and has therefore generally taken the initiative in Samoan matters'. Nor did the Australian governments greatly object to the final partition settlement. Victoria offered no criticism at all, and Queensland had only delayed its reply because it had attempted to learn the opinion of the other states—a fair indication of the lack of real interest in Samoa, which was too far away to bother them very much.[63]

Only the New Zealand government, therefore, was strongly critical of the settlement. When Seddon returned, he emphasized that 'Samoa is New Zealand's Alsace', and pointed out that the islanders had been sacrificed to political exigencies. This elicited a further lengthy explanation from the Colonial Office, which Herbert thought to be 'unusually apologetic' but which Chamberlain accepted, since 'It is desirous to keep them in good temper.' However, this failed to appease the deputy governor, Stout, who bluntly cabled: 'The Solomon Islands are of no interest to New Zealanders and though the Tongan Group may be of more value, for some reason or other greater interest has always centred in Samoa in New

---

62   Ibid., and also the drafts and minutes on paper 30930.

63   F.O.58/328, C.O. to F.O., 11/3/1899; F.O.58/330, C.O. to F.O., 28/4/1899; F.O.58/334, C.O. to F.O., Secret and Confidential, 11/11/1899; C.O. 209/259, papers 8146, 12605 and 11132; C.O.13/153, papers 10397 and 13571; Ross, *Aspirations*, pp. 249-50.

Zealand.' Nevertheless, even the New Zealand criticism was muted and kept from the public, since Seddon assumed that the Boer War alone had been the reason for the British withdrawal and was reluctant to embarrasss the imperial government. It is also interesting to note that the correspondence from the Australasian colonies at this time was full of details concerning colonial contingents for the war; in comparison to the events in South Africa, the Samoan question was of little significance, particularly in Australia. Moreover, since he could no longer affect the Samoan treaty, Seddon partly restrained his anger and concentrated upon using this British retreat to press for New Zealand control of Tonga and the Cooks as compensation.[64]

A similar pattern could be found in the colonial press also. Throughout the fighting, these newspapers had been generally very critical of the German proceedings, although several organs doubted the wisdom of supporting the young Tanu. When the settlement was made known, however, this unanimity no longer existed. The *Sydney Daily Telegraph* (10 November 1899) thought the treaty 'a wise and profitable one', while the *Sydney Evening News* was non-commital. Many newspapers commented favourably upon the clause allowing freedom of trade in the territories concerned, and were mollified by the approving reaction of such firms as Lever Bros. and Burns, Philp & Co. On the other hand, the *British Australian* (16 November 1899) was disturbed by the existence of a potential German threat to the proposed Pacific cable, and the *Melbourne Argus* (11 November 1899) criticized the 'slipshod statesmanship' of the British government and its disregard for colonial interests.

In New Zealand, the comment was more abrasive. The *New Zealand Times* and the *Auckland Herald* disapproved of the settlement, as did the *Otago Daily Times*. The *Auckland Evening Star* (22 November 1899) declared that 'The agreement was entirely a triumph for German diplomacy, and England appears to have received very little compensating advantage.' New Zealand opinion did not consider the acquisition of the Solomons as a great gain, and had tended to regard Tonga as already being in British hands. But here, too, the criticism was weaker because of the Boer War, and many organs agreed with the *Sydney Morning Herald's* view that, although the deal was disappointing, 'In a time like the present we must not embarrass the British government in preserving its foreign relations'. A meeting convened on 13 November by the

64 Ibid., pp. 251-52; C.O.209/259, paper 31513, Stout to C.O., 12/11/1899; C.O.225/58, papers 32244 and 36279, C.O. to Governors and Stout to C.O., 25/11/1899.

chairman of the Auckland Harbour Board also decided that it would be impolitic to discuss the treaty just then.

The attitude of the British press to the Samoan problem was even more complex. Generally speaking, they admitted that their sole interest in the group was to represent Australasia and that the affair was more of a nuisance than a serious matter. During the spring crisis, the *Times*, *Scotsman*, *Morning Post* and virtually every other paper except the *Daily News* made much of the solidarity of the Anglo-American naval forces and criticized the actions of the German officials, although the *Daily Mail* (13 April 1899) distinguished itself by declaring that 'as the friendship of Germany is the pivot of our foreign policy, her wishes should be respected in the final settlement.' Many organs, especially the *Daily Chronicle*, supported Salisbury in his struggle to obtain a commission which would decide by majority vote. After this, however, their interest swiftly turned to other, more important events, such as the impending conflict in South Africa. Both the German and British governments recognized that Samoa was not a burning issue for the British newspapers or public. The few parliamentary questions on it came from Irish Nationalist M.P.s, such as Hogan and Davitt, who seized upon the publicized connections between Chambers, Tanu and the London Missionary Society. Only these missionaries (fearing religious discrimination) and the British Empire League (fearing commercial discrimination) protested to the Foreign Office about the deal, and in both cases their fears were unjustified and quickly calmed.

Nevertheless, Salisbury was probably quite correct in warning Hatzfeldt that

> I could not give up our rights at Samoa without raising the angriest feeling, both here and in Australia. They care little enough about Samoa now; but the antagonism between German and Englishmen is in these countries intensely keen; and if either party thought that Samoa had been the cause of a humiliating bargain the most passionate interest in the islands would in either country take the place of their present indifference.[65]

Brodrick, too, was worried about this and urged Salisbury to 'lead public opinion' by a favourable Guildhall announcement of the treaty to avoid press criticism and the feeling abroad that it was 'a "climb-down" to square Germany for the moment'.[66]

In the event, the Foreign Office need not have worried, for the treaty was at first regarded sympathetically by the British

65 Salisbury Papers, A122/71, Salisbury to Hatzfeldt, 15/9/1899.
66 P.R.O. 30/67/4, Brodrick memo of 28/10/1899.

press on the whole. The *Standard* (9 November 1899) rather
naturally praised Salisbury for disposing 'of a number of
vexatious questions without any appreciable sacrifice of
British interests', while the *Times, Morning Post, Daily
Telegraph* and the *Globe* all thought that it was 'a fair bargain'
or 'a fair give and take arrangement.' However, the *British
Empire Review* was critical, the *Daily News* thought that the
prime minister 'has let himself be squeezed out of Samoa',
and the *Daily Chronicle* gloomily predicted further concessions
to other powers as a result of Britain's entanglement in
South Africa. Most organs expressed a wish to be on good
terms with Germany but without any firm alliance to that
country; Salisbury would appear to have read the British
mood in this matter more correctly than Chamberlain.

After Bülow's Reichstag speech of 2 February 1900, in
which he derided the concessions to Britain in the Pacific,
declared that Germany had the best of the bargain in the
Neutral Zone and pointed out that she would not give up
her rights in Zanzibar until the other powers did, the British
newspapers' mood changed somewhat—although this might
also have been due to the greater awareness of the anglophobia
in Germany. The *Daily News* (13 February 1900) repeated
its conviction that 'Germany has got the lion's share of the
bargain', and the *St. James' Gazette* was disappointed at the
news about Zanzibar. Even the *Standard* was uneasy at the
maritime importance Samoa would acquire when the Central
American canal was cut, and it felt disappointed that Bülow
had no friendly words for Britain in his speech. A growing
number of papers referred to the Germans as 'the professional
blackmailers' and as having made the British government
'stand and deliver'.[67] There was little criticism of Salisbury
by then, however, and the difficulties of his position were
realized. Finally, it might be noted that Opposition spokesmen
on foreign affairs, such as Kimberley, Ripon and Buxton,
readily agreed that the settlement was 'fairly satisfactory' and
rejoiced to be free of the 'ridiculous' tripartite system.[68]

Official criticism, therefore, was restricted to the New
Zealand government whilst the press reaction was mixed and
often not unfavourable to the British leaders. Even so, many
comments were resented by the Colonial Office. Anderson
wrote a searing, five-page refutation of the Australasian

67 For these various Australasian and British press comments, see the two collections
referred to in footnote 54, above; Ellison, *The Partition of Samoa*, pp. 267-87; Ross,
Aspirations, pp. 249-51; A.A./*Südsee-Inseln* 5 *nr*. 1, vol. 1; W. Bauermann, 'Die Times
und die Abwendung Englands von Deutschland um 1900' (Phil.diss., Köln, 1939), pp. 11-25.
68 Addit.Mss.43555 (Ripon Papers), Buxton to Ripon, 10/11/1899, and reply of
12/11/1899.

newspaper criticisms, concluding 'We have made a good bargain and those who criticise it unfortunately for themselves found all their objections on points which only show that they are ignorant of the actual facts in regard to the Islands.'[69] As Chamberlain's closest assistant during the negotiations and the most fervent convert to the settlement after he learnt of the Admiralty memorandum, Anderson simply could not understand how the terms of the treaty could be attacked. Years later, when the international situation at the beginning of the Boer War had been somewhat forgotten about and many Australasians pointed retrospectively to the 'surrender' of Samoa, Anderson returned to the defence of the British policy with a minute which summarizes the Colonial Office attitude to the entire matter and clearly reveals the chief motive for the withdrawal:

> Samoa had a high sentimental value for Germany & we made them pay accordingly, & got much the best of the deal, though Mr. Seddon & the Australians who know absolutely nothing as to the relative value of the concessions made by us & Germany at the time, profess to think otherwise.[70]

Even a brief examination of the Samoan crisis of 1898-99 could not escape the conclusion that it had provoked far more serious concern in Germany than in any of the other interested nations, and that it had worried the government in Berlin far more than those in London, Washington or even Wellington. Naturally, much of the German indignation came from the fact that the property and interests of fellow nationals had been damaged, and their rights ignored, during the Anglo-American naval actions. Secondly, there was the past German involvement in Samoa; as the pan-German deputy, Dr Hasse, put it, they had to have those islands 'where for many decades great German activity has been carried out, where German blood has been shed, where we have suffered deep humiliations . . .'[71] Nevertheless, there were more powerful reasons which went beyond this concrete historical link with Samoa. By the late 1890s, there existed a widespread feeling in Germany that their booming country simply had to expand, was no longer 'saturated', and was entitled and compelled to tread the world stage with Britain, America and Russia. Such feelings were common to other countries but they seem to have been more intense in Germany, perhaps because national self-consciousness was greater there,

---

69 C.O.209/259, memo of 18/11/1899, following paper 31513. Chamberlain wrote on this: 'I entirely agree'.

70 C.O.225/66, minute on paper 3625.

71 *Reichstag*, X Legislaturperiode, I Session 1898/1900, vol. 5, Sitzung 146 of 12/2/1900.

because it reckoned itself to be a 'have-not' country, because of the delicate internal situation, and because of the staggering increases in German population, trade and industrial strength. Colonial expansion, it was repeatedly stressed, was a necessity for Germany.[72]

Obviously, not all Germans felt this way and the working classes were largely indifferent to these affairs, but informed opinion (publicists, landowners, industrialists, academics, Reichstag deputies) in these years was remarkably unified in its general support of German expansion. Most important of all, this agitation was much more organized and developed in Germany than in any other country, and powerful pressure groups existed to represent the expansionist viewpoint; naturally, the demands of such bodies as the Colonial Society, the Navy League or the Pan-German League were quite enormous. Moreover, their campaigns well suited the entourage of the 'persönliches Regiment' in the policy of bolstering up the prestige and position of the monarchy and the establishment by obtaining glorious successes abroad, unifying the nation and diverting the attention of the electorate from internal political questions. For it is worth noting here that it was precisely those parties which favoured expansion which the government sought to enlist in the *Sammlungspolitik* at home. Finally, an aggressive colonial policy, while having aims in its own right, was also useful in the appeal for a larger navy with which to defend the new overseas possessions.

It is not surprising, therefore, to find Bülow writing at the end of March 1899, that 'The Samoan question stands now as before in the forefront of my interest.'[73] Within a few days, the government was under strong attack from the agrarian, colonial and Bismarckian press for its weakness in the face of the Anglo-American naval actions around Apia. The searing reproofs of the *Deutsche Zeitung* and the *Deutsche Tageszeitung*, which were virtually demanding a state of war with Britain and America as well as criticizing their own government, were quite extreme and many papers were content to rail against the Anglo-Saxon powers rather than Bülow. The *Berliner Neueste Nachrichten* warned the British that their 'suit for Germany's friendship' would be marred, while the *Börsen-Courier* thought that 'the leading circles in the United States are not wholly removed from the semi-savage standpoint.' Every organ commented angrily upon the supposed

72 Langer, *Diplomacy of Imperialism*, pp. 415-42; Steinberg, *Yesterday's Deterrent*, pp. 31-60; G. Mann, *The History of Germany Since* 1789 (London, 1968), pp. 257-70; F. Fischer, *Germany's Aims in the First World War* (London, 1967), pp. 3-24.
73 A.A./*Südsee-Inseln* 5, vol. 2, Bülow to A.A., tel. no. 1 of 29/3/1899.

insult to the *Falke* and the damage to German property, although after Bülow's hint of 3 April most of the attacks fell upon London rather than Washington. *Vorwärts* and a few other left-wing papers were isolated in their view that German colonial policy itself was to blame. Many journals, in criticizing the British officials in Samoa and the unfriendly attitude of 'perfidious Albion', called for closer links with Russia as a means of putting pressure upon Britain. Angry individuals wrote letters to Bülow, branches of the Pan-German League protested to the chancellor at the 'trampling under' of German rights by the Anglo-Saxon powers, and the expression *'die Schmach von Samoa'* was widely used.[74]

The *Wilhelmstrasse* naturally took the appropriate measures to control this outburst; Hamman's efforts to divert attention to the China expedition and to persuade the press to regard the Samoan affair a little more coolly have been noted in a previous section. At the same time, the editor of the *Hamburgische Zeitung* was sharply reproved for his 'tactless' article upon the lack of success of the German embassy in London. To counter the biased reports of Reuter and Associated Press, the semi-official *Kölnische Zeitung* sent its own correspondent to Samoa. However, the greatest help to Bülow was Dr Lehr's fiery interpellation against Britain and America in the Reichstag on 14 April, during which he called for a trade war against those countries, particularly the latter. This clear demonstration that the agrarian interests were merely using the Samoan affair to counter the United States commercial challenge and the vitriolic nature of Lehr's speech propelled the parties and most newspapers to criticize his standpoint and to praise the calm speech of Bülow, who declared that Germany would maintain all her rights without prejudicing her foreign relations.[75]

Nevertheless, the interpellation had given the Samoan episode a greater prominence than ever, and throughout the following months the colonial pressure groups were not backward in reminding Bülow of the government's pledges. In April the Pan-German League praised his firm Reichstag promises, and in June the Colonial Society reminded him that Samoa was 'a question of national honour'. On 19 June, when outlining the work of the commission thus far, Bülow therefore repeated his statement that Germany would

---

74 R.Kol.A.3048 contains many of these appeals and letters. See also, A.A./*Südsee-Inseln* 5, vol. 2, Monts to Hohenlohe, no. 41 of 13/4/1899.

75 A.A./*Deutschland* 135 *nr.* 2, vol. 1, Hammann report of 27/4/1899; *Reichstag*, X Legislaturperiode, I Session 1898/1900, vol. 2, Sitzung 65 of 14/4/1899; J. Lehmann, *Die Aussenpolitik und die Kölnische Zeitung während der Bülowzeit* 1898-1909 (Leipzig, 1937).

not retreat a hair's breadth from her rights. Government-influenced papers were asked to praise the expected damages agreement as 'a diplomatic victory' and when the *Kölnische Zeitung* appeared at one stage to be falling out of line, it was quickly warned by Bülow. Another editor was instructed to treat Samoa 'in a way which eases us in the diplomatic handling of the question abroad and at the same time strengthens the trust in our foreign policy internally'; but this did not reduce the pressure since many circles were clearly alarmed by the false rumours in October that the government was contemplating a withdrawal from the group. The Colonial Society, which gave 2,000 marks annually to the German school in Samoa to help counter English influence, petitioned Bülow not to give way, as did various branches of the *Bund der Landwirte*. These efforts were naturally joined by those of the Pan-German League, which had agitated about Samoa all summer and at a great meeting in Hamburg in August had called the naval actions 'a list of humiliations, for which the German people would never forget the Anglo-Saxons'.[76]

Consequently, the news that Germany was to retain Samoa was received with general approval. Congratulations flooded in to Bülow and the kaiser from the *D.H.P.G.*, the Colonial Society, the Hamburg Chamber of Commerce, the *Kolonialrat*, the *Verein für deutsche Auswanderwohlfahrt*, the kaiser's yacht club, Prince Heinrich, Francis Joseph of Austria, Eulenburg, the duke of Saxony, and many other bodies and individuals. In his joy, Wilhelm called Bülow his 'magician', bestowed decorations upon him, Hatzfeldt and Eckardstein, and cabled his 'sincere pleasure' to Queen Victoria. This exuberance was generally reflected in the government press, which was instructed by Bülow to print many of these messages and to emphasize the achievement. The *Berliner Post* exclaimed that 'The cry that Samoa has become German will find a joyful echo in German hearts', and the *Kölnische Zeitung* quietly reminded its readers that Germany had not relinquished her freedom of action by this deal. Kusserow, in an article in the *Deutsche Kolonialzeitung*, lavished praise upon the agreement, declaring it to be the greatest thing since 1870-71 and Bismarck's acquisitions of 1884-85. The *Berliner Neueste Nachrichten, Germania, Export, Tägliche Rundschau, Leipziger Zeitung, Münchener Allgemeine Zeitung, Dresdener Nachrichten, Dresdener Zeitung, Schwäbische Merkur* and many other

76 A.A./*Südsee-Inseln* 5, vol. 3, *Deutsche Kolonialgesellschaft* to Bülow, 8/6/1899; ibid., vol. 6, Stralsund Branch to same, 1/11/1899; ibid., vol. 4, Bülow to A.A., tel. nos. 129 and 130 of 16/9/1899.

journals praised the settlement, stressing that 'our national honour was engaged in Samoa' and that Bülow was 'an excellent diplomat', a veritable 'Sunday child'.

There were, however, several organs which, like the government's own experts and officials, felt that Germany had had to pay a great deal for her sentimental attachment to Samoa. The pan-German and agrarians predictably pointed out that Germany had not gained enough, and the *Deutsche Zeitung* bitterly declared: 'Everything beyond Tonga is far in excess of a fair price. Germany ought to have secured additional African rights.' The *Börsen-Zeitung* felt that the American possession of Tutuila 'appears to make the agreement less valuable', and several other papers expressed similar doubts. Even the slightest criticism irritated Bülow. While he could do nothing about the agrarian and pan-German attacks, he was annoyed that the influential *Münchener Neueste Nachrichten* had thought that Britain had obtained too much from the settlement; and Monts, who had good relations with that paper, was told that the *Wilhelmstrasse* expected no more criticisms of that sort. Similarly, Richthofen was asked to counter the attacks of the *Hamburger Nachrichten* by articles in 'a relatively independent paper' like the *Allgemeine Zeitung* or the *Weser Zeitung*—perhaps an indication of Bülow's own doubts that the government-controlled press had much influence outside the ranks of its own supporters.[77]

Of very great importance was the close connection of the Samoan affair to the two great trends of German public opinion in 1899—the growth of anti-British feeling and the widespread acceptance of the need for a large fleet. A careful study of the fleet propaganda in the 1897-1900 period has shown that the anti-British current did not really get under way until early 1899 and that 'The Samoan theme stretches like a red thread through the entire writings of the fleet movement ... .'[78] No longer did the publicists have to point to the lessons of history or the recent fate of Spain: now they had a genuine, German grievance and a clear example of where a larger fleet could apparently (though no one explained how) have helped to preserve the rights of their nationals. After the April crisis, though, much of this fleet agitation died down. Moreover, the daily pleas from the *Post* and *Berliner Neueste Nachrichten* for the construction of as many ships as the docks could handle (Wilhelm: 'Bravo!') were

77 For the German press reaction to the settlement, see J. B. Moore Papers, Box 241; BA, Richthofen Papers, vol. 5, Bülow to Richthofen, 18/11/1899; A.A./*Südsee-Inseln* 5 nr. 1, vol. 1; Ellison, *The Partition of Samoa, passim*; B.D., I, no. 155; *Letters of Queen Victoria*, Third Series, 3, pp. 416-17.

78 Meyer, *Die Propaganda*, pp. 102-05, 108-35.

based upon the belief that Tirpitz was almost ready to introduce a further fleet increase. When it was learnt that the *Reichsmarineamt* was still unprepared for this, much of the industrial-based clamour fell away.[79]

Nevertheless, the connection between Samoa and the need for a larger navy was continued in another form—the brochure, which was much in use at this time in Germany. The *Samoa-Flugblatt* of the Navy League was probably the most popular, 1,900,000 of these being produced. One pamphlet of that year was specifically called 'What are the lessons from Samoa?' Valois' polemic referred to the Samoan episode, as did Vice-Admiral Werner's brochure 'Our future lies on the water'. The so-called *Flottenprofessoren* also found Samoa a useful argument; Dr Weber used it in his pamphlet 'The importance of the German fleet for our present and future', as did Professor Sieger in his brochure 'On the fleet question'.[80] Pan-German League publications really exploited the Samoan affair for this purpose. Edmund Bassenge's brochure 'Germany's world position and the next tasks of German policy' virulently criticized the findings of the Samoan commission and called upon the government to reject them, while Dr Eisenhart wrote of 'the arrogant Admiral Kautz and the irresponsible Captain of the *Porpoise*' in a pamphlet ominously and appropriately entitled 'The reckoning with England'. Lehr also found much to say on this in his own work, 'Why the German Fleet must be increased'. Time and again these and other writers referred to the insults to German honour at Samoa and promised themselves satisfaction when the navy was built up.[81]

This very rapid growth of anglophobia soon worried the German government in case the British leaders and public recognized the depth of the hatred and began to take naval counter-measures; as the naval attaché in London put it when reporting upon the British capacity to respond in proportion to the proposed fleet increases, 'the German papers should not so often and loudly announce that we will create a strong fleet in order some day to be able to trample

79 BA/MA 3415, PG67332, *Schiffe, fremde*, vol. 1, kaiser's minute on *Post* of 14/4/1899; E. Kehr, *Schlachtflottenbau und Parteipolitik* (Historische Studien no. 197, Berlin, 1930), pp. 174-77.

80 Meyer, *Die Propaganda*, pp. 102-05, 182; Steinberg, *Yesterday's Deterrent*, pp. 57-58; Valois, *Seemacht, Seegeltung, Seeherrschaft* (Berlin, 1899); H. Weber, *Die Bedeutung der deutschen Kriegsflotte für unsere Gegenwart und Zukunft* (Berlin, 1900); W. Sieger, *Zur Flottenfrage* (Nuremberg, 1900); R. Werner, *Unsere Zunkunft liegt auf dem Wasser* (*Deutsche Revue* reprint, December 1899).

81 E. Bassenge, *Deutschlands Weltstellung und die nächsten Aufgaben deutscher Politik* (Munich, 1899); A. Lehr, *Warum die deutsche Flotte vergrössert werden muss* (Munich, 1899); K. Eisenhart, *Die Abrechnung mit England* (Munich, 1900). See generally, J. Husmann 'Der Alldeutsche Verband und die Flottenfrage' (Phil. diss., Freiburg, 1951).

upon England.'[82] For the same reason, Tirpitz strove his utmost to silence Valois, while Bülow anxiously cabled to the *Auswärtiges Amt* from Windsor that 'We will only help the business of the French revanchist politicians with our confused ravings against England.' When the *Münchener Neueste Nachrichten* bitterly attacked Britain's South African policy, Bernstorff himself reprimanded the editor; and the government-inspired press strongly criticized the *Münchener Allgemeine Zeitung* when it openly declared that the new fleet measure was due to the British treatment of Germany in the past year. The official line, as taken by the *Kölnische Zeitung*, was as a rule to give general reasons (increase of trade, etc.) for the Navy Law.[83]

Nevertheless, the German government itself had greatly contributed to anti-British feelings by its own directed press campaign for the fleet and by the frequent references to Samoa; for it proved to be impossible to separate anglophobic reactions from those two topics. Early in 1899, Bülow and Tirpitz had agreed to co-operate over press publications which could damage or assist their cause, and as soon as the news of the affairs in Samoa reached Berlin their respective offices got to work. *Nauticus*, edited in the News Bureau of the *Reichsmarineamt*, made references to the lessons of the episode and the *Kölnische Zeitung* could not restrain itself from noting:

> At least the new English rebuke has taught the German people the value and nature of a fleet. This is necessary in order that Germany will not one day be crushed against the wall, as has recently happened with our French neighbour.[84]

The latter article was a result of Bülow's own directive that the press should connect the Samoan affair to Germany's lack of a fleet. More interesting still, while the *Auswärtiges Amt* was moving to influence whatever newspapers it could, the navy was feeding clippings which urged an increase in the fleet to the kaiser to convince him of public feeling on this matter. On 5 April excerpts from three papers were presented to him, on the twelfth another eleven, and on 12 June a further one.[85] It seems curious and yet not altogether so

82   BA/MA 2340, PG94545, *Die Englische Marine*, vol. 1, Coerper to R.M.A., 3/1/1900; Meyer, *Die Propaganda*, p. 123; G.P., 15, p. 414 footnote.

83   A.A./*Frankreich* 105 *nr.* 1, vol. 15, Bülow to A.A., tel. no. 167 of 25/11/1899; A.A., *Preussen* 1 *nr.* 1 *nr.* 40, vol. 5, Bernstorff to Hohenlohe, no. 117 of 6/10/1899; Treue, *passim*; Lehmann, *Kölnische Zeitung*, pp. 57-64.

84   BA/MA 2233, PG93995, *Pressangelegenheiten*, vol. 1, Bülow to Tirpitz, 18/2/1899; Lehmann, *Kölnische Zeitung*, pp. 105-07; *Nauticus* (1900), p. 5.

85   BA/MA 3131, 1.1.1.5, *Immediatvorträge*, vol. 6, has these notices.

surprising that some of the clippings came from such organs as the *Kölnische Zeitung* or the *Berliner Neueste Nachrichten*; to a certain extent Wilhelm was being shown articles inspired by the *Auswärtiges Amt* under the guise of being true reflections of German public opinion.

All the same, Bülow still wished for fleet propaganda which would avoid being so anti-British. Particularly annoying were the demands of the *Deutsche Tageszeitung* for an alliance with Russia and the Boers. 'That's rubbish too!' he noted furiously, 'How did Russia and France behave during the Transvaal crisis? In what way should the Boers help us in Samoa? Have they a fleet? The correct solution (increase of the fleet) is always to be alluded to, in contrast to such high fantasies.' To a similarly-toned article in the *Deutsche Zeitung*, Bülow had the same answer: 'Have we already a strong fleet?' Will one be made up through such swagger?' and he sarcastically suggested that 'The *Deutsche Zeitung* is to give us fifty battleships. Without an English fleet an overseas policy à la England is certainly impossible.'[86] However, his criticisms were limited to the style and anglophobic content of these press utterances and not to their actual pleas for a larger navy; and by the end of the year both he and Tirpitz realized that they could no longer avoid anti-British reasons if the campaign for the Second Navy Law was to succeed. Wilhelm was by then determined to double the battlefleet, and was pushing the navy minister along faster than he wished to go and threatening to dissolve the Reichstag if the measure was rejected. On the other hand, the government was aware that the public had given only a mixed reception to the kaiser's Hamburg speech and, although many wanted an increased fleet, much more persuasion was needed before the wavering Centre party would accept such a large programme so soon after the First Navy Law. As Tirpitz himself admitted, the matter had become so important that parts of the anti-British 'risk theory' had to be publicly outlined.[87]

Both Bülow and Tirpitz did this in their Reichstag speeches in support of the future Navy Law on 11 December 1899. Bülow's statement on Anglo-German relations not only stood out by being much stiffer and cooler than his utterances over other nations, but appears doubly significant when one realizes that this was his answer to Chamberlain's Leicester speech and their conversation at Windsor on the bettering of those

86 A.A./*Südsee-Inseln* 5, vol. 2, minutes on *Deutsche Tageszeitung* of 30/3/1899 and *Deutsche Zeitung* of 31/3/1899.

87 Hohenlohe, *Denkwürdigkeiten der Reichskanzlerzeit*, pp. 534-36, 538; Meyer, *Die Propaganda*, pp. 14-15; Tirpitz, *Erinnerungen*, p. 105.

relations.[88] Referring to the lessons of Samoa and other events of the past two years, Bülow stressed that much political and commercial jealousy existed in the world against Germany. Despite this, they were going forward and would not be stopped in their expansion. 'In the coming century' he concluded prophetically, 'the German people will either be the hammer or the anvil.' As soon as he had finished speaking, Tirpitz rose to tell the deputies that Germany must equip herself with a fleet strong enough not only to defend her coasts but able to threaten the maritime supremacy of the most powerful navy existing. No names were mentioned but it was not difficult for his listeners to understand what nation he had in mind.[89]

What, finally, can one say about the German government's control of the press in these years? To outside observers, the matter was very clear. 'No doubt there is a sentimental interest in Samoa in Germany'. Anderson minuted sarcastically, 'but its manifestations break out with surprising opportuneness for the diplomatic exigencies of the Government'.[90] Sir Hugh MacDonell, the British minister at Lisbon, maintained that one word from above in Berlin would be sufficient to quell the anglophobic press utterances over the Boer War. Yet to this the kaiser angrily noted: 'One can do much from "above", but not silence the sense of justice of the Germans! Thank God!'[91] In fact, both viewpoints were false, the truth being somewhere in the middle. The government possessed a great and undeniable influence over many newspapers, and these consistently represented the official line. Through personal contacts with editors and owners, through the threat of denying the information in the press bureaus to wavering organs, and through general appeals for solidarity on 'national' issues, the government also exerted a certain, spasmodic influence upon the independent press. But it failed to control in any way the utterances of the agrarian, pan-German, anti-semitic and Bismarckian papers, not to mention those having socialist policies. If the latter did not matter so much, the former did and this became a great problem for Bülow. His policy was merely to insinuate and hint at anti-British ideas, which would attract much of the population without alarming Britain; instead, he was forced to see a press campaign of unequalled bitterness waged by these organs against 'perfidious Albion' in the years following 1899. Try as he did, he could not

88 Rich, *Friedrich von Holstein*, 2, pp. 614-15.
89 *Reichstag*, X Legislaturperiode, I Session 1898/1900, vol. 4, Sitzung 119, 11/12/1899.
90 C.O.225/58, minute on paper 9565.
91 G.P., 15, no. 4372, and Wilhelm's minute thereon.

suppress what he had been partly responsible for starting up. It was perhaps his first failure but it was a costly one. Within a short time, the British were aware that the Germans regarded them as the enemy and began to respond; and the consequences of this mutual distrust were to be very grave indeed. In the origins of this development, the Samoan issue had played no small part.

iii *Samoa and Tonga*, 1900-14

For the Samoans, their superficial and artificial state of independence disappeared completely with the signing of the partition treaties. In a sense, this was an advantage for them, too; for if the tripartite control had been a nuisance and an entanglement for the powers, it had certainly not helped the natives. Neither the economic nor the political development of the islands had been much furthered by the rivalries of the white groups, which had merely intensified the Samoan dynastic struggle fot the *Tafa'ifa*. If actual Samoan independence could not be recovered, was it not better for the islands to be ruled by one responsible and paternalistic government than to be subjected to the pressures of various, often irresponsible, influences?

Certainly, the white settlers thought so. Many Britons and Americans in Apia, together with the Malietoans, were naturally disappointed with the treaty, which came as a shock despite the press speculations upon the talks and the British diplomatic weakness due to the Boer War. Nevertheless, this feeling disappeared and the L.M.S. missionaries, who had originally feared the effects of the new arrangement, were soon praising the German administration and voluntarily started to learn German.[92] Much of this was due to the new governor, Dr Wilhelm Solf, who transferred from the post of municipal president upon the demise of the Apia municipality. Possessing intelligence and tact, a great degree of tolerance, and vital experience of native administration from his years in East Africa, Solf proved to be the ideal person for this delicate task; such was the widespread praise of the man that one could possibly lay claim for him being the best colonial administrator produced by Germany.[93]

From the very beginning, the Germans possessed clear plans for administering their part of the group and these were put into action after the flag was raised on 1 March

92   BA, Solf Papers, vol. 1, letter of 28/11/1899; L.M.S./S.S.L. 1900, no. 7805, Huckett to L.M.S., 17/5/1900.

93   On Solf's activities, see E. von Vietsch, *Wilhelm Solf: Botschafter zwischen den Zeiten* (Tübingen, 1961), pp. 42-101; Davidson, *Samoa mo Samoa*, pp. 76-90.

1900. The chief task was to restore lasting peace and prosperity to Samoa after the grievous events of 1899. To eliminate further dynastic struggles, the kaiser himself was proclaimed *Tupi Sili* (paramount king) although Mata'afa was recognized as *Ali'i Sili* (paramount chief). The latter's influence over five-sixths of the Samoan population made such an action very necessary, for, despite the opinion of the commission, the natives had in no way lost the idea of having some form of overall ruler. The departure of Tanu to Fiji to complete his education and the reconciliation of Tamasese to the new state of affairs assisted this step, although there still existed some bitterness among the Malietoans, many of whom hoped for the return of the British after the Boer War. Nevertheless, the recognition of Mata'afa's special position, linked with the German scheme to give the Samoans as much self-government as possible, was clearly a wise policy.[94]

Yet this was, it must be said, only a temporary and tactical measure by Solf. His real aim was to unite the Samoans under the kaiser and he thus planned to eliminate gradually the post of *Ali'i Sili* and also to reduce the importance of that group of talking-chiefs, the *Tumua* and *Pule*, who throughout the dynastic contests of the past years had plumped for one candidate or the other but always striven to augment their own standing. Even when Mata'afa's followers began to call him king of Samoa in April 1900, Solf knew that the old chief would have to be appeased 'to preserve the peace'. Possessing no armed force, and aware from the experiences of 1899 that a few warships were useless to cow the natives, he relied mainly upon moral influence and persuasion to get his way. 'The Samoans can be guided, but not forced' was a frequent saying of his. It was not until August 1905 that Solf felt able to replace the *Tumua* and *Pule* by a Samoan council of twenty-seven members, often chosen from districts which did not represent the old centres of native power. Yet whenever he was absent from the group, such as in 1904-05 and 1909, fresh political disturbances arose. In the latter year, they took a very serious form indeed, for Lauaki, the former spokesman of the *Tumua* and *Pule*, joined with Mata'afa to protest in favour of a return to the old ways and a promise that the next *Ali'i Sili* should be named before the aged chief died.[95]

94 A.A./*Südsee-Inseln* 5, vol. 7, Bülow to Wilhelm, 16/11/1899, enclosing memo on the future administration of Samoa.

95 BA, Solf Papers, vol. 20, memos of 5/4/1900 and 9/4/1900; ibid., despatches to R.Kol.A. of 19/4/1900, 26/6/1900, 4/9/1900 and 3/10/1900; W. H. Solf, *Samoa, the people, the missions and the Europeans*, 1907 (private manuscript in Rhodes House); Vietsch, *Solf*, pp. 59-64, 75-76; Davidson, *Samoa mo Samoa*, pp. 80-87.

In the event, this movement soon collapsed after Solf's return—but it had also required the presence of most of the German East Asian squadron, which deported Lauaki and nine others.[96] Moreover, it furthered Solf's determination to abolish the position of *Ali'i Sili* as soon as Mata'afa passed away. In fact, this did not occur until February 1912, some time after the first governor had left to be state secretary for the colonies; but a peaceful and sensible compromise had by then been reached, whereby Tamasese and Tanu were named as joint advisers to the governor. Equally important was the disappearance of the *Tumua* and *Pule* as an effective political body, although the individual members still possessed great influence. Nevertheless, Professor Davidson has righly queried whether the Samoan sense of grievance had fully vanished through these cautious German policies or whether economic discontents, which had led to the formation of a native co-operative movement until Solf forced its disbandment in 1905, would not have again become a source of trouble so long as the islands were dominated by the large plantation companies.[97]

Solf encountered many difficulties with the whites also. Strangely enough, these came not so much from the Anglo-Americans but from German settlers, who strongly objected to the governor's policy of offering local posts to people of other nationalities, of protecting the Samoan rights and of preventing excessive penalties being imposed upon the plantation workers. After he had won his struggle with interfering naval officers in 1900 over their right to participate in native affairs, Solf came up against a bitter opponent in one Richard Deeken, who had behind him a following of newly-arrived settlers, disgruntled with the governor that the paradise promised them in Deeken's own book *Manuia Samoa* (Hail, Samoa!) had not materialized. With the help of pan-German connections at home, these intriguers attempted for years to dislodge Solf from his post and were not above mixing in Samoan politics. Despite this campaign, however, he effectively retained Berlin's confidence.[98]

Economically, matters went well in the islands after 1900. Despite the troubles of the previous year, the copra crop had been a record, 8,500 tons of it being exported, producing a customs revenue of $31,000. The *D.H.P.G.* was particularly pleased with the new situation, and thereafter the annual

96 BA/MA 5121, II Deutschland 23b, *Deutschland, Kolonien in Australien*, vol. 2 Cruiser-Squadron to Admiralstab, 5/4/1909, and R.Kol.A. to same, 13/5/1909.

97 Davidson, *Samoa mo Samoa*, p. 90.

98 BA, Solf Papers, vol. 20, memo of 5/4/1900; Vietsch, *Solf*, pp. 65-75.

reports speak of the 'absolute peace and order' (1902) in place of their gloomy chronicles of the 'anarchic conditions' in previous years (1895). By 1902, their trading profit had risen to 623,336 marks; by 1913, it was 1,524,821 marks. Moreover, the planting of cocoa also proved to be a rapid success and in the years 1910-12 this commodity was exported to the average value of £35,000 per annum, second only to the average annual copra export of £173,400 in the same period. The customs receipts from this enabled the administration to devote money for roads, buildings, schools, etc. German Samoa very quickly became self-supporting: the imperial subsidy of 52,000 marks in 1900, which rose to a peak of 274,795 marks in 1904, gradually dropped and was not required after 1908. Only Togoland could claim a similar state of financial self-sufficiency.[99]

Nevertheless, the group was, relatively speaking, economically underdeveloped and insignificant. Its trade formed a very small part of Germany's colonial commerce, which in turn was only 0.5 per cent of that country's total foreign trade. It was less than Tonga's commerce for most of these years, and far inferior to Fiji's. The *D.H.P.G.* complained continuously of the lack of plantation workers, for the Solomons arrangement of 1899 did not work out adequately in practice. In 1903, a group of 350 Chinese were brought to the islands to fill this need and by 1914 over 2,000 coolies were employed on the plantations. This was a mixed blessing for the German administration, however, which was often involved in controversies with the Chinese government. Samoa also suffered from a lack of regular shipping communications with the outside world. In 1900, the Union Steamship Company of New Zealand abandoned its trans-Pacific service via Apia and Honolulu and the American-owned Oceanic Steamship Company transferred its port of call to Pago-Pago, while all attempts by the German government to interest German shipping companies in a subsidized line to Samoa failed miserably. Shipping, such as it was, remained firmly in the hands of small British-Australasian lines and in 1911 Germany's share of even the import and export trade was only 36.7 per cent.[100]

But, to anyone imbued with the glowing accounts of Samoa's future which filled the German newspapers in the 1890s, the biggest surprise and disappointment was surely

99 St. A.H., D.H.P.G.Archiv, *Bericht der Direktion*, 1895-1913; Davidson, *Samoa mo Samoa*, pp. 77-78, 89.

100 C.O.225/110, paper 8797, print copy of Sampson's memo on German colonies, 1910-11; Gray, *Amerika Samoa*, pp. 178-79; Weck, *Deutschlands Politik in der Samoa Frage*, p. 57; Zimmermann, *Kolonialpolitik*, pp. 300-02.

in the naval sphere. Where was the important naval station and cable landing post which Tirpitz had predicted for the group in his memorandum of 11 October 1899? As early as the spring of 1901, the commander-in-chief, Australia Station, had advised against even erecting an official coaling depot in Samoa. Because there were no German colonies in the islands further east, on the path to South America, he believed that the group 'will remain an outpost relatively'. His sole recommendation was that the *D.H.P.G.* should be contracted to provide coal for the few warships which called in at Samoa. But this, too, proved grossly unsatisfactory, as that monopolistic firm charged outrageous fees (61 marks per ton cf. 42 marks in Fiji) and the German navy preferred to coal at Suva or to slip secretly into Pago-Pago. The American fleet, on its famous 'round-the-world' cruise of 1908, declined to despatch their larger vessels to the 'dangerous Apia'; and even the ones that were sent there created such admiration and awe amongst the Samoans that Solf pleaded for a visit by equally large German warships to restore the government's prestige. Although this was agreed to, the Admiralty staff was very worried at sending the battle-cruiser *Scharnhorst* into such an unsafe harbour.[101]

Nor did the scheme for establishing a cable station at Samoa get under way, although all acknowledged that the delay in swift communication was a severe disadvantage in times of crisis. The Post Office had already pointed out how wasteful a cable connection to Samoa would be and even when they laid their Pacific line the group lay too far to the south-east and was too isolated to justify a branch-line. Nevertheless, the navy pressed for some means of communication (such as a powerful wireless) with the islands, so that messages could be sent swiftly to any warships there if war broke out. However, work did not start upon a Samoan station, which was situated in the hills a few miles behind Apia, until 1913 and it was not ready to go into service until the summer of the following year. Ironically, one of the first messages governor Schultz received was of the outbreak of war; and the apparatus had to be destroyed shortly afterwards to prevent it from falling into enemy hands.[102]

101 See the correspondence in BA/MA 4127, V.1.1.72, *Die Errichtung eines Kohlenlagers in der Südsee* 1901-1913, vol. 1; and BA/MA 4295, XIV.1.2.12, *Hafenanlagen in Samoa*, vol. 1. Also, A.A./*Südsee-Inseln* 5, vol. 10, Sternburg to A.A., no. 85 of 5/5/1908, and Solf to A.A., no. 286 of 26/9/1908.

102 BA/MA 5121, II Deutschland 23b, *Deutschland, Kolonien in Australien*, vol. 2, Admiralstab to R.M.A., 5/1/1909; BA/MA 5164, III 1.-3e, *Vorarbeiten u. Ausführungsbestimmungen zu den O-Befehlen. Australische Station. Ganz Geheim*, vol. 1, Admiralstab to C in C, Australia Station, 9/4/1912; A.A./Abt. II E (BA, Koblenz), R85/777, *Cormoran*, report no. 60 (copy), 29/5/1913.

Of course, it could be argued that Samoa did not become so important strategically because the Central American canal, the completion of which was expected by many experts to alter drastically the patterns of world trade with the antipodes, was not built for many years; but this excuse only serves to conceal the real fallacy in the predictions. The bald fact was that commerce across the South Pacific was very small and this would not noticeably increase with the opening of the canal. When Curzon had pressed the Admiralty in 1898 for information upon good strategic points in the South Seas, he had been repeatedly told by them that the area was really too remote to be considered; only the routes to the Far East mattered with regard to possible acquisitions by foreign nations. By 1908, a German officer engaged upon an operational study of British commerce in the Pacific and Indian oceans, had reached a similar conclusion. Trade in the Pacific was so meagre that the Australian squadron should attack the China routes in time of war, the best place of all being around Aden. He concluded that

> The well-known phrases, 'the centre of world history is moving inexorably towards the Pacific Ocean' (Marquis Ito), 'Who controls the Pacific controls the world' (Lord Palmerston), 'the great ocean', 'the Mediterranean of the future', etc. are historically weak and cannot be justified geographically, commercially or politically.[103]

There was, moreover, a far more basic reason for the German navy's neglect of Samoa and the Pacific: it simply did not fit into Tirpitz's strategy, which was founded solely upon the concept of a battlefleet in home waters which would neutralize the British. As he himself put it, 'The lever of our *Weltpolitik* was the North Sea: it worked indeed over the whole globe without us needing to deploy our ships anywhere.'[104] Since Tirpitz intended to recoup in the North Sea what he would lose in the South Pacific, little was done about the defences of Samoa. As early as 1902, the Admiralty staff thought that resistance was 'pointless' if an enemy force appeared over the horizon. While there were talks about creating a local militia, its main aim was to be protection from the Samoans; Schultz was very doubtful of the idea of arming the natives to resist an invasion lest the weapons be turned against the settlers themselves.[105] The vessels on the Australia

103 BA/MA 7840, *Winterarbeiten des Admiralstabes*, Wilke *Winterarbeit* of 1908.

104 Alfred von Tirpitz, *Politische Dokumente* 2 vols., (Stuttgart/Berlin, 1924), vol. 1, *Der Aufbau der deutschen Weltmacht*, p. 346.

105 BA/MA 5121, II Deutschland 23b. *Deutschland. Kolonien in Australien*, vol. 2, *Kondor* to Admiralstab, 21/6/1909; BA/MA 5164, III.1.-3e, *Vorarbeiten u. Ausführungsbestimmungen zu den O-Befehlen. Australische Station. Ganz Geheim*, vol. 1, Admiralstab to A.A., 17/3/1902; ibid., vol. 2, C in C, Australia Station, to Admiralstab, 11/11/1913.

Stations were consequently instructed to hide in the Pacific
islands and take to cruiser warfare if war did break out with
Britain, rather than attempt to support the German colonies
themselves.[106]

Not surprisingly, Samoa fell very easily when war came.
An expeditionary force of almost 1,500 men, sent up in troop
transports from New Zealand, took over the German part on
29 August 1914, without encountering any resistance. Upolu,
Savai'i and the smaller islands passed under new masters and
no one was more pleased at this than Sturdee. By then he had
risen to be Chief of War Staff at the Admiralty and as such
he personally supervised the naval arrangements leading to
the seizure of the islands he had striven so hard to keep out
of German hands some fifteen years previously.[107] When
Spee steamed past the group two weeks later with his squadron,
he found the New Zealanders commanding the shore and
decided that any attempt to re-take it would bring only
short-term advantages. After his force sailed away, the New
Zealand military hold upon Samoa was secure and the
D.H.P.G. and other firms were soon put into liquidation,
much to the delight of the Auckland Chamber of Commerce.

This grip the politicians in Wellington were unwilling to
relax. Throughout the war, they agitated for international
recognition of permanent New Zealand control of the islands,
pointing out the strategic reasons which made this necessary.
Sir Joseph Ward, the finance minister, put things at their
most extreme in his speech of 17 March 1917, to the Imperial
War Conference.

> The fine territory of Samoa was vital to the future of the British Empire,
> as it practically overshadowed New Zealand and Australia. It afforded
> one of the best places in the Pacific for a coaling station for the purposes
> of ships of war running into it, and having docks provided for their
> repair, and all that sort of thing: it was placing a base right in the Pacific
> Ocean and right in the very territory of the two great British possessions,
> Australia and New Zealand, which were vitally concerned in keeping
> that part of the Pacific clear, at least, of possible enemy countries.[108]

By the use of such arguments and by bitter attacks upon the
1899 treaty, the Australasians soon convinced the British
of the justice of their cause: indeed, unaware of the real
calculations in London's policy at the time of the partition,

106 BA/MA 5236, *Mobilmachungs-Uebersichten der Australische Station*, vol. 1, Top
Secret memo of 4/5/1910.
107 Sturdee Papers, private account. A short description of the takeover is in Gray,
Amerika Samoa, pp. 183-85.
108 C.O.537/989, Print of Imperial War Conference discussions, 17/3/1917. On this
theme generally, see W. R. Louis, *Great Britain and Germany's Lost Colonies 1914-1919*
(Oxford, 1967), *passim*.

the Foreign Office representative admitted that they had not had a very definite policy in the Pacific in earlier years. At the Versailles settlement, Western Samoa, as it was henceforward to be called, legally and officially obtained a new set of masters and entered upon a new phase in her history. It was to last until the beginning of 1962, when it became an independent state in its own right—a far cry from those days when it had been the cockpit of international rivalry in the south-west Pacific.[109]

The history of American Samoa since 1900 has been much more straightforward and, not surprisingly, more obscure, despite Hay's belief that Tutuila was 'the most important island in the Pacific as regards harbor conveniences for our navy, and a station on the trans-Pacific route'.[110] At its own special request, the Navy Department took over the administration of these eastern islands and on 17 April 1900, the United States flag was raised in Pago-Pago Bay. The consent of the Tutuilan chiefs to this had already been secured, although until 1904 it was found to be impossible to obtain a written acknowledgement of cession from the more independent people of Manua. The naval builders went ahead with their work, and German reports spoke enviously of the construction of the large coalshed and steel pier, of the dredging of coral from the harbour, and of the hubbub of activity inside Pago-Pago in the next few years. In 1900, its commander thought that 'the harbor of Pago-Pago is magnificent and one of the finest in the world, and will be of immense importance to the United States as a naval station', a view echoed by the commander-in-chief, Pacific station, in the following year.[111]

Shortly afterwards, however, a more realistic tone entered into the naval memoranda and by August 1902 Tutuila was reckoned to be a base of only third-grade importance by the General Board, which also even recommended abandoning the coaling station there. This move was strongly opposed by Bradford, by then a rear-admiral, who wanted Tutuila to 'be classed among stations of the first importance'. But although the Board dropped its own recommendation, it remained unconvinced of the harbour's strategic value to the navy and felt that Pago-Pago did not need to be fortified.[112]

109 For the period after 1918, see Davidson, *Samoa mo Samoa*, pp. 90ff.

110 Hay Papers, Box 26, Letterbook 1, Hay to Choate, 4/12/1899.

111 N.A.R.G. 45, Area File 9, M-625, roll 321, Long to McKinley, 17/1/1900; N.A.R.G. 80, File 3931, Box 416, Bureau of Equipment memo of 6/2/1900, and Rear Admiral Casey to N.D., 19/11/1901; Gray, *Amerika Samoa*, pp. 107-17.

112 Dewey Papers, Library of Congress, Box 56, memos of 27/8/1902 and 28/8/1902; General Board records, Letterpress volume 2, Dewey to the secretary of the navy, 10/10/1902.

It had not taken them long to realize that Crowninshield's prediction on the importance of the route to Australia was more correct than Bradford's optimistic assumptions; if no American warship had taken that route in the twelve years preceding 1898, there was little chance that this situation would suddenly alter after the partition of Samoa. America's outward drive in these years was towards China, not towards the south-west Pacific; the interest in Pago-Pago was as much a strategical aberration as the involvement in the tridominium had been a political one. To call Pago-Pago 'the Gibraltar of the Pacific' was to ignore the simple fact that it was Gibraltar's unique position, and not merely the physical characteristics, which made it one of the most important bases in the world; and since Tutuila did not lie upon any vital trade routes, the analogy was totally false. Only in 1942 was the base built up again to meet the Japanese thrust into the south-west Pacific; but after the battles of Guadalcanal, Pago-Pago's strategic importance declined once more.

On the non-naval side, the affairs of the American-owned islands were even more obscure. For years they were simply known as 'U.S. Naval Station, Tutuila', and only in 1904 was a de jure governor appointed. The same vagueness applied to the status of the Tutuilans themselves, who were refused American citizenship by Congress although they are recognized as being United States 'nationals'. The islands were not legally annexed until Congress ratified and confirmed the cession in 1929! Since 1951 they have been administered by the Department of the Interior but even today their whole future seems rather uncertain and an eventual re-unification with Western Samoa is not outside the bounds of possibility.[113]

It took much longer for the powers to execute the provisions of the damages agreement of 7 November 1899, than it did to carry out the partition treaty itself. This was partly due to the delays inherent in a complex international judicial investigation, and partly to a dispute over the wording of the agreement. Although King Oscar of Sweden and Norway agreed as early as 20 December 1899 to adjudicate in the matter, the collection and presentation of evidence by both sides delayed his judgement until 14 October 1902, when he announced that the military actions of the warships had been unwarranted. In his opinion, they were a form of individual control over the group, which the Berlin Act did not permit; and the policies which followed the arrival of Kautz ought to have been seen as exasperating the Mata'afans and endangering the peace.

113 Gray, *Amerika Samoa*, pp. 105ff. See also Professor Keesing's thoughtful foreword on pp. ix-xv.

While the British and American governments were made responsible for the losses, the king did not specify the amounts involved. Since the two defending parties agreed to compensate their respective nationals and jointly to pay half the sums found due to the subjects of other countries, he possibly assumed that matters would proceed smoothly following his decision.[114]

The judgement was received with pleasure in Germany, where it was regarded as a justification for their previous stand; but it aroused some surprise in Britain and especially in the United States, where the *Washington Times* noted bitterly that a decision by a monarch against a republic might well have been expected.[115] In any case, the negotiations soon reached a deadlock when the special legal agents of the two governments proceeded to examine all the German claims. Holding that only concrete damages arising from the actual military proceedings were involved, all compensation for native lootings and for arrest (the three Germans arrested for a short period demanded $35,000 damages) was rejected and the sum of $25,000 was offered as the total reimbursement.[116] Although this was considered in London and Washington to be very generous, as the agents believed that only $6,000—$7,000 should in strictness be paid out, it was sharply criticized by the German government, whose subjects had submitted claims totalling $111,745. Since Berlin considered that the destruction caused by the Samoan looters should also be compensated, the argument pivoted for months upon the validity and amount of these consequential damages. While finding no reason in international law for an increase, the agents recommended in August 1904 that the compensation should be raised to the sum of $40,000 to avoid further dispute. Even this did not satisfy the Germans, however, who asked for at least $60,000. At this, both Hay and Lansdowne stood firm and agreed to proceed no further—Berlin could either take it or leave it. By 1905, the Germans had decided to take it, since Lansdowne sharply told them that 'the sum *already* offered was considered to be far in excess of the true value of the German claims'.[117]

After this, matters went more smoothly and the French, Danish, Swedish and Norwegian claimants were all compensated with smaller sums. $18,000 was also paid out by the

114 W. S. Penfield, 'The Settlement of the Samoan Cases' in *American Journal of International Law*, 7 (1913), pp. 767-69.
115 A.A./*Südsee-Inseln* 5, vol. 9, Quadt (Washington) to Bülow, no. 402 of 27/10/1902.
116 F.O.58/340, Richards' reports of 7/4/1903 and 24/7/1903.
117 Ibid., F.O.58/341, Hurst to F.O., 12/4/1904; F.O.58/344, Villiers memo of 23/2/1905, and F.O. to Treasury, 19/4/1905.

British government to its own nationals although the American claimants had a much harder time. Not until 1911 did Congress make an allocation for this purpose but a fresh legal agent was called in by the State Department to re-investigate the various cases. Only in March 1913, therefore, did Congress recommend the amount of $14,812.42 for its own nationals.[118] Politically, the damages question was of little significance, apart from the fact that the State Department and the Foreign Office had co-operated closely and harmoniously in the affair, and joined together to resist what they considered to be the excessive demands of Berlin. Germany's reputation with both governments as a demanding and greedy power had received further small confirmation.

The corollary of the thesis that Samoa was chiefly discarded by the British government because it was no longer considered strategically valuable must be that Tonga's importance correspondingly increased; for if the Boer war and Germany's attitude rather than the Admiralty memorandum had been the determining factor for its withdrawal, then the acquisition of Tonga would only have been of moderate significance, a mere administrative consequence of the treaty rather than the raison d'etre of London's policy. In fact, the desire to secure the harbours of the latter group for the British Empire permeated official calculations after October 1899, as the documents clearly show. They also show that it was more difficult to achieve this aim than had been originally contemplated.

The first obstacle was the attitude of the United States, which had the right to establish a naval station in Tonga by their treaty of 1886 and which could only officially be abrogated by the action of Senate. Hay, although sympathetic to the British approaches in November 1899, baulked at the idea of asking that body to give up what were only *nominal* privileges. He therefore declined the British request, pointing out that America had abstained from the Anglo-German talks and that there had never been any previous mention of the renunciation of any rights (except those in Upolu and Savai'i) by the United States. Nevertheless, this was only his official answer, intended solely for the State Department records. Unwilling to see the treaty collapse because of this quarrel with London, he privately assured Pauncefote that until Britain formally annexed Tonga, which would extinguish the treaty rights of other powers in the group along with the native sovereignty that had granted them, the United States

118   Ibid., Hurst to F.O., 3/3/1905; Penfield, *Samoan Cases*, pp. 769-73.

would not take advantage of its rights there. Although this was less than the British had hoped for, they accepted Hay's promises and created no further delay in the signing of the tripartite treaty itself. After all, their concern for the group's future, and the security of Fiji, had been caused by German actions in the Pacific in 1898-99, not by American, and it was not expected that the United States would wish to erect a base in Tonga now that it was spending so much on nearby Pago-Pago.[119]

Nevertheless, the complications did not cease here, for the Colonial Office did not want to annex Tonga, but only to establish a protectorate over it; yet this, London feared, would not be considered enough to cause the rights of foreign powers in the group to be extinguished. For weeks, various officials tried to suggest ways around this obstacle and it was eventually agreed to proceed with the establishment of a protectorate, keeping open the option to annex if the Americans made 'an unfriendly move'. As Villiers pointed out, 'If we are to control the foreign relations of Tonga any base or concession would require our agreement, & this would afford time at least to consider the necessity of settling the matter by annexation.'[120] Drafts were therefore prepared for a treaty with the king of Tonga under which Britain would conduct all future relations with foreign states, have jurisdiction in all cases in which whites were involved 'to prevent any occasion or pretext for interference in the Group by foreign powers', place a Resident in the group to advise the king on these matters, and secure suitable sites for naval bases in the key harbours of Neiafu (Vavau) and Nukualofa (Tongatabu)[121]

To ensure the success of this scheme, the Colonial Office selected Basil Thomson, who already had some knowledge of Tongan affairs, to go to the group in a warship and negotiate with the king. They also sought to keep this plan a secret, suppressing evidence upon the superiority of Tonga's harbours and giving as little information as possible to New Zealand, which would be sure to publicize things, alarm the king and attract the attention of expansionist-minded Americans. The king, in fact, swiftly emerged as a major obstacle to the British plans, for he was determined to preserve his title of 'last independent King in the Pacific' and Thomson spent

---

119 This short section upon the Tongan aspect is a synopsis of the latter part of my *Britain and the Tongan Harbours*, 1898-1914, *passim*.

120 F.O.58/321, Villiers minute on Oakes memo of 21/12/1899.

121 C.O.537/447, paper 2500 (Secret. Mission of Mr Basil Thomson to Tonga) has the drafts and details.

many weeks endeavouring to persuade him to sign the treaty. On 18 May an agreement was signed, and Thomson also formally proclaimed a protectorate, but the king's great reluctance to give up control of Tonga's foreign relations made the Colonial Office most suspicious, especially when King George attempted to avoid exchanging the ratifications. 'We must keep this slippery gentleman to his treaty', minuted one of the clerks.[122] For years afterwards, London worried about the king's unreliability and in 1905 the Treaty of Friendship was re-written to give the British Resident a greater say in appointments and finance. Despite the mutual suspicions, the group's prosperity grew steadily and the careful eye of the Resident ensured that the administration functioned with a fair standard of competence and honesty.

As for the American naval rights in Tonga, nothing was ever done about them. The Colonial Office repeatedly sought to avoid annexing the group while Washington showed no interest in it; yet the Foreign Office always shrank from asking the Americans to make a unilateral renunciation of their privileges in Tonga and preferred to leave the matter alone. It was not until 1919 that London denounced the American-Tongan treaty, following a lengthy correspondence with the United States over the termination of one article therein. Two years later, Washington acknowledged the denunciation 'save and except as to Article VI, which is terminable only by mutual consent'—the naval station clause was still in force, therefore, but by this time it was of little importance in London and no further action was taken. The American right to a Tongan base, which had been a matter of concern to Salisbury and Chamberlain, was simply no longer an issue; and it has continued to exist, undisturbed and unused, to the present day.

122   C.O.225/59, minute on paper 24708. Thomson described his negotiations in his *Savage Island* (London, 1902), pp. 164-74; and *The Scene Changes* (London, 1939), pp. 186-210.

Conclusion

The Relations of Britain, Germany and the United States in the Light of the Samoan Question

In the Pacific itself, the partition of the Samoan and Tongan groups signified the end of an era. By the late 1890s, only a few small islands remained unannexed and disregarded, and all those of any importance had been picked up by the powers. The sudden expansion westwards of the United States in 1898 made the status of the two groups even more of an exception, and many observers must have joined Captain Mandt of the *Bussard* in thinking it 'surprising' that Tonga had not been annexed and in finding the 'most unfortunate' government at Samoa a regrettable aberration.[1] There was no room left in the age of high imperialism for an independent native kingdom, nor for a curious system of tripartite rule. For years, of course, changes had been anticipated but the difficulties inherent within the proposed alterations had prevented them from being carried out and had allowed the continuation of the status quo. By 1899, however, the critical internal Samoan situation, together with the state of international affairs, made necessary and simultaneously made easier the expected changes. The powers discovered that it was possible to arrange a partition of the two groups, and to put an end to their anomalous and unfashionable governmental systems. A 'shared' rule had been found to be impossible, therefore, at least for nations not possessing the higher motives of preserving an alliance or entente. Thereafter, apart from the Anglo-French administration of the New Hebrides, the Pacific was completely partitioned. Development and internal affairs filled the despatches on the Pacific, and imperial rivalries in the region no longer troubled the chancelleries of Europe.[2]

If the southwest Pacific had been most affected by the rivalries over Samoa, the question and its final solution was

1 F.O.58/318, Maxse to Salisbury, no. 53, Secret, of 22/10/1898, with enclosure.
2 The British records furnish a good example of this change. During the 1880s, an annual average of 8.5 volumes covers the Foreign Office Pacific correspondence, and a somewhat similar annual average of 7.3 volumes exists for the 1890s (16 volumes being needed to fill the 1899 correspondence). In the years 1900-1906 only 10 volumes of documents were filed and bound, much of it being on the Samoan claims; and by 1913 the Pacific Islands section had petered out completely. At the same time, the Colonial Office documentation on the Pacific rose rapidly, from an annual average of 2.7 volumes in the 1878-97 period to one of 5.0 volumes in the twenty years following.

also of significance to the powers themselves. For America, the affair revealed the changing attitudes of the government and people towards empire between the 1870s and the late 1890s. It was inevitable that as the industrial, commercial and naval power of the United States developed, she would expand her influence across the Pacific and come into contact with the peoples of the islands; although the true direction of this drive was across the North and Central Pacific, and only the temporary activities of the whalers and a few shipping concerns caused America to become involved in this group in the South Seas. Nevertheless, the commercial interest, which was soon reduced to the very smallest levels, did not imply territorial and political designs and throughout the 1870s and 1880s the policy of the United States was to preserve the independence of the native state, even to the extent of risking a confrontation with Germany upon this point. In the background, however, an additional interest had appeared and was growing larger—the strategic stake in the harbour of Pago-Pago. Although it cannot be overlooked, and schemes for the future use of their treaty rights there were possibly in politicians' minds and certainly in the mind of the U.S. Navy, this motive was not the dominant one in the 1880s. Indeed, having arranged a tripartite supervision of Samoa with the other two powers, Washington tended to lose interest in the affairs of the group and to regard them as an unnatural 'entanglement'.

The strategic interest was not fully extinguished, though, and it was powerfully revived as a result of the Spanish-American war and the sudden expansion into the Pacific and Far East after 1897. The feeling of distaste for the irksome obligation of running the tripartite government, especially with a restless Germany, also remained. Although the American administration stood firm against the actions of Raffel and Rose, it was not opposed in principle to the idea of a partition; neither was the American public and it became solely a matter of waiting for the other two nations to agree to their share, it being understood by all that the United States would receive Tutuila. By 1899, the attachment of Hay and the U.S. Navy to Tutuila was the basis for Washington's policy, and both greeted the eventual settlement with joy. By then, too, they were prepared to disregard the claims of the Samoans to rule themselves, and when Choate raised the matter of a clause in the treaty which would assure the Samoans of their political rights, Hay hastily answered that 'I do not think it would be advisable to insist especially upon any details of the participation of the natives in the government of the islands

. . .'³ It is to be wondered, in retrospect, whether the overall gain to the United States of this not-so-strategically-significant harbour was as great as Hay believed. In an imperialistic age, however, few people doubted the fact.

The Samoan episode also reflected, to a large extent, the relations of the United States to the other members of the tridominium. Even if the British activities in the group seemed peaceful, its tacit support of German policy in the 1880s confirmed the suspicion of the Americans that their natural foe would always back a European power against the young republic. If the greater part of their anger was directed against Germany, this should not obscure the powerful anglophobic strain running through the Congress and the press in these years, which fed upon a large number of other points of issue, particularly in regard to Canada. Because of this, the 1879 municipality treaty was not ratified, the 1889 conference was not held in London, and the British suggestions regarding the chief justice were refused by the Americans. Salisbury's obvious wish to see the Samoan matter settled by some partition arrangement and his great need for Germany's diplomatic support in Egypt and the Balkans had thrown him into Bismarck's camp, and the United States reacted accordingly.

Ten years later, things were entirely different. Following the Venezuela crisis, which alarmed influential circles upon both sides of the Atlantic, Anglo-American relations steadily improved, but the real breakthrough came only in 1898 and followed from the British government and press's attitude to the Spanish-American war. It is irrelevant to point out that the actual support from London was not as great as the rumours of the time indicated, or that the intentions of the continental powers were not as malevolent as the Associated Press made out. The crucial fact was, that the obvious pro-American feelings of the British at a time when the actions of the United States were being strongly criticized elsewhere was gratefully received in Washington. As Roosevelt himself put it: 'Indeed I shall not forget, and I don't think our people will, England's attitude during the Spanish war . . . '⁴ Moreover, those Americans in an official position, particularly in the U.S. Navy, were aware of a number of 'good turns' done for them by the British during the war. This is not to say that an Anglo-American alliance was possible, or even sought for, in the United States; with rare

3 Hay Papers, Box 26, Letterbook 1, Hay to Choate, 13/11/1899.
4 E. E. Morison, ed., *The Letters of Theodore Roosevelt*, 8 vols. (Cambridge, Mass., 1951-54), 2, pp. 889-90.

exceptions, it was still considered to be impossible and undesirable. Nor is it to deny that there were outstanding disputes between the two countries, over which the Americans in particular would bargain hard and over which the newly-formed friendship could break down. But the atmosphere had changed and this, together with the personalities of Hay and Pauncefote, promised a possible mutually satisfactory solution of these other difficulties.

This trend the Samoan dispute confirmed and, in an admittedly small way, assisted. First of all, the news of the combined stand in the South Seas came shortly after the breakdown of the Joint High Commission's talks upon the Alaskan boundary and fortuitously helped to obscure this more serious development. Secondly, it revived again the picture of Anglo-American forces standing together against German intrigues and misdeeds. Doubtless, the author of the *Philadelphia's* own magazine, *Our Flag*, was unduly biased and optimistic when he wrote in a leader entitled 'The Anglo-American Alliance':

> At last has come to pass that, which was looked forward to with hope by Americans and Englishmen and fear by the remainder of the world as to results: but which cannot but have a great effect on the future history of the world. We refer to the union of forces of the two great English-speaking nations of the earth. English and American sailors and marines are today side by side, shoulder by shoulder in a common cause . . .[5]

Nevertheless, in a more subdued form, this aspect was frequently mentioned by the majority of American newspapers. For the U.S. Navy in particular, the Samoan actions appear to have had some psychological importance; and in addition to the joint Anglo-American memorial to the dead officers and men erected in Samoa itself, a further one was constructed in the Mare Island dockyard chapel in 1902. Indeed, the whole Pacific fleet seems to have regarded the Manila and Samoan episodes as being very meaningful indications of their amity with the Royal Navy.

Naturally, the politicians were much more reserved. With the Irish and German groups in the United States making strenuous efforts against any pro-British policy, with the elections in the offing and with Chamberlain's imprudent Leicester speech appearing to throw doubt upon Hay's public denial of any alliance, the White House was forced to take

---

5 Quoted from *Our Flag*, vol. 1, no. 4, Samoan War issue, 18/4/1899, published on board U.S.S. *Philadelphia*, copy in August V. Kautz Papers, Box 8, Library of Congress.

6 N. M. Blake, 'England and the United States, 1897-1899' in *Essays in Honor of George Hubbard Blakeslee*, eds. D. E. Lee and G. E. McReynolds (Worcs., Mass., 1949), p. 282.

matters very cautiously by the end of 1899.[6] However, as Pauncefote reported

> the warmth & friendliness of manner shown towards me by the President and all his cabinet is very marked and evidently intended to show their desire to maintain and promote the entente cordial & the 'unwritten treaty' which undoubtedly exists in spite of the outcry about the word 'alliance'.[7]

It was, as noticed above, this 'extraordinary change of attitude toward Great Britain in the United States' which created the atmosphere of friendship that enabled the politicians to reach a satisfactory compromise upon the larger issues of the Canal treaty and the Alaskan boundary.[8] After those matters had been settled, there were no further crucial disputes left which threatened to divide the two nations. The change since the 1880s had been very great indeed, and one that the Samoan affair mirrored precisely. The joint naval actions, the American invitation to London to provide the next chief justice, Hay's refusal to press Britain into the partition settlement he so earnestly desired and his attitude over Tonga, all revealed a trust and a friendship which had not existed previously.

The British side of this development is easier to chronicle. In trying to avoid trouble with the United States over the insignificant Samoa in the 1880s, London's policy was purely negative, that of refusing to add a further problem to the long list of existing ones throughout the world. By the end of the century, this reasoning had not changed; if some of Britain's international worries had disappeared, they had been replaced by fresh ones, especially in China. It was not surprising, therefore, that the Anglo-American rapprochement was welcomed so enthusiastically by the British press and by British politicians, since it was thought that this development might ease them of many foreign burdens. Thus, the London newspapers made much of the joint naval actions and the 'solidarity of arms' during the Samoan episode and Chamberlain's first reaction to the German feelers was that 'We certainly must not do anything to break the present "entente" between the U.S. and ourselves.'[9] The same concern for the difficult position of the British Empire and the same wish to keep upon good terms with the Americans as a consequence were present in the later negotiations also; in fact, had it not been for the British decision to give way on important points

7 Salisbury Papers, A140/24, Pauncefote to Salisbury, 19/1/1900.
8 C. S. Campbell, *Anglo-American Understanding*, p. 346.
9 C.O.225/57, minute on paper 1480, F.O. to C.O., 18/1/1899.

in all these matters, from Alaska to the Caribbean, the entente would have foundered.

However, there was a positive side to the British attitude which had not existed before, although this is harder to define and describe. To the single idea of avoiding trouble with the United States was added the one of wanting to go along with her, not just because of the China situation or Britain's isolation in Europe, but because the two peoples had so much in common, they represented the same culture and ideals, and stood for the same things. In other words, the growth of 'race patriotism' produced a positive feeling that Britain and America ought to be friends, and this also helps to explain the extensive British concessions made in regard to the Clayton-Bulwer treaty and the Alaskan boundary. It is the change of mind, above all else, which really indicates this all-important development in Anglo-American relations in these years.[10]

The same can be said, though with different implications, for German-American relations. Until the Samoan crisis of 1889, the feelings between those two countries had been relatively friendly. But the confrontation there, where the Americans appeared ready to go to war and their attitude was certainly interpreted that way by Bismarck, indicated a turning point. After 1890, with the anti-imperialistic Cleveland and Caprivi in charge of their respective governments, points of conflict died away—although the tariff war between them boded no good for their future relations. In 1897, as a result of the mutual resurgence of expansionist activities, the German-American rivalries began to re-emerge. The hostile attitude of the German press during the Spanish-American war, the suspicious activities of Diederichs' squadron at Manila, and Berlin's pressure for colonial compensations at a time when the United States was engaged in battle, were never forgiven by the American government or people, despite the frantic efforts of the *Wilhelmstrasse's* propaganda machine to repair the damage afterwards.[11]

These mutual suspicions were confirmed by the Samoan clash of 1899. Once again, Germany was seen as a restless, greedy, intriguing power by the majority of Americans; and once again, the United States was seen as an obstructive and hostile force by the majority of Germans. At the height of the

10   R. G. Neale, *Britain and American Imperialism*, applies a useful corrective to earlier interpretations of the effect of the Spanish-American war; but the points made by A. E. Campbell, *Great Britain and the United States*, pp. 186-211, regarding the *pyschological* changes, are important.

11   G. P., 17, no. 5151, for Roosevelt's later comment on this to Sternburg.

crisis, Tirpitz even seems to have believed that it would lead to a German-American war;[12] and several American senators obviously thought the same way. Certainly, the bitterness upon both sides was very high because of this, their colonial rivalry in general, and their tariff warfare. Neither the harmony between Tripp and Sternburg, nor the activities of the German-Americans, could erase the deep suspicions; and most American newspapers, and the government itself, breathed a sigh of relief when they were freed of the tridominium and the contact with Germany which it involved. In Berlin, the press was equally bitter, and the agrarian and pan-German newspapers in particular kept up a fierce attack upon the United States. If public opinion was any guide, Samoa seems to have played its part in the gradual alienation of the two countries.[13]

More important still were the official attitudes. Neither the German government, eager to restore its good name in the United States and to prise that country away from the British entente, nor the American government, electorally sensitive to its German voters, could openly express their distrust; and if one took as guides the presidential messages or the kaiser's telegrams to McKinley, one's impression would be that the two administrations were upon friendly terms with each other. Looking at the military and naval planning of both countries, however, an entirely different picture emerges.

No thought was given on the German side to the military problems posed by war with America, for example, until the Samoan crisis of 1889. Thereafter, the matter lay in abeyance until 1897-98, when a young officer was detailed to reconsider the topic in a *Winterarbeit*. By the following year, it became more urgent to examine possible preparations and a top secret memorandum of 7 February 1889 (the most critical period of all, in Bülow's estimation), declared that *since America had become a colonial power and was taking an interest in the Pacific*, it would be necessary to draw up plans against her in case the two nations clashed in the future.[14] These were begun in March and soon became the subject of earnest discussion between Schlieffen and Diederichs, with the kaiser taking an active interest in the whole matter. Indeed, Wilhelm's desire to possess the means to frighten or, if necessary,

12 *Monts, Erinnerungen und Gedanken des Botschafters Anton Graf*, ed. K. F. Nowak and F. Thimme (Berlin, 1932), pp. 386-87.

13 On this, see C. E. Schieber, *The Transformation of American Sentiment towards Germany* 1870-1914 (New York/Boston, 1923). There is no comparable German study, although Vagts does provide examples of German press utterances.

14 BA/MA 5174b, III.1-16, *Vorarbeiten zu den Operationspläne gegen die Vereinigten Staaten von Amerika*, vol. 1, Admiralstab memo, 15/6/1898; BA/MA 5161, III. 1.-3b, *Geheime-O-Angelegenheit. Andere Schiffe im Auslande*, vol. 5, Top Secret memo, 7/2/1899.

defeat the Americans made him the partial instigator of these plans, and he kept an anxious eye upon the naval development of the United States. 'I fervently hope so', he once minuted upon the *Scientific American's* wail that they would be outmatched in the future as a result of the German naval increases.[15]

On the American side, too, matters had drastically changed in the last few years of the nineteenth century. In 1890, the only operational scheme in any form was Mahan's famous plan in the case of war against Great Britain. Ten years later, that country had lost this unenviable position and Germany was taking its place as a direct result of the events in the Pacific. As Braisted notes, 'American naval strategists would not soon forget that, at every disputed point in the Pacific, Germany contested the American wishes during 1898 and 1899 while England seemed invariably to favor the United States.' As early as 1900, the American planners were considering the problems arising out of a general war in which Britain and America were part of one coalition and Germany was part of the rival one. Moreover, as they sensed Berlin's eyes being cast upon Latin America, the maintenance of the Monroe Doctrine against German naval might become the number one problem of the strategists in Washington: 'the most important war problem to be studied is based on the supposition that Germany is the enemy', the General Board firmly stated in 1903. Furthermore, for the decade after 1900 the Royal Navy's support in this question was often hoped for and Roosevelt continually urged the British to strengthen their fleet against Germany, while anti-German feelings and suspicions permeated the U.S. navy in these years.[16] A whole host of recent studies utterly destroys the view that 'for Americans the tangible threat of British sea-power was more real than the hypothetical threat of German land-power',[17] for Roosevelt and Lodge were as concerned as their planners that the Germans might just dare to attempt an invasion during a war, which is indeed what Diederichs planned.

---

15 BA/MA 3557, *Zeitungsausschnitte mit allerhöchsten Randbemerkungen*, vol. 1, minute on *Scientific American* of 31/3/1900. On the German plans, see Herwig and Trask, *German-American Operations Plans*, passim.

16 Ibid.; Braisted, *U.S. Navy*, pp. 113-18, 149-53, 170-72, 189-90, 232-35; Vagts, *Weltpolitik*, 2, pp. 1,393-97; Vagts, *Hopes and Fears*, sections 1 and 2; Grenville and Young, *Politics, Strategy and American Diplomacy*, pp. 305-19; Grenville, 'Diplomacy and War Plans in the United States 1890-1917' in *T. R. Hist. Soc.*, Fifth series, II (1961); D. M. Smith, *The Great Departure: The United States and World War I* 1914-1920 (New York, 1965), pp. 10-14.

17 G. Barraclough, *An Introduction to Contemporary History*, Pelican ed. (Harmondsworth, 1967), p. 111.

In truth, the military and more especially the naval staffs of both America and Germany were measuring each other up in the years after 1898. Both countries had burst into the outside world and come into conflict upon a number of occasions, including the clash in Samoa. Although war did not result from these events, both sides took note of them and prepared themselves accordingly. At the end of his exhaustive study of German-American relations, Professor Vagts was forced to the conclusion that the rivalries of these two imperialist powers prevented any accord being reached between them. Uneasily, they watched the other's actions all over the globe, suspecting (often correctly) designs upon Liberia, the Dutch and Danish West Indies, the Galapagos Islands, China and especially Latin America.[18] Had not European affairs claimed Berlin's prior attention, then possibly the rivalry in the latter region would have caused a conflict, for the kaiser was seeking the abolition of the Monroe Doctrine and a 'Free Hand' for Germany there, something the Americans would have felt bound to resist.[19] Yet if the mutual distrust was already deep by the first decade of the twentieth century, it had arisen from simple origins, from the disputes and actions of several naval commanders in the Philippines and the South Seas and the antagonisms this had produced at home.

If Britain had stood neutral during the 1889 crisis, she was clearly an active participant by the time of the 1898-99 troubles. Indeed, the Samoan question also reflects the changes in her own attitudes and position from the early 1880s to the 1890s. Firstly, the imperialistic feelings seem to have been missing in 1885 and in the years following, despite the actions of Weber and Brandeis, but they showed themselves in 1894 and were quite evident in 1899. Even if the English newspapers then often admitted that their stake in the group was not considerable, they willingly defended Salisbury's firm policy and strongly advocated that Australasian interests should not be disregarded. They also gave sharp retorts to the criticisms in the German press, although the coming of the Boer War modified their tone somewhat. Nevertheless, although many organs welcomed the partition arrangement, others did not and there was a strong feeling of resentment against Germany's opportunism, captured vividly in Chirol's comment: ' I should strongly deprecate any surrender to the thumbscrew & especially at the expense of our kinsmen's interests at the other

18 Vagts, *Weltpolitik*, 2, pp. 2,105-09, and the relevant chapters.
19 Herwig and Trask, *German-American Operations Plans, passim*; Grenville and Young, *Politics, Strategy and American Diplomacy*, pp. 306 07.

end of the world. There is something specially mean in their exploitation of the visit question.'[20] For the British press and public to have feelings upon Samoa at all, and particularly such strong ones, was in marked contrast to the situation in 1878 or 1885.

It is in Salisbury's foreign policy itself, though, that the Samoan affair is particularly informative. Well aware of the group's comparative unimportance and deeply anxious to improve Britain's weak diplomatic position after 1885, he deliberately subordinated the Samoan question to the demands of the overall international scene. For four years, despite protests from Australasia, the disapproval of the Colonial Office, and his own distaste, he virtually allowed Bismarck to 'do his worst' in the islands. Nor was this entirely motivated by the prime minister's need to please Berlin, for even after the German retreat he was in favour of a partition arrangement whereby Britain would step out of the group. Rosebery continued this policy of deference to Germany but as the gap between the two powers widened during his administration, the long-desired German dream of obtaining Samoa was brusquely rejected in the colonial quarrels of 1894. Apart from the personal feelings involved, there were two important long-term developments on the British side which pointed to a stiffening of their attitude: firstly, imperialistic sentiment was apparently rising and the government felt obliged to take account of this, especially that in Australasia; and secondly, for a number of reasons London no longer felt dependent upon Berlin.

Salisbury's return witnessed the continuation of this changed policy and for four years German overtures regarding a partition failed miserably. Even when the native war of 1899 brought matters to a head, he steadfastly refused the solution so ardently desired by the kaiser. The contrast with his earlier attitude is amazing and can only be explained, as he himself attempted to do in his letter to Hatzfeldt of 15 September, by the fact that he now believed that he must have regard for public opinion and he no longer considered that Germany's friendship 'had any special value for England separately'. Although many would have said that Britain's international position in 1899 was as critical as in, say, 1886, the prime minister himself was not going to ask for Berlin's support and pay colonial compensations for this. Juxtaposing quotations from his letters on this topic exposes the glaring differences: his belief that he had to sit upon the Colonial

20 Times Archives, Foreign Letter Book (green), no. 4, Chirol to Saunders, 15/10/1899.

Office and to go with Germany 'in all matters of secondary
importance, indeed in all matters where we have not an
imperative interest to the contrary' (1886) sounds completely
out of place in 1899; while his claim that Britain must possess
Upolu (1899) could never have been seriously made in the
1880s. Samoa, more than anything else, mirrored the change
in Salisbury's attitude towards Germany.

In view of his feelings during the partition negotiations, the
prime minister's unconditional rejection of an alliance with
Germany two years later is hardly surprising. If he did not
recognize the need for Berlin's special friendship in 1899,
how could one expect him to recognize the need for her full
support in 1901, when the situation to his mind was certainly
no worse? If he did not wish to pay the price of one-third part
of a distant island group, would he ever consider paying the
far larger price of tying his country to the Triple Alliance?
Salisbury's wish was for normal relations with Berlin, not for
an alliance with her, nor for dependence with her, nor, if he
could help it, for even working very closely with her. He was
cool over any Moroccan 'deal' and when Hatzfeldt asked him
in November 1899 about the truth of the rumour (which
Germany had privately received from the Queen-Regent of
Spain) concerning a recent Anglo-Portuguese treaty, the prime
minister blatantly denied its existence.[21] Hence, too, his firm
refusal of the kaiser's demands on Samoa, a rejection which
embittered Anglo-German relations for almost the whole of
1899 and might have proceeded further had not the Admiralty
memorandum offered a satisfactory way out for both sides.

How far one can detect any signs of British hostility to
Germany in these Samoan talks is hard to say. Rather than
causing any new feelings in London about that country, it
merely confirmed old attitudes: Germany was already known
to them as a pushing and greedy power, although never
thought of as an enemy. It is interesting to note, in this
respect, that of ninety overseas bases of possible use to foreign
powers listed in the Admiralty-Foreign Office correspondence
of 1898-99, Germany was regarded as having designs upon a
large number of them. Moreover, the methods used and the
threats made to Salisbury by Berlin during the Samoan
negotiations cannot but have increased his own distaste for
dealings with the *Wilhelmstrasse* and furthered his desire to
settle outstanding problems with France and Russia, which
he knew would ease this pressure and make his hands even freer.

---

21 A.A./*England* 78 *nr.* 1 *Secr.*, vol. 14, Hatzfeldt to A.A., 2/11/1899. Chamberlain's
deception was less blatant and he admitted that there had been negotiations on the entry
of arms *via* Delagoa Bay; ibid., same to same, no. 346 of 22/10/1899.

If he suffered in silence, the Foreign Office staff were less stoical and one already detects signs of their distrust of Germany. Bertie's attitude was shown in the Portuguese colonies negotiations, in the discussions on the Atlantic cable question, and in his reaction to the Windsor meeting with Bülow; while Crowe, though not involved in the Samoan negotiations, was very cynical about 'honest & straightforward cooperation between the 3 Powers' when he learnt privately in July 1899 that the German navy was confident of securing the islands.[22] When Berlin attempted to dispute the boundary line in the Solomons soon after the treaty, Villiers minuted: 'The Germans are behaving in a very shabby way as they have done in all matters respecting the Pacific.' Even Sanderson felt irritated that 'to preserve German favour we are to pay and give way everywhere.'[23]

All that this shows, however, is the dislike of German methods which Salisbury and his staff possessed. While it naturally caused them to seek to decrease their dependence upon Berlin, which the prime minister did not admit to in any case, there is no sign that they were moving into a position of hostility to Germany. Resentment of her was checked by the many disputes with France and Russia in these years, while the belief that Britain was getting the best out of the partition treaty also helped to mollify any indignation. For the British press, who only saw the outside facts, it was a somewhat different matter and there was much resentment at the exultant jeers of the German newspapers, one of which went so far as to proclaim: 'All hail and victory, brave Boers! You have fought for us and have won us Samoa!'[24] For the younger men of the Foreign Office, also unaware of the satisfaction felt at the partition, this interpretation of German 'blackmail' seemed to fit into the picture they later possessed of a predatory, aggressive power; and Crowe in his famous memorandum of 1907 pointed to it as one of the many examples of German bullying which had slowly forced Britain to look around for more reliable nations to ally with.[25]

Chamberlain, of course, would have admitted to few of these facts in the early winter of 1899. Although he felt very strongly about German opportunism, once he had perceived a solution to the Samoan problem he pursued it with the deliberate intent of erasing a sore point in Anglo-German

22 F.O.58/332, Crowe to Villiers (private), 27/7/1899.
23 Villiers minute on German Embassy *Aide-Memoire* of 20/2/1901 in F.O.83/1878; Sanderson minute quoted in Louis, *Britain and Germany's Lost Colonies*, p. 28.
24 Quoted in Hale, *Publicity and Diplomacy*, p. 193.
25 B.D., 3, pp. 411, 423-24.

relations so that the two countries could come closer again. Hence his famous Leicester speech, in which he appealed for an Anglo-American-German alliance, severely embarrassing the two other governments in question. His attitude (if not his method) was shared by Balfour and Brodrick, both of whom applauded the Samoan treaty for its political aspect rather than for the solid gains involved. Even Bülow's cold reply to the Leicester speech, although Chamberlain found it bitterly disappointing, did not prevent the colonial minister from favouring a German alliance in 1900 and 1901. It was to take the alarming growth of German naval power and the extreme anglophobia in that country, in both of which Samoa had played its part, to cause this section of the cabinet to realize how wide the gulf between the two nations had become.

If the alterations in British and American attitudes which the long drawn-out Samoan question reflected are worthy of note, then beyond doubt the German ones are even more so. The whole focus of German imperialism seems in some way to have slipped and the emphasis to have changed between the time of Bismarck and that of Bülow. It cannot be denied that the former's colonial policy in the 1884-85 period was opportunistic, for he could appreciate that his quarrels with Gladstone's government would help him politically at home and abroad; but it does seem, at the bottom, to have had genuine commercial motives. As he candidly explained to London during their quarrels, he intended to establish protectorates over all regions where German commerce predominated and another power's flag had not been raised. Since Samoa fell into this category, its acquisition was steadfastly pursued by Berlin, although this intention was often hidden in dealings with the Americans by recourse to the idea of the most interested power acting as the mandatory administrator. Yet while Bismarck fully believed that his aim was the protection of legitimate German interests by putting an end to the native depredations in Samoa, he also recognized that this policy had its limits. It certainly was not going to involve him in a war with the United States, nor to endanger his good relations with Britain, although he went a long way before retreating before such dangers. But once he recognized the priorities and made his withdrawal, it was a fairly complete one. German colonial interests were subjugated to diplomatic exigency and in 1889 he even told Malet that 'he much wished that New Zealand would buy the interests of the German Co. at Samoa'.[26]

26   Salisbury Papers. A62/22, Malet to Salisbury, 26/2/1899.

For his successors, however, there were different priorities. German commercial predominance was the excuse, and not the real reason, for their wish to annex the Samoan Islands; hence the disapproval of the *Wilhelmstrasse* at the news that the *D.H.P.G.* was involved in talks concerning a merger with, or takeover by, British companies. Looking at this particular incident through purely businessman's eyes, as Bismarck had been prepared to do at the end of 1889, there could have been little objection. But now the *Primat der Innenpolitik* was becoming more obvious in distant colonial affairs, particularly for politicians uncertain of their position and sensitive to criticism, although it still remains hard to believe Marschall's diary entry over Samoa, that 'the reputation of the New Course depends upon it'.[27] After 1897, this trend grew stronger as these matters were linked with the *Sammlungspolitik*. For this reason, Bülow dared not back down over Samoa: having deliberately striven 'to direct the gaze from petty Party disputes and subordinate internal affairs on to the world-shaking and decisive problems of foreign policy', a success had become essential for him. The theme running through the 1899 documents was not Germany's commercial predominance in Samoa, although this was naturally emphasized to the British, but the need to satisfy the kaiser and public opinion with this bauble. While Bismarck had raged at his consul's concern over 'prestige' questions, Bülow found it all-important. Hence the deep concern over a matter which Richthofen privately asserted was not worth the telegrams spent on it.

Nothing could more clearly illustrate the difference between this age and Bismarck's than the *Kolonialrat* discussion of 16 October 1889, where the 'realists' were outvoted by the 'idealists'; one member openly declared, 'In our colonial policy we cannot get by with a strictly *Realpolitik* and commercial policy'.[28] As the older commercial-based majority in that body was gradually giving way to the 'nationalists', so the same change had occurred in the government.

This can be over-stressed: many of Bülow's colonial policies had concrete economic foundations, and Bismarck's were also based upon reasons of national prestige. But the emphasis had clearly changed. While Germany's industrial growth at the end of the century seemed to demand markets and territories rich in raw materials in Africa, the Near East, China and

27 H. Pogge von Strandmann, *The Kolonialrat*, p. 293.
28 A.A., Kolonial-Abteilung/*Akta betreffend Verhandlungen des Kolonialrats* (Transcript from Dr H. Pogge von Strandmann), vol. 19, von der Heydt speech, 16/10/1899.

South America, economic considerations could hardly have caused the future of a few South Sea islands to become a matter of such concern that it threatened to disturb her entire foreign policy. The German government's determination to secure at least Upolu and then to trumpet this gain to the nation in order to enhance the monarchy's prestige and to divert attention from domestic issues provides one of the clearest examples of 'manipulated social imperialism' and strongly confirms the researches and theories of Kehr, Hallgarten and Röhl in this respect. Without repeated reference to the internal political situation, Berlin's attitude over these islands cannot be explained. All other considerations were subordinated to this greater calculation. Thus, no longer did the government ride roughshod over colonial pressure groups if the national interest required it; on the contrary, Bülow seemed reluctantly prepared to break off Anglo-German relations over Samoa, even though he no longer possessed that line to St Petersburg which had kept France isolated and Britain respectful.

Of course, Bülow would rarely admit that Britain's need for Germany to remain friendly or at least neutral while London encountered the rivalries of France and Russia throughout the world was not as great in 1899 as it had been a decade earlier. Yet his manoeuvres during the Samoan negotiations beautifully illustrate how precarious Berlin's self-claimed position of the 'third hand' really was. The threat of joining the Dual Alliance was a useful ploy with which to gain colonial morsels like Samoa from the British but Bülow was aware that to enter the Franco-Russian camp would so arouse London's anger and distrust that Germany would never again obtain concessions. Moreover, he declined to consider any alliance with Russia until France publicly and permanently renounced her ideas of recovering Alsace-Lorraine; and this, as he discovered in 1889 and 1900, Russia would not press the French to do. The foreign minister was also conscious at this time that France was in no way willing to consider such a step. His wish that she should wallow deeper into the mire of the Dreyfus affair and thus scandalize the world is hardly an attitude one would hold about a potential ally.[29] Bülow's panic-stricken realization in the early part of November that he might have to carry out his threats against Salisbury clearly revealed the hollowness of his stance. Would he but admit it, he occupied the middle position

29 A.A./*Deutschland* 137 *Secr.*, vol. 3, memo of 15/8/1899; Bülow, *Deutsche Politik* p. 32; H. von Nostitz, *Bismarcks unbotmässiger Botschafter: Fürst Münster zu Derneberg, 1820-1902* (Göttingen, 1968), pp. 234-35, 241.

between Russia and Britain because there was no other. A move to one side endangered Germany's European position; a move to the other endangered her world policy.

Yet as soon as the Samoan crisis was over, Berlin's confidence returned. The double success of announcing a partition settlement on the same day as the Czar's visit obscured the more ominous lessons of the previous week. The whole operation was staged as a bluff and Waldersee admitted beforehand that, although the Czar's trip was an act of 'cold politeness', it would suffice for the public 'who do not know the proceedings'.[30] Yet despite the artificiality of it all, they always believed that the antagonisms of the other two powers were too great to ever cause them to turn against Germany. Holstein's remark to Monts early in 1899 that

> The Powers, which can become dangerous for us, are at present so occupied with internal or external worries or both that a coalition, which was once and quite rightly a subject of lasting concern to Bismarck and Moltke, is now unthinkable without the presupposition of a great German error.[31]

seems in retrospect terribly ironic when one realizes that this was written at the same time as Germany was creating a direct challenge to Britain by the doubling of her battlefleet and simultaneously a direct challenge to Russian interests by the Bagdad Railway and the growing involvement at Constantinople. Furthermore, Berlin's continued refusal to intervene in the Boer War was to cause Delcassé to give up any hope of reaching an understanding with Germany and to turn to London instead. If fear and nervousness characterized German policy after 1911, over-confidence was the chief feature of it at the turn of the century. Occasionally Hatzfeldt would have brief glimpses of the truth and warn that if Germany demanded too much, the British might think it eventually cheaper to settle their differences with the French; but he himself often relapsed and at the end of 1899 he advised that Berlin should keep Chamberlain hoping for an eventual alliance so that they could extract further concessions from him.[32] Ignoring Salisbury, and relying upon Chamberlain, was one of the few lessons which the Germans believed they had learned from the Samoan quarrel.

There was one further lesson, the consequences of which were eventually to be disastrous for Anglo-German relations:

30 Waldersee, *Denkwürdigkeiten*, 2, p. 437.
31 Monts, *Erinnerungen und Gedanken*, p. 357.
32 A.A./*Aegypten* 3 *Secr.*, vol. 1, Hatzfeldt to Holstein (private), 10/2/1899; cf. G.P., 15, no. 4401.

the need to construct a great German fleet. This desire already existed and it may indeed be said to have dominated German foreign and defence policy since 1897, but by 1899 it was reaching peak proportions, with the naval propaganda campaign in full swing and the kaiser pressing for a new measure. In such an atmosphere, Samoa played a vital part in two ways: firstly, by offering the best example of where an increased fleet (so it was asserted) would have protected Germany's overseas interests and her honour; and secondly, by confirming in the minds of her leaders the belief that only by creating a large navy would they escape future humiliations from, and dependence upon, the British.

The first aspect, the use of the Samoan affair for fleet purposes, has been referred to already. One final example remains to be chronicled. Despite the naval agitation throughout the country in 1899, the attitude of the parties to the idea of doubling the battlefleet was rather reserved. It grew more receptive after the seizure by the British of the *Bundesrath*, upon which Bülow immediately instructed the Press Bureau that

> His Majesty desires that the seizure of the *Bundesrath* should be utilised (without impolitic bitterness or heat against England but factually) with vigour and persistence for the fleet measure. My latest speech for the fleet (no-one can know today what consequences the war in South Africa would have, etc.) can also be alluded to.[33]

Nevertheless, although the British action enraged the German press and was greeted with secret rejoicing by Wilhelm and his entourage for the boost it gave to their campaign,[34] the Centre party was still dubious and needed to be convinced of the necessity of the enormous increase contemplated by the Second Navy Law. During the secret discussions of the Budget Commission in March 1900, therefore, Bülow felt it necessary to speak more plainly to the party representatives, naturally only stressing the defensive aspect of the battlefleet. It was, he pointed out, 'above all to secure peace for us against England'. Their overseas expansion was leading them into more potential points of conflict with this world power, and a war could come from the growing chauvinistic feeling in Britain or as a result of the Anglo-German trade rivalry, since London was now dominated by spirits who felt called upon to maintain their economic supremacy of the globe. Germany aimed at a peaceful expansion but she could no

33 A.A./*Deutschland* 138, vol. 2, Bülow to Hammann and Esternaux, 31/12/1899.
34 See Wilhelm's own *Ereignisse und Gestalten aus den Jahren* 1878-1918 (Leipzig/Berlin, 1922), pp. 196-97.

longer endure 'humiliations'. Relations with Britain had become very critical over Samoa and over the seizure of the German steamers, and these crises had only been solved satisfactorily due to intense German pressure at a time when London was diplomatically weak. This state might not always last and in any repetition of an affair like Samoa Germany would be faced with the choice 'of a great humiliation or a calamitous war'. Through repeating this argument in other forms, Bülow succeeded by the end of the Budget Commission meetings in convincing the wavering Centre party to vote for the bill.[35] Never, one suspects had the clashes in that distant archipelago proved more useful to him than upon these particular occasions.

Yet it must not be thought that this was entirely exaggeration or propaganda upon Bülow's part, for he did fear a conflict with Britain *while the German navy was still weak*. For him and Tirpitz, Britain had become their most dangerous foe, 'the one power which could attack us without special risk to itself'.[36] If the admiral believed that Samoa had brought them near to war, so too had the foreign minister, at least momentarily, and he never wavered from his conviction that London had been attempting to force them out of the islands. This, in part, explains much of his anxiety in early April; a conflict with Britain and the United States, he later told Eulenburg, would have resulted in a 'catastrophe' for Germany.[37] His policy, he informed the *Kolonialrat*, was to achieve a pleasing settlement 'without compromising the peace, which a conscientious government ought not to endanger in view of the present position of our naval forces against the two other powers'.[38] It was with incidents such as this in mind that Bülow told the Budget Commission that

> in 1897, as the fleet measure was introduced, the possibility of a clash with England did not seriously appear to be at hand. But I dare not conceal that since then the circumstances have so changed that today such an eventuality is not outside the bounds of possibility.[39]

This attitude requires some explaining in view of the fact that Bülow returned from his Windsor visit aware that the

35 BA, Bülow Papers, vol. 24, draft of speeches to Budget Commission, 27/3/1900 and 28/3/1900.
36 Ibid.; See also Waldersee, *Denkwürdigkeiten*, 2, pp. 426, 428-29, and Hohenlohe's own *Denkwürdigkeiten*, ed. F. Curtius, 2 vols. (Stuttgart/Leipzig, 1907), 2, p. 537, expressing the same sentiments.
37 BA, Eulenburg Papers, vol. 54, Bülow to Eulenburg, 6/12/1899.
38 A.A., Kolonial-Abteilung/*Akta betreffend Verhandlungen des Kolonialrats* (Transcripts from Dr H. Pogge von Strandmann), vol. 19, Bülow speech, 16/10/1899.
39 BA, Bülow Papers, vol. 24, draft of speech to Budget Commission, 28/3/1900.

bitter anglophobic feelings in Germany were not reciprocated in England, and equally aware that London sought only friendly relations with Berlin. Why was it then, that an important *Admiralstab* memorandum of these days could state that certain factors 'made a clash sooner or later very probable?'[40] The factors themselves were made clear in Tirpitz's meaningful remark to the Saxon military attaché upon the need to clothe the real motive for the Second Navy Laws.

One could not say directly that the fleet increase is in the first line against England, with whom we must doubtless come into conflict in the next century in some part of the earth, be it out of economic rivalry or as a consequence of colonial disputes.[41]

The key lay in his awareness that his country intended to expand commercially and territorially into the outside world wherever the opportunity occurred, whether the British agreed or not. Imbued with the belief that for internal political and economic reasons Germany had to do this, the Foreign and Navy Ministry files for this period are full of documentation over colonies and fleet bases in Malaya and Siam, the West Indies, the Red Sea and Persian Gulf, Morocco, China, Liberia, and over the future of such 'dying' empires as the Dutch, Danish, Spanish and Portuguese. When they collapsed, Germany was determined to have her share. Senden talked of a 're-division' of the globe, and in his Reichstag speech of 11 December 1899, Bülow bluntly declared: 'We cannot permit any foreign power, any foreign Jupiter to tell us: "What can be done? The world is already partitioned."' Salisbury's obstructive attitude over Morocco, the Portuguese colonies and Samoa showed that little could be expected from him unless he respected Germany more, however, and this the fleet was meant to bring about.

Hence Tirpitz's promise of a forty-five battleship force for the kaiser, following which 'England will have lost every inclination to attack us and as a result concede to Your Majesty such a measure of naval mastery and enable Your Majesty to carry out a great overseas policy'. Hence, too, the *Admiralstab's* fears that Britain, if provoked, would be able 'to stunt Germany's ability to carry out *Weltpolitik* for generations'. In his *Immediatvortrag* of 28 September 1899, Tirpitz candidly admitted that Germany's great commercial expansion overseas was more or less bound to lead her 'to

40 BA/MA 5656, VI. 1.-3, *Flottenerweiterungsprogramm—Ganz Geheim*, Grapow draft of 19/1/1900.
41 Quoted in Berghahn, *Zu den Zielen*, pp. 67-68.

points of contact and conflict with other nations, therefore power (sea-power) vital if Germany will not quickly go under'. A few years later, another memorandum stated that 'if we wish to promote a powerful overseas policy and to secure worthwhile colonies, we must in the first place be prepared for a clash with England or America.'[42]

Because of a series of colonial quarrels with Britain, one of these being the Samoan affair, Bülow and Tirpitz had come round to the belief that there existed a fixed connection between *Weltpolitik* and their sea-power relationship to Great Britain. For the former to be safely and fully realized, the latter had to be substantially altered. There were, of course, other reasons, based upon economic or personal or internal factors, which would have led to an increase of the fleet but not necessarily to an anti-British policy. These general factors do not explain why, in the operation plans, the fleet manoeuvres, the *Winterarbeiten* and the overall strategic calculations, the German navy was becoming obsessed with the idea of a war with Britain; or why Tirpitz was striving for an ultimate force of sixty battleships or more. The neutralization of possible British attempts to obstruct the outward expansion of Europe's most powerful state emerges as the clear-cut aim of the German fleet construction. Though a long-term plan, it was in fact a short cut to world power. If things did not work out the way they were planned, if Germany's favourable European position collapsed and her naval hopes crumbled after a few years, and if the chief question became one of 'encirclement', this should not obscure the fact that her leaders were optimistically expansionist at the turn of the century.

The Samoan question, because it had lasted from 1878 until 1900 and followed rather than made more general trends, had been a remarkably good mirror of the developments of the treaty powers over that period, in their attitudes both to imperialism and to each other. For Anglo-German relations in particular, it had been a useful and fairly accurate barometer of the state of their regard for one another; just as their understanding regarding the islands in the late 1880s mirrored the generally good relations of Britain and Germany at that time, so the disagreement in 1899 reflected the uneasy relationship which had since developed. More important still, perhaps, it pointed to a further widening of the gulf in the future. The eventual partition arrangement has often

42 On German naval calculations towards Britain in this period, see ibid. and also P. M. Kennedy, *Tirpitz, England and the Second Navy Law of* 1900, from where the above quotations are taken.

been seen as a good sign, in that it removed a thorn from their relations. This is true only in the short-term; the deeper aspects of the quarrel, Salisbury's stubbornness, Bülow's exploitation of the affair in the press, the growth of anglo-phobia, and the contribution to the German wish to build a great fleet, were ominous portents for the future.

Finally, one might enquire what light, if any, the Samoan episode threw upon the general nature of imperialism in this period. Why, in particular, was so much written and debated about a small island group in the Pacific? There were doubtless economic interests involved, especially on the German side; there were also strategic interests, especially on the Austral-asian and American sides, and missionary and cultural interests, especially upon the British side. Yet the sum total of these interests does not seem to have amounted to much. Why, therefore, were Salisbury and Chamberlain, and also Cleveland, so reluctant to give up their share? How could Samoa be referred to by Seddon as 'New Zealand's Alsace'? Why were the Americans so pleased with their acquisition of Tutuila? Why especially did it become a matter of such grave concern in Germany? 'Anyone ignorant of geography', Professor Hale had acutely noted, 'would have assumed by the racket made by the German press that a continent was at stake rather than a small island'.[43]

Clearly, the answer lies at home and not in the group itself. By the end of the nineteenth century, as the kaiser was wont to remark often and bitterly, all the more valuable colonial territory had been occupied. What remained therefore assumed an exaggerated value, particularly in view of national rivalries, Social Darwinism, economically-based worries about the future, immoderate newspaper commentaries and a 'manip-ulated social imperialism'. The sheer distance of the islands appeared to magnify rather than reduce their worth: it was not what Samoa was that mattered, but what people at home thought it was. And since the politicians and diplomats themselves paid a healthy regard to their own public opinions, then they too were affected by this exaggerated belief in Samoa's value; or, more pertinently, they valued the group because the colonial and naval circles at home did. If this case has any general applicability, and reference to the almost simultaneous debate about the future of China suggests that it has, the later stages of imperialism in the nineteenth century were 90 per cent illusion and 10 per cent reality. Even if it has not, the Samoan dispute must remain as one of the most

43   O. J. Hale, *Publicity and Diplomacy*, p. 192.

interesting examples of great power rivalries which accompanied that growth of European and American influence and activity into the rest of the globe at that time, and as an almost perfect mirror of the way the relationships between three of those powers were drastically changing as the twentieth century approached.

Bibliography

Note: The following select bibliography briefly lists the archival sources used, together with all other works mentioned in the footnotes. For a more detailed breakdown of the published and unpublished sources, see my thesis, 'The Partition of the Samoan Islands, 1898-1899' (D.Phil.thesis, Oxford, 1970), pp. 406-74.

A) *Unpublished Sources.*

 (1) Official
  (*a*) British
  (*b*) German
  (*c*) American
 (2) Private
  (*a*) British
  (*b*) German
  (*c*) American
 (3) Miscellaneous

B) *Official Published Sources.*

 (1) Debates, Blue Books, Trade Reports
 (2) Diplomatic Document Collections

C) *Secondary Sources.*

A) *Unpublished Sources.*
 (1) Official
 (*a*) British
Admiralty records, Public Record Office, London.
 Admiralty 1, Admiralty 50, Admiralty 116, Admiralty 167 series.
Cabinet records, Public Record Office, London.
 Cabinet 8, Cabinet 9, Cabinet 11, Cabinet 37, Cabinet 41 series.
Colonial Office records, Public Record Office, London.
 C.O.13, C.O.201, C.O.209, C.O.225, C.O.234, C.O.309, C.O.323, C.O.418, C.O.537, C.O.879, C.O.881 series.
Foreign Office records, Public Record Office, London.
 F.O.2, F.O.5, F.O.27, F.O.58, F.O.63, F.O.64, F.O.83, F.O.97, F.O.115, F.O.244, F.O.343, F.O.366, F.O.371, F.O.425, F.O.800 series.
Foreign Office Confidential Prints, Rhodes House Library, Oxford.

 (*b*) German
Auswärtiges Amt (Political Division) records, German Foreign Ministry Archives, Bonn.
 Deutschland, Preussen, Sachsen-Coburg-Gotha, Europa Generalia, England, Frankreich, Russland, Spanien, Afrika Generalia, Aegypten, Marokko, China, Vereinigten Staaten von Nordamerika, Südsee-Inseln series and sub-divisions.
 London Embassy records, colonial series and *Geheim-Akten* series.
 Rome Embassy records.
Auswärtiges Amt (Commercial Division) records, Bundesarchiv, Koblenz.
 R 85/699 and 777.

Reichsschatzamt records, Bundesarchiv, Koblenz.
R 2/1617-1618, 24490-24491, 24529.
Imperial German Navy records, Bundesarchiv-Militärarchiv, Freiburg i.Br.,
Fach (bundle) nos. 623, 624, 625, 630, 666, 689, 692, 697, 1143, 2015,
2023, 2024, 2034, 2035, 2036, 2223, 2235, 2236, 2240, 2254, 2262, 2278,
2298, 2340, 3131, 3195, 3388, 3402, 3415, 3419, 3456, 3533, 3543, 3557,
3677, 4127, 4265, 4266, 4295, 4324, 4325, 4346, 4348, 4349, 5078, 5079,
5084, 5090, 5121, 5124, 5159, 5160, 5161, 5164, 5166, 5167, 5174a, 5174b,
5186, 5187, 5188, 5236, 5496, 5586, 5587, 5656, 5774, 7146, 7537, 7560,
7562, 7577, 7639, 7840.
Kolonialamt records, Deutsches Zentralarchiv I, Potsdam.
R.Kol.A. volume numbers 2477-2479, 2518-2519, 2560-2561, 2601,
2624-2627, 2642-2656, 2663, 2719-2721, 2807, 2808-2833, 2834-2837,
2839-2840, 2841-2845, 2846-2864, 2867-2872, 2873-2877, 2882-2886,
2888-2901, 2902, 2905-2910, 2912, 2913, 2915-2917, 2927-2929, 2933,
2938, 2947-2948, 3011-3067, 3068.

(*c*) American
State Department records, National Archives, Washington, D.C.
Record Group 59, various sub-divisions.
Record Group 43, various sub-divisions.
Record Group 84, Apia Consulate-General records section.
American Navy records, National Archives, Washington, D.C.
Record Group 45, various sub-divisions.
Record Group 80, various sub-divisions.
General Board records, U.S. Navy Yard, Washington, D.C.

(2) Private
(*a*) British
The papers of Robert Arthur Talbot Gascoyne Cecil, third marquis of
Salisbury, Christ Church Library, Oxford.
The papers of Joseph Chamberlain, Birmingham University Library.
The papers of Arthur James Balfour, first earl of Balfour, British Museum.
The papers of Sir Michael Hicks-Beach, First Earl St. Aldwyn, Gloucester
County Record Office.
The papers of Sir Frank Cavendish Lascelles, Public Record Office, London.
The papers of Sir Edward Malet, Public Record Office, London.
The papers of George Saunders, *Times* Archives, Printing House Square,
London.
The papers of Admiral of the Fleet Sir Doveton Sturdee, c/o Captain W.
D. M. Staveley, Ivy Hatch, Kent.
The papers of Archibald Primrose, fifth earl of Rosebery, National Library
of Scotland, Edinburgh.
The papers of St. John Brodrick, first earl of Midleton, Public Record
Office, London.
The papers of George Leveson-Gower, second earl of Granville, Public
Record Office, London.
The papers of Edward, Viscount Grey of Fallodon, Public Record Office,
London.
The papers of George Nathaniel, First Marquis Curzon of Kedlestone,
India Office Library, London.
The papers of Sir Stafford Henry Northcote, First Earl Iddesleigh, British
Museum.

(*b*) German

The papers of Bernhard, Prince von Bülow, Bundesarchiv, Koblenz.

The papers of Oswald, Baron von Richthofen, Bundesarchiv, Koblenz.

The papers of Chlodwig, Prince zu Hohenlohe-Schillingsfürst, Bundesarchiv, Koblenz.

The papers of Wilhelm Solf, Bundesarchiv, Koblenz. (See also a typescript report by Solf of 1907, entitled 'Samoa, the people, the missions and the Europeans', which was prepared for, but not sent to, the *Reichskolonialamt*; in Rhodes House Library, Oxford.)

The papers of Philipp, Prince zu Eulenburg-Hertefeld, Bundesarchiv, Koblenz.

The papers of Karl von Eisendecker, German Foreign Ministry Archives, Bonn.

The papers of Friedrich, Baron von Holstein, photostat copy in Foreign Office Library, London.

The papers of Paul, Count von Hatzfeldt-Wildenburg, c/o Oberstudienrat G. Ebel, Bad Nenndorf.

The papers of Admiral Alfred von Tirpitz, Bundesarchiv-Militärarchiv, Freiburg i.Br.

The papers of Admiral Wilhelm Büchsel, Bundesarchiv-Militärarchiv, Freiburg i.Br.

(*c*) American

The papers of John Hay, Library of Congress, Washington, D.C.; also a collection at Brown University Library, Providence, Rhode Island.

The papers of William McKinley, Library of Congress, Washington, D.C.; also here is the so-called 'Cortelyou addition', which are McKinley papers which passed into the hands of his private secretary.

The papers of John Bassett Moore, Library of Congress, Washington, D.C.

The papers of Joseph Choate, Library of Congress, Washington, D.C.

The papers of John D. Long, Massachusetts Historical Society, Boston.

The papers of Admiral George Dewey, Library of Congress, Washington, D.C.

The papers of General August V. Kautz, Library of Congress, Washington, D.C. (See Box 8, correspondence relating to Admiral Kautz.)

(3) Miscellaneous

The *Times* Archives, Printing House Square, London. Foreign Letter Books.

Archiv der deutschen Handels- und Plantagengesellschaft der Südsee-Inseln zu Hamburg, Staatsarchiv, Hamburg.

London Missionary Society records, Livingstone House, London. South Seas Letters.

B) *Official Published Sources*
　　　(1) Debates, Blue Books, Trade Reports

Hansard
Accounts and Papers (Blue Books and Trade Reports)
Congressional Record
Stenographische Berichte über Verhandlungen des Reichstages (Debates and *Weissbücher*)

(2) Diplomatic Document Collections

Die Grosse Politik der Europäischen Kabinette, ed. J. Lepsius et al., 40 vols., Berlin, 1922-1927.

British Documents on the Origins of the War, eds. G. P. Gooch and H. Temperley, 11 vols., London, 1926-38.

Papers relating to the Foreign Relations of the United States, annual, Washington, D.C.

Documents diplomatiques francais 1871-1914, Paris, 1929 et seq., Series 1.

Dokumente, neue Ruissische, 'Die englisch-deutsche Annäherung im Jahre 1898' in *Berliner Monatshefte*, 11, 1933, translated from *Krasny Archiv*.

C) *Secondary Sources*

Allen, H. C. *Great Britain and the United States: A History of Anglo-American Relations* 1783-1952. London, 1954.

'American Imperialism in 1898'. Symposium in The Problems of American Civilisation series, selected by Amherst College Department of American Studies. Boston 1955.

Anderson, P. R. *The Background of Anti-English Feeling in Germany*, 1890-1902. Washington 1939.

Andrew, C. *Théophile Delcassé and the Making of the Anglo-French Entente*. London 1968.

Barraclough, G. *An Introduction to Contemporary History*. Pelican ed. Harmondsworth 1967.

Bassenge, E. *Deutschlands Weltstellung und die nächsten Aufgaben deutscher Politik*. Munich 1899.

Bauermann, W. 'Die Times und die Abwendung Englands von Deutschland um 1900'. Phil. diss., Köln 1939.

Bayer, T. A. *England und der neue Kurs*. Tübingen 1955.

Beazley, R. C. 'Britain and Germany in the Salisbury-Caprivi Era, 1890-1892' in *Berliner Monatshefte*, 12. 1934.

Bemis, S. F. *A Diplomatic History of the United States*, 5th ed. New York 1965.

Berghahn, V. R. 'Zu den Zielen des deutschen Flottenbaues unter Wilhelm II' in *Historische Zeitschrift*, 210. February, 1970.

Bismarck, Graf Herbert von, *Aus seiner politischen Privatkorrespondenz*, edited by W. Bussmann. Göttingen 1964.

Bittner, L. 'Neue Beiträge zur Haltung Kaiser Wilhelm II in der Faschoda Frage' in *Historische Zeitschrift*, 162. 1940.

Blake, N. M. 'England and the United States 1897-1899'. In *Essays in Honor of George Hubbard Blakeslee*, edited by D. E. Lee and G. E. McReynolds. Worcs., Mass., 1949.

Bowers, C. G. and Reid, H. D. 'William M. Evarts'. In *The American Secretaries of State and their Diplomacy*, edited by S. F. Bemis. vol. 7. New York 1963.

Braisted, W. R. *The United States Navy in the Pacific* 1897-1909. Austin, Texas, 1958.

Buckle, G. E. ed. *The Letters of Queen Victoria*, Third Series, 3 vols. London 1930-32.

Bernhard von Bülow, *Deutsche Politik*. Berlin 1916.

—— *Denkwürdigkeiten*. 4 vols. Berlin 1930.

Bünemann, R. J. P. 'The Anglo-German "Colonial Marriage", 1885-1894'. B.Litt. thesis, Oxford 1955.

Busch, B. C. *Britain and the Persian Gulf*, 1894-1914. Berkeley Los Angeles 1967.

Butler, J. 'The German Factor in Anglo-Transvaal Relations'. In *Britain and Germany in Africa: Imperial Rivalry and Colonial Rule*, edited by P. Gifford and W. R. Louis, with A. Smith. New Haven/London 1967.

Campbell, A. E. *Great Britain and the United States* 1895-1903. London 1960.

Campbell, C. S. *Anglo-American Understanding* 1898-1903. Baltimore 1957.

Carroll, E. M. *Germany and the Great Powers* 1866-1914: *A Study in Public Opinion and Foreign Policy*. New York 1938.

Cecil, G. *The Life of Robert, Marquis of Salisbury*. 4 vols. London 1921-32.

Churchward, W. B. *My Consulate in Samoa*. London 1887.

Davidson, J. W. *Samoa mo Samoa: The Emergence of the Independent State of Western Samoa*. Oxford 1967.

Dulles, F. R. *Prelude to World Power*. New York 1965.

Eberhard, K. 'Herbert von Bismarcks Sondermissionen in England 1882-1889'. Phil. diss. Erlangen 1949.

Eckardstein, H. von. *Lebenserinnerungen und politische Denkwürdigkeiten*. 2 vols. Leipzig 1919-20.

Eisenhart, K. *Die Abrechnung mit England*. Munich 1900.

Ellison, J. W. *The Opening and Penetration of Foreign Influence in Samoa to 1880*. Oregon State monograph, Studies in History no. 1, Corvallis, Oregon, 1938.

—— 'The Partition of Samoa: A Study in Imperialism and Diplomacy' in *Pacific Historical Review*, 8. 1939.

Eyck, E. *Das persönliche Regiment Wilhelm II*. Zurich 1948.

Fischer, F. *Germany's Aims in the First World War*. London 1967.

—— *Krieg der Illusionen*. Düsseldorf 1969.

Gilson, R. P. *Samoa 1830 to 1900: The Politics of a Multi-Cultural Community*. Melbourne 1970.

Goetz, W. ed., *Briefe Wilhelm II an den Zaren* 1894-1914. Berlin 1920.

Grattan, C. H. *The Southwest Pacific to* 1900. Ann Arbor, Michigan 1963.

Gray, J. A. C. *Amerika Samoa*. Annapolis 1960.

Grenville, J. A. S. *Lord Salisbury and Foreign Policy*. London 1964.

—— 'Diplomacy and War Plans in the United States 1890-1917' in *T. R. Hist. Soc*. Fifth Series, 2. 1961.

—— and G. B. Young, *Politics, Strategy and American Diplomacy. Studies in Foreign Policy* 1873-1917. London/New Haven 1966.

Gwynn, S., ed. *The Letters and Friendships of Sir Cecil Spring Rice*. 2 vols. London 1929.

Hale, O. J. *Publicity and Diplomacy with Special Reference to England and Germany* 1890-1914. New York/London 1940.

Hallmann, H. *Der Weg zum deutschen Schlachtflottenbau*. Stuttgart 1933.

Herrmann, W. *Dreibund, Zweibund England* 1890-95. Beiträge zur Geschichte d. nachbism. Zeit u. d. Weltkrieges, Heft 6, Stuttgart 1929.

Hertslet, Sir E. *The Map of Africa by Treaty*. 3rd ed. 3 vols. Reprint, London 1967.

Hertz, R. *Das Hamburger Seehandelshaus J. C. Godeffroy und Sohn*. Veröffentlichungen des Vereins für Hamburgische Geschichte, Bd. 6, Hamburg, 1922.

Herwig, H. H. and Trask, D. F. 'Naval Operations Plans between Germany and the United States of America 1898-1913. A Study of Strategic Planning in the Age of Imperialism' in *Militärgeschichtliche Mitteilungen*. 1970(2).

312 *The Samoan Tangle*

Fürst Chlodwig zu Hohenlohe-Schillingsfürst, *Denkwürdigkeiten*. Edited by F. Curtius. 2 vols. Stuttgart/Leipzig 1907.
—— *Denkwürdigkeiten der Reichskanzlerzeit*. Edited by K. A. von Muller. Stuttgart/Berlin 1931.
The Holstein Papers, edited by N. Rich and M. H. Fisher, 4 vols. Cambridge 1955-63.
Holt, W. S. *Treaties defeated by the Senate*. Baltimore 1935.
Hubatsch, W. *Die Aera Hubatsch*. Göttingen 1955.
Husmann, J. 'Der Alldeutsche Verband und die Flottenfrage'. Phil. diss. Freiburg 1951
Ide, Henry C. 'The Imbroglio in Samoa' in *North American Review*. June 1899.
Jacobs, M. C. 'The Colonial Office and New Guinea' in *Historical Studies. Australia and New Zealand*, 5. 1952.
Keesing, F. M. *Modern Samoa*. London 1934.
Kehr, E. 'Englandhass und Weltpolitik' in *Zeitschrift für Politik*. 1928.
—— *Schlachtflottenbau und Parteipolitik*. Historische Studien no. 197. Berlin 1930.
Kennedy, P. M. 'The Royal Navy and the Samoan Civil War, 1898-1899' in *Canadian Journal of History*. vol. 5, no. 3. March 1970.
—— 'Tirpitz, England and the Second Navy Law of 1900: A Strategical Critique' in *Militärgeschichtliche Mitteilungen*. 1970(2).
—— 'German Colonial Expansion: has the "manipulated Social Imperialism" been ante-dated?' in *Past and Present*, 52. February 1972.
—— 'Britain and the Tongan Harbours, 1898-1914' in *Historical Studies. Australia and New Zealand*, 15. April 1972.
Kluke, P. 'Bismarck und Salisbury: Ein Diplomatisches Duell' in *Historische Zeitschrift*, 175. 1953.
Koch, H. W. 'The Anglo-German Alliance Negotiations. Missed Opportunity or Myth?' in *History*, 56, no. 182, October 1969.
LaFeber, W. *The New Empire. An Interpretation of American Expansion 1860-1898*, New York, 1963.
Langer, W. L. *The Diplomacy of Imperialism*. 2nd ed. New York 1951.
—— *European Alliances and Alignments 1871-1890*. New York 1964.
Lehmann, J. *Die Aussenpolitik und die Kölnische Zeitung während der Bülow-Zeit 1897-1909*. Leipzig 1937.
Lehr, A. *Warum die deutsche Flotte vergrössert werden muss*. Munich 1899.
Louis, W. R. *Great Britain and Germany's Lost Colonies 1914-19*. Oxford 1967.
Lowe, C. J. *The Reluctant Imperialists*. 2 vols. London 1967.
Mann, G. *The History of Germany since 1789*. London 1968.
Marder, A. J. *The Anatomy of British Sea Power*. Hamden, Conn., 1964.
Mastermann, S. R. *The Origins of International Rivalry in Samoa 1845-84*. London 1934.
McCormick, T. J. *China Market. America's Quest for Informal Empire 1893-1901*. Chicago 1967.
Meinecke, F. *Geschichte des deutsch-englischen Bündnisproblems 1890-1901*. Munich 1927.
Meisner, H. O., ed. *Waldersee, Denkwürdigkeiten des General-Feldmarschalls Alfred Graf von*. 3 vols. Stuttgart/Berlin 1923.
—— *Aus dem Briefwechsel des General-Feldmarschalls Grafen Waldersee*. Berlin/Leipzig 1928.
Meyer, J. 'Die Propaganda der deutschen Flottenbewegung 1897-1900'. Phil. diss. Bern 1967.

Moller, R. 'Bismarcks Angebot an England vom Januar 1889' in *Historische Vierteljahresschrift*. 1938.
—— 'Noch Einmal Bismarcks Bündnisangebot an England vom Januar 1889' in *Historische Zeitschrift*, 163. 1941.

Monger, G. *The End of Isolation*. London 1963.

Morison, E. E. ed. *The Letters of Theodore Roosevelt*. 8 vols. Cambridge, Mass., 1951-54.

Morison S. E. and Commager, H. S., *The Growth of the American Republic*. 4th ed. 2 vols. New York 1950.

Morrell, W. P. *Britain in the Pacific Islands*. Oxford 1960.

Neale, R. G., *Britain and American Imperialism 1898-1900*. Queensland 1965.

Nostitz, H. von, *Bismarcks unbotmässiger Botschafter: Fürst Münster zu Derneberg 1820-1902*. Göttingen 1968.

Nowak, K. F. and Thimme, F., eds. *Monts, Erinnerungen und Gedanken des Botschafters Anton Graf*. Berlin, 1932.

Pacific Islands, Geographical Handbook series, B.R.519A. 4 vols. Naval Intelligence Division, London 1943-45.

Penfield, W. S. 'The Settlement of the Samoan Cases' in *American Journal of International Law*, 7. 1913.

Penson, L. 'The New Course in British Foreign Policy' in *T.R.Hist.Soc.*, Fourth Series, 25. 1943.

Penzler, J. and O. Hötzsch, eds. *Fürst Bulows Reden*. 3 vols. Berlin 1907-1909.

Pogge von Strandmann, H. 'The Kolonialrat, its Significance and Influence on German Politics from 1890 to 1906'. D.Phil. Oxford 1970.
—— 'Domestic Origins of Germany's Colonial Expansion under Bismarck' in *Past and Present*, 42, February 1969.
—— and Smith, A. 'The German Empire in Africa and British Perspectives'. In *Britain and Germany in Africa: Imperial Rivalry and Colonial Rule*, edited by P. Gifford and W. R. Louis, with A. Smith. New Haven/ London 1967.

Ramm, A. ed. *The Political Correspondence of Mr. Gladstone and Lord Granville 1876-86*. 2 vols. Oxford 1962.

Rich, N. *Friedrich von Holstein*. 2 vols. Cambridge 1965.

Ritter, G. *Die Legende von der verschmähten englischen Freundschaft 1898-1901*. Freiburg 1929.

Robinson, R. and Gallagher, J. with Denny, A. *Africa and the Victorians*. London 1961.

Röhl, J. C. G. *Germany without Bismarck*. London 1967.

Ross, A. *New Zealand Aspirations in the Pacific in the Nineteenth Century*. Oxford 1964.

Routledge, D. J. 'Mr. Lundon in Samoa' in *Historical Studies. Australia and New Zealand*. 11, 1964.

Ryden, G. H. *The Foreign Policy of the United States in Relation to Samoa*. New Haven 1933.

Sanderson, G. N. *England, Europe and the Upper Nile*. Edinburgh 1965.
—— *The African Factor in Anglo-German Relations*, 1892-95. Private paper of the Commonwealth and Overseas Seminar, Cambridge University.

Scarr, D. *Fragments of Empire: A History of the Western Pacific High Commission 1877-1914*. Canberra 1967.

Schieber, C. E. *The Transformation of American Sentiment towards Germany*, 1870-1914. New York/Boston 1923.

Schmack, K. *J. C. Godeffroy und Sohn, Kaufleute zu Hamburg*. Hamburg 1938.

Schüssler, W. *Deutschland zwischen England und Russland*. Leipzig 1940.

314   *The Samoan Tangle*

—— 'Noch Einmal Bismarck zwischen England und Russland 1889' in *Historische Zeitschrift*, 163. 1941.
Sell, M. *Die deutsche öffentliche Meinung und das Helgoland Abkommen im Jahre 1890.* Berlin/Bonn 1926.
Sieger, W. *Zur Flottenfrage.* Nuremberg 1900.
Smith, D. M. *The Great Departure: The United States and World War I 1914-20.* New York 1965.
Sontag, R. J. *Germany and England: Background of Conflict*, 1848-94. New York 1969.
Steinberg, J. *Yesterday's Deterrent.* London 1965.
Stevenson, R. L. *A Footnote to History: Eight Years of Trouble in Samoa.* London 1892.
—— *Vailima Letters.* London 1895.
Suchan-Galow, E. *Die deutsche Wirtschaftstätigkeit in der Südsee vor der ersten Besitzergreifung* 1884. Veröffentlichungen des Vereins für Hamburgische Geschichte, Bd. 14. Hamburg 1940.
Tansill, C. C. *The Foreign Policy of Thomas F. Bayard* 1885-1897. New York 1940.
Tate, M. 'Great Britain and the Sovereignty of Hawaii' in *Pacific Historical Review*, 31. November 1962.
Taylor, A. J. P. *The Struggle for Mastery in Europe* 1848-1918. Oxford 1954.
—— 'British Policy in Morocco 1886-1902' in *English Historical Review*, 66. 1951.
Thomson, B. C. *Savage Island.* London 1902.
—— *The Scene Changes.* London 1939.
Tirpitz, Alfred von, *Erinnerungen.* Leipzig 1919.
—— *Politische Dokumente.* 2 vols. Stuttgart/Berlin 1924.
Thayer, W. R. *The Life and Letters of John Hay.* 2 vols. Boston/New York 1915.
Townsend, M. E. *The Rise and Fall of Germany's Colonial Empire* 1884-1918. New York 1930.
Treue, W. 'Presse und Politik in Deutschland und England während des Burenkrieges' in *Berliner Monatshefte*, 11. 1933.
Turner, H. A. 'Bismarck's Imperialist Venture: Anti-British in Origin?' In *Britain and Germany in Africa: Imperial Rivalry and Colonial Rule*, edited by P. Gifford and W. R. Louis, with A. Smith. New Haven/London 1967.
Vagts, A., *Deutschland und die Vereinigten Staaten in der Weltpolitik.* 2 vols. London/New York 1935.
—— 'Hopes and Fears of an American-German War, 1870-1915'. Part 1. In *Political Science Quarterly*, 54. December 1939.
Valois, von, *Seemacht, Seegeltung, Seeherrschaft.* Berlin 1899.
Vietsch, E. von, *Wilhelm Solf: Botschafter zwischen den Zeiten.* Tübingen 1961.
Warhurst, P. R., *Anglo-Portuguese Relations in South-Central Africa 1890-1900.* London 1962.
Weber, H., *Die Bedeutung der deutschen Kriegsflotte für unsere Gegenwart und Zukunft.* Berlin 1900.
Weck, A., 'Deutschlands Politik in der Samoa Frage'. Phil. diss. Leipzig 1933.
Wehler, H.-U., *Bismarck und der Imperialismus.* Cologne/Berlin 1969.
—— '1889: Wendepunkt der amerikanischen Aussenpolitik. Die Anfänge des modernen Panamerikanismus—Die Samoakrise.' In *Historische Zeitschrift*, 201. 1965.
—— 'Bismarck's Imperialism 1862-1890'. In *Past and Present*, no. 48. August 1970.

Werner, B. von, *Ein deutsches Kriegsschiff in der Südsee*. Leipzig 1889.
Werner, R., *Unsere Zukunft liegt auf dem Wasser*. *Deutsche Revue*. Reprint. December 1899.
Wertheimer, M. S., *The Pan-German League* 1890-1914. New York 1924.
Wilhelm II, *Ereignisse und Gestalten aus den Jahren* 1878-1918. Leipzig/ Berlin 1922.
Witte, E. *Revelations of a German Attaché: Ten Years of German-American Diplomacy*. New York 1916.
Zimmermann, A., *Geschichte der deutschen Kolonialpolitik*. Berlin 1914.

Index

A'ana district, 102
Adams, U.S.S., 15
Adler, S.M.S., 75-6, 86
Albatros, S.M.S., 16, 54
Alexander of Battenberg, 56
Ali'i Sili question, 273-4
Allgemeine Zeitung, 267
Alvensleben, Graf Friedrich von, German ambassador in Washington, 52-3, 65-6
Anderson, Sir John, C.O. under-secretary, 215, 227, 243-4, 258, 262-3, 271
Anderson, Sir Percy, F.O. under-secretary, 102
Angra Pequena, 42
Apia, main town of Samoa, 2, 6, 14, 18-22, 40, 44, 51, 69, 92-3, 97, 151-5, 194, 217, 221, 223, 246, 276
Ariadne, S.M.S., 15-6
Arthur, U.S. president, 51
Arundel & Co., Messrs J., 107
Ashley, C.O. parliamentary under-secretary, 48
Associated Press, 141-2, 161, 265
Atlantic cables negotiations, 162
Atua district, 12, 102-3
Auckland, relations with Samoa, 7-8, 90, 259-61, 278
Auckland Evening Star, 260
Auckland Herald, 260
Austin, chief of U.S. Bureau of Statistics, 250
Australia, attitudes to Pacific, 32-4, 38-9, 41, 156, 201, 258-63

Badger, U.S.S., 154
Balfour, A. J., British minister, 131, 137, 156-7, 209, 233, 241-2, 245, 297
Bamberger, German radical leader, 16
Baring & Co., bankers, 22, 29
Barracouta, H.M.S., 9, 14
Bartlett, General, in Samoa, 15-6
Bassenge, Edmund, 268
Bates, George, U.S. Samoan commissioner, 64-5, 88-9, 92
Bayard, Thomas F., U.S. secretary of state, 14, 51-3, 55, 63-8, 71-3, 78-9, 84, 87-90, 93, 95
Bayer, T. A., historian, 110
Bear Island dispute, 187
Becker, German consul in Samoa, 67, 69-75

Beckmann, *D.H.P.G.* manager, 108
Bemis, S. F., historian, 134
Bendemann, Vice-Admiral, German Navy, 217-8
Berlin West Africa Conference, 37, 42, 45
Berliner Neueste Nachrichten, 165, 264, 266-7, 270
(*Berliner*) *Post*, 116, 266-7
Bernstorff, Graf, Foreign Ministry official, 269
Bertie, Sir Francis, F.O. under-secretary, 242, 296
Biermann, German consul in Samoa, 104
Bismarck, Fürst Otto von, German chancellor, 16-7, 22-3, 25-99 *passim*, 109, 119, 151, 157, 164, 199, 201, 213, 287, 290, 294, 297-9
Bismarck, Graf Herbert von, secretary of state for foreign affairs, 45-6, 54, 67, 71-3, 89, 91, 93, 97, 215, 228
Bismarckian press, 141, 264, 267, 271
Bismarck, S.M.S., 19
Blacklock, U.S. vice-consul in Samoa, 76, 78
Blaine, James G., U.S. secretary of state, 87-91, 94-6, 105
Börsen-Courier, 116, 264
Börsen-Zeitung, 267
Bougainville, Louis de, passes Samoa, 4
Boulanger, French general, 81
Bradford, Captain, U.S. Navy, 143, 250, 279-80
Braisted, W. R., historian, 292
Brandeis, activities of, in Samoa, 65, 69-75, 77, 98, 106, 293
British Australian, 260
British Empire League, 261
British Empire Review, 262
Broderick, St. John, F.O. parliamentary under-secretary, 163, 167-8, 179, 195, 210, 242, 246, 248, 261, 297
Bryan, U.S. politician, 134
Buchan, Dr Gerhard, *Kolonial-direktor*, 222, 224
Büchsel, Captain, German Navy, 221
Bülow, Bernhard von, secretary of state for foreign affairs (1897—1900), 122-3, 139-42, 144, 148, 156-72, 180-8, 190-211, 215-9,

221-43, 245, 248, 251, 262-72, 291, 297-305

Bund der Landwirte, 266

Bundesrath, seizure of, 301

Burns, Philp & Co., 260

Bussard, S.M.S., 146, 148, 285

Buxton, Sidney, C.O. parliamentary under-secretary, 119, 262

Calliope, H.M.S., 86

Campbell, C. S., historian, 172

Canisius, U.S. consul in Samoa, 51

Caprivi, Graf Leo von, German chancellor, 109, 117, 290

Caroline Islands, 28, 48, 125, 139, 143, 159, 234, 250

Cedercrantz, Conrad, first chief justice of Samoa, 100

Central Polynesian Land and Commercial Company, 11

Chagos Islands, 218-9

Chamberlain, Joseph, colonial secretary, 122, 128-31, 137, 159, 162, 164, 178-83, 194-7, 199-217, 220-35, 241-9, 258-9, 262-3, 270, 284, 288-9, 296-7, 300, 305

Chambers, Frank T., 143

Chambers, William Lee, chief justice of Samoa, 105, 108, 145-55, 158, 161, 171-6, 185, 188, 256-7, 261

Chicago Chronicle, 256

Chicago Tribune, 79

Chirol, Valentine, foreign editor of the *Times*, 242, 293-4

Choate, Joseph, U.S. ambassador in London, 233-4, 252-3, 286

Churchill, Randolph, chancellor of the Exchequer, 56, 60

Churchill, U.S. consul in Samoa, 3, 145

Churchward, British consul in Samoa, 34, 40

Clayton-Bulwer treaty, 172, 290

Cleveland, U.S. president, 51-2, 79, 105, 107, 113, 252, 290, 305

Coëtlogen, British consul in Samoa, 99

Coghlan, Captain, U.S. Navy, 256

Connaught, Duke of, 180

Cook Islands, 260

Cornwall, Frank, land claims of, 101f.

Cridler, State Department assistant secretary, 250

Crowe, E. A., F.O. official, 296

Crowe, J. A., Berlin Conference delegate, 91f., 95

Crowninshield, Captain, U.S. Navy, 143, 280

Currie, Sir Philip, F.O. permanent under-secretary, 61

Curzon, George, F.O. parliamentary under-secretary, viceroy of India, 179, 277

Cusack-Smith, British consul in Samoa, 100, 122, 145

Daily Chronicle, 261-2

Daily Mail, 261

Daily News, 261-2

Daily Telegraph, 262

Daily Tribune (New York), 71, 255

Davidson, J. W., historian, ix, 274

Davis, U.S. senator, 251

Davitt, Irish M.P., 261

Dawson, U.S. consul in Samoa, 15, 21

Day, U.S. secretary of state, 140

Deeken, Richard, intrigues in Samoa, 274

Delcassé, Théophile, French foreign minister, 192, 194-5

Derby, 15th Earl of, colonial secretary, 39-43, 46, 48

Derenthall, Foreign Ministry official, 223

Deutsche Handels- und Plantagen-Gesellschaft der Südsee-Inseln zu Hamburg (D.H.P.G.), 22-3, 28-35, 44-5, 57-8, 60, 65-7, 71, 73-7, 85, 91, 94, 102, 106-8, 147-8, 194, 206, 216, 224, 235, 266, 274-6, 278, 297-8

Deutsche Kolonialzeitung, 266

Deutsche Seehandels-Gesellschaft, 22

Deutsche Tageszeitung, 164, 264, 270

Deutsche Zeitung, 164, 264, 266-70

Devonshire, Duke of, 195, 209, 244-5

Dewey, Admiral George, 137, 139-40, 256

Diederichs, Vice-Admiral von, 139-40, 290, 292

Disraeli, Benjamin, British prime minister, 17

Dresdener Nachrichten, 266

Dresdener Zeitung, 266

Eber, S.M.S., 86

Eckardstein, Baron Hermann von, attached to London embassy, 191, 199-211, 215-7, 222-35, 245-7, 266

Egypt, role of, in Anglo-German relations, 37, 39, 48, 57, 61-2, 118, 121

Eisenhart, K., 268
Eliot, C. N. B., British Samoan commissioner, 169-78, 184, 189-90
Eulenburg-Hertefeld, Fürst Philip zu, 126, 131-2, 186-7, 190-1, 219, 240, 266, 302
Evarts, U.S. secretary of state, 13, 21
Export, 266
Eyck, E., historian, 184

Fairfax, British rear-admiral, 76
Falealili, harbour of, 15
Falke, S.M.S., 152, 167, 226, 265
Fashoda crisis, 133, 157, 186, 192
Ferguson, Sir James, F.O. parliamentary under-secretary, 59-60
Fiji, 6, 11, 13, 17, 28-9, 32-3, 42, 46, 49, 108, 176, 212-6, 275, 283
Flag, The, 288
France, relations with Britain and Germany, 5, 27-8, 37, 39-40, 47-8, 57, 61, 69, 81-3, 114-5, 120-1, 127, 130, 157-8, 161, 163, 178-9, 183, 186-7, 192-6, 203, 248, 285, 295-6, 299-300
Francis Joseph, emperor of Austria-Hungary, 192, 266
Frankfurter Zeitung, 165
Freisinnige Zeitung, 116
Fritze, German naval commander in Samoa, 77-8, 80
Frye, U.S. senator, 79

Gaunt, Lt., 153
Gazelle, S.M.S., 29
George Tupou I, king of Tonga, 64
George Tupou II, king of Tonga, 283-4
German-American Review, 171, 257
German Colonial Society (*Deutsche Kolonialgesellschaft*), 144, 264-6
German Navy League (*Flottenverein*), 264, 268
Germania, 226
Germany
    Admiralty, 67-8, 76, 78, 103, 120, 138-9, 217-21, 269, 276-8 (*see also* Tirpitz)
    Auswärtiges Amt, 67-8, 71, 75-6, 98, 102-4, 121, 139, 193-4, 197
    imperialist feelings in, 22-3, 26-7, 33, 82, 107-20, 126, 130, 136, 139, 144, 163-5, 171-2, 197-8, 208, 216, 218-9, 222-4, 231-2, 244, 263-72, 274, 290-1, 297-9, 301-2, 305
    internal politics of, and relationship to Samoa, 26-7, 82, 86-7,
109-120, 122-33, 144, 148, 155-6, 163-6, 171-2, 197-8, 203, 218-9, 222-4, 227-41, 263-72, 301-3, 305
    policy towards Samoa, 7, 10, 14-7, 22-3, 25-122, 136, 155-211, 215-39, 297-300
    Reichstag, 16, 22-3, 27, 35, 45, 58, 78, 84-5, 110, 123, 160, 166, 219
    relations with Great Britain, 17-9, 26, 29, 33, 36-50, 53-75, 81-97, 105, 108-33, 136, 141-3, 155-169, 178-211, 215-7, 219-20, 225-43, 251-3, 267-71, 281-2, 294-305
    relations with United States, 16-7, 21, 51-6, 63-97, 101, 105, 112-3, 118, 135-44, 156, 159-61, 163-6, 170-2, 193, 233-4, 251-3, 256-8, 281-2, 290-3, 302-4
Gilbert Islands, 6, 110-1, 159, 164, 200, 206, 208, 215, 219, 222, 223
    and Ellice, Phoenix and Union Groups, 208
Gilson, R. P., historian, ix, 12
Gladstone, William, British prime minister, 8, 17, 21, 26, 32, 37, 39-48, 112, 297
Globe, 262
Godeffroy, J. C., and Son, German firm in Samoa, 6-7, 9, 11, 19, 22-3
Gordon, General, death of, 39
Gordon, Sir Arthur, high commissioner for the Western Pacific, 13-5, 17-20, 23-4, 30, 35, 40, 42
Gorrie, acting high commissioner for the Western Pacific, 17-8
Goechen, George, first lord of the admiralty, 195, 209, 211-2, 245
Gosselin, Martin, chargé at Berlin embassy, 119-20
Grant, U.S. president, 9
Granville, Earl of, foreign secretary, 22, 39-45
Grattan, C. H., historian, 11
Great Britain
    Admiralty, 102, 111, 211-4, 295
    Cabinet, 38, 206, 209, 230
    Colonial Office, 8, 18-9, 38, 40-1, 44, 47, 49-50, 53, 59-62, 68-70, 111-3, 122, 158-9, 213-7, 227-8, 236, 243-7, 283-4
    Foreign Office, 17, 22, 44, 53, 60, 168, 213, 246, 297, 284, 295-6
    imperialist feelings in, 8, 17-8, 38-44, 107-9, 116-22, 191, 243-8, 293-4, 305

internal politics of, and relationship to Samoa, 39, 118, 122, 205, 243-8
policy towards Samoa, 5, 8, 10, 14-5, 17-22, 24, 38-63, 66-75, 88-97, 99, 105-22, 136, 146, 156-70, 181, 184-5, 189, 195-217, 225-49, 258-63, 293-7
regard for Australasian opinion, 8, 10, 33, 38-9, 41-4, 46-7, 49, 59-63, 70, 88-9, 107-8, 112-20, 136, 156, 161, 178, 200-2, 205, 213-7, 226-8, 243-6, 257-63, 278-9, 293-5
relations with Germany, 16-7, 26, 29, 36-51, 53-63, 65-75, 81-4, 88-97, 105, 108-22, 128-32, 136, 141-3, 155-69, 178-211, 215-7, 225-43, 247-8, 257-63, 281-2, 294-7, 299-305
relations with United States, 13-4, 17, 21, 70, 82-3, 88-94, 129, 136-8, 142-3, 163, 171-2, 176, 261, 281-4, 287-90
Greenebaum, U.S. consul in Samoa, 55, 64
Grenville, J. A. S., historian, 195
and Young, G. B., historian, 52
Gresham, U.S. secretary of state, 105, 113
Gray, Sir George, ambitions in Pacific, 7, 18, 33
Grierson, Lt.-Col., British military attaché, 181-2, 235
Griffin, U.S. consul in Samoa, 12-3, 15
Grosse Politik der europäischen Kabinette, die, deliberate omissions in, 117-8, 130f., 131, 132f., 156f., 181f., 231, 233, 248

Haedicke, Dr, 161
Haggard, Bazett, British land commissioner in Samoa, 101
Hale, O. J., historian, 305
Hallgarten, G. W., historian, 299
Hamburg, interests in Pacific, 6-7, 28-34, 45 (*see also D.H.P.G.*)
Chamber of Commerce, 266
Hamburger Korrespondent, 165
Hamburgische Zeitung, 265
Hamilton, Lord George, secretary for India, 195, 242
Hammann, Otto, head of Foreign Ministry Press Bureau, 164-5, 265
Hannoverscher Korrespondent, 165
Hannoverscher Kurier, 165
Hansemann, Adolf von, German banker, 22-3, 224
Harcourt, Sir William, Liberal

minister, 39, 112
Harrison, U.S. president 82, 94-5
Hasse, Dr, Pan-German, 263
Hatzfeldt, Graf Paul von, German ambassador in London, 50, 53-5, 58-61, 69-70, 75, 82-5, 89, 97, 112-21, 126, 136, 138-9, 155-6, 161, 164-8, 175, 180-4, 189-211, 215, 217, 222-38, 241, 245-7, 261, 266, 294-5, 300
Hawaiian Islands, 11, 28, 65-8, 75, 112-3, 133-6, 138, 214
Hay, John, U.S. secretary of state, 141, 146-7, 160, 163, 170-2, 175-6, 233-4, 249-58, 279, 281-3, 286-9
Hayes, U.S. president, 14
Heinrich, prince of Prussia, 138, 266
Herbert, Sir Robert, C.O. permanent under-secretary, 19, 41-3, 47, 59-61, 69, 72, 107, 215-6, 244, 258-9
Hernsheim, German firm, 28
Hertslet, F.O. librarian, 44
Hesse, Grand-Duke of, 182
Heusner, Commodore, German Navy, 68-9, 73
Heydt, von der, member of *Kolonialrat*, 224
Hicks Beach, Sir Michael, colonial secretary, 19
Hogan, Irish M.P., 261
Hohenlohe-Schillingsfürst, Fürst Chlodwig zu, German chancellor, 122, 136, 141
Holleben, Theodor von, German ambassador in United States, 141-2, 156, 161, 166, 170-1, 175, 248, 254
Holstein, Baron Friedrich von, *Vortragender Rat* in Foreign Ministry, 76, 82, 85, 91-5, 126, 128, 132, 159, 161, 165, 190, 193, 196, 198-9, 204, 206, 209-10, 222, 224, 228, 231-8, 241, 300
Howe Island, 236-7
Hull, U.S. congressman, 255
Hunter, H., British consul in Samoa, 175

Iddesleigh, Earl of, foreign secretary, 48, 56, 59-61
Ide, H. C., chief justice of Samoa, 101, 104, 256
Iphigenie, 187
Irene, S.M.S., 140
Irmer, Dr, German colonial official, 145, 149, 223-4, 235

Journal of Commerce (New York), 135

Kalakaua, king of Hawaii, 65
Kane, British naval captain, 86
Kasson, John A., U.S. Samoan delegate, 88, 90, 93, 96, 170
Kautz, Rear-Admiral Albert, 152-5, 163, 167, 171, 174, 250, 256, 268, 280
Kayser, Paul, *Kolonialdirektor*, 117
Kehr, Eckert, historian, 299
Kiaochow, seizure of, 128, 135
Kimberley, Earl of, colonial secretary, foreign secretary, 8, 24, 41, 114-9, 121, 262
Kimberley, Rear-Admiral, 79-80
Knappe, German consul in Samoa, 77-8, 84-5, 94
Knorr, Admiral Viktor, 138, 221
Kölnische Zeitung, 116, 161, 165, 265-6, 269-70
Kolonialrat, discusses Samoa, 222-4, 227, 240, 266, 298, 302
Krämer, Dr, anthropologist in Samoa, 149
Krauel, Dr Friedrich, *Kolonialdirigent*, 46-7, 54, 58-60, 67, 71, 84
Kruger Telegram, 120, 149, 180
Kusserow, Heinrich von, colonial expert in Foreign Ministry, 22, 36, 45, 266

Lackawanna, U.S.S., peace settlement on, 25, 29-31, 40, 51
Lansdowne, Marquis of, British foreign secretary, 281
Lascelles, Sir Frank, British ambassador in Berlin, 131, 158, 166, 180, 184, 192, 201, 223, 225, 231, 234-6
Lauaki, Samoan talking-chief, 273-4
Leary, U.S. captain, 76
Lehr, Dr, Pan-German, 171, 265, 268
Leipziger Zeitung, 266
Le Mamea, Samoan emissary, 13-5
Leopold, II, king of Belgium, 115
Lever Bros., 260
Leyds, Dr, Boer emissary in Europe, 225
Liardet, British consul in Samoa, 13-4
Liebert, governor of German East Africa, 162
Lister, T. V., F.O. under-secretary, 17
Lodge, senator Henry Cabot, 141, 292
Lokal-Anzeiger, 165
London Missionary Society (L.M.S.), in Samoa, 5, 11, 30, 106, 147-8, 261, 272

Long, John D., U.S. Navy secretary, 171, 250, 254
Lundon, intrigues in Samoa, 32-4, 41

MacDonell, Sir Hugh, British ambassador in Portugal, 271
Mahan, Captain A. T., 124, 141, 292
Mail and Express, 257
Malet, Sir Edward, British ambassador in Berlin, 43-4, 53, 59, 62, 75, 83-4, 86, 89-93, 110, 113, 120-1, 297
Malietoa family and party, 3, 15, 24-5, 29-38, 98, 156
Malietoa Laupepa, Samoan chief, 9, 11-2, 15, 19, 24-5, 29-38, 21-4, 49, 54-5, 58, 62-75, 85, 92-3, 98-104, 145-6, 148, 156
Malietoa Tanumafili (Tanu), Samoan chief, 150-5, 166, 176-7, 260-1, 273-4
Malietoa Tavalou, Samoan chief, 19-22, 24-5, 30, 35
Malietoa Vai'inupo, Samoan chief, 5, 11, 19
Mandt, Captain, German Navy, 285
Marist Fathers, in Samoa, 148
Marschall von Bieberstein, Baron, German secretary of state for foreign affairs, 112-5, 118-9, 298
Marshall Islands, 85, 98, 102, 146, 148, 234
Masterman, S. R., historian, x, 24
Mata'afa Iosefo, Samoan chief, 75-8, 85, 88, 92-102, 145-55, 173-4, 177, 190, 255-6, 273-4, 280
Maudslay, A. P., acting British consul in Samoa, 15-8, 20, 23-5
Maxse, British consul in Samoa, 145-55, 158, 161, 169-70, 174-5, 190
McArthur & Co., traders in Samoa, 73
McDonell, S. K., Salisbury's secretary, 217
McKinley, William, U.S. president, 133-4, 140-3, 160, 165-6, 170-1, 249-51, 257, 291
Meade, Commander, U.S. Navy, 8-9, 14
Meade, Sir Robert, C.O. under-secretary, 111
Melbourne Argus, 260
Metternich, Graf Paul von, 185, 242
Meyer-Delius, of *D.H.P.G.*, 224
Miquel, Johannes, Prussian minister of finance, 123-7
Monts, Anton Graf, 267, 300

Moors, H. J., trader in Samoa, 73, 256
Morning Oregonian, 140
Morning Post, 156, 261-2
Morocco, Anglo-German relations over, 184, 190, 194, 241, 248, 295, 303
Morrison & Co., Messrs John, 107
Möwe, S.M.S., 31
Mulinu'u, native capital of Samoa, 2, 19, 34, 75, 153
Mulligan, U.S. consul in Samoa, 104, 256
Mumm von Schwarzenstein, Baron Alfons, *Vortragender Rat* in Foreign Ministry, chargé in Washington, 193, 233, 251-3
Münchener Allgemeine Zeitung, 266
Münchener Neueste Nachrichten, 267
Münster, Count, German ambassador in London, 43
Muraview, Russian foreign minister, 157, 186-8, 192, 195, 202, 232, 237-8
Muscat crisis, 163

Narragansett, U.S.S., 9
National Zeitung, 165
Nauticus, 269
Naval War Board (U.S.), 143, 279
Neutral Zone (in West Africa), 201, 205-7, 211, 215-6, 223-4, 227, 230, 233, 235, 239, 262
New Guinea, 25, 27, 32, 37, 39-43, 46, 57, 136, 159, 195-6
New York Herald, 79, 85, 159
New York Post, 255
New York Sun, 258
New York World, 79
New Zealand, attitudes towards Samoa, 7-8, 10, 32-4, 38-9, 41, 50, 107, 115-9, 156, 201, 258-63, 278-9 (*see also* Auckland)
New Zealand Times, 260
Nicholas, czar of Russia, 127, 192, 204, 232, 234, 237-8, 259, 300
Nipsic, U.S.S., 80, 86
Norddeutsche Allgemeine Zeitung, 116, 171
North American Review, 256

Oceanic Steamship Co., 275
Oertzen, German consular agent in Pacific, 32
Olga, S.M.S., 86
Osborn, U.S. consul in Samoa, 145-55, 170-1, 175
Osborne, Lloyd, Stevenson's son-in-law, 256
Otago Daily Times, 260

Pacific Ocean, trade and communications in, 1-2, 6-8, 28, 106, 135, 211-4, 275-8, 286
Pago-Pago, harbour of, 2, 8-9, 14, 20-1, 59, 80, 89, 96, 143-4, 156, 175, 212, 241, 249-50, 253, 275-6, 279-80, 286-7
Pan-German League (*Alldeutscher Verband*), 109, 116, 124, 136, 171, 264-8, 271, 274.
Pauncefote, Sir Julian, F.O. permanent under-secretary, ambassador in Washington, 54, 69, 76, 78f., 161, 164, 254, 282, 288-9
Penjdeh crisis, 39-40
Perouse, visits Samoa, 4
Phelps, William W., Berlin Conference delegate, 88
Philadelphia, U.S.S., 152-3, 160, 166, 288
Philippines, 134-5, 138-40, 142-3, 159, 163, 257
Plessen, Baron von, chargé at London embassy, 63
Porpoise, H.M.S., 151-2, 268
Portuguese colonies, Anglo-German negotiations over, 125, 130-1, 156, 189-90, 193, 203-4, 228, 241-2, 295, 303
Powell, Wilfred, British consul in Samoa, 56, 92
Press and public opinion, 254-72, 285 (*see also* Germany; Great Britain; United States, imperialist feelings in)
Prince of Wales, 209
Pritchard, George, British consul in Samoa, 5

Raffel, Dr, president of Apia municipality, 105, 108, 145, 149-52, 158, 160, 171, 250-1
Reuter's Press Agency, 161, 164, 265
Rhodes, Cecil, 161-2, 187, 209
Richmond, S.S., 78
Richter, Eugene, 116
Richthofen, Baron Oswald von, under-secretary of state for foreign affairs, 140, 143, 156, 175, 191-3, 198, 201, 241, 267, 298
Ripon, Marquis of, colonial secretary, 106, 111, 116, 119, 262
Roggewein, Jacob, discovers Samoa, 4
Röhl, J. C. G., historian, 127, 299
Roosevelt, Theodore, 141, 287, 292
Rose, German consul in Samoa, 145-55, 158, 160-1, 169-71, 174, 190, 224, 240, 250-1, 255, 286

Rosebery, fifth Earl of, foreign secretary, prime minister, 53-6, 102f., 111-9, 294

Rothschild, Alfred, 186, 192, 217, 230, 233-4

Ruge, German firm, 28

Russia, relations of, to Britain and Germany, 39-40, 47-8, 56-7, 69, 81-2, 110, 114-5, 121, 127-37, 163, 178-9, 183, 186-94, 196, 202-4, 209, 226-8, 231-8, 241-2, 248, 259, 270, 295-6, 299-300

Salisbury, third Marquis of, prime minister and foreign secretary, 17, 47-75, 78, 82-3, 88-90, 93-6, 99, 105, 109-13, 119-20, 124, 128-32, 136-7, 142, 156-60, 164-75, 178-217, 222, 226-38, 241-9, 252-3, 261-2, 284, 287, 293-6, 299-300, 305

Saluafata, harbour of, 15-6, 20, 156, 217, 221, 223

Samoa

commerce and plantations in, 6-8, 29-35, 61, 74, 83, 89, 93, 106, 147, 224, 237, 274-5

early white settlers in, 4-12, 23-4

foreign labour in, 7, 30-2, 147, 239, 275

land acquisitions in, 4, 6-7, 10-1, 16, 20, 23-4, 33-4, 91, 98, 100-2

missionaries in, 4-5, 7 (*see also* L.M.S.; Marist Fathers)

native political and social structure of, 2-4, 7, 10-1, 107, 150 (*see also* Tafa'ifa)

overestimation of value of, 2f., 211-2, 275-80, 305-6

population of, 2f.

strategic significance of, 2f., 211-4, 217-21, 246-9, 275-80

Samoa and the powers, establishment of treaties with (1878-9), 12-25, 30, 42

German treaty with (1884), 34-7

International Commission on (1886), 54-61, 64

Washington Conference on (1887), 60, 64-7

Berlin Conference and Treaty on (1889), 87-98, 150, 155, 168, 173-4, 176-7, 254

Tripartite control of (1889-98), 98-108

civil war in (1898-9), 145-55

International Commission on (1899), 164, 166-78, 193-4

arbitration of war damages in, 185, 190, 250-1, 280-2

partition negotiations on (1899), 155-239, 252-4

after partition, 272-80, 285

role of, in Anglo-German-American relations, x, *passim*, but especially, x, 285-306

Samoa Times, 78

San Francisco Call, 256

San Francisco Examiner, 79

Sanderson, G. N., historian, 122

Sanderson, Sir Thomas, F.O. permanent under-secretary, 101, 164, 168, 195, 235-7, 296

Saunders, George, *Times* Berlin correspondent, 149, 242

Savage Island, 195, 197, 205-6, 208, 211, 215, 223-4, 227-39

Savai'i, 2, 31, 113, 153, 211-2, 215-39, 254

Saxe-Coburg-Gotha, succession dispute, 180-5, 188

Saxony, Duke of, 266

Scharnhorst, *S.M.S.*, 276

Schlieffen, Generalfeldmarschall Graf von, 292

Schmidt, president of Apia municipality, 101, 104-5

Schmidt-Dargitz, Foreign Ministry official, 148, 224, 240

Schoenfelder, Captain, German Navy, 152, 226

Schultz, Erich, governor of Samoa, 276-7

Schurz, Carl, German-American leader, 81, 83

Schwäbische Merkur, 266

Scientific American, 292

Scotsman, 261

Scott, C. S., Berlin Conference delegate, 91f.

Seddon, Richard John, New Zealand prime minister, 107, 116, 119, 258-60, 263, 305

Seitz, member of *Kolonialrat*, 224

Selborne, Earl of, C.O. parliamentary under-secretary, 206, 244, 258

Senden-Bibran, Admiral Gustav von, 128, 225, 303

Senfft von Pilsach, Baron, first president of Apia municipality, 100

Sewall, U.S. consul in Samoa, 69-74, 79, 92, 256

Seward, U.S. secretary of state, 13

Sherman, U.S. senator, 80

Sieger, W., 268

Solf, Dr Wilhelm, governor of Samoa, 174-5, 272-6

Solomon Islands, 57, 195, 201, 216-7, 219, 222-4, 226-30, 239-40, 244, 249, 258-9, 275

Soveral, Marquis of, Portuguese ambassador in London, 204, 210

Spain, 48, 133-4, 137-9, 287

Spring-Rice, Sir Cecil, embassy secretary at Washington, 66, 71, 138

St. James' Gazette, 262

Standard, 262

Stanhope, Edward, colonial secretary, 59-60

Staudinger, member of *Kolonialrat*, 224

Steinberger, A. B., activities in Samoa, 9, 12, 19

Sternburg, Speck von, German Samoan commissioner, 80, 169-78, 189, 193, 224, 252, 291

Stevenson, R. L., author, in Samoa, 99, 256

Stewart, U.S. senator, 255

Stout, Sir Robert, New Zealand minister, 259

Stuart, Captain Leslie, 153

Stuebel, O., German consul in Samoa, 31-8, 44-5, 54-8, 64, 99

Sturdee, Captain Doveton, 149-55, 184, 268, 278

Sweden and Norway, king of, role as neutral adjudicator on Samoan affairs, 94, 185, 251, 280-1

Sydney (Inter-Colonial) Convention of 1883, 32-3, 38-41

Sydney Daily Telegraph, 260

Sydney Evening News, 260

Sydney Morning Herald, 260

Tafa'ifa (kingship question), 3-5, 19, 31, 34, 74, 147, 150-1, 155, 173-4, 272-4

Tägliche Rundschau, 266

Ta'imua and *Faipule*, 12-9, 24, 31

Tattenbach, Count Christian von, German ambassador in Portugal, 190

Tauranga, H.M.S., 153

Taylor, A. J. P., historian, 129

Thomson, Basil, mission to Tonga, 283-4

Thurston, Sir John, (deputy) high commissioner for the Western Pacific, 41, 46-7, 55, 58-61, 74, 77, 88, 169

Times (London), 116, 149, 209, 242, 261-2

Tirpitz, Vice-Admiral Alfred von, 123-8, 132, 138, 165, 167, 171, 178, 184, 217-26, 240, 249, 268-71, 276-7, 291, 302-4

Tongan Islands, 6, 17-8, 29, 42-3, 46-7, 59-63, 69-70, 75, 82, 84, 106, 112-3, 121, 136, 156-61, 194-7, 201, 205-24, 233-5, 237-40, 244-5, 253, 258-60, 275, 282-4, 289

Vavau Harbour in, 29, 64, 213, 219, 225-7, 241, 244-9, 282-4

Torch, H.M.S., 154

Townsend, Mary, historian, 26

Travers, German consul in Sydney, Samoan commissioner, 58-9, 62, 64

Trenton, U.S.S., 86

Tripp, Bartlett, U.S. Samoan commissioner, 169-78, 193, 249, 252-3, 291

Truth, 256

Tucher, member of *Kolonialrat*, 224

Tumua and *Pule*, activities in Samoa, 273-4

Tupua family and party, 3, 25, 29-38, 98, 149-50

Tupua Tamasese Lealofi, Samoan chief, 103, 150-1, 173-4, 273-4

Tupua Tamasese Titimeae, Samoan chief, 25, 44, 48, 54-5, 58, 63, 66-75, 77-8, 92, 98, 102

Tutuila, 2, 5, 9, 31, 89, 153, 177, 212, 215-39, 249-54, 257-8, 279-80, 286 (*see also* Pago-Pago)

Uncle Sam's American Eagle, 171

Union Steamship Co. of New Zealand, 275

United States of America

imperialist feelings in, 7, 13-4, 52, 64, 73, 79-81, 88, 95-6, 113, 133-5, 140-1, 159, 172, 249, 254-8, 286, 290-1, 305

internal politics of, and relationship to Samoa, 51-2, 64, 66, 73-5, 79-81, 88, 96, 113, 133-5, 250-1, 305

Navy Department, 96, 137, 143, 249-54, 279-80, 286-93 (*see also* General Board)

policy towards Samoa, 5, 8-10, 13-4, 51-3, 55-6, 63-97, 102, 105, 143, 146-7, 249-58, 279-80, 286-93

relations with Germany, 16-7, 21, 51-6, 63-97, 101, 113, 135-44, 159-66, 170-2, 175-6, 193, 251-3, 257-8, 281-2, 286, 290-3

relations with Great Britain, 13-4, 21, 70, 88-94, 136-8, 142-3, 171-2, 176, 251-3, 281-4, 287-92
State Department, 3, 21, 51, 105, 146-7
Unshelm, August, Godeffroy agent in Samoa, 6
Upolu, 2, 31, 211-2, 215-39, 254 (*see also* Apia)

Vagts, A., historian, 293
Valois, Vice-Admiral von, 221, 268-9
Vandalia, U.S.S., 86
Venezuela crisis, 135, 287
Verein für deutsche Auswanderwohlfahrt, 266
Victoria, queen of England, 38, 126, 157-8, 180-5, 209, 246, 266
Villiers, Sir Francis, F.O. undersecretary, 211, 213, 283, 296
Vogel, Julius, New Zealand prime minister, 8, 60
Volta Triangle, 205-7, 211, 215-6, 223-4, 227
Vorwärts, 265
Vossische Zeitung, 116, 165

Waldersee, Alfred Graf von, 81, 95f., 300
Walfisch Bay, 218-9, 249
Ward, Sir Robert, New Zealand minister, 278
Washington Post, 141, 171, 257-8
Washington Times, 281
Webb, W. H., interest in Samoa, 8-9
Weber, H., 268
Weber, Theodor, activities in Samoa, 6-7, 10-3, 15-7, 19, 30-8, 44-5, 54, 58, 66-7, 91, 293

Wehler, H.-U., historian, 134f.
Werner, Vice-Admiral R., 268
Weser Zeitung, 116, 267
West, Sir Lionel Sackville, British ambassador in Washington, 65-6, 83
Western Pacific High Commission (British), 14, 18 (*see also* Sir Arthur Gordon)
White, A. D., U.S. ambassador in Berlin, 140, 143, 160, 170
White, Henry, secretary at U.S. Embassy in London, 252, 257
Wilhelm II, German kaiser, 78, 81, 95, 112, 117-8, 120-33, 138-41, 144, 155-8, 162-6, 171, 176, 179-94, 197-8, 200-8, 211, 219-22, 225-8, 231-2, 235-7, 240-3, 248, 256, 266-71, 291-5, 298, 301, 305
Wilkes, Captain, U.S. Navy, visits Samoa, 5, 8
Williams, John, missionary in Samoa, 4-5
Williams, John C., British consul, American commercial agent, in Samoa, 5, 11
Williams, W. E., reporter, 256-7
Wingfield, Edward, C.O. permanent under-secretary, 197
Witte, Dr Emil, 161, 171
Woermann, Hamburg shipowner, 223
Wolf, S.M.S., 99
Wolff, Sir Henry Drummond, mission to Constantinople, 63

Zanzibar, 48, 55-6, 61, 83, 195-6, 207-8, 215, 218, 223, 227-9, 239, 249, 262
Zembsch, German consul in Samoa, 23, 30-1, 33, 42